Springer Series in Design and Innovation

Volume 32

Springer Series in Design and Innovation (SSDI) publishes books on innovation and the latest developments in the fields of Product Design, Interior Design and Communication Design, with particular emphasis on technological and formal innovation, and on the application of digital technologies and new materials. The series explores all aspects of design, e.g. Human-Centered Design/User Experience, Service Design, and Design Thinking, which provide transversal and innovative approaches oriented on the involvement of people throughout the design development process. In addition, it covers emerging areas of research that may represent essential opportunities for economic and social development.

In fields ranging from the humanities to engineering and architecture, design is increasingly being recognized as a key means of bringing ideas to the market by transforming them into user-friendly and appealing products or services. Moreover, it provides a variety of methodologies, tools and techniques that can be used at different stages of the innovation process to enhance the value of new products and services.

The series' scope includes monographs, professional books, advanced textbooks, selected contributions from specialized conferences and workshops, and outstanding Ph.D. theses.

The volumes of the series are single-blind peer-reviewed.

Keywords: Product and System Innovation; Product design; Interior design; Communication Design; Human-Centered Design/User Experience; Service Design; Design Thinking; Digital Innovation; Innovation of Materials.

How to submit proposals

Proposals must include: title, keywords, presentation (max 10,000 characters), table of contents, chapter abstracts, editors'/authors' CV.

In case of proceedings, chairmen/editors are requested to submit the link to conference website (incl. relevant information such as committee members, topics, key dates, keynote speakers, information about the reviewing process, etc.), and approx. number of papers.

Proposals must be sent to: series editor Prof. Francesca Tosi (francesca.tosi@unifi.it) and/or publishing editor Mr. Pierpaolo Riva (pierpaolo.riva@springer.com).

Nuno Martins · Daniel Raposo
Editors

Communication Design and Branding

A Multidisciplinary Approach

Springer

Editors
Nuno Martins
Research Institute for Design, Media and Culture
School of Design
Polytechnic Institute of Cávado and Ave
Barcelos, Portugal

Daniel Raposo
Research Centre for Architecture Urbanism and Design
Polytechnic Institute of Castelo Branco
Castelo Branco, Portugal

ISSN 2661-8184 ISSN 2661-8192 (electronic)
Springer Series in Design and Innovation
ISBN 978-3-031-35384-0 ISBN 978-3-031-35385-7 (eBook)
https://doi.org/10.1007/978-3-031-35385-7

This Springer imprint is published by the registered company Springer Nature Switzerland AG
The registered company address is: Gewerbestrasse 11, 6330 Cham, Switzerland

Preface

The various channels of communication and interaction have undergone important evolutions in recent years, resulting in major challenges to designers and marketers in the design, strategy, and management of branding solutions. Communication Design and Branding are complementary areas of knowledge, which traditionally cooperate in brand creation and strategic business management although not always they are jointly considered in research. In this sense, it is important to deepen knowledge through different and connected scientific contributions which present a broader—and therefore more reliable—perspective of brand communication.

From a branding perspective, developing a competitive product requires an appropriate design project. Brand awareness, user interface design, and user experience design play a key role in customer engagement, customer experience, customer satisfaction, loyalty behaviors, innovation, and brand image. The biggest companies and organizations are known for their ability to combine appropriate design principles with the best branding practices.

Considering branding from the perspective of communication design means defining a brand from an integrated, systemic perspective, throughout different stages, from brand conceptual definition, to brand evaluation, from the way technology for design and communication can be used in the design of brand marks and brand management.

This book intends to provide readers with literature and empirical cases supporting the importance of combining design and branding in research, business management, and academy. It gathers original contributions, in the form of both preliminary data and final findings, representing an advance in the scientific and practical knowledge in the areas of communication design (graphic design, identity design, user interface design, web, multimedia, and audiovisual communication) and branding (brand image and positioning, brand identity, brand equity, promotion effectiveness, and social media technology), among other intersection areas.

This book can be both viewed from a global perspective of communication design and branding research, as well as observed from every single specific area, as mentioned above.

Our aim is to open new perspectives and research paths, explaining the diverse processes and experiences carried out by different research groups, centers, and institutions, on an international scale.

The main research directions in communication design and branding are reflected by the organization of this book into four thematic parts, namely:

1. Visual Identity Design and Communication Design
2. Communication Design and Brand Advertising
3. Brand Image and User Experience
4. Design, Innovation, and Brand Management

In all of them, theory and practice are inextricably intertwined.

Written by renowned researchers and professionals, the chapters of this book were subjected to a rigorous evaluation by both the book editors and a scientific committee. They address and seek to inspire both researchers and practitioners, in the broad field of communication design and branding, by covering the following main topics:

- Design of Brand Marks and Dynamic Visual Identities
- Visual Identity of Non-profit Organizations
- Outdoor Advertising and Poster Design
- Social Media and Storytelling
- Hospitality Branding, experience, and image
- Strategic Design, Marketing, and Management

Barcelos, Portugal — Nuno Martins
Castelo Branco, Portugal — Daniel Raposo

Contents

Communication Design and Brand Advertising

Brand Image and User Experience

Visual Identity Design and Communication Design

Mapping Out the Narrative Dimensions of Visual Identities: A Typological Classification

Catarina Lelis and Elizete A. Kreutz

Abstract Brands are the carriers of stories that help us in framing our understanding of society and in knowing the world. Logos, which are graphical elements that aim at quickly and in a condensed manner translating a brand's identity, are just one of such bearers of rich and meaningful information. However, in hypermodern times, several brands' visual identities adopt a dynamic, interactive, mutant approach, potentially comprising diverse visual narratives, semantically multidimensional, fuzzy, and hardly quantifiable. The complexity of this phenomenon is mostly a consequence from the fact that brands are no longer the unique sources of their branded messages since audiences are increasingly opinionated, vocal, and active. The main goal of this chapter is to illustrate a tentative proposal on how to map visual identities against their narrative dimensions, resorting to a few destination brands and their visual identities, both Conventional and Mutant. Relying on the advantages and the shortcomings of natural languages, a typology is proposed, which is then used to map the logos of the selected brands, based on their narrative-oriented characteristics. Despite the obvious lack of objectivity which describes the semantic richness and fuzziness of brands' stories the presented visualisation resources are expected to be of value for, at the very least, benchmarking activities.

Keywords Visual identity · Narrative dimensions · Mutant brands · Fuzzy classification · Mapping typologies · Visualisation

C. Lelis (✉)
University of Aveiro, Aveiro, Portugal
e-mail: lelis@ua.pt

E. A. Kreutz
Marcas Mutantes Consultoria, Rio Grande do Sul, Brazil

N. Martins and D. Raposo (eds.), *Communication Design and Branding*,
Springer Series in Design and Innovation 32,
https://doi.org/10.1007/978-3-031-35385-7_1

1 Brands and Narratives

In general, until the 1990s, the rational view of brands was common. Classic authors such as Kotler [17], Al Ries [32], Aaker [1], among others, defined the brand as a product/service whose main function is to differentiate itself from its competitors. However, studies in neuroscience, such as those carried out by Damásio [5] helped in changing the way we see the world, including brands. According to Kreutz and Fuhr [21], in the contemporary world, emotion is recognised as an important part both in the lives of people and in brands. And we observe that contemporary authors such as Beverland [3] and Troiano [38] among many others, consider the brand as an emotional factor to generate public involvement. Therefore, we can state that:

> Brands are symbolic forms that interact with their audiences to win them over. This interaction can vary in intensity according to the positioning of the brand, the characteristics of the public and the society in which the latter is inserted, as well as the technical means of production and transmission of messages. Therefore, the brand is a multisensory symbolic representation, whose meanings are socially constructed through multimodal discourse [21: 1].

Brands have been known to ease recognition throughout the years due to the implementation of sound and consistent communication strategies, but contemporary dynamic brands, which adapt to the context in which they operate, must embrace a level of flexibility that will allow them to develop and closely accompany a constantly evolving world, hence not necessarily bound to strict approaches [22]. In fact, many renounce the traditionally consistent and immutable storytelling, where such openness to new communication opportunities naturally impacts a brands' visual discourse.

Following the assumption that a brand is a live construction [29], and supported by Zadeh's [43] idea that natural language is not easily translated into the absolute and dichotomic terms of True or False, or Yes and No, on a previous research we proposed a set of six dimensions that aim at explaining how contemporary brands approach visual narrative through their logos [23]: (1) *hierarchy* between a main/central logo and its possible variations, (2) *linearity* of logo variations and included narratives, (3) *predictability* of both the logo variations and the narratives within contained, (4) *longevity* of the brand, of its visual identity and its story, (5) *interactivity* allowed to and with the audiences, and (6) *synchronicity* between the moment of creation of the logo variation and it reaching the intended audiences.

This chapter assumes that brands' narratives include the various fuzzy and hardly quantifiable states in between each of the binary options. The issue with such subjective states is that they are extremely difficult to classify and distinguish. Hence, the main goal is to illustrate a tentative proposal on how to map visual identities against their narrative dimensions, to some extent operationalising our framework [23] and resorting to a few destination brands and their visual identities as case studies.

2 Contemporary Dynamic Brands

In the early 2000s, Kreutz [18, 19] identified two main visual brand identity systems: one where she grouped brands labelled as Conventional, which main characteristics are standardisation and fixedness, and another one that the author categorised as Non-Conventional or Mutant Brands, where brands would present as flexible, dynamic, plural, fragmented and heterogeneous. Mutant brands are also those that assume a changing visual identity (VI), where their logos are no longer constant and static, but instead they vary or change in some of their essential features (e.g., colour, typography, shape, etc.), potentially carrying different messages in every single variation and subsequent application. Within this group, a brand's VI can be split into two categories: Programmed, including VIs that respond to predefined variations, and Poetic, where VIs can be completely free of rules, in close communion and interaction with their audiences [19].

The adjective "Mutant", representing this contemporary practice, results from a few observations: the world keeps changing, but the word "mutation" still is either almost exclusively (and naturally) attached to the biological sciences, or a synonym of freak creations and/or of awkwardness. Generally, whatever goes against the standards in force is not well accepted and, indeed, in the early 2000s, the reaction of many branding professionals regarding these non-traditional approaches to corporate visual identity was toward opposition. However, if we observe the evolution of life on earth, mutation has been intrinsically related to it, since it is the ability to adapt that allows life to constantly evolve. A mutant being is, therefore, the one with the ability to reinvent itself, to adapt. According to Maturana and Varela [27] this process is known as *autopoiesis*, a term whose origin is linked to the Greek words *auto* (self) and *poiesis* (creation), to designate the ability of entities to adjust and evolve through maintaining interaction with the environment.

Dynamic brands and their VIs are, in comparable terms, like princess Scheherazade, whose intricate multileveled stories were the powerful resources that, through engagement and interaction, kept her alive and made her queen.

3 The Fuzziness of Multilevel Stories

The level of mutations in a brand's VI can be analysed using Fuzzy Logic. Unlike classical logic, fuzzy logic is diffuse, nebulous, non-linear, supporting approximate modes of reasoning, instead of exact ones. Lotfi Zadeh, the mathematician who first coined this expression in 1965, extols the virtues of imprecision, based on life being subject to imperfections and after observing that people make decisions resorting to non-numerical information. Purely structuralist approaches where the possible answers are polarised with options such as Yes or No, True or False, lead to dualities that often do not live up to the complexity of life [43]. The author's theory proved to be useful in many areas, such as in the natural languages, which do not always contain enough terms to express subjective variables. *Age*, for example, is such a variable since it may be defined by opposing values such as *young* and *old*, in this case adjectives. Even for *young* there is an enormous amount of imprecision as it can relate to a young child or a young adult. We can also build additional (but still fuzzy) values such as *rather old* or *somewhat young*. According to Zadeh, between *Yes* and *No* there are thousands of *Maybes,* uncountable instances of data that "play an important role in human thinking, particularly in the domains of pattern recognition, communication of information, and abstraction" (1965: 338).

Brands and their associated advertising practices have been making use of this kind of fuzziness for decades, and most of their storytelling is grounded on both the strong points and the shortcomings of natural languages. Therefore, to study and research storytelling in the context of contemporary dynamic brands, a diffuse logic is especially valid for the analysis of the variations of visual identities and their intrinsic narratives, and in assessing whether they lean toward a Programmed approach (hence, *timider*, *fairly modest*, or *rather shy*) or toward a Poetic attitude (where visual identities can be *daring*, *considerably unreserved,* or *somewhat sociable*).

4 The Strength of Stories, Emotions and Brands

Based on current marketplace trends, Kim and Sullivan [15] suggest that storytelling is one of the strategies to appeal to emotions in the operative context of brands. In fact, it is widely accepted that storytelling is currently essential in branding a product [8, 24]. Narratives provide brands with a personality by facilitating the creation of associations with familiar human traits [11].

In this highly competitive market, brands from diverse sectors and industries struggle to distinguish themselves, especially when customers are becoming increasingly loyal to the digital sales channels rather than to the brands, a phenomenon that is linked to the growth of brand agnosticism [35]. The establishment of emotional relationships is seen by many brands as a competitive way to engage their customers. Brands do so by relying less on product features and facts, but mostly in meaningful, personal feelings and experiences, which can be narrated and transformed into a story that can be told and shared. Hence, brands can differentiate themselves through authentic stories that resort to meaningful features or characters [9] which establish a link between the reality of their offer and the reality of their audiences.

5 Narratives of Destination Brands

A territory brand (representing a city, a country, or a touristic destination) is a symbolic representation of a certain place, which encompasses specific characteristics that can be economic, political, commercial, historical, cultural and/or socially relevant to their audiences, along with landscape, geography and population characteristics and specific representative elements such as flags, anthems, celebrities, among others [6]. Another important expression in this context is place branding, which can be defined as "the practice of applying brand strategy and other marketing techniques and disciplines to the economic, social, political and cultural developments of cities, regions and countries" [14: 278].

It is through their stories that brands capture the public's attention and connect them emotionally. Brands become harbours and hubs of narratives in which events of a certain fictional structure are linked, and the more extraordinary they are, the more they enchant and provoke the participant's identification, activating their imagination and remaining in their memory, thus building on connections and bonds.

In the case of territory and destination branding, such as in the case of cities and countries, there are a multitude of facts, events, characteristics related to the place that can successfully fuel the creation of these stories. And to represent the multiplicity, to draw the public's attention and to promote their interaction, some of these brands have adopted a dynamic and mutant strategy.

6 Brand Narratives and the Power of Social Media

It is widely acknowledged that in the hypermodern current times, brands are no longer the unique sources of their branded messages. Since the boom of social media in the first decade of this century, we have been experiencing great demand for narrative content [42]. Memorable, powerful stories that create connections with the audiences lead individuals into liking or following a brand [39]. Stories have a great persuasive effect on individuals and when people deeply engage with a story, their attitudes and aims change to reflect that story [41]. Brands with a presence in social media use storytelling to provide rational, emotional, and relational experiences that can nudge their audiences into action [31]. Users develop an attachment as they identify with the brand's identity through emotions that are, from their perspective, essential for a meaningful experience. This is particularly true in the case of place branding, the effort to use strategies that are usually developed for and implemented in the commercial sector to manage the attractiveness of a geographical location [40], whether at the national, regional, city or town level, whether for political and social reasons, or for cultural and touristic ones. However, it is in the sphere of the latter, which includes travelling and being away from home, that an understanding of place branding is most developed. In fact, according to Hanna and Rowley [10: 64] "the general supposition that a *destination brand* denotes the tourism dimension of a place is widely supported". Thus, *place branding* involves the creation, design, strategy, and maintenance of territory brands, including, but not limited to, the concept of destination brand, which can be defined as a.

> …name, symbol, logo, word or other graphic that both identifies and differentiates the destination; furthermore, it conveys the promise of a memorable travel experience that is uniquely associated with the destination; it also serves to consolidate and reinforce the recollection of pleasurable memories of destination experience [33: 103].

Tourists, visitors and even citizens' shared stories are valuable and powerful assets since they crystallise important conceptions and characteristics [25] to a group of individuals with similar expectations. These are transported into the story's universe through relatable visual resources and imagery, and also by empathising [31] with contents and meanings that result from consumer-brand interactions [37], and that lead, to some extent, to the subsequent snowballing production of co-created designs and narratives about a place.

The downside of this is that, increasingly, social media users are also harming brands through their posts [23]. Hence, the need to carefully define a narrative strategy for brands' visual identities, since well-told, sound, and consistent stories are better remembered and more convincing than facts [7] – and that entails knowing where such VI's narrative is located within a vast range of narrative and discourse possibilities. The approaches around the possible narratives of a brand should therefore be organised/processed, classified, and visualised, so that storytelling co-creation can be as fruitful as it can, for both brands, their audiences and the places represented by the brands as well.

7 Maps as Tools of Organisation, Classification, and Visualisation

Data is, in a summarised way, an abstract representation of the world and of what we know. In essence, narratives make use of data to transform it into intelligible (yet fuzzy) information, which can, in turn, contribute to knowledge creation. Horttanainen and Virrantaus [12] have shown that information visualisation improves data analysis and Shen et al. [36] argue that to make critical decisions, decision-makers must easily visualise the scenarios with highest frequencies through instantly understandable indicators, whilst simultaneously the scenarios indicating outliers or threats must be equally visualised so they can be known and adequately circumvent.

These processes have become increasingly more complex and difficult due to the ever-growing sheer volume of data produced and collected from a vast variety of sources. Nevertheless, it is always easier when the data in question is crisp and objective, rather than when fuzzy and imprecise (such as co-created brand-related stories), namely when both a fixed structure of rules and an objective orientation to clustering (of information) are completely absent.

Clustering involves grouping objects in categories. According to Newman [30], recent forms of categorisation include *conceptual clustering* and *prototype theory*. In conceptual clustering the characteristics (data) of an object are considered as much as the language used to describe the category. Through this method of categorisation, the produced visualisations (henceforth *maps*) include an area that is spacio-cognitive, disregarding any sense of order and not necessarily including a specific catalogue of possible answers or typologies. Thus, the interpretation of mapped concepts is made based on their position or hierarchy in the map. Prototype theory, introduced in the 70s by psychologist Eleanor Rosch [34], defends that humans remember the differences between things and concepts based on prototypical exemplars they come across with or experience throughout life. This categorisation system defends that human cognition is grounded on experiencing the world, mostly through the use of metaphors, i.e., our ability to relate one idea in terms of another, based on our empirical (and fuzzy) confrontations with the world. This is particularly true in the context of brands since, according to Batey [2], they extensively resort to semantic spaces to understand and measure meanings that are both a consequence and a determiner of real-life behaviour.

Hence, resorting to this method, we can generate maps that explain phenomena via operational but not definitive categories (idem), since:

> The utility of mapping as a form of visualization isn't on accuracy or precision, but rather the map's capacity to help us make and organize hypothesis about the world of ideas and things [30: 97].

8 The Cases Under Study

To exemplify how the fuzziness of VI's narratives can be mapped, and acknowledging the two previously mentioned systems of categorisation, four destination brands have been selected: three of them were designed within the last 15 years, which means they are creations from a web 2.0 era, and all of them are extensively used as case studies in the existing research and discussion on dynamic brands (City of Melbourne, Colombia and Rio450). They also fall within the category of Mutant Poetic brands. In addition, out of more than a dozen destination brands we reached out, these were the ones from which we received some sort of answer and clarification on the use of their variations, either by the brands themselves or by the respective design studio.

The fourth brand has been designed and implemented in the 80s (Spain), thus a creation pre-Internet and pre-cybercultural times. This one is considered a Conventional brand.

To analyse these brands' VIs, we resorted to official sources: the brands' websites and the websites of respective designers/agencies, brand manuals and the brands' recorded social practices (i.e., in events or in social media).

9 City of Melbourne

Melbourne is a dynamic city that enjoys international recognition for its diversity, innovation, sustainability, and quality of life. It offers its audiences countless experiences, whether in culture, art, gastronomy, entertainment, education, tourism, or commerce. The previous visual identity, which was used until the first decade of the twenty-first century, no longer fulfilled its function – it was static, and it disputed visibility with other distinct brands. A more flexible and future-focused identity system was needed. The current VI was created by Landor & Fitch, in 2009. It represents an M (Fig. 1) as the basic visual resource that, besides being immediately recognisable, is expected to provide an infinite number of possibilities for representing Melbourne's multi-faceted, creative, cultural, and sustainable offer (Fig. 2).

Fig. 1 City of Melbourne's main logo

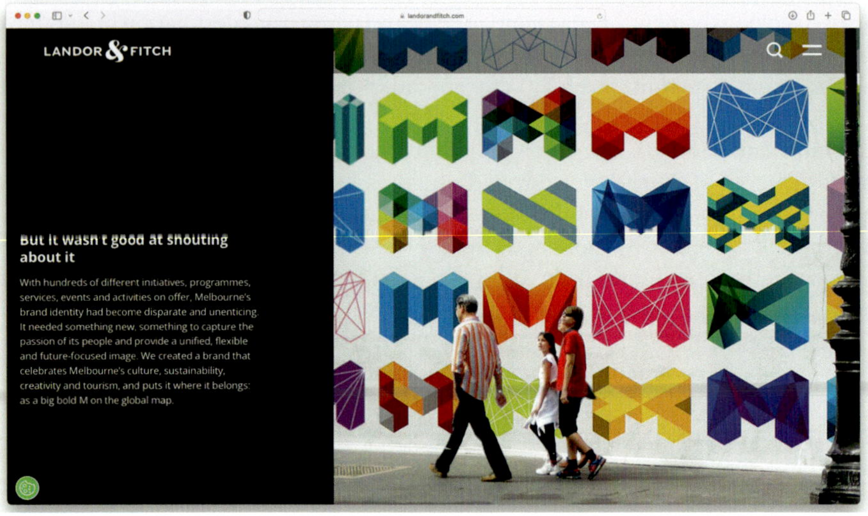

Fig. 2 Outdoors example of City of Melbourne's VI application (Landor & Fitch's website)

10 Colombia

This is a country where 10% of the whole world's biodiversity can be found and with hundreds of indigenous ethnic groups, rhythms, cultural particularities, and gastronomy in abundance. It is also a growing economy, thanks to recent campaigns that aimed at changing the collectively held image of a violent and corrupt country – mostly due to the drug war – to a prosperous and promising place. Colombia's VI, known as "CO", with its motto "La respuesta es Colombia" (The answer is Colombia), was created by Sancho BBDO in 2012 (Fig. 3). It represents the mega diversity of the country and is presented through geometric and colourful shapes, taking advantage of the wide variety of icons and national symbols, in addition to allowing popular appropriation, to link audiences to the brand and, with that, generate narratives and promote interaction among stakeholders (Fig. 4).

Fig. 3 Colombia's main logo (CO)

Fig. 4 CO's logo variations (*potenciadores* webpage)

Fig. 5 Rio450's main logo

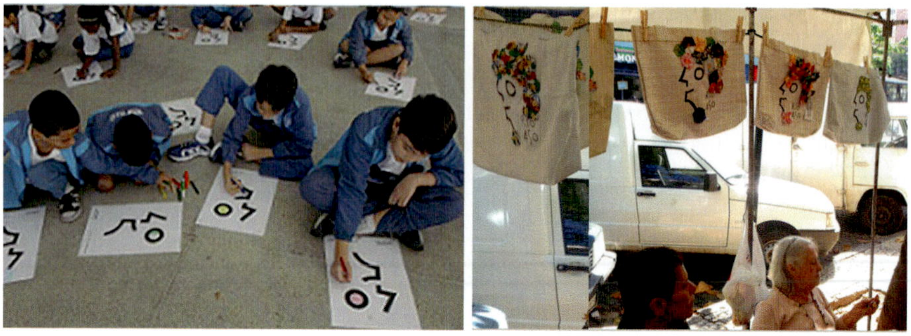

Fig. 6 Appropriation of Rio450 by the public. On the left, a workshop in a Rio de Janeiro primary school; on the right, a crafts market

11 Rio450

Created by Brazilian agency Crama Design Estratégico in 2016, to commemorate the 450th anniversary of the city of Rio de Janeiro, the brand Rio450 represents a unique lifestyle that is shared by 6 million people who live in the "Wonderful City", another example of a multicultural, multi-ethnic, and multifaceted place. The basic element of this VI is the number 450 which was humanised into a Carioca's[1] profile (Fig. 5) and which was largely appropriated by the public (Fig. 6) and even by other brands (Fig. 7), inspiring and creating new meanings, new narratives. Appropriation by the public is encouraged through workshops in schools, events, actions on public spaces, resorting to crafts and artistic creation.

12 Spain, a Conventional VI

Spain's brand was created in 1983 by renowned Spanish artist Joan Miró. Quick splashy strokes and three colours mainly (red, yellow, and black) constitute an abstract, simple, and extremely distinctive design (Fig. 8). If the main function of a

---

[1] Carioca is the official gentilic of Rio de Janeiro's municipality; it can also refer, as an adjective, to everything that belongs to Rio de Janeiro, such as its citizens, its neighbourhoods, its infrastructures, etc.

Fig. 7 Appropriation of Rio450's VI by Coca Cola

Fig. 8 The "Sun of Miró", Spain's official destination brand since 1983

visual identity is to represent the essence of the brand, for at least 40 years the "Sun of Miró" has fulfilled its function. Unlike the previous three VIs, on this one we observe the characteristics of conventional brands, such as rigidity in the form used for identification purposes, standardisation, and immutability. Its main application is as an overlay (like an accreditation seal) on promotional materials (Fig. 9).

13 A Typology of Visual Identities Mutability

The selected brands were analysed according to the narrative dimensions of their VIs, following our own framework [23] and, to a certain degree, demonstrating it in further practical terms.

Fig. 9 Homepage of "You Deserve Spain", by Turespaña, the state marketing company responsible for promoting the country

To classify dimensions Hierarchy, Longevity and Predictability we analysed the brands' manuals, the visual guidelines and the logos' applications that have been made available online. The definition of dimension Linearity relied on the model for the analysis of VIs proposed by Martins et al. [26]. The authors identified eight mechanisms that are associated with the most common variations in VIs: *colour variation, combination, content variation, positioning, repetition, rotation, scaling,* and *shape transformation*. For dimensions Interactivity and Synchronicity, the brands' websites and social media, and the respective communication agencies online presence were scrutinised.

For the definition of the expected levels of fuzziness of each of these dimensions, a typology was constructed. A typology is usually multidimensional and conceptual, and it is well represented using matrices or tables, in which each cell includes labels or names that define the conceptual types. Hence, for each dimension of VI's narratives, we used two frames to construct our classification: the dimension itself and the brand's mutability. When these two frames are combined, a fourfold typology emerges, as presented in Table 1. These four categories per dimension (the conceptual types) are the classifications grounded on the fuzziness of spoken natural language that will be used to create a map.

Table 1 Typology of visual identities mutability: fuzzy classifications

Narrative dimensions of visual identities [23]		VI's mutability [18, 19]	
		Programmed	Poetic
Hierarchy	Nuclear	*Largely Crucial*	*Fairly Specific*
	Peripheral	*Moderately Additional*	*Fully Digressive*
Linearity	Sequential	*Really Structured*	*Evenly Deviating*
	Non-linear	*Considerably Varying*	*Positively Wandering*
Longevity	Permanent	*Thoroughly Enduring*	*Creatively Stable*
	Transitory	*Kind of Momentary*	*Utterly Ephemeral*
Predictability	Anticipated	*Considerably Foreseen*	*Relatively Certain*
	Open-ended	*Rather Loose*	*Wholly Unpredictable*
Interactivity	Interpretative	*Remarkably Illustrative*	*Quite Allegorical*
	Appropriative	*Tolerably Embraced*	*Substantially Adoptable*
Synchronicity	Asynchronous	*Mainly Nonparallel*	*Pretty Uncoincidental*
	Synchronous	*Reasonably Concurrent*	*Massively Simultaneous*

14 Classifying and Mapping the Selected VIs

After analysing all the collected materials, we found the following regarding each of the selected VIs:

14.1 City of Melbourne

- *Moderately Additional*, in the sense that its original proposal includes predetermined peripheral variations depending on a central logo (Hierarchy).
- *Considerably Varying*, since it resorts to four variation mechanisms: colour variation, combination, content variation and repetition (Linearity).
- *Creatively Stable*, because in 2009 it came as a fresh approach to replace the previous VI (Longevity).
- *Considerably Foreseen*, as the public is, to a large degree, aware of the co-existence of logo variations, although the municipality has been resorting to only a few (Predictability).
- *Quite Allegorical*, since it allows the interpretation of a wide range of logo variations, with a low degree of possible intervention by the public or any other entities (Interactivity).
- *Asynchronous*, given that the definition of the narrative through logo variations occurs solely at design time, in this case, by Landor & Fitch (Synchronicity).

Its VI includes predetermined expressions that may result in stories with different nuances, that the public is expected to interpret and live (Fig. 10).

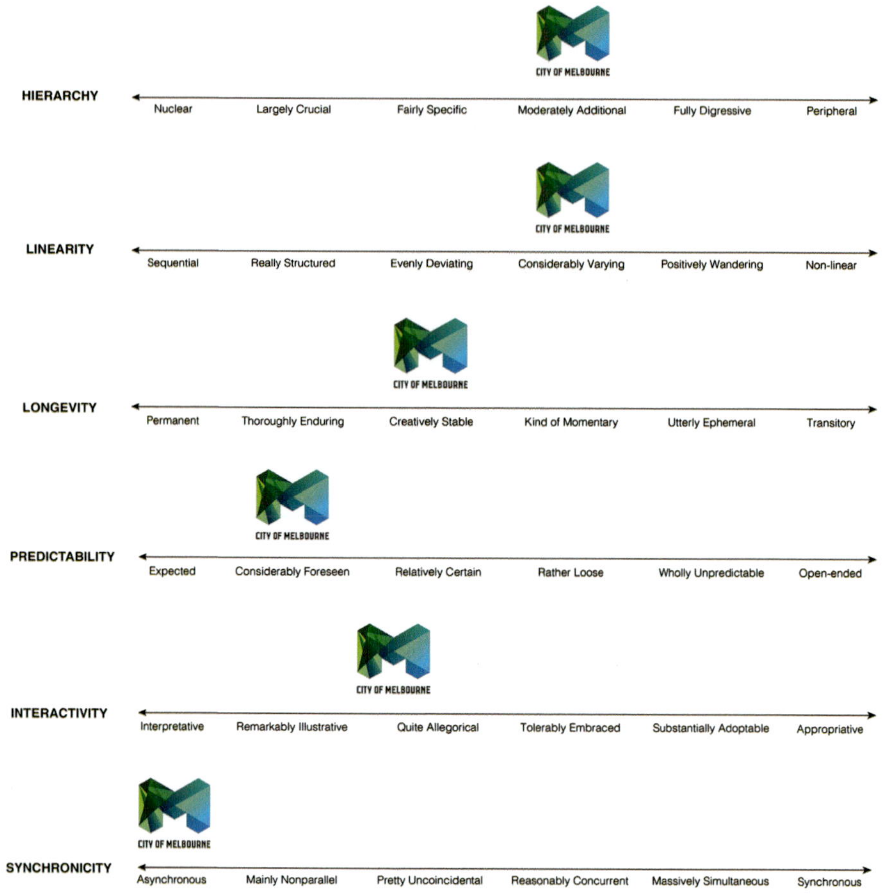

Fig. 10 Mapping City of Melbourne's logo against the narrative dimensions of VI

14.2 Colombia

- *Moderately Additional,* to *Fully Digressive*, in the sense that it includes predetermined peripheral variations depending on a central logo but, unlike City of Melbourne, it allows the creation of new variations by anyone, provided these get official clearance before application (Hierarchy).
- *Considerably Varying*, since it resorts to three variation mechanisms: colour variation, combination, and content variation (Linearity).
- *Creatively Stable*, because it exists since 2012, i.e., for more than a decade as of the day this chapter was published (Longevity).
- *Rather Loose,* as the public is aware of the co-existence of logo variations, both predetermined and recreated (Predictability).

- *Tolerably Embraced*, since it allows the appropriation of the VI for the creation of new logo variations subject to approval (Interactivity).
- *Pretty Uncoincidental,* given that the definition of the narrative through logo variations occurs at design time, but also at subsequent times, since other entities are allowed to create new variations (Synchronicity) (Fig. 11).

Its VI includes predetermined expressions that may result in stories with different nuances, and the public is expected to both interpret and possibly engage with, by adding their own views of Colombia's multi-diversity.

Fig. 11 Mapping Colombia's logo against the narrative dimensions of VI

14.3 Rio450

- *Fairly Specific* to *Moderately Additional*, in the sense that it is presented to the public, not only via a couple of possible variations, but mostly through a nuclear predetermined logo which may lead to several co-created variations (Hierarchy).
- *Positively Wandering*, since it potentially resorts to all eight variation mechanisms (Linearity).
- *Utterly Ephemeral to Transitory*, because it is attached to a specific commemorative occasion, in this case, a year, but it has remained for longer then, probably, the expected (Longevity).
- *Open-ended,* as the public is very aware of the coexistence of logo variations and extensively contributes to their variety with unexpected individual versions (Predictability).
- *Substantially Adoptable to Appropriative*, since it allows the public to appropriate the nuclear version of the logo for the creation of an unquantifiable range of variations (Interactivity).
- *Massively Simultaneous*, given that the definition of the narrative through logo variations occurs mostly at the public's use-time, except for variations generated in the context of possible partnerships and created by other brands (Synchronicity).

Its VI includes a minimum number of predetermined expressions but the variety of stories is expected from the public as co-designers and co-owners (Fig. 12).

14.4 Spain

- *Nuclear*, in the sense that it includes a predetermined nuclear and unique version of the logo (Hierarchy).
- *Sequential*, since the VI resorts to a sequential logo narrative, without any variations (Linearity).
- *Permanent*, because it persists for about 40 years (Longevity).
- *Expected,* as the public is totally aware of this logo (and this version only) in its applications (Predictability).
- *Interpretative*, since it only permits the interpretation of the logo and its contained unchanged narrative (Interactivity).
- *Asynchronous*, given that the definition of the narrative through logo variations occurs exclusively at design time (Synchronicity).

Its VI includes one predetermined and very stable expression that strongly communicates a single kind of narrative, which the public can interpret and elaborate on, with the support of brand applications (such as advertising campaigns), that play the role of augmented storytelling resources (Fig. 13).

The previous four maps showcase how we can classify one brand according to the dimensions of narrative of its VI. Another visualisation mode is possible when the

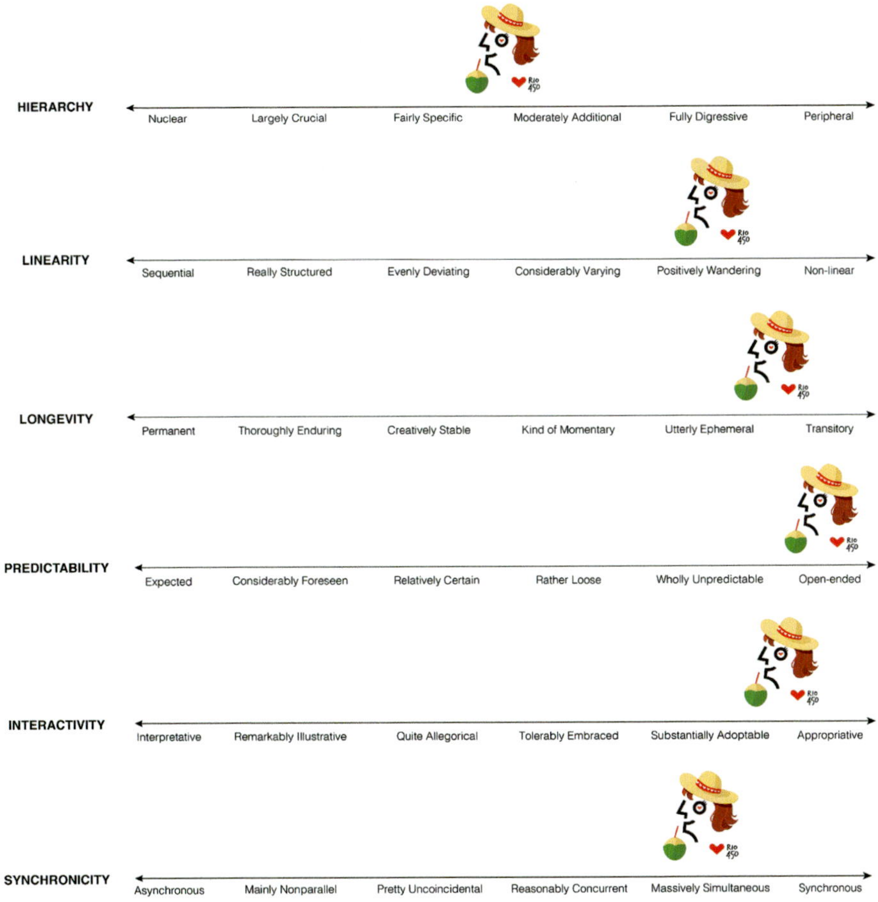

Fig. 12 Mapping Rio450's logo against the narrative dimensions of VI

analysis focuses on each individual dimension and knowing its prevalence within a certain group of brands, for example, brands from the same industry sector—which may be of interest for benchmarking purposes.

By making such a comparative visual analysis using the selected brands, it becomes clear that Spain's VI location on the map coincides with the left-hand territory, in which classification resorts to semantically precise terms, hence, and going back to Zadeh, either 0 or 1. For the purposes of reading a VI's mutability, in this case 0 applies best, since Spain's different narrative possibilities are not associated to its unchangeable logo (Fig. 14).

Once again, on these maps we can observe, when considering the Mutant Brands framework proposed by Kreutz [18, 19], that more rigid and less dynamic VIs are those leaning toward the left-hand side (Programmed), and VIs presenting a higher level of openness and lower number of predefined features (hence allowing

Fig. 13 Mapping Spain's logo against the narrative dimensions of VI

an increased number of possible, shared and co-created stories that were not predicted nor thought at design-time) are those that tend to the right (Poetic). Hence, should we find the average horizontal position of each of the analysed VIs, the representation depicted in Fig. 15 would be achieved.

Rio450 adopts a considerably poetic approach, where changes to its visual representation and to overall behaviour (impacting both creativity and strategy) are allowed and welcome. Equally evident – although for quite opposite reasons – is the case of Spain, whose level of mutability is fully zero, thus classifying as a Conventional brand. Colombia and City of Melbourne include a certain propensity to a poetic attitude but with a medium to high number of programmed features.

Again, as mentioned before, whereas Spain is almost a relic brand – mostly due to its heritage and artistic value, which certainly explains why this VI has been in force for so many years – the other three are twenty-first century and modern VIs, designed

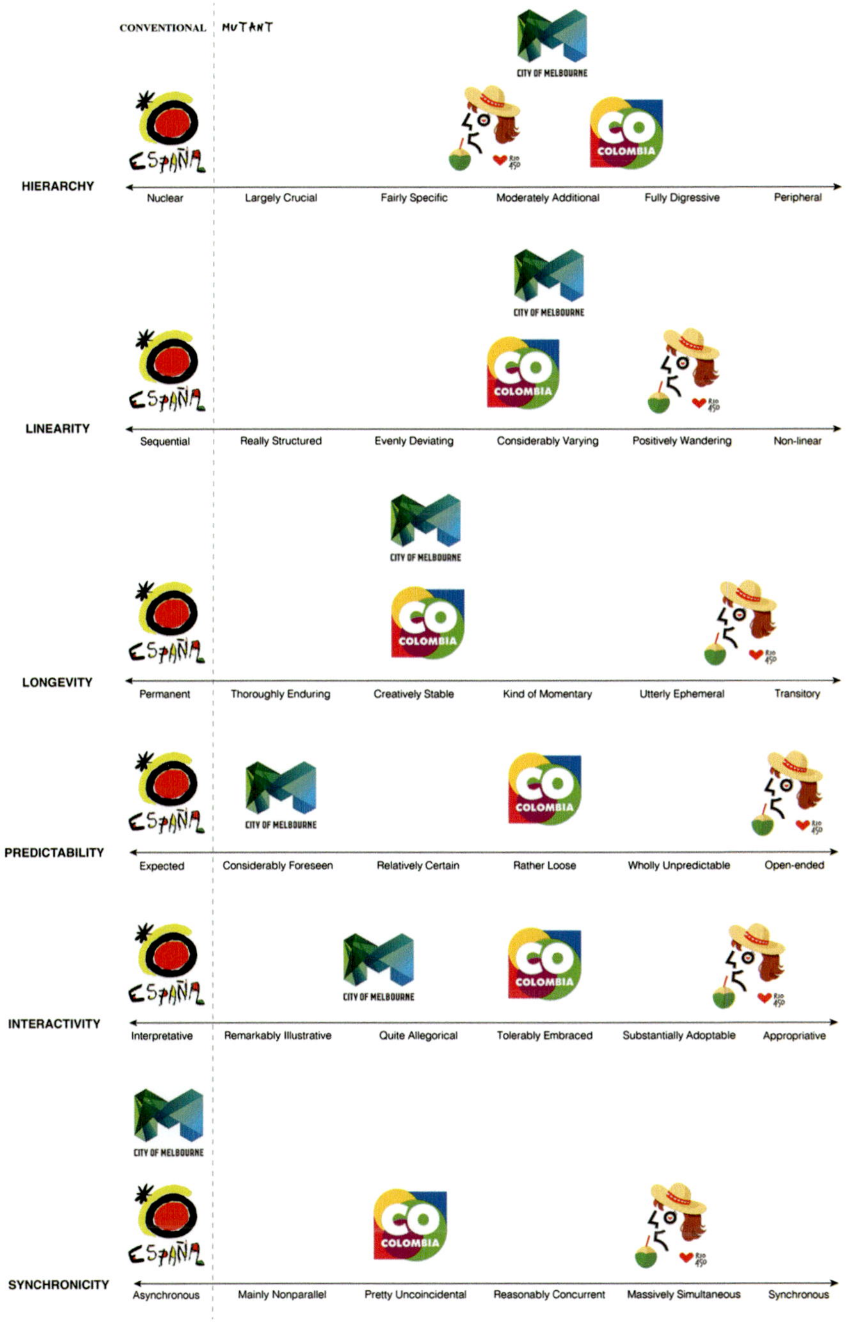

Fig. 14 Mapping the four selected VIs against the narrative dimensions of VI

Fig. 15 Mapping the selected VIs according to their mutability

with a hypermodern, informed, opinionated, and naturally participatory audience in mind, to whom storytelling is a commonplace and everydayness asset.

Hence, going back to the table where the fuzzy classifications are broken down into a proposed typology of VIs mutability, it is possible to define clearer boundaries to support a more accurate clusterisation of VIs regarding their storytelling potential. Table 2 replicates Table 1, but now with some colour coding where conceptual types in light grey cells can be used to categorise mutant VIs, whereas conventional ones can only resort to the adjectives in darker grey cells.

Table 2 Typology of visual identities mutability: light grey for mutant VIs and dark grey for conventional VIs

Narrative dimensions of visual identities [23]		VI's mutability [18, 19]	
		Programmed	Poetic
Hierarchy	Nuclear	*Largely Crucial*	*Fairly Specific*
	Peripheral	*Moderately Additional*	*Fully Digressive*
Linearity	Sequential	*Really Structured*	*Evenly Deviating*
	Non-linear	*Considerably Varying*	*Positively Wandering*
Longevity	Permanent	*Thoroughly Enduring*	*Creatively Stable*
	Transitory	*Kind of Momentary*	*Utterly Ephemeral*
Predictability	Anticipated	*Considerably Foreseen*	*Relatively Certain*
	Open-ended	*Rather Loose*	*Wholly Unpredictable*
Interactivity	Interpretative	*Remarkably Illustrative*	*Quite Allegorical*
	Appropriative	*Tolerably Embraced*	*Substantially Adoptable*
Synchronicity	Asynchronous	*Mainly Nonparallel*	*Pretty Uncoincidental*
	Synchronous	*Reasonably Concurrent*	*Massively Simultaneous*

15 Final Thoughts

Narratives are deeply rooted in cultural and social practices, and brands use them to activate the collective imaginary and promote engagement among their audiences. It is important to reinforce the idea that stories may produce change, for which reason they cannot be ignored. Brands tell their stories through a diverse set of assets and resources (e.g., salespeople, advertising, the size and location of their premises, store design, etc.), but also through their logos, those tiny elements that appear everywhere the brand is, and which can both encapsulate visual narratives, and successfully tell a story through pictorial and graphical elements. Hence, the storytelling of a brand is also crystallised by its visual identity and, as in any other story context, it can be either foreseeable or unpredictable, rational or emotional, limited or infinite, it may allow the public to either interpret it or co-create it (establishing a different kind of bond, grounded on shared ownership).

These dichotomic values are just the limits of an array of possibilities, since many contemporary brands have been investing in VIs which flexibility makes them fall in an unprecise location (or classification), somewhere in between these poles – for example, some brands may purposedly include in their VI's narratives some foreseeable elements amidst unpredictable ones.

In this chapter we assume that brands' (visual) narratives may include the various fuzzy and hardly quantifiable states in between each of the binary options, and we propose that to be the case of those brands whose greater or lesser dynamism and flexibility puts them in a category known as mutant. Mutant brands are exactly those that augment the possibility of discursive approaches and potential new narratives because they acknowledge change and diffuseness as a normal condition of what it means to be alive.

The issue with such diffuseness and its subjective states is that they are extremely difficult to classify and distinguish. Hence, the main goal of this chapter was to illustrate a tentative proposal on how to map visual identities against their narrative dimensions, to some extent operationalising our framework [23], resorting to a few destination brands and their visual identities as case studies, both conventional and mutant.

Therefore, we propose a typological mapping process as a means to relate the imprecision with some form of visual representation. These visualisations seek only to give a general sense of the position of values. The task of reading the exact and precise values of such positions (should they exist) is not the intention. The purpose is to achieve a balance between a representation that attracts the user whilst offering them a sense of where these brands sit regarding their VI's storytelling potential or past/current performance. Above all, the idea is to provide a big picture through a brief scan [18] so that brand professionals can creatively and strategically initiate or restart the definition of the best possible ways to establish meaningful and emotional links between the reality of their offer and the reality of their audiences.

With this chapter we aimed at proposing a way for brand designers, brand storytellers and brand strategists to surface the Scheherazade in each of the brands they work for/with, namely:

1. *During the visual identity's creation phase* – to explore, analyse, organise, and explain the insights they get from researching the brand, its audiences, and its markets, mostly aiming at showcasing and defending the storytelling tactic that will best make justice to the brand's vision and purpose.
2. *During a brand's maintenance* – get an overall view of how its VI's narrative is structured, how it is being used, and where it should go next, extracting recommendations, inspirations, and possible action plans in everything brand narrative and VI -related.

Ultimately, the proposed mapping process may both confirm existing quantitative data or nudge towards the collection of figures that have not been retrieved yet. Eventually, visualisations resorting to this model may even underpin the formulation of data points of view (DataPOV), a sentence that includes a call to action and a proposal of what is at stake, whether the storytelling-related recommendation is followed or not.

Regardless, it is important to note that whatever the approach to storytelling, all will depend on the brand's positioning, since the VI is inherently part of a brand's multimodal and overall discourse and must be loyal to it. As we have seen through the analysed and presented examples, there is no issue whatsoever in being a Conventional brand (e.g., Spain) rather than being a Mutant one. Above all, consistency is expected to be one of the main rules and VIs should always (graphically) reflect the essence of the brand.

References

1. Aaker D (1998) As marcas – Brand Equity: gerenciando o valor da marca. Elsevier, São Paulo
2. Batey M (2008) Brand Meaning. Routledge, NY
3. Beverland M (2018) Brand Management. Sage, London
4. Correll M, Heer J (2017) Black hat visualization. In: Workshop on dealing with cognitive biases in visualisations (DECISIVe). IEEE VIS 2017
5. Damásio A (1995) O Erro de Descartes: Emoção, Razão e Cérebro Humano. Publicações Europa-América, Lisboa
6. Dinnie K (2008) Nation Branding: Concepts, Issues, Practice. Butterworth-Heinemann, Oxford
7. Escalas, J. E. (2004). Imagine yourself in the product. Mental simulation, narrative transportation, and persuasion. *Journal of Advertising*, 33(2), pp. 37–48.
8. Fog K, Budtz C, Yakaboylu B (2005) Storytelling: Branding in Practice. Springer, Germany
9. Gunelius S, Hedges K (2013) *5 Secrets to Use Storytelling for Brand Marketing Success*. Available at: http://www.forbes.com/sites/work-in-progress/2013/02/05/5-secrets-to-using-storytelling-for-brand-marketing-success/#33de8f5e3dd9. Accessed 30 Nov 2022.
10. Hanna S, Rowley J (2008) An analysis of terminology use in place branding. Place Brand Public Dipl 4, 61–75 (2008). https://doi.org/10.1057/palgrave.pb.6000084.
11. Herskovitz S, Crystal M (2010) The Essential Brand Persona: Storytelling and Branding. J Bus Strateg 31(3):21–28

12. Horttanainen P, Virrantaus K (2004) Uncertainty evaluation of military terrain analysis results by simulation and visualization. In: Conference on Geoinformatics - Geospatial Information Research: Bridging the Pacific and Atlantic, pp 473–480
13. Ind N (2001) Living the Brand: How to Transform Every Member of Your Organization into a Brand Ambassador. Kogan Page, New York
14. Kerr G (2006) From destination brand to location brand. J Brand Manag 13(4–5):276–283
15. Kim YK, Sullivan P (2019) Emotional branding speaks to consumers' heart: the case of fashion brands. Fash Text 6(1):2. https://doi.org/10.1186/s40691-018-0164-y
16. Kirk A (2019) Data visualisation: a handbook for data ddriven design, 2nd edn. SAGE, London
17. Kotler P (1981) Administração de marketing: análise, planejamento e controle, 1ª. Atlas, São Paulo
18. Kreutz EA (2001) As Principais Estratégias de Construção da Identidade Visual Corporativa. Master's Dissertation. Pontifícia Universidade Católica do Rio Grande Do Sul
19. Kreutz EA (2005) Identidade visual mutante: uma prática comunicacional da MTV. Doctorate Thesis. Pontifícia Universidade Católica do Rio Grande Do Sul
20. Kreutz EA (2011) O Discurso Multimodal das Marcas Mutantes. XXXIV Intercom. Retrieved from http://www.intercom.org.br/papers/nacionais/2011/resumos/r6-2423-1.pdf. Accessed 10 Dec 2022
21. Kreutz EA, Fuhr IF (2014) Storytelling: rituales contemporáneos para la consolidación de la marca. Brand J. Pathways to Brand(ing): from representation to practice. Year 4. Vol. 07. 07.
22. Lelis C (2019) Like a chameleon: the polychromatic virtue of flexible brands. Journal of Product & Brand Management. https://doi.org/10.1108/JPBM-10-2017-1621
23. Lelis C, Kreutz, EA (2022) The HOW behind the story: a framework for the design of brand narratives. In: Raposo D (ed) Design, visual communication and branding. Cambridge Scholars Publishing, Newcastle, ISBN: 1-5275-8054-7, pp 132–159
24. Lund NF, Cohen SA, Scarles C (2018) The Power of Social Media Storytelling in Destination Branding. J Destin Mark Manag 8:271–280
25. Martin D (2010) Uncovering Unconscious Memories and Myths for Understanding International Tourism Behaviour. J Bus Res 63:372–383
26. Martins T, Cunha JM, Bicker J, Machado P (2019) Dynamic Visual Identities: from a survey of the state-of-the-art to a model of features and mechanisms. Visible Language 53(2):4–35
27. Maturana HR, Varela FJ (1991) Autopoiesis and cognition: the realization of the living, vol 42. Springer Science & Business Media
28. Mena P (2021) Reducing misperceptions through news stories with data visualization: The role of readers' prior knowledge and prior beliefs. Journalism.https://doi.org/10.1177/146488492 11028762
29. Neumeier M (2006) The brand gap. New Riders, San Francisco CA
30. Newman WE (2017) Data visualization for design thinking. Routledge, NY
31. Pera R, Viglia G (2016) Exploring How Video Digital Storytelling Builds Relationship Experiences. Psychol Mark 33(12):1142–50
32. Ries A, Trout J (1993) Posicionamento: a batalha pela sua mente, 4ª. Pioneira, São Paulo
33. Ritchie JR, Ritchie JB (1998) The branding of tourism destinations, in *Annual Congress of the International Association of Scientific Experts in Tourism*, Morocco, September.
34. Rosch E (1975) Cognitive representations of semantic categories. J Exp Psychol Gen 104:192–233
35. Sharma R (2017) Building customer-based brand equity of domestic brands: Role of brand equity dimensions. Metamorphosis 16(1):45–59
36. Shen H, Bednarz T, Nguyen H, Feng F, Wyeld T, Hoek PJ, Lo EH (2019) Information visualisation methods and techniques: State-of-the-art and future directions. J Ind Inf Integr 16:100–102
37. Thompson CJ, Rindfleisch A, Arsel Z (2006) Emotional branding and the strategic value of the doppelgänger brand image. J Mark 70(1):50–64
38. Troiano J (2017) Brand Intelligence: Construindo Marcas que Fortalecem Empresas e Movimentam a Economia. Estação das Letras e Cores, São Paulo

39. Tussyadiah I, Fesenmaier D (2008) Marketing Places through First-Person Stories —An Analysis of Pennsylvania Roadtripper Blog. J Travel Tour Mark 25(3/4):299–311
40. Van Ham P (2008) Place branding: The state of the art. Ann Am Acad Pol Soc Sci 616(1):126–149
41. Van Laer T, De Ruyter K, Visconti LM, Wetzels M (2014) The Extended Transportation-Imagery Model: A Meta-analysis of the Antecedents and Consequences of Consumers' Narrative Transportation. Journal of Consumer Research 40(5):797–817
42. Van Laer T, Feiereisen S, Visconti LM (2019) Storytelling in the Digital Era: A Meta-analysis of Relevant Moderators of the Narrative Transportation Effect. J Bus Res 96:135–146
43. Zadeh LA (1965) Fuzzy sets. Inf Control 8(3):338–353. https://doi.org/10.1016/S0019-9958(65)90241-X

Principles for the Design of Brand Marks

Alice Vieira, João Brandão, Daniel Raposo, and Nuno Martins

Abstract This chapter aims to deepen the understanding about the Design of Brand Marks in the design-symbolic-perception relationship to clarify concepts and contribute to the advancement of knowledge in this theme, assisting in the design, standardization, and use of brand marks. A qualitative non-interventionist methodology was selected, namely a literature review to clarify, delimit and discuss the concepts and different taxonomies of graphic brands, as well as to identify graphic brand design principles; furthermore, the case study methodology, based on six Graphic Standards Manuals, allowed the identification of design principles, and confront them with the knowledge obtained by the literature review. The methodology was relevant insofar as it allowed us to identify the principles necessary for the Design of Brand Marks. The literature review showed a lack of consensus and some points of convergence in taxonomic classifications and in the definition of concepts and design principles for Brand Marks. The case study allowed us to observe that even the Brand Marks designed by professional designers present structural and formal errors, standardization errors, as well as incorrect or imprecise technical terminology. We consider that this chapter contributes to the deepening of knowledge in the field of Brand Mark Design, through the clarification of concepts, terms, and principles for the development of Brand Marks.

Keywords Brand Marks · Graphic Principles · Logotype · Symbol

A. Vieira · J. Brandão
Lisbon School of Architecture, Universidade de Lisboa, Rua Sá Nogueira, 1349-063 Lisboa, Portugal
e-mail: joao@b2design.pt

D. Raposo (✉)
Research Centre for Architecture, Urbanism and Design, Polytechnic Institute of Castelo Branco, Castelo Branco, Portugal
e-mail: draposo@ipcb.pt

N. Martins
Research Institute for Design, Media and Culture, School of Design, Polytechnic Institute of Cávado and Ave, Barcelos, Portugal
e-mail: nmartins@ipca.pt

N. Martins and D. Raposo (eds.), *Communication Design and Branding*,
Springer Series in Design and Innovation 32,
https://doi.org/10.1007/978-3-031-35385-7_2

1 Introduction

The success of a given company, product or service depends on several facts that ensure its notoriety and differentiation in the market and an effective communication, which includes: a visual identity system, quality in the product and service, a good consumer experience, a selection of media appropriate to the profile of the audiences, articulated media, and advertising, among others.

Regarding the creation of awareness, brand dimension and brand positioning in the market, the Visual Identity System plays a strategic role in the process of identification, differentiation, and memorization, creating conditions for the effectiveness of the brand communication media over time.

According to Raposo et al. [1], the Visual Identity Systems are a supersystem, insofar as it includes other systems (a set of correlated components articulated by their meaning and graphic similarity to form a coherent whole), such as the Brand Mark, the base and secondary chromatic palette, typography, imagery, formats, and other graphics. The elements of the Identity System and its design principles (rules for selection and use) define the brand language and ensure visual coherence in all media, whether physical, digital, virtual, two-dimensional, three-dimensional, spatial, or audiovisual.

In the Brand Visual Identity System, the Brand Mark stands out as the graphic signs whose meaning is the brand. After the name, the Brand Mark is the most used and most seen identity element. The Brand Mark works as a signature of the brand, identifying what belongs to it or is of its authorship/responsibility and differentiating the brand, its property, products, and services from those of its competitors.

A Brand Mark is a graphic element that is marked on products for identification and on branded media, while a brand is a network of intangible concepts about something.

Since a Brand Mark plays a role of identification and differentiation, its selection and design have perceptual requirements on a symbolic, graphic, and aesthetic level, articulating denotative with connotative meanings. The Brand Mark needs to be graphically aligned with what the brand represents.

This chapter discusses the Brand Mark concept and the different classificatory taxonomies, presenting some design principles, as a result of a master's thesis.

The investigative process was designed considering a set of associated problems, namely:

- The lack of consensus on key concepts in this theme, as well as publications dedicated to the design of Brand Marks that merely present cases and portfolios, lacking reflection, systematization, and in-depth theoretical study of this practice;
- Wrong or inaccurate use of technical terminology about Brand Mark types, in books, papers, Visual Identity Guidelines, brand standards manuals, brand centers, namely the confusion between Brand Mark, logo, logotype and symbol;
- Translation problems in the terms Brand Mark, logo, logotype and symbol;

- The great diversity of communication media (enhanced by globalization and the Internet) that demand more of the Brand Marks' design, namely the need for reduction and recognition;
- Misconceptions in the selection and design of Brand Marks, disregarding the context of use, technical and perceptual limitations, as well as brand communication needs.

Considering the problematic, two research questions were defined:

- What are the relevant concepts, terminologies, and principles in the process of designing a Brand Mark?
- What are the graphic characteristics of brands of companies with an international dimension, success and history? How to use these characteristics in the design of new ones?

Additionally, the following research objectives were defined:

- To deepen the knowledge about the design of Brand Marks, in the design-symbolic-perception relationship;
- Clarify concepts and terms specific to Brand Marks design;
- Identify general design principles of Brand Marks.

In order to answer the research questions and objectives, a qualitative non-interventionist methodology was adopted. The literature review allowed to proceed to the study framing, as well as to discuss concepts and morphological classifications and contributed to the definition of Brand Marks design principles. On the other hand, the descriptive case study allowed the analysis of the Brand Mark section in six digital Graphic Standards Manuals (three in E-pub format and three in PDF format), with the purpose of identifying Brand Marks design principles. The results of the case study were confronted with those of the literature review, allowing conclusions to be drawn.

2 Theoretical Framework

2.1 Brand Marks Concept

The concept of brand has been discussed in several areas, namely management, marketing, communication and design, with no consensus on concepts or a common lexicon. Kotler and Keller [2, p. 386] state that "a brand is a name, term, sign, symbol or design, or a combination thereof, that is intended to identify the goods and services of a seller or group of sellers and differentiate them from those of competitors." However, for Costa [3, p. 18] the concept of brand is more than that, defining it as "a socio-economic, political and cultural phenomenon, but also legal, formal, semiotic, etc.". Raposo [4, p. 241] considers that "the brand is a consequence of associations arising from the experience and culture of the receiver, taking into account messages received directly or indirectly from the organization (…) that work as groups and systems of signs and that culminate in the collective social imaginary".

Thus, in the scope of this work, we consider that a brand is a network of related meanings formed in the collective imagination (the brand image) of the people who know the brand. The brand image results from experiences and contacts with the brand and includes reputation and secondary associations, establishing the brand equity of the corporation, business, product or service.

As for the Brand Mark, Raposo [5] defines it as the visual graphic sign that represents the brand, namely a logotype or a symbol (separately or as a group), and may include a designation, slogan or descriptive. In the same sense, Chaves [6] states that a Brand Mark is a visual sign capable of representing and synthesizing the identity and image of a company. The Brand Mark is a sign, something that means and that is used in the communication and identification of the brand, being subjected to different conditions that require flexibility in the reduction, recognition in different contexts and ease of retention and memorization [5].

Brand Marks are logotypes or symbols used separately or in combination. A logotype is a graphic representation of the brand name to be seen and read, so its design is made with typography (predefined letters or numbers), modified typography, or lettering (designed exclusively for that purpose) [7, 8]. The symbol is a conventionalized graphic representation of an idea that synthesizes the meaning of the brand or something that has meaning in its narrative, and can be iconic, schematic, abstract or generative [9].

Thus, a Brand Mark must follow certain principles of design and use, so that they can contribute to the awareness of the brand identity and its adequate positioning in the market. Calderón [10] explains that the Brand Mark identifies the brand, whose communication oversees presenting arguments and building a narrative that informs, guarantees symbolic differentiation, and establishes an agreement or commitment about quality and the relationship with stakeholders in the short and long term.

The study Logos Now by Siegel + Gale [11], focused on the perceptions of different global brands, states that the brand mark can connote or arouse secondary associations, emotions and feelings in the person who perceives it, even if this person has had no previous contact with the brand.

Brand image begins to form in the first visual, consumer, communicational, advertising, or reputational contact between a stakeholder and a brand, organization, business, product or service. It is in this context that branding seeks to manage the public perception of the brand, while the Visual Identity System aims to ensure the correct identification, differentiation, and communication [5].

A Brand Mark is a sign of identity that establishes the correlation between products, product ranges, services and other goods and equipment, differentiating and identifying the brand in buildings, in its media and in what it sells.

The design of a Brand Mark includes structural, formal factors, and the graphic features that correlate its sub-components. It also includes the perceptual and symbolic strategies of style and level of iconicity or abstraction, capable of ensuring that the Brand Mark is fixed in the collective memory in a manner consistent with the brand. The Brand Mark can be measured, touched, and seen and registered for commercial use, while the trademark is essentially an immaterial idea or concept [9].

2.2 *Taxonomy*

The taxonomy, that is, the morphological classification of the elements of a Brand Mark and its organization by classes or typologies, helps in the analysis and understanding of the various types of Brand Marks [12]. In the process of developing a de-terminated Brand Mark it is important to know it's different typologies, in order to choose the one that best fits the brand concept, values, means and needs of identification and communication. However, among the authors who study Brand Marks there are distinct visions as to their taxonomy. We consider some classifications unnecessarily complex, while others are not very useful for categorizing Brand Marks.

2.2.1 Chaves and Bellucia Classification

According to authors Chaves and Bellucia [13], Brand Marks are divided in two main categories: logotypes and symbols. Logotypes are subdivided into four subclasses: "typographical" (use of an already designed typeface); "exclusive" (use of a typeface designed specifically for the brand; "retouched" (use of an already existing typeface with changes in certain elements, such as spaces, sizes, proportions, lengthening or compression of some elements, creation of special ligatures, among others, with the aim of increasing the uniqueness of the Brand Mark); and "iconized" (use of an existing typeface, replacing some letters with icons that correspond formally); The authors also add two other subclasses: "singular logotype" (a set designed as a whole, with an exceptional shape that does not respond to any existing typeface); and "logotype with stable accessory" (use of certain complementary elements to strengthen contrast and differentiation, such as, underlining, small symbol, dot or just a background with, usually, geometric shape).

The symbols are divided into three categories: iconic (use of something representative and recognizable in the real or imaginary world with a high level of formal similarity or its encoding); abstract (use of a representation without similarity to an object, whose form connotes sensations, such as "hardness", "fragility", "softness", "tradition", among others); and alphabetic (use of initials of the brand name or letter to represent the brand). Graphically, the symbols can be designed in more organic or geometric shapes and can be combined with the various types of logotypes, which they call a combined Brand Mark.

2.2.2 Cassisi, Bellucia and Chaves Classification [14]

In 2011, Cassisi, Bellucia and Chaves [14] proposed another classification that is divided into nominal and symbolic identifiers. However, it has similarities with the classification presented previously.

Nominal identifiers encompass logotypes with background (inserted in a dependent background); pure logotype (representation of the name through typography, calligraphy, or lettering); and logotype with accessory (accompanied by a dependent symbol).

On the other hand, symbolic identifiers cover logotypes with symbol (accompanied by an independent symbol); and logo-symbols (integration of the logotype into the symbol).

2.2.3 Mollerup Classification [12]

In Mollerup's classification [12] Trademarks are divided into Non-Graphic Marks and Graphic Marks, which in turn are subdivided into Picture Marks and Letter Marks.

The Picture Marks are divided into Figurative Marks (representing a concrete object) and sub-divided into Descriptive Marks (describing what it represents), Metaphoric Marks (describing a recognizable idea or one that has meaning in context) or Found Marks (arbitrary selection and abstract form); and Non-Figurative Marks (use of images).

Letter Marks are organized into Name Marks or Abbreviations. The Name Marks are subdivided into five classes: Proper Names; Descriptive Names; Metaphoric Names; Found Names; Artificial Names.

Abbr are subdivided into Initial Names or Non-Initial Abbreviations. Initial Names decline into Acronyms and Non-Acronym Initial Abbreviations.

We can observe that Mollerup's classification [12] is based on what it is and how it is designed. However, in the case of the logotype, the classification follows less the morphological or typographical logic and adopts the structure according to the naming and connotation of the brand name.

2.2.4 Classification Raposo et al. [1]

Raposo et al. [1] present a classification focused on the morphological structure of the Brand Marks and by their graphic style, organizing them into two major groups: sym-bols and logotypes.

A symbol can be classified as iconic (descriptive or metaphoric), schematic (organic or geometric), abstract (organic or geometric), alphabetic (with letters) or dynamic (dynamic is when the shapes undergo some kind of graphic change in structure, color or texture, or are replaced from a set of possibilities, are customized or obey to a script or generative programming). In the case of the logotype, it can be typographic, lettering, calligraphic or dynamic.

The authors also consider Brand Marks combining symbol and logotype. For Raposo et al. [1], the needs and limitation of brand communication should determine the typology of Brand Mark and as well the visual hierarchy between symbol and logotype, if used together.

2.2.5 Adoption of a Brand Marks Classification

Chaves [14] states that many poor-quality Brand Marks result from inadequate choices in the typology to be used. In this sense, Chaves [14] states that the design of a Brand Mark should start by selecting the typology and factors such as: respect or rupture in the sectorial codes; extension and layout of the designation; the various points of contact; the brand architecture; the alignment and semantic compatibility with the brand.

By analyzing the different taxonomic classifications of Brand Marks it was possible to identify the common typologies.

In a first stage, we tried to adopt for this study the classification of Cassisi, Bellucia and Chaves [14]. However, we found that some Brand Marks could fit into more than one class, while others could not fit into any typology. In this sense, the classification proposed by Raposo et al. was adopted [1].

3 Case Studies

The case study was selected as a non-interventional research methodology, including the direct observation method and a descriptive analysis of the common chapters on graphic brands in six digital Graphic Standards Manuals (three e-pub and three Brand Center). The six cases were selected considering three criteria: being brands with an international dimension, having representativeness, and considering its level of complexity in graphic standardization. Two cases were selected from each sector: technology, automobiles, and university institutions, including cases with dynamic visual identity.

The study focused on the standards manuals (e-pub version) of the brands Edp, Kia and OCAD University and the brand centers of the brands IBM, Audi and Aalto University and on the sections: brand anatomy, construction (grid), variations of brand shape, brand versions (horizontal and vertical), protection area, minimum size, positioning (in physical and digital media), application, use on backgrounds (colored and photographic), composition (layout), prohibitions (don’ts), and the relationship of the graphic brand with other elements (typography, sub-brands, partners, and signature).

In a complementary manner, the 15 most representative brands from each of the sectors were selected: food industry, transportation, university institutions, place identities, and sports, for a total of 75 Brand Marks.

The evolutionary process of each Brand Mark was observed to verify its relationship with fashion phenomena; furthermore, an empirical analysis was made of the graphic characteristics of the current brands: anatomy, composition, colors, logotype, typographic class (through Vox Classification), typography variant, sign type, symbol type, iconicity scale, favicon existence, minimum size, blur and pixelation performance, behavior in monochrome (black and inverted), and Vienna Classification. Brand Mark anatomy (classification by typology) and morphology (symbol-logo relationship) and syntax (subcomponents, colors, etc.) were also compared [9].

4 Principles of Graphic Design for the Brand Marks

When we refer to design principles, we consider the criteria and fundamentals that determine the selection, design, configuration, and composition of the components that make up a Brand Mark as a single and coherent whole. In this case, we are particularly interested in those that can contribute to the memorization and recognition of the Brand Marks by the stakeholders. As Raposo [9] states, Brand Mark design principles are not rules, checklists, nor recipes or guidelines, but rather basic fundamentals on how to proceed during the design and use of a Brand Mark.

The definition of principles for the design of Brand Marks has been discussed in greater depth by several authors, such as Solas [15], Mollerup [12], Leitão et al. [16], Calderón [10], Cuéllar [17], Shumate [18], and Raposo [9].

According to Solas [15] the design principles of a Brand Mark come from the identity strategy and the strategies of its visualization. Solas [15] considers that from the identity strategy result: the representation principle or symbolic principle (the global image in its entirety represents an identity); formalization principle (refers to the image as a whole); integration or consistency principle (guarantees visual coherence in the various supports, in order to produce a global image, through the standardization of the various components); universality principle or image globalization, which is divided into: cultural universality, temporal universality (preference for simplicity and generic and racionalized forms for greater durability); and universality of the addressees (divided into three classes: superior, considered in some way as prescribers of the entity; the intermediate class, composed of emulators; and the type of publics; principle of normalization (guidelines for the reproduction of the Brand Mark in the various media); and principle of differentiation (rupture of the sectorial codes or formal assimilation to its major competitor).

Concerning the principles that come from visualization strategies, Solas [15] considers geometrization, sharpness and legibility. The author mentions that combining geometry, with sharpness and legibility strongly impacts the categorization of the normalization principle insofar as it makes it flexible to use in various media and printing materials and processes. Furthermore, he considers that the legibility of the Brand Mark is determined by its size and context of use.

Calderón [10] considers as principles of design of Brand Marks the universality, the originality (differentiation), the standardization and adds the graphic synthesis or simplicity (the fewer features the Brand Mark has, the better its perception and easy memorization).

On the other hand, Mollerup [12] states that a Brand Mark must be quickly identifiable and transmit the values of the company or product it represents, being necessary to consider requirements such as: recognition, application, differentiation, legal protection, simplicity, attention value, decency, color reproduction, black and white reproduction, applicability in products and media, its eye-holding power, description, tone of voice, its relation to fashions, timeless character, graphic excellence, the ability to say "buy me", to be a trademark, to be able to be used in digital and video, three-dimensionally, associable with non-verbal sounds, discretion and likeness.

Mollerup [12] considers it essential to first identify the brand's competitors and media, noting that a word mark may be stronger in certain media than a pictorial mark. Moreover, its ability to differentiate itself from competing brands is fundamental.

For Cuéllar [17] designing a Brand Mark should imply principles such as: the concept of the brand; its flexibility (possibility of use in different brand communication media); its originality (possibility of registration as a unique brand); its durability (ability to last at least five years); its timeless character (not to be defined by trends); its adaptability (ability to adapt to various scales and media); its legibility (easy reading, recognition and subsequent memorization); its identification (ability to recognize the main components of the Brand Mark, such as shape, typography—if any—and color); its representation (alignment with the values and mission of the company it represents); and its aesthetics (secondary associations or connotation by the graphic appearance).

From another perspective, Shumate [18] argues that a Brand Mark should ensure the following requirements: instant recognition; ability to transpose into monochrome, especially black, without altering the visual perception of the original version; consistency and ability to reproduce in various situations; mass, i.e. density enough to be legible in reduced formats; contrast with the background where the Brand Mark is applied; formal and style coherence; the non-overlapping of elements; the form should be a synthesis that works as a cohesive whole.

In his study, Raposo [9] agrees with other authors about the need for differentiation, timelessness and flexibility of use, adding the possibility of visual declination, monochromatic use with true negatives, the form's contrast through a skeleton or structure recognizable at a distance and with low vision, the level of schematization or iconicity, the semantic compatibility with the brand and its positioning in the market, the graphic synthesis and the power of fascination (state of attention on the subject and the ability to retain the look or seduction). Also, the principle of exaggeration (artificial appearance and formal accentuation of certain features improve the contrast in the media and environments), stating that the artificial character allows a Brand Mark to contrast more in a natural, urban or audiovisual world [19].

In another perspective, Shumate [18] argues that a Brand Mark must ensure the following requirements: instant recognition; ability to transpose to monochrome, especially to black, without changing the visual perception of the original version; consistency and ability to reproduce in various situations; mass, i.e., enough density to be readable in reduced formats; contrast with the background where the Brand Mark is applied; formal and style coherence; the non-overlapping of elements; the form must be a synthesis that works as a cohesive whole.

In his study, Raposo [9] coincides with other authors regarding the need for differentiation, timelessness and flexibility of use, adding the possibility of visual declination, monochromatic use with true negatives, the contrast of the shape through a skeleton or structure recognizable at a distance and with low vision, the level of schematization or iconicity, the semantic compatibility with the brand and its positioning in the market, the graphic synthesis and the power of fascination (state of attention in the subject and the ability to retain the look or seduction). Also the principle of exaggeration (artificial appearance and formal accentuation of certain characteristics improve contrast in media and environments), stating that the artificial character allows a brand mark to contrast more in a natural, urban or audiovisual world [19] (Fig. 1).

5 Conclusion

The methodology of the present study seems adequate to the extent that it allowed us to identify principles for the design of Brand Marks. In the literature review, we observed the existence of several taxonomic classifications of Brand Marks. After analyzing the selected classifications, we observed that some are unnecessarily complex, while others do not allow us to adequately categorize certain Brand Marks. We understand that a typological classification should be explicit and easy to categorize as the one proposed by Raposo et al. However, the study of other classifications was important as it allowed us to increase our knowledge on the subject under study. The literature review also allowed us to identify common and different denomination of Brand Marks design principles.

From the case studies, it was concluded that many existing Brand Marks have performance gaps because of design errors and standardization of use. Several problems were observed in the technical lexicon and that in the placeholder there is a tendency to use a rectangle or square with the same perimeter area, which is a clear optical problem. The data indicates that most of the Brand Marks combine logotype and symbol, being particularly evident in the university and Place Brands. Regarding color, there was a predominance of red, particularly in the food industry and university sector. More than half of the Brand Marks have a single color, with emphasis on the transportation sector.

It was possible to observe that in digital applications logotypes perform worse than a symbol than a symbol, due to their horizontality. Many Brand Marks have little mass (spot or contrast), especially logotypes, implying the use of containing shapes

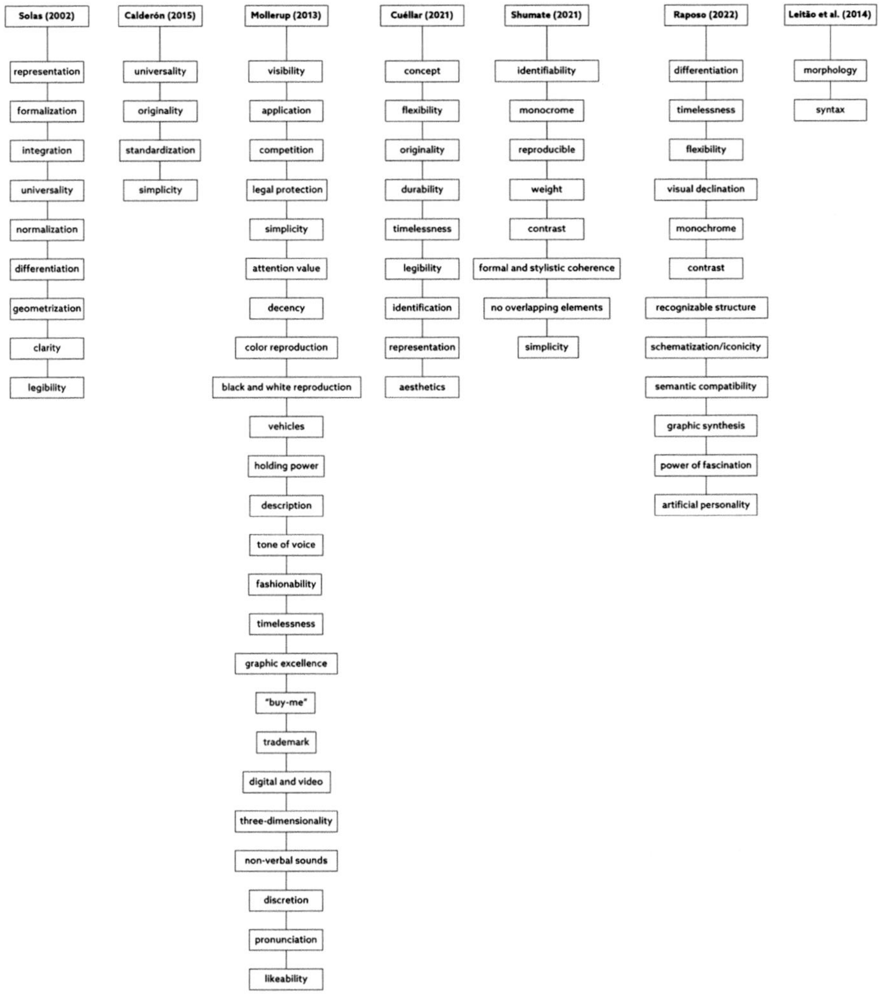

Fig. 1 Diagram principles for the design of graphic brands

to ensure contrast; There are Brand Marks unsuitable for applications in monochrome for light or dark backgrounds; In the automotive industry, it was observed that, until the end of the twentieth century, the Brand Marks were flat and that, in the transition to the XXI century became three-dimensional. From around 2007 and especially after 2015 there has been a trend towards two-dimensional design.

In summary, it is considered that the design of Brand Marks requires knowledge of certain concepts and principles, namely: visual coherence, sufficient contrast, legibility, flexibility, transposition to monochrome—especially to black, timelessness, excellence of graphics, semantic compatibility, adaptability, the power of fascination, the exaggeration of the form/structure, the hierarchy between symbol and logotype, originality and formal balance of the whole. Many of these principles are present both in the Brand Marks and in the various means of communication of successful companies with an international dimension and a history of success.

The study allowed clarifying the Brand Mark concept, as well as understanding the imprecision in the use of technical terminology and the translation problems in Visual Identity Guidelines, brand standards manuals, brand centers.

It also allowed us to understand that the diversity of media, and digital media in particular, pose greater challenges to the design of Brand Marks, especially in the reduction and recognition at a distance and in small formats such as favicon and avatars on social networks.

It was also realized the importance of establishing design principles and standards considering the Brand Marks in optical and perceptive terms and not only geometric ones.

It was possible to define Brand Mark, Logotype and Symbol and to study the characteristics of Brand Marks of brands with international dimension, namely their evolution over time and how they resist fashion phenomena. The study allowed us to contribute to the knowledge about the design of Brand Marks in the design-symbol-perception relation and to identify general principles for their design.

For future developments, it is considered relevant the development of a digital platform, in website format, that presents, classifies, analyzes and compares several Brand Marks. This website is intended to be a form of visual education and a support to clarify and explain concepts and principles specific to Brand Marks design.

Acknowledgements This article is a synthesis of the Master's dissertation, within the scope of the course in Communication Design at the Faculty of Architecture of the University of Lisbon, defended in February 2023, entitled Principles for the Design of Graphic Brands, under the supervision of Professors João Brandão and Daniel Raposo, following Daniel Raposo Post-Doctoral research.

References

1. Raposo D, Silva F, Correia R, Ribeiro R, Neves J, Silva J (2022) Brand Marks examination. Empirical study of graphic parts in their relation to contrast, recognition, and memorization. In: Rebelo F (ed) ergonomics In design. AHFE (2022) international conference. AHFE open access, vol 47. AHFE International, USA. https://doi.org/10.54941/ahfe1001985
2. Kotler P, Keller KL (2016) Marketing management, 5th edn, global edition. Pearson Education
3. Costa J (2004) La imagen de marca: Un fenómeno social (1a ed., 5a imp). Paidós
4. Martins DR (2005) Gestão de identidadecorporativa: do signo ao código. Universidade, Aveiro, 258 p. Dissertação de Mestrado
5. Martins DR (2012) La letracomo signo de identidad visual corporativa [DoctoralThesis, Universidade Técnica de Lisboa, Faculdade de Arquitectura]. https://www.repository.utl.pt/handle/10400.5/17758?locale=en
6. Chaves N (2015) La marca: señal, nombre, identidad y bla-són. EME Exp Illus, Art & Des 3(3):40–49. https://doi.org/10.4995/eme.2015.3432
7. Wheeler A (2018) Designing brand identity: an essential guide for the entire branding team, 5th edn. Wiley

8. Peón ML (2003) Sistemas de Identidade Visual. 2AB, vol 3, p 104
9. Raposo D (2022) Análise de Marcas Gráficas: Marcas portuguesas de produtos alimentares destinados à exportação [Investigação Pós-Doutoral]. CIAUD
10. Nive Flórez Calderón B (2015) Guía para diseñaruna marca. Editorial UOC
11. Siegel+Gale (2015) A study of logo treatments and brand perceptions. Recuperado de http://simple.siegelgale.com/acton/attachment/9371/f-0160/1/-/-/-/-/Logos%20Now.pdf
12. Mollerup P (2013) Marks of excellence: the history and taxonomy of trademarks (Second edition (revised, expanded and updated)). Phaidon Press Limited
13. Chaves N, Bellucia R (2003) La marca corporativa: gestion y diseño de simbolos y logotipos. Buenos Aires, Paidós
14. Chaves N (2012) Pensamento tipológico. ForoAlfa. https://foroalfa.org/pt/artigos/pensamento-tipologico
15. Solas JG (2002) Identidad visual corporativa: La imagen de nuestro tiempo. Síntesis
16. Leitão SML (2014) Princípios estruturantes e orientadores da identidade visual de marcas em ambientes multimeios [MasterThesis, Universidade de Aveiro]. https://ria.ua.pt/handle/10773/15166
17. Cuéllar-González R (2021) Logo: ten essential characteristics
18. Shumate AM (2021) Logo design theory: how branding design really works (2.1). Elfstone Press
19. Laginha C, Raposo D, Neves J (2016) La Escala de Iconicidad en el ámbito de las Marcas Gráficas. Em E. Herrera, & L. Fernández, Actas del Primer Congreso de Diseño Gráfico: Marcas Gráficas de Identidad Corporativa. UPV/EHU, pp 153–160

Dynamic Visual Identities: Fundamental Principles of Their Design

Pedro Fonte, Nuno Martins, Daniel Raposo, and Leonardo Pereira

Abstract This article analyzes Dynamic Visual Identities (DVI) intending to present a set of principles that designers should take into account when designing such systems. It starts with a literature review, approaching a set of reference authors, to clarify the key concepts around the DVI; its relationship with brands, brand identities, visual identity systems; the socio-historical context that leads to the expansion of dynamic identities; the typology of DVI constructions, categorizing them and demonstrating some of their guiding and structural principles in their construction. A chronological overview of some pioneering DVI systems that introduced mechanisms designed for dynamism is also presented. Finally, based on the study carried out, the main potentialities and risks in the use of the DVI are presented and a set of principles to be taken into account in its design are identified.

Keywords Dynamic visual identities · Logo design · Brand identity

P. Fonte
School of Design, Polytechnic Institute of Cavado and Ave, Barcelos, Portugal

N. Martins (✉)
Research Institute for Design, Media and Culture, School of Design, Polytechnic Institute of Cávado and Ave, Barcelos, Portugal
e-mail: nmartins@ipca.pt

D. Raposo
Research Centre for Architecture, Urbanism and Design, Polytechnic Institute of Castelo Branco, Castelo Branco, Portugal

L. Pereira
DigiMedia, Department of Communication and Art, University of Aveiro, Campus Universitário de Santiago, 3810-193 Aveiro, Portugal

N. Martins and D. Raposo (eds.), *Communication Design and Branding*,
Springer Series in Design and Innovation 32,
https://doi.org/10.1007/978-3-031-35385-7_3

1 Dynamic Visual Identities

1.1 Context

Since the late 1950s, there have been noticeable changes in the way brands present and communicate themselves. Factors such as technological advancements, distinct features of various media, and evolving market expectations have encouraged new types of relationships and altered the contexts in which brands operate. As a result, there has been a proliferation of new approaches to visual identities.

However, dynamic visual identities (DIV) approaches differ from conventional or traditional methods in several aspects. In the past, brands rationalized and controlled their presence in different media by standardizing and predicting their visual homogeneity [7]. The focus was on achieving easy recognition through consistent and predictable visual identity systems [1]. However, with the emergence of profound contextual changes, such as technological advancements, digital printing, the internet, new media, the customization, and transformations in brand communication needs, this rigid and standardized approach began to show its limitations. As a result, brands, companies, and institutions had to change their positioning to stand out in an increasingly competitive and media-saturated market. They sought to build stronger, lasting, and irreplaceable emotional connections with customers through various means [21]. Additionally, they used surprise tactics to draw attention and provoke consumers [14] as part of their overall strategy.

1.2 Brand Identity

The need to establish strong connections between brands and people has brought about a shift in visual identity systems. Brands and organizations have started to develop new strategies for creating identities that adapt to their own needs and those of their audiences, while reflecting the socio-historical context in which they operate [20]. However, this new context, not only created new needs, desires, and perspectives of the world, but also led to the evolution of techniques, styles, media, and platforms [6]. The evolution of media and platforms, in particular, was decisive for brands, as it provided access to a multitude of new touchpoints that increased brand recognition and loyalty among audiences and customers. This new type of presence crystallized the brand's identity, making it tangible and enabling more effective communication of differences, ideas, and meanings that appeal to the senses of consumers and users [21]. This is one of the reasons why design plays a crucial role in this context. It is essential for creating and constructing brands, not only because it can differentiate them from others, but also because it can incorporate and convey the intangible qualities that they aim to achieve through their identity systems to different types of consumers.

1.3 Dynamic Visual Identities

DVIs can have different names. In addition to the term used throughout the article, the following terminology has been identified: flexible visual identities [3], adaptive visual identities [4], and mutant brands [6]. However, regardless of the assigned name, there is broad agreement on certain traits that characterize them. For example, [5] distinguishes between two large groups of corporate visual identities: conventional and unconventional. The former is characterized by rigidity, standardization, and immutability, while the latter is characterized by flexibility and dynamism, indicating a new approach to construction and communication. Felsing [3] also refers to conventional ones as static (without variable components) and non-conventional or mutant ones as flexible (with variability based on the interaction between constant and variable elements). Budelmann et al. [1] refer to an earlier time when monolithic consistency was the prevailing wisdom to create recognizable and memorable identities, and to a later time, with stronger graphic identities that inaugurate a new trend of customization, as in the example of MTV.

These two major groups or ways of visual identity building, along with their logos, have led to a consensus on the characterization of temporal periods. In the first case, the period is described as modernist, and in the second as postmodernist. According to various authors, this change has been caused by profound contextual shifts that occurred during the transition from the 20th to the twenty-first century [6, 7]. Political, technological, and sociological changes, not only drove the development of new approaches to a visual identity that are more flexible, multifaceted, and fluid, but also transformed various features of brand communication, usage, relationships with audiences and consumers, performance contexts, and market expectations [1, 5, 19]. Irene [19] highlights successive technological, technical, and media evolutions, such as the strong expansion of the internet and its influence on markets and the global context, as the fundamental factors that have driven brands to behave like living organisms that are in constant adaptation.

Another common feature is found in the graphic standards manual. As an element that was part of the traditional identity construction process, it ensured that both brands and organizations adhered to established assumptions regarding the correct use and application of identities. The identity manual anticipated and regulated hypothetical behaviors that the brand would acquire in different physical supports and forms of contact with the public [7]. In traditional systems of visual identities, after designing the identity or logo [6, 7], the manual helped ensure the correct use of the brand, and consequently, its recognition and memorization [1, 8]. However, with the evolution and emergence of more flexible approaches to visual identities, this posture changed. The rigidity of the rules that the manual entailed was replaced by identity programs that prioritize variety through customization and personalization [1, 7].

The authors also identify the types of brands that adopt the strategy of dynamic visual identities to represent their companies or institutions [15]. These types of brands are mainly found in the cultural and public sectors [3], or more specifically, in organizations such as galleries, public relations consultants, music companies, or brands associated with designers themselves, where creativity, experimentation, and the unexpected are valued [17]. Felsing [3] argues that the reason for this trend is related to the design process itself, including the variation process and the lack of control over the outcome, as well as the wide spectrum of variation and its complexity. These aspects make it difficult to recognize the connection between the different variations, which can pose enormous risks for organizations and their visual identities: they may become imperceptible or not memorable in the eyes of the public.

1.4 The Construction Processes of DVI

The analysis of the construction processes of DVI will focus on the perspective of three authors: Van Nes [19], Kreutz [6], and Felsing [3]. Van Nes [19] summarizes the brand's visual identity system in six components (and the connections they make between them): typography, imagery, logo, language, graphic elements, and color. However, she explains that to build a dynamic identity, one or more of these components must be of a variable nature and that it is through their manipulation that the flexibility of the identity will be determined. And she concludes that fixed components, through consistency, favor brand recognition, and variability gives it room to live and evolve.

Van Nes [19] classifies the construction of DVIs into six groups:

1. *Container*: approach the logo as a box or container that can constantly change its content. Manipulating a single variable, such as color or image, is enough to create great variety while still being recognizable;
2. *Wallpaper*: placing variables behind a constant logo. The general form varies, but the impression of a unique identity remains;
3. *DNA*: dynamic identities created from a set of pre-established "ingredients" that can be combined in different ways, each combination offering a different result;
4. *Formula*: instead of allowing the ingredients to form the core of the identity, the system is allowed to form its own content. Whether it's a grid or a set of rules, it forms a language, a formula, that unifies the whole;
5. *Customized*: addresses customization as a current fashion trend that allows the customer to interact and be part of the brand, or even own it. It is the first step in allowing the identity to reflect a certain sense of community, thus creating an emotional bond;
6. *Generative*: using computational techniques based on rule sets that allow identities to react to external data.

Kreutz [6], varying the form and nomenclature, subdivides Mutant visual identities into Programmed (a certain number of variations for a given period of time) and Poetic (spontaneous variations, without pre-defined rules and yielding to the creative appeal of designers). However, concerning the construction process, it establishes the following stages:

1. Identify the nature/essence of the brand: each brand has its own vision of the world and its mission and designs its personality throughout its existence through its multimodal discourse;
2. Determine the desired brand perception: the organization needs to determine what image it wants the public to have of the brand;
3. Consider the desirable characteristics: the most recurrent of an VI are concept, originality, clear meaning, persuasive and memorable, usability (appropriate colors, suitable in black and white, suitable for vehicles, suitable for media, 3D renderable, pronounceable), and dynamism;
4. Determine the base VI: the function of the VI is the visual representation of the essence of the brand, that is, it must be the graphic synthesis of the organization's values and can contain: name, typography, symbol, and colors. It is the skeleton, the main identity subject to registration at the National Institute of Industrial Property (INPI), and from which mutations may arise;
5. Mutant (Dynamic) Characteristics: the most recurrent are fragmentation, color, typography, shape, name/word, and movement, among others;
6. Mutant Visual Identities Collections: sets of variations of an VI on the same theme;
7. Interactive field: opening given so that the public can interact with the brand. Interaction can be interpretive and/or appropriative (action of modifying the brand graphically).

Felsing [3] defines flexible visual identities by their ability to exhibit variability, context-dependency, processability, performativity, non-linearity, coherency, and variety. These characteristics can be present in varying degrees within visual identities. However, to attain a fully developed visual identity, several criteria must be fulfilled. One of the most prominent criteria is the incorporation of variation, which goes beyond mere form and instead reflects the organization's context-based content. Unlike static identities, which often rely on transposing symbolic or ideal values, conventions, or common symbols, a flexible visual identity delves into the analysis of the organization or context to explore its intrinsic and unique characteristics. This approach generates a "theme" or "idea" that guides the design principles and overall derivation of the visual identity. As Felsing [3, p. 225–226] asserts, a differentiated visual identity emerges when the organization's significant content, rather than general values or cliché ideas, is translated into a visual form. This concept is exemplified in the ERCO typographic logo, designed by Otl Aicher. The logo skillfully represents the organization's activity as a manufacturer of architectural lighting systems with discreet visibility by using four weights of the Univers font in descending order to depict the loss of light intensity with increasing distance. This principle is transferred to the typogram (see Fig. 1).

Aicher, by reproducing the typical behavior of light, transforms the brand's mark into something meaningful and gives the necessary substance to the identity, making it useful in building a quality experience in different media.

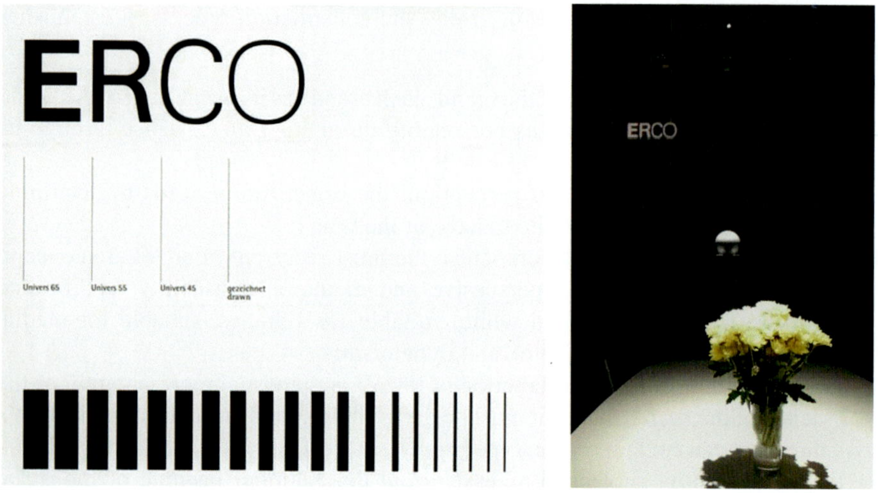

Fig. 1 ERCO visual identity (1976). *Source* https://medium.com/fgd1-the-archive/erco-1976-b7625d7829dc

Felsing [3] then describes the other two fundamental criteria for obtaining fully developed visual identities: a wide spectrum of variation—a basic design principle or theme that allows implementation in various forms of expression, dimensions or media, and differentiation—which creates tension in dynamic visual identities (which distinguishes, for example, between the association as a whole and its subsections; between permanent presence and temporary events; and between various communication channels).

With regard to building flexibility, Felsing [3] describes the following steps:

1. Content and external form: flexibility generated by the interaction between constant and variable elements. The outer shape, which can be a mask or a grid, is fixed and the content—the inner area—is variable, or vice versa;
2. Element and sequence (movement, change of perspective): representation of movement, which can take different forms, in visual identities; examples include animations, pulsating structures, illustrated or photographic sequences, and two- or three-dimensional photos;
3. Theme and variations (transformation): variation processes applied to unique signs of identity expression, such as size, shape, and color; degree of abstraction; and means of representation or communication;
4. Combinatorics (rapports, modules, elementary construction kits): the variability of identities is as dynamic as the variation of the elements that are reinforced by the combination;
5. Element and structure (permutation): identities that present a high number of variations of combined elements that can reach complex forms; generated by computer programs that play a central role in determining the sequence of signs, even if they are initially designed by hand;

6. Interaction (control factors, transfer, and open form): identities that dynamically incorporate in the design real-time processes or data; in these visual identities, organizations provide information about their activities while building their own identity; highly significant and authentic character signs.

Chronology and evolution of DVI. DVI systems have followed underlying evolutions in technologies, media, and processes. In the initial phase—between the industrial revolution and the Second World War—efforts were made to build solid reputations and, through the creative mechanisms of the VI system, facilitate the recognition or identification of companies and organizations [1]. From the mid-twentieth century (the 1950s), there was an increase in new DVI approaches.

Therefore, the consolidation of the idea of a Visual Identity Systems, based on coherence and uniformity, was largely due to the Olympic Games and multinationals companies or major brands. And alongside these, the embryo of Dynamic Visual Identities systems began still in printed media, before personal computers and internet, through brands such as Boîte à Musique (1959), the textile Albitex (1961), Hadfields Limited (1967), Prince Hotels (1968), Priba (1973); and on television with MTV (1981) and Nickelodeon (1984). However, DVI systems became associated with segmentation and technological and territory brands such as Google (1998), Optimus (2008), Melbourne City, Swisscom, Wook (2009), AOL (2010), edp (2011), New York City, Oi, Nordkyn (2012), è Bologna, MIT Media Lab, Porto City (2014), among many others [12].

Among them was Karl Gerstner's approach, defending systematic design and defining a design program as "a set of rules to construct a variety of visual solutions" [10, p. 125]. Gerstner's identity project for Boîte à Musique, from 1959, presented a system of elements that changed according to the context [10], which means that it was already a flexible system (see Fig. 2). The same approach was seen in the Zahn-Nopper store's DVI, designed by Anton Stankowski between 1961 and 1963, where the identity system was based on a programmatic approach to design. Lupton [10, p. 124] describes it as "using a limited set of elements to build diverse but genetically linked solutions" and "the system is not governed by a fixed logo, but by flexible constructive rules".

Another example worth mentioning is the Hadfields paint brand. The identity, elaborated by Wolff Ollins in 1966, already translates the concept of dynamic identity. As Siswanto and Dolah [16, p. 434] points out, "if we think that dynamic identity depends on digital and technology, this could be wrong" and he demonstrates this through the dynamic fox—the "mascot," in the author's words—which comes to live through the different poses it takes on each paint can (see Fig. 3). In the end, he concludes that dynamic identity is not a new concept and that a printed media can also be dynamic.

Next, we present the identity for MTV, developed by Manhattan Design in 1981 (see Fig. 4), where a variation system was established before the introduction of the concept itself [16]. Irene [19, p. 7] categorizes the identity as a container, structured in a system where 'M' and 'TV' have a fixed shape and position, but thousands of variations can be built through colors, patterns, textures, animations, and illustrations.

Fig. 2 Boîte à Musique (1959). *Source* https://www.underconsideration.com/speakup/archives/004431.html

Fig. 3 Identity for Hadfields (1966). *Source* https://www.londondesignfestival.com/stories/in-conversation-michael-wolff

However, despite all variations, visualizations, and changes in appearance—moving, changing, or transforming - it maintains consistency [16].

Continuing this timeline, we present the case of Walker Expanded, by Andrew Blauvelt, Chad Kloepfer, and Emmet Byrne (see Fig. 5), which in 2005 developed an identity that acts as a letter type: instead of using bold and italic, it groups related words or vocabularies and repeated patterns [7]. Felsing [3] categorizes this identity as 'Element and Structure: Permutation'.

Fig. 4 Variations of the MTV logo (1981). *Source* https://customneon.co.uk/logo-statistics/

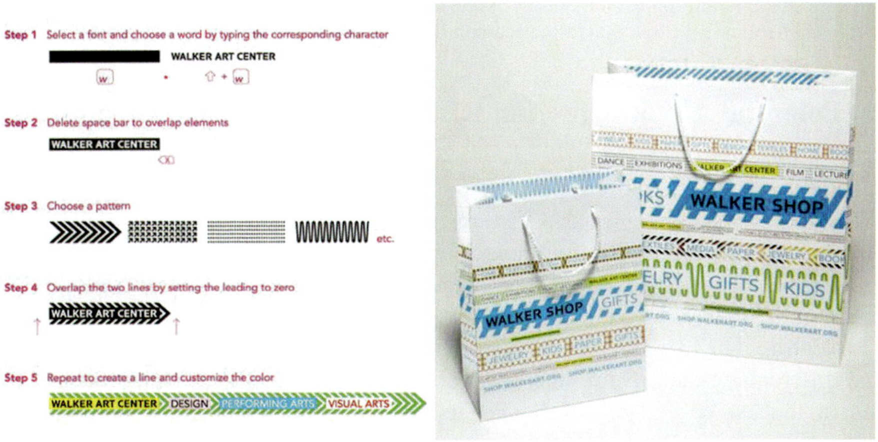

Fig. 5 Walker Expanded (2005). *Source* https://br.pinterest.com/pin

Finally, the logo of the Casa da Música, designed by Stefan Sagmeister, Matthias Ernstgerger, and Quentin Walesch in 2007, is presented (see Fig. 6). Here, the problem of representing the iconic building has been resolved by imitating the architectural shapes of different points of view, and a logo generation system was used to allow flexibility in the color application by the user and to allow the variation of themes from application to application or from media to media, like a chameleon [17], depending on the context [1].

Fig. 6 Variations and application of the Casa da Música logo (2007). *Source* https://nevolution.typepad.com/theories/2011/03/casa-de-musica-contingent-solutions.html/

2 Potential Advantages and Risks of a DVI

As previously mentioned, in the conception and building of a DVI it's essential to maintain the consistency of the VI through the established coherence between its mutations/alterations, restricting some of the elements that compose it to certain rules, either through the way in which the change will be operated or through the behavior of some static elements [2, 3].

According to [3], for VIs to be easily recognizable and have characteristics that differentiate them from others, variable elements should refer only to specific content that can be changed, and static elements, as fundamental base elements, thus safeguarding the coherence of the identity itself.

Assuming these aspects are achieved, particularly in terms of consistency, the potential advantages and risks involved in creating and maintaining an DVI are listed in Table 1.

As for the qualities that can be added or the benefits that the use of an DVI can offer, the table highlights the constant renewal of the brand, the attribution of different functionalities, as many as possible, to the logos themselves (associated with content), as in the case of Nordkyn and Australian Design Radio. The dynamism provided by the variations can be more representative of the tone or spirit of the brand, and can contribute to greater visibility or prominence in different media, in addition to presenting greater adaptability and customization when answering to the target audience, granting space for user intervention in constructing identities, and, not least, the impossibility of determining limits for variations [1–3, 6, 21].

Table 1 Survey of the potential advantages and risks of DVIs

Advantages	Risks
The dynamic and flexible aspect of DVIs are factors that, by themselves (for example: through the transmission of new content), contribute to the constant renewal of the brand	The visual identity standards manual tends to oppose the concept of dynamism. Increase in the complexity of the design principles or guidelines and the need for brand centers
Versatility in assigning functionalities and content to brand marks	Greater difficulty in registering variations
The DVI system denotes greater permeability in capturing and representing the spirit of the brand	Greater complexity in the process of managing and applying brand marks
The impact of variation and the effects of surprise/novelty can generate greater interest or visibility in the media	Possibility of some lack of control over the result in generative and participatory VI
Adaptation and customization of responses to the target audience	Failures in the interpretation of results
Unlimited variations in the brand's discourse and visual language	Use of specific software
Flexibility in adapting to different media, platforms, and situations	Dissolution increases as the range of variation in VI grows; therefore, there is a risk of it becoming less recognizable and memorable
Greater ability to reflect changes and/or evolutions in the strategies of organizations and brands	
Openness to new interpretations (of the logo or brand mark)	
The variations of DVI allow for greater differentiation within the organization and against the competition	
VI that denote greater openness to public involvement, through customization and collaboration, in the construction of the final result	
Greater potential to reference changing contexts due to the coherence maintained between the constant aspects, which provide stability, and the variable aspects, which generate dynamics	

On the other hand, and in what may represent a risk or threat, the norms' manual is opposed to the concept of dynamism, and in terms of the result of variations generated, the difficulty in registering, managing, and applying the logos, recognizing versions, the lack of control over the result, interpretation failures, and also the need to use specific software [3, 6, 7].

3 Principles to Consider When Designing a DVI

The design of a DVI does not differ, in some respects, from a static visual identity. Both are united in the goal of reflecting the context in which the organization is inserted, being fundamental, for this, to answer to the needs of a briefing, to determine what makes the organization distinct or essential (through the definition and study of values, mission, collaborators, cultural and historical context, etc.), as well as the analysis of its competitors and potential consumers. A set of steps that make it possible to outline a strategy, taking into account the most appropriate market positioning and the representation of the image with which the organization or brand aspires to project itself [2, 9, 19, 21].

If DVIs are distinguished from static ones by one or more of their elements undergoing variations and by the interaction between static and variable elements in the VI system [3, 9, 11, 15, 19] suggests some steps that should guide the design of a flexible system. The first two steps:

(1) define the communication problem and
(2) decide where your solution will be applied—are already diluted in the introduction of this topic, namely in the response to the briefing's needs, in the outlining of the strategy, and in the positioning chosen by the organization. While the remaining ones are listed below:
(3) Select a shape—the form conveys messages and influences the tone of the visual language;
(4) Build your assets—the visual identity will be more differentiated from competitors;
(5) Test your assets on different formats—test your visual system in all types of media: narrow, wide, large, small, loud, quiet, moving, and static;
(6) Present your system on mock-ups—this is essential to understand how the visual system reacts to different formats and contents and to imagine how the visual identity will work in context. It also suggests the development of a design manual that documents the process and the defined rules, which is also essential to verify if the rules were designed and applied consistently.

Lorenz [9, p. 9] also highlights what he calls transforming systems, which are "like a filter that distorts an image, font, or graphic in a recognizable way". For him, the transformation becomes "the identifiable element of visual identity and not necessarily the transformed".

On the other hand, [11], after analyzing the terminology applied by several authors to DVIs and the perspectives on their classification, present us with a model based on how variation is visually performed and identify the three aspects to consider when designing a DVI: identity focus, variation mechanisms, and characteristics.

Identity focus is important in determining whether or not a VI is focused on a brand mark. By way of distinction, they present two examples: the VI of the Priba supermarket chain, designed by Allied International Designers and Geoff Gibbons in 1973, in which the entity is identified and recognized by a brand mark that frames a series of images, colors, and patterns that reflect the diversity of products and services; and the VI of the Walker Art Center, where the focus is on graphic language, which explores a set of tools: bars, stripes, and chevrons [11].

Variation mechanisms (VM) specify how VIs change visually, and the authors clarify that a VI can use more than one VM and that the same VM can be applied to more than one element of the VI system [11]. The VMs are described as follows:

Color Variation—a graphic element changes color. Example of the VI from Casa da Música, where the colors of the brand mark are picked from images related to events.

Combination—a combination of different graphic elements in the VI system. Example of the La Fonda del Sol restaurant, designed by Alexander Girard in 1960, with the combination of a set of facial features, sun rays, enclosing shapes, and colors, which create a wide range of sun designs.

Content Variation—area or space where different images are placed, either in the background or in the figure. Example of the VI for Design Academy Eindhoven, created by The Stone Twins in 2010, where the content changes with each interaction, every time a person writes the name of the school, creating countless versions.

Positioning—a graphic element is positioned in different ways. MV applied to the Boolab VI, designed by Mucho in 2009, exploring numerous arrangements of the four lines and five circles that form the word "boolab".

Repetition—repetition of the same graphic element, subject or not to a grid. VI for the Mobile Media Lab, created by FEED in 2008, reproduces symbols independently or overlapping each other.

Rotation—a graphic element is rotated. VI of the Optica store, designed by Vlad Likh in 2013, through the rotation of a pair of glasses in a three-dimensional space.

Scaling—a graphic element changes size. Example of the IV for IDTV, created by Lava in 2008, is based on the combination of four distinct modules with different scales.

Shape Transformation—a graphic element changes shape. MV applied to the IV of the Brooklyn Museum, created by 2 × 4 in 2004, to continuously morph a seal.

According to the authors, these characteristics refer to the properties that distinguish an IV, or that they retain—as a kind of personality—and that can be cumulative [11]. They identify the following:

- Flexible—identities that adapt to different contexts in which they are applied, both in terms of media and content. The VI of Boîte à Musique, an example of adaptation to the media, reconfigures itself to adapt to different formats (paper sizes), while Casa da Música VI adapts to different content through color variation to change the graphic identity according to the images related to each event;
- Fluid—an identity that changes continuously, usually with a wide spectrum of possible variations. Kamnin bank VI, created by b2s6 in 2013, is based on a three-dimensional shape composed of layers, which creates a sense of continuous movement;
- Generative—variations generated by an algorithm, with a certain degree of autonomy and sometimes randomness. For example, 2007's Lovebytes VI was

code-generated, which gave rise to a new type of image and personalized design. Otherwise, the VI of the Rhizome organization, designed by Surface in 2001, is generated by querying the website, depending on the IPs of the last four users, defining the mode of interaction with people and/or reaction to input data in real-time. Most generated VIs have a "logo generator" (a computer program that generates variations of the graphic identity);

- Informative—identity that provides information to its audiences; used to communicate messages or to identify products, services, sections, or personnel. Google regularly changes its brand mark with the Google Doodles, designed by Dennis Hwang in 1998, to celebrate significant events or special dates;
- Participatory—DVI that allows the involvement and influence of the user, in addition to the designer, in obtaining the final result. In some cases, the user provides the content, as in the graphic identity of OCAD University, designed by Bruce Mau Design in 2011, where the public is invited to fill a frame (with illustrations, doodles, or photos). In other cases, users configure a set of elements provided by the identity itself, as in the VI of the GetUp hair salons, designed by Alexis Rom studio in 2007, where customers and stylists create brand marks through the stamping process;
- Reactive—DVI that reacts to input data, whether real-time or not, and that is generated programmatically, such as the graphic identity for Visit Nordkyn, designed by Neue in 2010, which is affected by a feed of meteorological statistics;
- Unlimited—the variations of DVIs are infinite. For example, the VI for the Web Aol., designed by Wolff Olins in 2009, features an ever-changing background that evokes the multiplicity and dynamic nature of the Web, featuring a wide variety of objects (content).

4 Conclusion

The decision to develop DVI appears to be in line with the current market trend of providing personalized and customized product and service solutions by brands and organizations. The number of DVIs has been increasing steadily in recent years, indicating a growing interest in this type of strategy. This may be because DVIs offer various benefits, such as representing a dynamic and ever-changing world or brand, adapting to new communication needs that arise due to the evolution of contemporary society, enabling greater originality and flexibility in identity creation, and allowing for the transmission of references and content to audiences in ways that can generate unique stimuli and surprising effects. Additionally, DVIs can facilitate the renewal of concepts or the identity itself, making them an attractive option for organizations seeking to stay ahead of the curve.

To create effective DVIs, there are two important design requirements to consider. The first is to ensure that the brand mark is memorable and recognizable so that the VI doesn't lose its identity and become indistinguishable [3]. The second requirement is related to the complexity and maintenance of the system. Since DVIs don't rely on a traditional logo or brand mark, they may require additional communication efforts to maintain consistency across different platforms and avoid confusion. This could mean repeating the logo or brand mark to reinforce memorization and recognition or adapting it for different media to encourage creativity and consistency. Overall, attention to both requirements can help ensure that the DVI is effective and meets its intended goals.

In conclusion, in terms of design, it is important to highlight that most of the DVIs analyzed by Martins et al. [11] focus on the brand mark as the main element for creating variation in the identity's appearance. In some cases, it is the only element of the identity that undergoes variation. Regarding the variation mechanisms, (81%) use one or more MV in the brand mark, and (54%) use one or more MV in the system. However, only (35%) use MV simultaneously in both the brand mark and the system. As for the characteristics, the most common is the unlimited characteristic, followed by flexible, fluid, generative, informative, participatory, and reactive. These are important factors to consider when constructing a DVI, as they reveal endless possibilities for the combination that can lead to unexplored or innovative paths, and they allow professionals to test the limits of visual representation and have greater creative freedom.

References

1. Budelmann K, Kim Y, e Wozniak C (2010) Brand identity essentials: 100 principles for designing logos and building brands. Rockport Publishers, Inc, Beverly, Massachusetts
2. Capsule (2007) Claves del diseño//Logos 01. Barcelona: Editorial Gustavo Gili, SL
3. Felsing U (2010) Dynamic identities in cultural and public contexts. Lars Müller Publishers, Germany
4. Junior LAP, Costa MJ, e Torres SSM (2018) Identidades visuais adaptativas: Inovações no processo de criação e suas tecnologias. In: Revista sistemas e media digitais, Abril de 2018, Vol 3 No 1, pp 1–10
5. Kreutz EA (2007) Identidade Visual Corporativa Mutante: uma estratégia comunicacional contemporânea. In: Intercom—XXX Congresso Brasileiro de Ciências da Comunicação, 29 de Agosto a 02 de Setembro de 2007. Santos
6. Kreutz EA (2012) Construindo Marcas Mutantes. Chasqui. Revista Latinoamericana de Comunicación, (119), pp 61–65
7. Leitão S, Lélis C, Mealha Ó (2014) Marcas Dinâmicas: Haverá forma de as orientar? In: 1st International Congress on Branding, ESTG, 2–4 October 2014, Leiria, Portugal
8. Lelis C (2019) Like a Chameleon: the polychromatic virtue of dynamic brands. J Prod & Brand Manag 28(4):445–461
9. Lorenz M (2021) Flexible Visual Systems: the design manual for contemporary visual identities. Slanted Publishers, Karlsruhe, Germany
10. Lupton E (2004) Thinking with type: a critical guide for designers, writers, editors & students. Princeton Architectural Press, Estados Unidos
11. Martins T, Cunha JM, Bicker J, Machado P (2019) Dynamic Visual Identities: from a survey of the state-of-the-art to a model of features and mechanisms. Visible Lang 53(2):4–35
12. Raposo M, Oliveira F (2017) As marcas tipo-gráficas e a metamorfose: A tipogradia enquanto elemento unificador do sistema de identidade visual. Conference: CIDAG-4. ªConferência Internacional em Design e Artes Gráficas. ISEC/IPT/Salesians de Sarrià. pp 84–89

13. RTP Homepage, rtp.pt/notícias/cultura/. Accessed 10 Dec 2022
14. Sääksjärvi M, Hende E, Mugge R (2015) How exposure to logos and logo varieties fosters brand prominence and freshness. J Prod Brand Manag 24(7):736–744
15. Silva R, Martins N (2018) MIT Media Lab's dynamic identity. In: DIGICOM 2018—2nd International conference on design and digital communication: proceedings. November 9–10, 2018, Barcelos, Portugal. Edições IPCA. pp 33–43. ISBN: 978-989-99861-8-3. https://digicom.ipca.pt/docs/DIGICOM2018-Proceedings.pdf
16. Siswanto R, Dolah J (2018) Exploration to the most fundamental form of dynamic visual identity. Adv Soc Sci, Educ Huml-Ties Res 197:432–438
17. Stones J (2009) No rules logos: radical design solutions that break the rules. RotoVision, SA, Switzerland
18. Twemlow A (2007) Para que serve o Design Gráfico? Editorial Gustavo Gili, SL, Barcelona
19. Van Nes I (2012) Dynamic identities: how to create a living brand. BIS Publishers, Amsterdam, Holanda
20. Vasconcelos J, Martins N, Brandão D, Penedos-Santiago E (2023) Visual Identity of Non-profit Organizations: Escola Oficina, a Case Study Plan. Advances in Design and Digital Communication: Proceedings of the 6th International Conference on Design and Digital Communication, Digicom 2022, November 3–5, 2022, Barcelos, Portugal. Springer Series in Design and Innovation, vol 27. Springer, Cham. pp 675–686. https://doi.org/10.1007/978-3-031-20364-0_57
21. Wheeler A (2009) Designing brand identity: an essential guide for the entire branding team. Wiley, Estados Unidos da América

Redesigning the Visual Identity of Non-profit Organizations: The Case Study of Escola Oficina

João Vasconcelos, Nuno Martins, Daniel Brandão, Leonardo Pereira, and Daniel Raposo

Abstract This article seeks to analyze the importance of Corporate Visual Identity (CVI) for non-profit and social solidarity organizations. It starts from the case study of Escola Oficina (EO), where an evaluation and consequent redesign of its CVI was developed. This study, developed within the ECHO research project, funded by the Fundação para a Ciência e Tecnologia (FCT), arose from a problem, identified by EO itself, that consisted of making known the activity developed and, above all, to minimize the generalised distrust of consumers regarding its products. EO is a social project located in Vila Nova de Gaia, in northern Portugal, and its main goal is to empower and prepare unemployed citizens, namely from vulnerable communities, for a future integration into the labour market. This chapter is based on a Case Study methodology, supported by a literature review and exploratory interviews. The main results were the development of a new corporate visual identity solution for Escola Oficina, in response to the problems identified in this study.

Keywords Visual identity design · Communication design and branding · Social design · Logo design · Non-profit organization

J. Vasconcelos
School of Design, Polytechnic Institute of Cavado and Ave, Barcelos, Portugal

N. Martins (✉)
Research Institute for Design, Media and Culture, School of Design, Polytechnic Institute of Cávado and Ave, Barcelos, Portugal
e-mail: nmartins@ipca.pt

D. Brandão
CECS, Institute of Social Sciences, University of Minho, Braga, Portugal

L. Pereira
University of Aveiro, DigiMedia, DeCA, Aveiro, Portugal

D. Raposo
Research Centre for Architecture, Urbanism and Design, Polytechnic Institute of Castelo Branco, Castelo Branco, Portugal
e-mail: draposo@ipcb.pt

N. Martins and D. Raposo (eds.), *Communication Design and Branding*, Springer Series in Design and Innovation 32,
https://doi.org/10.1007/978-3-031-35385-7_4

1 Introduction

Escola Oficina (in english *School Workshop*) is a social project, created in 2015, in the Balteiro social enterprise in Vila Nova de Gaia, with the goal of enabling assistance for local citizens who are in a situation of professional precariousness, providing training, occupation and employability. It is a community practice that has as its philosophy the promotion of environmental sustainability and economic development, having as its principle the circular economy, giving to unemployed people social integration opportunities in the labour market. The organisation maintains a system of self-sustainability, financially supported by the commercialisation of the products it develops. It is a recognised success story, both in the training and empowerment of unemployed citizens and in their integration into the labour market [39].

The trainees of this school are qualified in different areas, with the main focus on sewing and cardboard. The knowledge they gain is exploited in a practical way in the workshop, starting projects in a real work context, which translate into the transformation of non-hazardous industrial waste and residues, provided by textile and waste companies, into final products with added value.

However, Escola Oficina's (EO) external communication has been almost non-existent, which has naturally hindered the dissemination of its activity and, above all, the sale of the products that the EO develops with its trainees. Moreover, the EO's managers feel that customers have a generalized mistrust of its products' quality, given that they're produced by unemployed trainees.

So, the insufficiency of its communication strategy and the possible less positive reputation identified by the institution's management may constitute an obstacle to sales' growth of EO's products; to the growth of the added value of its products; and, consequently, to the increase of the needed revenues to ensure the sustainable development of the organisation.

This study arises, therefore, with the goal of answering to these problems. We believe that Design can be an important tool that helps to overcome difficulties such as the ones identified in EO and that, generally, are common to this type of organisations that operate in the social environment. Through this case study, it is intended to present an effective action methodology and the potential replication in other similar cases. From this article arises an analysis of relevant themes regarding identity design in non-profit and social organisations and the presentation of the solution designed for EO.

So this article starts with a literature review about the Brand concept and the influence that its valuation (branding) may have on the customer, where the perspectives of Wheeler [41] and Keller and Lehmann [22] are analysed. The main adversities common to Non-Profit Organizations (NPOs), which constitute themselves an obstacle to the development of their brand, are identified according to Grau's beliefs [18]. The article also explores the concept of Social Design and visual communication for social change, studying the points of view of several authors [6, 14, 17, 20,

23, 25, 31, 36, 37, 38]. Also in the mentioned literature review, it is sought to define the concepts of Identity, Image and Corporate Visual Identity [5, 9, 11, 26].

Finally, the new Corporate Visual Identity (CVI) proposal designed for EO is presented, based on Design Thinking methods [3, 7, 8, 13, 34].

2 The Brand

In a study of this nature, it's important to have a full grasp of the key concepts, as well as asking the right questions. In this case one has to ask:

> What does an identity brand represent? This question is not interested in what the brand objectively "is", but in what it means to the public [11, p. 83].

A Brand enables organisations to create strong connections with consumers. People fall in love with brands, trust them, and believe in their superiority. The way a brand is interpreted influences its success, both in a Non-Profit Organisation (NPO) and a product [41].

It is, therefore, necessary to understand some of the attributes of brands and, particularly the elements that affect communication and how the brand will be perceived by stakeholders. Among these attributes are brand identity and positioning.

A Brand's identity is tangible and appeals to the senses. It fuels recognition, amplifies differentiation, and makes big ideas and meanings accessible [41].

Positioning a brand or making a strategic choice that seeks to give a credible, different and attractive position of its offering in the minds of consumers [12] in order to make it irreplaceable, requires a constant and methodical will: Branding is a process used, in order to create awareness, attract new consumers, and expand consumer loyalty [41] by employing the distinctive characteristics of the brand, forming an engagement with the target audience while mirroring the mission and values of the organization [18].

According to [22], branding has become a priority in the management of companies due to the growing perception that brands are among the most valuable assets (resources) held by organizations. One of the topics explored by the authors is *brand intangibles*, which they define as means of differentiating it and adding value to its physical products. Intangibles can encompass various types of associations to the brand, related to its identity. However, they do not involve physical and concrete, as the name implies, tangible attributes.

Notwithstanding the obvious opposition (tangible versus intangible) between the way Wheeler and [22] present their definition, their associations regarding identity are, in fact, literally intangible. However, the tangibility characterised by [41] is targeted to the consumer's perspective, because through the exploitation of these intangible assets, the mental image that a brand may have, will influence the consumer's decisions towards products or services that, effectively, may be tangible. In other words, since "brands mirror the complete experience that consumers have with products" [22], through the tangible experiences associated with the brand, the human being is able to identify this materiality by the connection that he creates (via his senses) between the brand and the product.

The brand is developed by designers, marketers, brand managers and other professionals, but it lives in people's minds [18]. It can be described as the idea that lives in consumers' minds and that emerged from of all their impressions with them: they are emotional connections between the institution and the consumers based on a consistent delivery of quality and trust [18]. Thus, "it seems that the brand increasingly belongs to the public and less to the company" [35], while branding seems to belong more to the institution and its employees, because it corresponds to the brand's development process.

EO is a brand that belongs to the social sector. The social segment of brands has shown a paradigm shift, where activities such as marketing and branding have become, in recent decades, methodologies used more often by Non-Profit Organizations (NPOs) to achieve their mission and goals (Eikenberry & Kluver, 2004). This change is related to the increased competitiveness in this sector. According to [1], Non-Profit Organizations not only value, but also deploy more capital in their image when they find themselves in a more competitive environment, where they perceive that the public has a hard time distinguishing between different organizations and what they represent [18].

EO, similarly to these NPOs, did not initially give importance to its image and visual identity, but with the gradual evolution of the organisation, it faced the need to review the strategies used [28].

The management of the EO assumed the almost non-existence of external communication with its potential audiences. This shows that the idea that underlies the work developed by the school (identity), its interests and how it wants to be perceived by the public (positioning) is not passed on. This situation causes consumers to spontaneously create, in relation to their products, their own idea, little or not conditioned by the decision-makers of the organisation [12].

Thus, the organisation does not establish a connection that allows showing what the brand is (such as, for example, the values of sustainability and circular economy; and the production quality of its products), thus being limited to the image of being a solidarity institution that supports people in a situation of professional precariousness.

Creating a convergent perception in consumers' minds with the brand's values requires a studied and continued work. It is, therefore, necessary to establish in EO tools that are traditionally explored by branding.

3 Branding in Non-profit Organizations

In the organisational context and in the literature, branding is often associated with commercial goals. However, "*Branding can be as important to nonprofit organisations as it is for large for-profit companies*" [18, p. 33].

Notwithstanding its importance, branding in the social sector has adversities that are different from the ones faced by organizations in the for-profit market. These adversities, characteristic of the social environment, increase the difficulty in the institution evidencing process, of the brand's branding. Grau [18] identifies some of the reasons underlying these difficulties:

1. **Complexity of target audiences:** It is common for a NPO to have both clients and beneficiaries of its programmes and services, who generally have different relationships with the organisation (although there are cases where these audiences overlap). These different audiences require different communication methods, their own messages, appropriate to their connection with the organisation;
2. **Nature of programmes and services:** Many of the programmes and services that define NPOs are complicated to explain and this does not favour audiences to identify with the NPOs' mission and goals;
3. **General perceptions:** The public positively accepts NPOs and understands that they are worthy of support because of their role in the community. However, this can have a negative impact because when organizations assume that they are socially relevant due to the service they provide, they neglect branding needs and are subject only to perceptions spontaneously generated by the public;
4. **Branding costs and requirements:** Apart from the large NPOs, most small and medium organisations do not enjoy the advantages that companies benefit from and boast, be they monetary advantages or advantages at the level of human resources and their skills.

Like EO, a large portion of Non-Profit Organizations lack the capacity to sustain the expertise that is essential to build and maintain their brand. In the reality of a NPO, human and financial resources are limited and, at the same time, they still have to strive to achieve their mission [18]. As a result, they end up neglecting the potential of their brands' specific traits and personalities, which are essential for brand enhancement and to strengthen the emotional connection with the public.

According to Huang and Ku [21], NPOs should use their brand as an identification system in order to differentiate themselves from other organisations [in agreement with [18]]. They should devise branding strategies to create the intended brand image.

Focusing on the benefits of institutional image enhancement, [18] adopts the Interbrand (a global brand consultant company) method for classifying the value of brands worldwide, with the aim of exploring in more detail the aspects that can enhance their development.

This model is made up of three components: financial analysis (revenues); the role of the brand (estimation of how important the brand itself is in the purchase); and *brand strength* (the strength of the brand). In *brand strength*, there are several attributes, with internal dimension factors: clarity; commitment; management; and responsiveness; and external dimension factors: authenticity; consistency; differentiation; *engagement*; presence; and relevance.

These factors are important considerations for an NPO's management, that should, therefore, be weighed up by the EO in order to: strengthen its brand; extend its competence [18], and genuinely represent the brand's core.

The brand's core is the vision of the organisation and includes the mission, purpose, values, actions and principles. This vision is the basis of what makes an organisation of great value. However, as noted above, the brand needs to stand out. Like other institutions, NPOs' brands have personalities (set of characteristics that reflect their vision, mission, values, etc.) and it is relevant that the brand is not only attractive but also unique [18].

In general, the foundation of managing an effective brand's image is consistency. It needs to be communicated to stakeholders consistently, over a long period, in order to form, not only an intellectual relationship with customers, through knowledge and understanding of the organization, but also by the emotional bond [18].

It is easily understood that the core of EO's brand is unique, within the geographical, economic and social universe in which it is integrated. We argue that its communicational inconsistency demotivates the latent emotional bonds, leaving gaps in the image it intends to convey. The idea that consumers feel compassion for the trainees' situation may be overlapping with the representation that EO intends to preach [supported by the idea of generalised perceptions referred to by [18]]. However, only the institution itself can take the initiative to make the paradigm shift achievable.

4 Social Design in Identity Design

The social landscape is one of the defining aspects of responsibly conducted Design: current societal challenges (such as environmental crises, inequality, ageing, etc.) put pressure on the discipline of Design and its professionals to integrate goals and indicators of success that go beyond profits [20].

As mentioned before, EO is inserted in a universe of its own, with challenges typical of an organisation of this nature. The type of Design service that is developed, particularly in EO's ecosystem (organisation-community), is part of the so called Social Design discipline. Social Design is the broad term used in the academic literature that seeks to highlight design practices that aim at social change or social improvement rather than (solely) financial gain [20]. So, the change in the public's attitude towards EO is the expectation that best meets the goals of this project.

As Social Design is a subject of multiple nuances, it was important to understand, in this study, how this subject is academically interpreted and approached.

Koskinen and Hush [23] explain different concepts within Social Design. They divide social Design into three categories: utopian, molecular and sociological.

Utopian social design stems from convictions and desires for utopian social change [25, 31].

From another perspective, molecular social design stems from the idea that many designers working on social topics prefer to move away from utopian and revolutionary ideals. These designers accept that they can contribute to " the improvement of the world, albeit a little at a time", regardless of whether these "few" add up to a large-scale change. This is [6] and Frascara's et al. [17] point of view.

In Sociological Social Design, design is guided by sociological theories. It is based on social sciences' knowledge, which makes it different from utopian design. This definition contemplates both previous categories of Social Design. In it it's accepted that design can be molecular in its strategy, as it can also seek to aim at changes in structures that concern persistent social problems.

These different categories demonstrate and prove the large depth of the Social Design topic. However, for EO, design might not be the solution to achieve major changes in the structures of society. This project is therefore a resource that will try to answer to a social challenge.

Thorpe and Gamman[38] clarify that design challenges are complex, and characterised by factors that, sometimes, may be competing among them or even contradictory. Adding to these factors, there are still scenarios in which there may be more than one right solution to answer to design problems. The aforementioned complexity requires designers and other actors in the design process, to be responsive to the context in which the design activity is integrated. Given the context (with its own resource requirements, goals and needs) it is important to consider and, mainly, to decide which factors should be prioritised in what will be the design answer.

The authors also point out that designers not belonging to a particular community should keep in mind that it is not necessary to take responsibility for solving that community's problems. The approach to the problem, as a designer, will be to do whatever is within his reach, working with social factors to leverage community assets, in order to provoke positive change in the community.

EO's ambition, in wanting to implement new communication strategies, goes beyond the financial gains these can bring. The basis of its self-sustainability is the support that EO brings to the citizens. Support which, without doubt, is the organisation's priority. It was, therefore, crucial that this philosophy had been intrinsically present in all the stages of this research work, in the same way it is present in EO.

For this project, Identity Design will be the means to give EO a new way of being identified in the community where it intervenes, as transparently as possible. The inherent complexity of a design project for the social environment requires a responsive connection between the Designer and the constituents of the Institution, in this case EO (Management, trainees, employees, etc.).

As one of the significant agents in the transmission of an organisation's identity, Identity Design is deeply grounded in and aided by Visual Communication, topic which we will address in the next section.

5 Visual Communication

The willingness to improve the EO's inconsistent communication was demonstrated by its management. Admitting that, initially, communication was not considered relevant, given the size of the project, EO is now in a different situation: it is the brand of a self-sustainable project, covering the metropolitan area of Porto; it has already trained hundreds of citizens and aims to train even more; it manufactures a wide variety of products, but still has no means to communicate with its public. The public forms its perceptions based on the tangible messages transmitted by organisations: if these perceptions differ from reality, this is then the consequence of an ineffective strategy or it means that the perception of the organisation itself needs to be modified [4].

According to Argenti [4], the rhythm in the production of messages and the speed with which they are communicated give greater importance to Corporate Communication. On the other hand, as the same author underlines, people demand and are more suspicious of corporate messages, and so there are new approaches. On the other hand, we add that every year more companies are created and that markets and communication are more international, global and digital.

Taking into account that the current means of communication, between organizations and their publics, are grounded in the visual communication field, we conclude that the visual branch is symbiotically linked to the corporate image. The purpose of transmitting information through the visual format (photos, videos, illustration or graphic design) is grounded on the principle that it is fast and efficient. The dynamic nature of the visual medium is the result of the fusion of technology with forms of visual expression (photography, cinema, television and, lastly, the internet) [24].

Visual Communication as an object of research isn't recent. Munari [29], already in the sixties, identified the basis of the aspects of Visual Communication in a single characteristic: objectivity [idea reinforced [14]]. The author explains that if a message isn't objective, it has a lesser chance to visually communicate something: it is necessary that the used image is legible and visible to everyone in the same way. Otherwise, there is no visual communication, but visual confusion. Human beings are subject to seeing and disseminating visual artefacts. What we see has an effect on what we do, feel and even in who we are. With experience and experimentation, the perception of the 'visual world' continually grows simultaneously with its influence [32].

Virtually everything we see is Visual Communication: images can take on different values depending on the context in which they are embedded, giving different information. However, there are two distinctions between the messages that reach our eyes: they can be casual or intentional [14, 29].

We can assume that, so far, the message conveyed by EO has not always been intentional. As already mentioned, that message was, for years, predominantly spontaneous, spread through word-of-mouth. Communication resulted from what was done or said, of free will by the people who related to the EO, without the visual segment of communication being structured or prioritised. This is reflected in the scarce materials that EO has at its disposal (discussed more specifically in Sect. 6.1).

In addition to this broader vision of visual communication, the OE needs to prepare its Visual Communication strategy for the social environment in which the organisation lives. This environment, with its own needs, corresponds to the space where the message will be disseminated.

5.1 *Visual Communication for Social Change*

The communication intended for EO should achieve an image readjusted to its claims and, thus, consolidate the interconnection with the community. As discussed in Sect. 4, we must take into account that we're in the presence of a social nature brand, as mentioned by nature brand, as mentioned [36]. In the process of socially driven design, when working in order to achieve results targeted at a particular community, the intrinsic factors of that community must be taken into account. By allowing these characteristic factors to work for and with a community and by giving them the necessary focus, the found design solution can become more accessible to the audience and, thus, achieve greater effectiveness in communication [36, 38].

Shea [37], proposes relevant strategies in the development of design solutions for a given community, which can be applied in combination (with each other) or restructured according to the needs of each project. They are the following:

1. engaging with the community;
2. building trust;
3. promising only what can be delivered;
4. prioritising the process;
5. facing controversy;
6. identifying the community's strengths;
7. using local resources;
8. creating with the community's voice;
9. maintaining commitment with the community.

Visual Communication Design alone certainly cannot eradicate crime, narco-dependency, accidents or unjustified discrimination. However, concerted strategies, including communication, can help reduce the intensity of these problems significantly [17]. Frascara infers that the visual dimension of visual communications should always be contextualised within the pragmatic dimension in which it is found [in agreement with [14, 29]], that is, it enacts the communication event, which takes place on the part of the audience [17]. Bearing in mind the previous statement, it should be noted that "*In graphic communication, the message is prefabricated and carefully crafted before it is sent, so there is no improvisation which is typical in a dialogue. Ambiguities and visual noise are, as far as possible, avoided or abolished by the designer, who seeks a clear message, a game of unambiguous meanings, with which he intends to ensure the correct transmission-comprehension of the overall meaning*" [11, p. 56].

In building effective communications, it should be kept in mind that the goal of all visual communications is to produce a change in the audience's knowledge, attitudes and behaviour. For this change to happen, the communication has to be detectable, discriminable, attractive, understandable and convincing. It has to be built on knowledge of visual perception, cognition and human behaviour, and bearing in mind the personal preferences, cognitive abilities and value systems of the audience [17].

Furthermore, it is also important to refer [33], who indicates that the human being attributes a symbolic value to the "product", (as a result) of the design: the ability to have meaning, which provides an additional value to the communicated message.

From this literature review it is possible to conclude that the importance of design is associated with the ability to communicate visually, in a homogeneous way, the values and convictions of an organisation-community. Consequently, it is possible to strengthen the emotional connection established, or intended to be established, with the audience.

It is, thus, assumed that the effectiveness of the Design, as a tool for connecting the organisation and the interested parties, through the development of identity signs (exclusive and long-lasting), will be correlated to the quality (the ability to transmit them with fidelity to the institution's characteristics) and to the memorability of the mental image it will imprint in the target audience's mind, which is so necessary in EO.

6 Identity and Image

Once identified the need to improve the impact of EO's Brand and its communication, it is important to take into account the concepts of image and Corporate Identity. These concepts are transversal to this study, so it is important to understand them in order to clarify their nuances. Fetscherin and Usunier [16] makes the analysis of the evolution of academic literature in the field of corporate branding over the past decades, and reports a diffuse terminology in this medium. The author uses the example of the term identity, in which he finds more than one terminology: identity can both be defined as the unique and specific attributes of an institution and it is also used to designate the visual solution of a Corporate Visual Identity. Having said this, in the analysis of these subjects, it is relevant not to leave this concept's definition and interpretation dubious and make it as clearly described as possible.

Identity and Image (corporate) are concepts that, although they seem equivalent, they are, in fact, two different things that work in a symbiotic and complement way.

Identity is a network of concepts internal to the organisation, which can be selected (for their value) to characterise the brand's identity and which can be communicated. So, "*The term "identity" has a strategic cultural meaning. It is what makes each company different from the others, unique and unrepeatable. It is a matter of company management, like administration, organisation, production, staff relations,* etc. *However, identity is invisible and much less variable than those other aspects of organisations, but at the same time more substantial*" [11], p. 87).

According to [11], in the identity lies the future potential that is in the essence of the organisation. It is, therefore, "a valuable potential, but intangible" [11]. To substantiate the identity of a company, making it noticeable and memorable, it is necessary to create unique and lasting symbols: a set of elements that combined in a particular way are the constituents of the company's signs (symbols that belong to the image of the organization). These iconic signs communicate in a universal language, focusing on functions of remembrance, aesthetics and empathy with the public.

Corporate identity is fundamentally the reality of what an organisation is, i.e. its strategy, philosophy, history, business scope, type of products and services offered, and its formal and informal communication [26]: the substance in its institutional nature [11].

Costa [11] also makes clear the difference between identity images (visual) and mental images: The company image is not precisely a set of visible figures, but the general image that it raises in the collective memory.

The corporate image is not only a function of what design conveys, but above all what the overall conduct of the organisation reveals: it is what is perceived. "In short, the identity is what the company 'is' (whether it knows how to transmit it or not) and the image is what we think it is" [11], p.88). Therefore, we observe that the image that EO raises in the collective memory is not being properly understood, which means that there are difficulties in the transmission of its identity, as referred by [4] in Sect. 5.

In the line of thought of [40], and subscribing to [11] identity principles, a CVI is then a well-considered visualisation of an organisation's strategy. And in that way, it is a tool that communicates the desired identity of an organisation [40].

6.1 Corporate Visual Identity

Communication and Visual Identity are the bases of the relationship between the organization and the public. [26] makes its segmentation into four categories: Corporate Communication, Uncontrollable Communication,Architecture and Location; and Corporate Visual Identity (CVI) [26].

Regarding the physical and graphic dimension of corporate image, the notion of CVI emerges. [27] simplify this concept proposing that it consists of:

1. corporate name [the first element of a corporate identity to pay attention to. The whole identity revolves around it, as the logo is the name designed [11]];
2. logo and/or symbol;
3. typography;
4. colour;
5. and slogan.

In this study, we found that the EO had an implemented CVI. This CVI included a logo, two main colours and several typographies used regularly in the communication materials it communicates with (Figs. 1, 2, 3, and 4). But, even so, this CVI is limited as it is not graphically very flexible and, above all, it is visually inconsistent, given the vagueness of its guidelines. Although there is a visible improvement in the graphic design materials that EO has recently developed for its communication (catalogues, brochures, etc.), this effort and limitations highlights the weaknesses and deficiencies of EO's CVI system.

Fig. 1 Current EO's corporate image. *Source* Escola Oficina (2021)

Fig. 2 Example of EO's corporate image. *Source* Escola Oficina (2021)

eo escolaoficina

Fig. 3 Current EO's logo

Fig. 4 Flyer with EO's CVI. *Source* Escola Oficina (2021)

Taking into account the subjects analysed throughout this article and the need assumed by those responsible to renew EO's CVI, our project then proceeded or moved forward into the renewal and Design of EO's new CVI.

According to Bosch et al. [9], a new CVI can be considered the first step to build organisational reputation. For these authors, the development of a new CVI begins with the process of discovery, thus revealing the organisation's current corporate identity, its roots, culture, strategy and structure. Once the essence of the organisation is known (what it stands for, what it seeks to be, and how it differs from others) the design process can begin, with the intended outcome being a CVI system that is appropriate to the organisation as it will be developed to represent it (Bosh et al. 2005).

The fundamental principle of CVI is differentiation (the fruit of identity). Both the verbal name and the visual signs must possess a high degree of differentiation from their competitors. The more a CVI possesses this distinctive and exclusive value, the faster it is distinguished and retained in memory. Differentiation and recallability are the essential principles of good identity design, and it will not turn its back on the target audience [11, p. 89].

The signs that [11] refers to are iconic symbols that communicate a visual language that is universal, where its translation is not necessary. These attributes focus on "the functions of remembrance, aesthetics and empathy with the public". As we have seen previously, and in convergence with this author, the success of Visual and Identity Communication is united to the emotional connection that it awakens or promotes [26].

Corporate Identity is the basis of the communication strategies of an organisation [5] and in this identity the vision of the institution should manifest itself with consistency in all identity elements, from the logo to the behaviour of employees [4].

The challenge for designers is then to create design solutions that are aesthetically appropriate and visually appealing to the target audience, but at the same time possess functional readability and support the coding of communication messages so that they are decoded as intended [30].

The literature review we conducted addressed theoretical issues that are essential to a design project such as the EO's one. Given the context of EO, an organization that operates in the social environment, it is important to decide which of its characteristics should be highlighted by the Design in its answer to the identity problem [38]. The following section describes the process of building the proposal for the new EO's CVI.

7 Development of EO's CVI

To guide this project of renewal of EO's CVI, the methodology of Design Thinking was adopted, which is present in all stages of the iterative process that is the Identity Design. Considering the points of view of different authors regarding Design Thinking [3, 7, 8, 13, 34], a similar structuring of this methodology was found among them. However, and notwithstanding the different delineation of its stages, [7] presents a simplified terminology of Design Thinking, defining the procedure in only 3 stages (but keeping the principles):

1. **Inspiration:** stage of information gathering, analysis and problem definition;
2. **Ideation:** stage of idea generation, improvement of creative solutions and their respective prototyping;
3. **Implementation:** execution stage, where the design is developed into its final state.

Ambrose and Harris [3] and Pressman [34] highlight another stage (which suits this type of design project), called validation, where the critical evaluation of the final product is performed. This step helps to improve the performance of the designer, who should seek feedback from the target audience (his or her client) to understand whether the design solution has achieved the defined goals [3].

We then began with the first stage (which includes the preceding literature review), where the problems were identified and an attempt was made to empathise with the institution and its community. In line with [36] and [37], design achieves better results when the factors specific to a community are taken into account.

The main problem observed during the study and found in the analyzed visual identity (see Sect. 6.1), was the discrepancy between the brand core and what the identity elements represent. The authors [11] and [4] point out that the brand always has an identity, but sometimes it fails to present it properly to the public. Moreover, EO, as a non-profit organization, has its own personality [18], but it is still subject to these problems. It was therefore necessary to clearly understand the core of the EO brand, so that the new elements of its identity could transmit it objectively and, above all, intentionally. This step is crucial, and its inadvertence may cause a disconnection between brand identity and brand image.

To this end, and given the relevance of this step, interviews were conducted with EO's coordination; visits were made to the establishment, during working hours; and internal discussion meetings were held within the working group responsible for restructuring the means of communication of EO (ECHO project Research Group). From these interactions, it was learned what this social project genuinely was, how it operates, its roots, ideology, vision, values and mission (which determine the core of the brand [18]). The factors that best characterise this brand and that contributed to achieving the most faithful representation of the nature of the institution to the public were thus recognised. These factors that define the conceptual foundation of the new CVI of EO are as follows:

1. Openness to the community (capacity to receive);
2. Humanity in relationships;
3. Recreation/Renewal;
4. Inclusion;
5. Sharing/Union;
6. Cooperation;
7. Sustainability and revaluation;
8. Circular economy;
9. Modernity/Innovation;
10. Minimalism/Simplicity.

7.1 Graphic Brand

After identifying the basic characteristics of the EO's brand core, which allowed the concept to be defined, we moved on to the project's ideation. In this stage different possibilities for the design of the new EO symbol were explored.

The developed symbols will be a means to represent the brand (Bosh et al. 2005), but its distinctive capacity is what will dictate its retention in the public's memory [11].

As Costa [11] points out, symbols communicate a universal visual language, where no translation is required. The new EO symbol's design went through several iterations. This was the procedure that required a longer and deeper work, aiming to optimise the clarity of the transmission of the ideas, defined in the concept.

After meeting with the work team, it was considered that the following graphic model would be the interpretation that best suited the above concept:

The basic shape of the graphic brand is a circle, representing the circular economy and unity (Fig. 5). The pair of hands symbolises the human side of the institution, the cooperation and sharing it fosters. The hands, which can also be interpreted as arrows, stand for the connection to the sustainable side of EO. They are the symbol of recycling and the mark of recreation (Fig. 6).

In addition to the symbol, other elements were decided upon: the typography and the chromatic palette (Figs. 7 and 8). All these elements should work in harmony, thus forming the foundation for the graphic resources of this CVI.

Two topics commonly highlighted by authors in the field, as fundamental features to consider in the development of an effective Visual Identity, are consistency and

Fig. 5 Set of symbolic and explanatory elements that support the concept of the new graphic brand proposal for EO. *Source* Own formulation (2023)

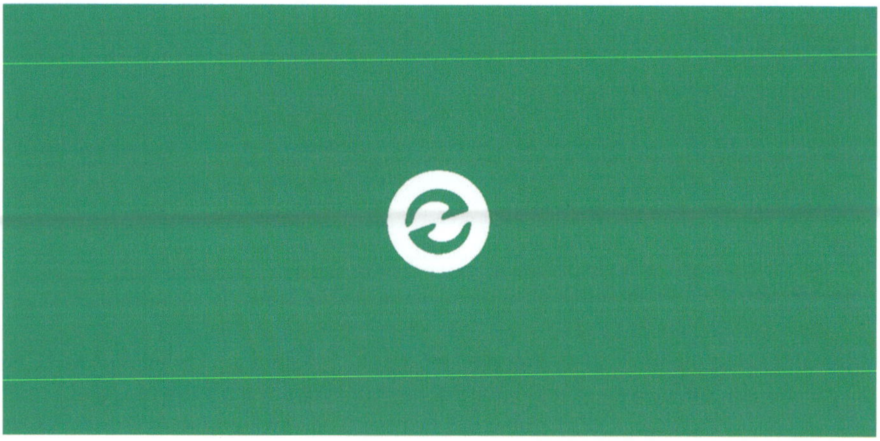

Fig. 6 Proposed symbol for the graphic brand of EO. *Source* Own formulation (2023)

Fig. 7 Proposed graphic brand (symbol and logo). *Source* Own formulation (2023)

Fig. 8 Proposed graphic brand for EO, tested on and against different colour backgrounds. *Source* Own formulation (2023)

distinctiveness [4, 11, 18, 41]. In the opinion and point of view of these authors, and as discussed in the literature review, consistency and distinctiveness are directly related to the emotional bonds that are intended to create with the public: the consistency of the image of a brand goes beyond visual and graphic elements, and should manifest itself throughout the institution.

The typography stipulated to complement the graphic brand is the so-called Montserrat font. This not only allows the values of the identity to shine through, but fundamentally improves the consistency of the Visual Identity, giving concrete options for its future use in different media and situations (one of the inconsistencies found in previous CVI applications). It's a typography without serifs, sober, simple and modern; it works both in analogue and digital form; and it has a range of 9 weights, from *Light* to *Bold* weights, therefore increasing the flexibility of contents' graphic management, which is obtained through contrast and hierarchy.

As for colours (Fig. 9), they influence human beings and their behaviour, both physiological and psychological. The same colour can arouse different feelings, which is directly related to the context in which it is used, i.e. there is a dependence on the other colours with which a particular colour is applied [15, 19]. The chromatic solution found for this project consists of a main colour (turquoise green) and a

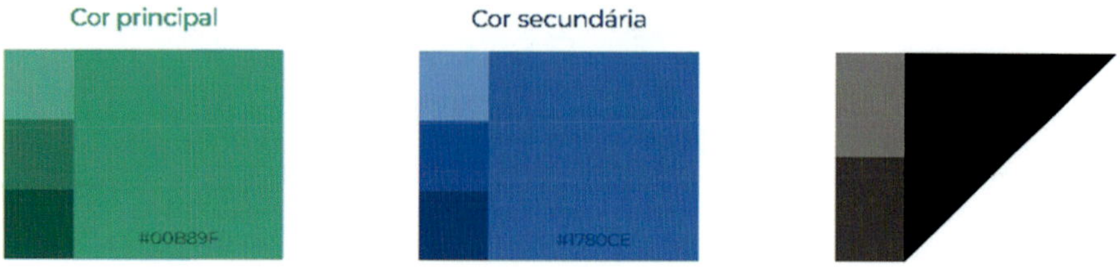

Fig. 9 Chromatic palette. *Source* Own formulation (2023)

secondary colour (blue), paired with black and white. The colour green is the colour of nature and sustainability. Used together, these colours can symbolise harmony, confidence, security and tranquillity [19]. It is an analogous palette, and in the same way as the typographic choice, this one is simple and prepared for the digital medium.

8 Conclusions and Future Work

The success of EO, an NPO, is based on the social contribution (employability, training, etc.) to the community where it operates (Porto Metropolitan Area). Notwithstanding its social importance in that territory, difficulties were observed in advertising itself to the public as a brand: not only by what was observed during the research, but also identified by the institution's own management [28].

The vagueness of the image presented by the institution's communication department, as well as its inconsistency, resulted in heterogeneous communication, which hindered the growth of the brand's reputation and may even be a factor conducive to unintended generalisations [18] by the target audience (such as the generalised distrust of EO's products): the organisation can only be what it shows it to be.

Considering the aforementioned weaknesses of the brand (lack of identity signs, unstructured and inconsistent communication) the EO was not objectively transmitting to customers the way it wanted to be perceived, which meant that its identity was not being materialised through the emotional connections that the brand could create with its target audience.

In short, it became necessary to revitalize EO's communication, through a visual support (the identity symbols of the new CVI) that had versatility in its application, consistency and distinguishability, but kept clear its interconnection to EO's brand core. Moreover, it should be noted that, despite the visual change, the essence that portrays EO was maintained.

Taking into account that this is a social project, the process of building the new visual identity was approached in accordance with the philosophy of Thorpe and Gamman's Social Design [38], which explains (as mentioned in Sect. 4) that due to the complexity of the challenge, designers and other actors involved in this process should work together, without the burden of responsibility to eradicate the problem, but only with the aim of leveraging the community's assets. Alongside the principles of Design Thinking, these factors determined the stage of extensive research and continuous collaboration between the institution and working team.

The graphic solution developed in this project was presented to the people involved and responsible for EO. Proposals for the new website and a mobile application for textile waste management were also presented, in order to expand the means of communication. The remaining proposals were developed by members of the research team, where the new graphic image has already been implemented. The proposal for the renewal of EO's Visual and Corporate Identity, developed in this study, was well received, approved and authorised for implementation by EO's managers.

For the future progression of this Design project, it will be essential to continue the implementation stage and subsequently measure and validate the results of its use, namely as audiences beyond those involved and those in charge of EO. It will be important to understand if the conclusions of the study are really in tune with the interpretation of the EO's publics, or not.

Acknowledgements This project was founded by the Portuguese Foundation for Science and Technology (FCT) under the reference EXPL/ART-DAQ/0037/2021.

References

1. Adams C, Perlmutter F (1991) Commercial venturing and the transformation of America's voluntary social welfare agencies. Nonprofit Volunt Sect Q 20(1):25–38
2. Ambrose G, Harris P (2010) Basics design 08: design thinking. Bloomsbury Publishing
3. Ambrose, G., & Harris, P. (2009). Basics design 08: design thinking. AVA Academia.
4. Argenti PA (2009) Corporate communication. McGraw Hill
5. Baker M, Balmer J (1997) Visual identity: trappings or substance? Eur J Mark 31:366–382. https://doi.org/10.1108/eb060637.
6. Branzi A (2013) Seven degrees of separation. In: Annicchiarico S, Branzi A (eds) The new Italian design. Triennale di Milano, Milan, Italy, pp 14–17
7. Brown T (2008) Design thinking. Harv Bus Rev 86(6):84
8. Brown T, Katz B (2011) Change by design. J Prod Innov Manag 28(3):381–383
9. Bosch ALM van den, de Jong MDT, Elving WJL (2005) How corporate visual identity supports reputation. Corp Commun: Int J 10(2):108–116. https://doi.org/10.1108/13563280510596925
10. Chen DS, Cheng LL, Hummels CCM, Koskinen I (2016) Social design: an introduction. Int J Des 10(1):1–5
11. Costa J (2011) Design Para os Olhos: Marca, Cor, Identidade, Sinalética. Dinalivro
12. Dionísio P, Lendrevie J, Lévi J, Lindon D, Rodrigues JV (2008) Mercator XXI – Teoria e prática do Marketing (11ª edição). Publicações Dom Quixote, Lisboa
13. Dolak F, Uebernickel F, Brenner W (2013) Design thinking and design science research
14. Fahmy S, Bock M, Wanta W (2014) Visual communication theory and research: a mass communication perspective. Springer
15. Farina M, Perez C, Bastos D (2011) Psicodinâmica das cores emcomunicação. Editora Blucher
16. Fetscherin M, Usunier JC (2012) Corporate branding: an interdisciplinary literature review. Eur J Mark
17. Frascara J, Meurer B, van Toorn J, Winkler D (1997) User-centered graphic design: Mass communication and social change. CRC Press

18. Grau SL (2014) Marketing for nonprofit organizations: insights and innovations. Oxford University Press, USA
19. Heller E (2018) A psicologia das cores: Como as cores afetama emoção e a razão. Editorial Gustavo Gili
20. Hernandez RJ, Goñi J (2020) Responsible design for sustainable innovation: towards an extended design process. Processes 8(12):1574
21. Huang SL, Ku HH (2016). Brand image management for nonprofit organizations: exploring the relationships between websites, brand images and donations. J Electron Commer Res 17(1)
22. Keller KL, Lehmann DR (2006) Brands and branding: research findings and future priorities. Mark Sci 25:740–759
23. Koskinen I, Hush G (2016) Utopian, molecular and sociological social design. Int J Des 10(1):65–71
24. Khorin A, Ekaterina V (2021) The role of visuals in the communication process. Filosofija Sociologija 32(1)
25. Margolin V (2015) Social design: from utopia to the good society. In: Bruinsma M, van Zijl I (eds) Design for the good society. Stichting Utrecht Biennale, Utrecht, the Netherlands, pp 28–42
26. Melewar TC, Bassett, K, Simões C (2006) The role of communication and visual identity in modern organisations. Corp Commun: Int J. 11:138–147. https://doi.org/10.1108/135632806 10661679.
27. Melewar TC, Saunders J (1998) Global corporate visual identity systems: Standardization, control and benefits. Int Mark Rev 15(4):291–308
28. Mota D (2021) Entrevista conduzida por videoconferência a Diana Mota em 10 de dezembro 2021
29. Munari B (1968) Design e Comunicação Visual. Edições 70
30. O'Connor Z (2013) Colour, contrast and gestalt theories of perception: the impact in contemporary visual communications design. Color Res Appl 40:85–92. https://doi.org/10.1002/col. 21858
31. Papanek V (1984) Design for the Real World; Van Nostrand Reinhold: New York, NY, USA, 1984.
32. Parkinson M (2012) The power of visual communication. Billion Dollar Graphics
33. Pereira J (2015) the contribution of communication design as a strategic constituent for the development of organizations—the input of digital media
34. Pressman A (2018) Design thinking: a guide to creative problem solving for everyone. Taylor & Francis, United Kingdom
35. Raposo D. (2011) Sistemas de Identidade Visual Corporativa Corporate Visual Identity Systems
36. Scott D (2012) Designing for social change—social responsibility and the graphic designer
37. Shea A (2012) Designing for social change: strategies for community-based graphic design
38. Thorpe A, Gamman L (2011) Design with society: why socially responsive design is good enough. CoDesign 7(3–4):217–230
39. Vasconcelos J, Martins N, Brandão D, Penedos-Santiago E (2023) Visual identity of non-profit organizations: Escola Oficina, a case study plan. In: Advances in design and digital communication: Proceedings of the 6th international conference on design and digital communication, Digicom 2022, November 3–5, vol 27, 2022, Barcelos, Portugal. Springer Series in Design and Innovation. Springer, Cham. pp. 675–686. https://doi.org/10.1007/978-3-031-20364-0_57
40. Wendy B, Menno DT de Jong, Annette LM van den Bosch (2018) Corporate rebranding: effects of corporate visual identity changes on employees and consumers, J Mark Commun 24:1, 3–16. https://doi.org/10.1080/13527266.2015.1067244
41. Wheeler A (2017) Designing brand identity: an essential guide for the whole branding team. Wiley

Certification of Vegan and Vegetarian Products: V-Label's Redesign

Joana Silva and Álvaro Sousa

Abstract This article is a response to a problem detected in the identification and distinction of the labels of the certification program of V-Label, a non-profit organization that advocates for the plant-based movement. Currently, the certification is based in two existing labels, one of which identifies and guarantees that the products that contain it are vegan, while the other does the same for vegetarian products. However, the visual similarity between the two increases the likelihood of confusing them when making a purchase. Thus, this article can be inserted in graphic design and communication area, but also in the area of branding, and intends to reflect on how to reconcile the familiar sense of an identity already widely recognized with solutions that communicate it in a more clear and efficient way, reinforcing trust in the brand and in the labels that represent it. V-Label presents itself as a means for reflection on the contribution of design to the plant-based movement which, for ethical, ecological, and social reasons, deserves to be encouraged and helped to grow. For these reasons, the project presented proposes not only to find solutions that correct the initial problem and lead to a more effective identification and distinction between vegan and vegetarian products, but also proposes to demonstrate the contribution that design can have for the growth and visibility of plant-based movement.

Keywords Certification labels · Communication · Rebranding · Identity

J. Silva · Á. Sousa (✉)
University of Aveiro, Aveiro, Portugal
e-mail: alvarosousa@ua.pt

N. Martins and D. Raposo (eds.), *Communication Design and Branding*, Springer Series in Design and Innovation 32,
https://doi.org/10.1007/978-3-031-35385-7_5

1 Introduction

V-Label is a quality and certification label for vegan and vegetarian products, managed by an NGO of the same name. The V-Label is a project supported by the European Vegetarian Union (EVU), being recognized for its high experience in animal and environmental protection and legislative intervention within the European Union. This article derives from the observation that the current design of the labels of the certification program managed by V-Label is fragile and contains graphic problems, which was seen as an opportunity for an intervention both in terms of the graphic component and strategic communication. The results that will be presented will focus on the analysis of existing problems in the brand and its respective labels, with subsequent development of a new design proposal for them, based on theoretical knowledge such as branding, shape, typography, color, and composition.

Products bearing the V-Label on their packaging mean that consumers do not need to look closely at the list of ingredients of a product to be sure that it is vegan or vegetarian. Companies and producers who decide to join the certification program can, if their products meet the criteria set by the organization, include one of the labels on their packaging. The V-Label, which has been asserting itself as a remarkable and highly recognized project, has accompanied and helped the growth of the plant-based market. The labels immediately attract potential buyers and are also a graphic indicator of a growing trend in the demand for more sustainable, healthy, and ethical products.

Efficient label design is important, not only for the companies that purchase such labels and wish to include them on their products without printing and/or production issues, but also for consumers by helping them make choices quickly, clearly and with confidence.

V-Label currently manages two labels—one vegan and one vegetarian—which are visually very similar, which turned out to be the starting point for this study. Vegan and vegetarian products are usually placed in proximity in the same sections in a store. Given that these are included in the packaging layout with reduced dimensions, it is natural and common for them to get confused. This confusion is mainly relevant for the vegan public, who do not consume products with any type of animal derived ingredient. Therefore, even if a product holds a V-Label, it may not be enough to avoid mistakes. Thus, this factor can contribute to a sense of distrust in the organization, on the part of consumers.

It should also be noted that, although "vegans remain a niche with a little over 1 percent of the population" [13], that number extrapolated to the 445 million people in the European Union [8] gives a perception of the magnitude of consumers that can potentially be affected. If the V-Label aims to help consumers interested in plant-based products to identify them clearly and quickly, the simple fact that the design of the two labels is so similar goes against the values and goals outlined by the organization, in addition to going against the principles that lead to the distinction of any object or design.

2 Thematic Framework

"Although veganism (100% plant-based lifestyle) is not a new phenomenon as such, in recent years vegan eating has gained heightened visibility in public discussion in many Western countries. The reasons for this include the intensifying discourses on animal rights-related aspects which lie at the heart of veganism, the environmental and health-related problems caused by animal production and consumption, and a new interest in vegan eating as part of sustainable lifestyle political movements" [12].

The World Health Organization defines plant-based diets as "a diverse range of dietary patterns that emphasize foods derived from plant sources coupled with lower consumption or exclusion of animal products" [31].

Therefore, plant-based diets are grouped into 6 that are considered the most common:

(a) *Vegan diets*—omit all animal products, including meat, dairy, fish, eggs and (usually) honey.
(b) *Lacto-vegetarian diets*—exclude meat, fish, poultry, and eggs, but include dairy products such as milk, cheese, yoghurt, and butter.
(c) *Lacto-ovo vegetarian diets*—include eggs and dairy, but not meat or fish.
(d) *Ovo-vegetarian diets*—exclude meat, poultry, seafood, and dairy products, but allow eggs.
(e) *Pesco-vegetarian (or pescatarian) diets*—include fish, dairy and eggs, but not meat.
(f) *Semi-vegetarian (or flexitarian) diets*—are primarily vegetarian but include meat, dairy, eggs, poultry, and fish on occasion, or in small quantities (Ibidem).

With the growing discussion regarding healthier and more ethical consumption with less environmental impact, the demand for, and consequent offer plant-based alternatives has increased. These alternatives also "provide an example of how material change may instigate reconfiguration in eating: the recent rise of vegan foods on the market has opened up opportunities for the development of novel meanings and competencies, enabling changes in everyday performance also among non-vegans" [12]. Vegan certification and labelling are increasingly established and evolving for non-food consumption [13].

On World Vegan Day 2020, the German company Veganz conducted a market study with around 2,600 participants from seven European countries, from vegans to omnivores, to understand their eating and shopping habits. According to the study, the vegan trend is strongest in Germany. Extrapolated for the current population of 83.1 million people (as of June 2020), the study results show that 2.6 million people—around 3.2% of the population—are vegan and about 3.6 million (4.4%) are vegetarian [30]. Compared with previous studies carried out in 2016, which pointed out that the number of vegans in Germany were 1.3 million, it is concluded that in just 4 years the number of vegans doubled [22, 30].

In this study, it was also possible to understand that more than 30% of participants claimed to follow a diet that aims to reduce or exclude meat, which means that there is many Europeans who are within the spectrum of plant-based diets: 1.9% are vegan, 3.1% are vegetarian, 2.9% are pescatarian and 22.9% are flexitarian [30].

According to another recent study within the framework of the "Smart Protein" project by ProVeg, it is also visible a huge growth in the plant-based market in Europe. The plant-based food sector has grown by 49% over the past three years and is now valued at €3.6 billion. The meat alternatives sector grew by 68%, the vegetable drinks (a.k.a. vegetable milk) sector grew by 36% and the vegan cheeses sector saw a triple-digit increase—112%. And the highest of all, "plant-based fish with a 623% growth rate over the past two periods", says the report [19].

In the case of processed foods, as the ones mentioned above, consumers cannot easily determine or verify whether a product is vegan (in comparison with unprocessed food, such as fruits and vegetables). "The list of ingredients is only of limited help as it is only listing the substances that belong to the ingredients per legal definition. In addition (…) various components of food do not legally belong to the ingredients and therefore do not need to be declared in the ingredients list. These include processing aids, carrier substances, food additives and food enzymes". When purchasing or consuming a product consumers can neither prove if a product is really vegan nor if it was produced without animal derived products. "Consumers have to rely on their trust that a product labelled as vegan is truly vegan" [9].

Hence the need for labels to contain all relevant information regarding the product, even though Regulations and legislation on food labels vary enormously from country to country. "One of their primary functions is to enable consumers to make informed decisions by showing key product information and claims. Food labels can also help consumers with storage advice and give dates for safe consumption, which can help reduce food wastage. Food labels typically offer guidance on specific contents or allergens, helping people manage their consumption of these ingredients, nutrients, and calories" [17].

With so much offer available, it becomes useful for the consumer that the labels contain information to that can be read quickly so that they can understand which options are more in line with their preferences or dietary restrictions. For this reason, companies and producers choose to submit their products to a certification process. Numerous organizations offer certification for specific standards and each of them works within a different scope. From religious institutions to independent certification bodies and government institutions, there are hundreds of groups that inspect, test, and certify food products around the world using a wide range of standards. After the certification process, these organizations allow food and beverage companies and suppliers to use their certification logos or marks on their product labels to indicate that they meet those standards [15], helping them make informed choices based on their preferences: a quality label. This works as a guarantee for the producer that certain product has gone through a process and has been independently certified for meeting the necessary requirements to carry the label. The same applies to plant-based products. To be able to navigate in a sea of options and to avoid limiting issues such as reading the ingredients list, a recent V-Label report shows that consumers are increasingly relying on independent labelling to help them identify vegan and vegetarian options quickly, confidently, and transparently [24].

Due to the importance of such labels, several nonprofits that advocate for the plant-based movement also started offering certifications programs for vegan and vegetarian products. These services operate mainly (but not exclusively) in the food sector and at the same time encourage the creation of new products. The growing number of products, in turn, helps perpetuate concrete changes in society and helps to protect the animals and the environment. The certification programs consist of a license that can be acquired for any vegan or vegetarian product, if the attribution parameters are met, so that a logo or label related to the organization responsible for certification can be included on the packages. These labels are a guarantee for the consumer that the product they are purchasing actually meets all the requirements to be considered vegan or vegetarian. The labels are also visible to consumers interested in plant-based products and help vegans to shop without constantly consulting ingredient lists. They also help companies recognize a growing vegan market, as well as bringing the word Vegan—and the lifestyle it represents—into the mainstream [29].

The labels also provide a temporary solution to another dilemma that arises in the European context: presently there is no consensus around the concept 'vegan' and 'vegetarian' throughout Europe and without explicit and accurate legislation, consumers may be misled by product labeling [21]. Since there is no legally binding definition or regulation of the use of the term 'vegan' and 'vegetarian', that can lead to a lack of transparency in communication from the producers' side and there are no guarantees even if the product is described on the label as "vegan" and "vegetarian". Article 36, paragraph 3(b) of the European Food Information Regulation (EU) No. 1169/2011 lays down that the European Commission should issue an implementing act defining the requirements for the voluntary labelling of food suitable for vegans or vegetarians. Until today, this has not happened since there is no deadline for the implementing act. Despite numerous initiatives from vegetarian and vegan associations and consumer protection organizations emphasizing the importance of a uniform definition and regulation for the labelling of vegan food, especially in the light of increasing numbers of vegan consumers [9].

This is a regulatory problem that allows the existence of products with information that is not transparent or even incorrect. Many companies and producers use their own labels for their products. When creating these labels, however, they define their own criteria for vegan and vegetarian products, which results in inconsistencies. These self-made labels are not subject to checks by independent bodies, which means that incorrect labelling can sometimes go unnoticed by consumers [26]. That's why it is recommended, in order to increase credibility, that producers of vegan food should certify their products with third-party labels at least until the European Commission achieves an agreement on a legally binding definition and issue uniform regulations on the use of the term 'vegan' and 'vegetarian' [9].

3 Project Development

V-Label is an internationally recognized, registered seal for labelling vegan and vegetarian products and services [25]. It is considered an independent certification, which means that companies interested in including the label on their product contact the organization responsible for certification. After an analysis of the composition and the manufacture process, the guarantee that the products meet all the requirements and the payment of the stipulated amount, the company that invested in the label can start carrying it on the packaging of their products and including it in communication materials.

For consumers, V-Label is a guide to identify plant-based choices at a glance and for businesses is a way of increasing their trustworthiness and transparency in vegetarian and vegan labelling [27]. The Switzerland-based V-Label GmbH coordinates international cooperation on the V-Label, as the holder of the trademark rights, and is supported by the European Vegetarian Union (EVU), "an umbrella organization for numerous European organizations active in the field of veganism and vegetarianism" [28].

Following a critical analysis of V-Label's current vegan and vegetarian labels according to criteria of shape, typography, color, and composition, in order to understand whether the current design is appropriate for the target audience, whether it evokes the intended symbolic connotations, whether it is properly perceived and whether the communication of the message is clear and legible.

Terms

In this analysis, some specific terms will be used to describe the labels. For the sake of simplification and to avoid repeatedly explaining their meanings, we will present their definitions below:

Label the current design in its entirety; the term that encompasses all visual elements (Fig. 1).

Fig. 1 Visual representation of the term "label"

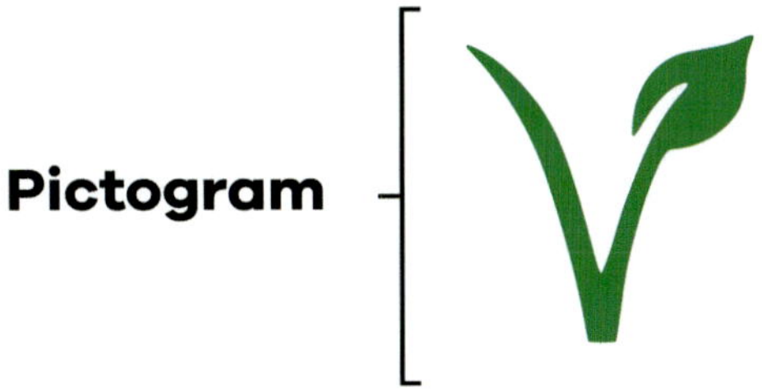

Fig. 2 Visual representation of the term "pictogram"

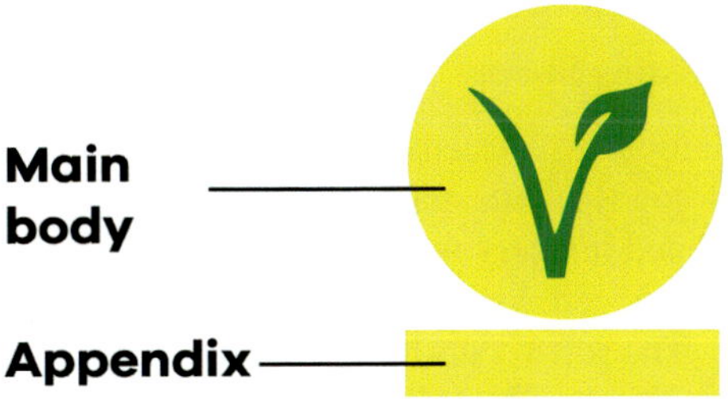

Fig. 3 Visual representation of the terms "main body" and "appendix" in terms of shape

Pictogram the icon of the letter "V" with a leaf on the upper right corner (Fig. 2).

Shape Main body and appendix: when it comes to the shapes that constitute the label, the circle that contains the pictogram will be defined as the main body, while the rectangle situated below will be defined as appendix (Fig. 3).

Text information this term will be used to define the text located in the appendix that indicates whether the product we are purchasing is vegan or vegetarian.

The text information appears translated depending on the country where the product is purchased, for example, a product certified in Portugal will be indicated with the word 'vegano' or 'vegetariano', but the same product in Germany will be indicated with the word "vegan" or 'vegetarisch'. The english version will be used for this analysis (Fig. 4).

Additional information the text placed inside the main body that follows its circular shape will be defined as additional information. It contains generic information, such as the indication of V-Label's website (V-Label.eu) and the name of the organization that originated the project (European Vegetarian Union) (Fig. 5).

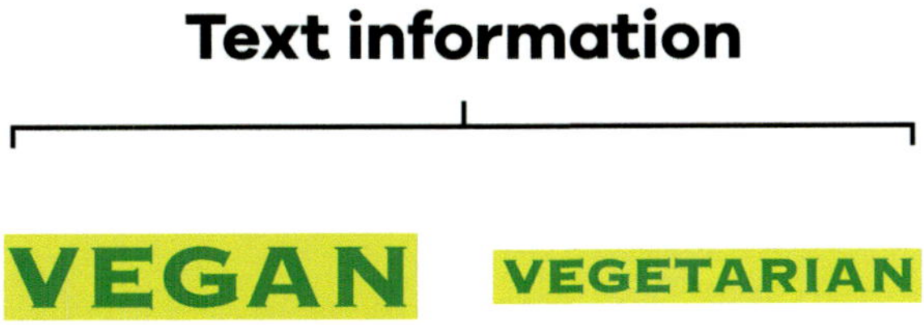

Fig. 4 Visual representation of the term "text information"

Fig. 5 Visual representation of the term "additional information"

Existing Shape

Jiang et al. concentrated their research on a basic, potentially eye-grabbing feature of logos: their shape. Consumers spontaneously generate product- or company-related imagery when processing the information, and shape-activated associations are utilized during imagery generation.

The soft versus hard associations elicited by circular and angular shapes, respectively, are found to be critical to the evaluation of physical product attributes (comfortableness and durability) and nonphysical attributes (a company's customer sensitivity). So, they came up with the hypothesis that a circular logo is likely to result in the company being perceived as more customer sensitive than an angular logo. And during their research, they demonstrated that the mere circularity/angularity of a logo is powerful enough to influence the inferences that consumers draw about products and the attitudes they have toward them [11].

The label is composed by two shapes: a circle that contains part of the information and a rectangular appendix below. It is considered that the shape chosen for the main body—the circle—works due to its simplicity, effectiveness, and appealing character. But also, for the symbolic connotations that we can associate with the brand—sensitivity, care, and nature protection (Fig. 6).

Fig. 6 Analysis of the shapes that constitute the labels

Fig. 7 Isolated word "vegan" for font analysis

Despite the choice of shape for the main body being so efficient and eye-grabbing, making the consumer associate certain qualities with the brand, a part of the information, probably the most important, is in the appendix: the information that is, nonetheless, the indication that the product we are purchasing is vegan or vegetarian.

If there are two labels and each ones serves to certify different products, it is pertinent to question whether it makes sense for both labels to have the same shape.

Main Information

As mentioned above, the label contains the information that indicates whether the product is vegan or vegetarian in the appendix located below the main body. A bold fond, with serifs (Cooperplate) in all capital letters was used for the text information (Fig. 7).

The same font was used for the additional information, but on a smaller scale within the composition of the label, when compared to the text information.

"When talking about typefaces, designers and researchers discuss two main issues: readability, overall ease of reading; and legibility, recognizing individual letters. The conventional wisdom is that serifed typefaces have higher readability. This is because the serifs lead the eye in a line across the page" [20].

Serifs can be described as extensions, protrusions, or finishing strokes extending from the ends of a character. They also serve to distinguish typefaces with similar shapes from each other are said to enhance readability by guiding the eye from one character to the next [23].

However, in the case of the label, the text information consists of a single word that is usually applied in small bodies of text. So should the ease of movement of the eye across the page even be a concern?

When selecting text type, production issues should be considered. For instance, when going very small, there's a possibility for disappearing thin strokes and other details, especially when printed [23].

Assuming that the label will mostly be perceived in reduced size, as it is usually added to packaging without being its focus and without overpowering the design composition, it makes sense to question whether the use of a serif font is appropriate. In this case, a serif font contains details that not only can be lost in the printing process but will also not add much legibility to the single word text information.

The usage of a serif for the additional information can also be questioned for the reasons mentioned above. These reasons are exacerbated by the fact that the additional information is present in an even smaller size within the composition of the label, which suggests that even more details could be lost in the printing process.

It is considered the usage of capital letters and a bold font as positive points.

The use of boldface is a good way to achieve emphasis by way of weight contrast and works even better for stand-alone words or phrases. If na even stronger emphasis is desired, all caps can be very useful if utilized sparingly and intentionally, as it creates a very noticeable emphasis [23].

Due to the importance of the message that wants to be conveyed in the text information, it makes perfect sense it appears in a bold font in all caps.

Color Palette

Of the design elements available to the designer of visual communications, color and contrast play key roles in visual perception, and the strategic use of these can contribute to the effectiveness of visual communications design. Color and contrast have the capacity to enhance the cognitive organization of incoming visual information as per the Gestalt 'laws' of visual perception, a theory that remains a reference to design practices.

When it comes to visual communications design, line and form are clearly important design elements; however, it is color and contrast that plays a more important role in terms of visual communications design due to their role in attracting attention and their capacity to enhance or mitigate the Gestalt laws of perception [18].

The label contains the pictogram, the text information, and the additional information in a dark green color over a bright yellow background. It is considered that these are two highly contrasting shades, which is a very positive aspect. But if there are two labels and if each serves to certify different products, it is again pertinent to question whether both labels should have the same color (Fig. 8).

It can also be questioned if a consumer suffers from a condition that makes it difficult to distinguishing colors, what solutions can be put into practice to handle such situations.

For example, in the case of a colorblind consumer, the condition doesn't mean that they can't see any color at all, or that they see things in grayscale. It's a decreased ability to see color, or a decreased ability to tell colors apart from one another. Color blindness should be taken into consideration for anyone in the design field, since color theory is an integral feature in successful design, and a lot of decisions are

Fig. 8 Analysis of the colors that constitute the labels

based on the feeling and emotion derived from colors. It is important to cater for a widest audience and mitigate possible issues with the design [7].

4 Composition

In V-Label's case, the label doubles as the seal quality for vegan and vegetarian products and as the company's logo.

Logos (or labels in this case) are particularly important in stores as a means of speeding recognition of products [10]. If the labels are critically analyzed, it can be seen that these are basic compositions, with just a few elements, but that the only difference between them is the text information located in the appendix. Even so, that difference will only be noticed after an effort to read the text—"Vegan" or "Vegetarian" (Fig. 9).

The rationale is that pictures are perceived faster than words. This is important because many company communications are seen for only a brief time, for example when walking by products on shelves a supermarket [10], like in the case of V-Label.

If logos should accelerate the recognition of a brand or company, if images carry more weight than text and if the consumer, generally, only perceives the logo in a short period of time, it can be questioned whether the visual strategy of basing the entire distinction between the two labels on a small text body is the most efficient.

4.1 Problems Survey

Globally, consumers are increasingly looking for healthy, ethical, and cost-effective products with low environmental impact, which is driving the demand for vegan and vegetarian alternatives.

Fig. 9 Visual representation of the conclusions drawn from the visual analysis of the labels and their distinctive elements

Fig. 10 V-Label's vegan and vegetarian labels with application of the Gaussian Blur effect in Photoshop at 15 pixels

With the growing number of options available, consumers are increasingly relying on independent labelling [24]. Thus, the importance of V-Label's work but also the importance of an effective design.

After an analysis of V-Label's current label design, it was possible to identify a series of issues that can be easily resolved through the intervention of the designer. The questions raised during the analysis were:

Does it make sense that both labels have the same shape?

Does it make sense the usage of a serif font that contains details that could be lost in the printing process and that will not add legibility, or even identity to the text?

Does it make sense that both labels have the same color?

Does it make sense to base the whole distinction between labels in the text information located in the appendix? (Fig. 10).

If the labels are submitted to a blur test (applying the Gaussian Blur filter at 15 pixels on Photoshop), simulating the way they could be perceived by a consumer with a poor sight, there is proof that there are not enough elements that allow for a proper distinction between the vegan and the vegetarian labels. This similarity can cause confusion and demands an extra effort to carefully examine the label.

This visual similarity between these two seals is not in accordance with the company's own identity—to bring clarity and security to the consumer.

This article's goal is to answer each of the questions raised through a redesign project and, in the end, obtain distinct solutions, which communicate a clear message, in accordance with the company's values and which respond to the anxieties of consumers.

The relevance of this project lies in the fact that the V-Label sells two similar labels for different attribution criteria. This alone is proof enough that there are big differences between plant-based products. And the difference them products should be clarified and communicated.

4.2 Project Program

A redesign project should take into consideration the equity the company has already built around their identity. Many times, however, significantly change brand identity might mean going a step too far when all that's needed is a refinement of the design. When the identity has become a little dated or has communication issues but consumers' familiarity with it is high, it is often enough to make small adjustments and fine-tune the design. These improvements should refine and consolidate the visual identity [1].

As concluded in the critical analysis, the current label has some deficiencies in terms of design and communication, but it also has positive aspects that can and should be considered when redesigning it. The degree of recognizability points to the fact that the current label should not be radically altered, and principle of continuity should be adopted.

Familiarity

"Logo recognition occurs at two levels. First, consumers must remember seeing the logo (correct recognition). Second, logos must remind consumers of the brand or company name (recall). The former depends largely on the design itself. Given equal exposures, a more memorable design will be recognized more easily than a less memorable one. Therefore, facilitating recall of the company logo starts with selecting a design that is recognized easily" [10].

Some logos will create a sense of familiarity even when they have never been seen before. This could be the result from a logo evoking a familiar meaning or from the design being like well-known symbols. Familiar-looking stimuli tend to be perceived and processed faster, which is particularly important for logos.

Either way, familiarity can benefit a logo because it can increase affect, create more consensually held meanings and a more cohesive image. and even enhance choice of a brand if brand experience is limited. A sense of familiarity can be maximized by selecting a unique, but easily interpreted, design of a familiar object (Ibidem).

"Collectively, color, symbol, shape, and lettering contribute to what Lightfoot and Gerstman define as visual equity. Visual equity is the value derived from 'visual form', that is the 'look and feel' of the brand. Visual equity contributes towards brand recognition (…) helps to communicate a brand's desired image" and, especially in V-Label's case, it enables a brand to stand out on the supermarket shelf [2] (Fig. 11).

Based on these concepts and the brand's own history, it makes sense that the redesigned labels do not radically break with the current V-Label design. Thus, in

Fig. 11 Pictogram with the letter "V" with a leaf at the top right top as the familiar element to bridge the gap between the current design and the redesign proposal

order to adopt a principle of continuity with the pre-existing label, it was decided to keep the pictogram of the "V" with a leaf that both characterizes and makes the current label recognizable. Thus, a familiar element is maintained for the consumer, which allows both correct identification and recall of the brand.

Shape

The choice to keep the pictogram implies the use of other strategies to increase the distinction between the vegan and vegetarian labels. Color and typographic composition will play an important role, but other strategies should be explored. This is especially important to avoid possible confusion in case the consumer suffers from a condition that makes it difficult to distinguishing colors or even when printing in high contrast.

"Form is generally more resistant to environmental variation relative to color. Perception of color is sensitive to changes in the angle from which a viewer perceives them as well as by the brightness of the environment. Shape and form, by contrast, are less affected by such situational variation. Form more so than color detail provides information about the essential nature of depicted objects. (…) Although there may be times in which color can be critical for identification—such as when the color of a tomato (green vs. red) signals its palatability (less edible vs. more edible, respectively)—generally speaking, color relative to form is less informative about the essential nature of objects and is treated as redundant or unnecessary information" [14].

As for the issue of the base shape being the same for both labels, this appears not to make much sense, since the shape is a key element in communication. Not only is it an element that is easy to work with and adapt within the composition, but it also has the greatest resistance to variations in situation.

As such, it is intended to make the distinction not only through color and typographic composition, but also through shape, by choosing two basics but clearly different shapes. As previously mentioned, the circle was a good choice for the current V-Label and can clearly be used for the redesign of one of the labels, leaving only a second shape to be chosen for the other label.

Form can be analyzed according to different criteria and functions. Chen et al. developed a study on recognition with the argument starting with the degree of simplicity and raised some new questions that concern the memory and recognition of form. It was questioned whether regular figures are better remembered than irregular ones simply because they contain more synthetic visual information. There was an observable bias in perception for simple configurations, straight lines, circles, and other simple orders in opposition to random shapes in their day-to-day lives [3], 365–74).

Chen et al. also mentioned a visual perception experiment conducted by Hochberg, that presented silhouette forms, where it was concluded that the threshold for recognition was the lowest with the simplest form: first the circle; secondly the rectangle (Ibidem) (Fig. 12).

Having these concepts in mind, it makes even more sense to keep the current shape of the V-Label—the circle—for one the labels. And it also makes sense to use

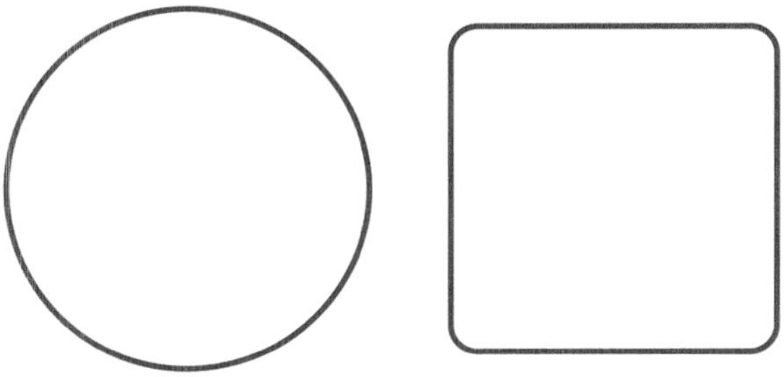

Fig. 12 Distinct shapes chosen for the labels' redesign proposal

a square shape for the second label. Since the word "vegetarian" is longer than the word "vegan", the square shape will be assigned to the vegetarian label. The square will have rounded corners to maintain the same visual language as the circle.

Typography

"Typefaces create atmosphere. They spark emotions and express historical, contemporary, or cultural connotations — all before the text is read. Subtle messaging via the physical characteristics of typefaces prompts viewer participation. Some faces are casual or dignified, others mechanical or playful". A fitting typeface personality makes an impression and when text in limited quantity, such as title pages or short headings, striking display faces work nicely [5].

If early roman letters designed for printing were based upon early handwritten manuscripts and the roman capitals carved on the buildings of the Roman Empire.

It seems, therefore, logical to reason that traditional and historical factor played a major part in the custom of using typefaces with serifs for text in the Western world.

The legibility theory of roman typefaces was developed after romans had been used a considerable time for text, and not because they are presumably superior in legibility. It was only in the beginning of this century that sans serifs were designed in greater numbers.

According to McLean the first sans serif appeared in Britainin 1816 and the first lowercase sans serif in 1835.

If first letters designed for typographic printing were based in imitating the black-letters that copyists drew with a pen, in order to make the printed book equal to the book made in the medieval scriptorium, they rapidly shifted form and sought inspiration from the *capitalis monumentalis* carved on buildings of the Roman Empire—upper case—and the Carolingian alphabet (commanded to be drawn by Carlos Magno) —lower case—also inspired by Roman manuscripts, made on waxed boards or papyrus. It therefore seems logical to conclude that there were factors based on history and tradition that played a role in the current use of serif fonts. In contrast, the emergence of sans serif fonts dates to a more recent period, more precisely from the grotesque typefaces of the early nineteenth century [6].

With these concepts in mind and circling back to the choice of a serif font: in addition to the problems already mentioned, namely the possibility lost details in the printing process without any increase in the legibility, a font with serifs has an

VEGAN

VEGETARIAN

Fig. 13 Text information when applied the chosen font for the redesign proposal

associated historical component and a more conservative personality. For the labels' redesign, it was decided to adopt a more modern and striking approach through typography, proceeding with a bold, geometric, with high readability sans-serif font (Fig. 13).

Choosing a geometric and sans-serif font also tackles any potential issue that a serif font could bring to the printing process. This font will be used for both the text and the additional information.

Composition

It's often explored the idea that graphic simplicity allows for a better identification and recognition of images, objects, or ideas. But how can the concept of simplicity be inserted in the context of V-Label's redesign—where the labels are already, by themselves, simple compositions widely recognized by the public?

Graphic simplification aims to express the characteristics of an object clearly and additionally make it more recognizable and memorable. Simplifying a design can be more difficult than adding elements to it—simplification means not only deleting the details of the objects, but also emphasizing key points on specific details [3], 365–74).

Taking this concept into account, it can be argued that V-Label's original design, despite its simple composition and recognizability, the detail that there are two distinct vegan and vegetarian labels was not emphasized. That said, one might even argue its total recognizability—the public may be familiar with the colors and shapes of the label and may even look for it while shopping. But they also may fail to properly identify the label of the product they are purchasing, confusing the vegan with the vegetarian label.

Murchie and Diomede explained that the signal to noise ratio is a useful concept to determine the amount of information to present where clearly communicating information (high signal) with minimal degradation due to excess material (low noise) is the goal. When in doubt, simplicity should be chosen over complexity, by taking away everything in a visual (including text) until there are only the essentials there [16].

In the redesign proposal, in addition to the changes already mentioned earlier in terms of familiarity, shape and typography -, it was decided to take advantage of some elements of the current composition—namely the pictogram of the "V"—and part of the additional information that mentions the V-Label website. The remaining additional information—namely the indication of the organization European Vegetarian Union—and the appendix, will not be included. These were considered as non-essential elements that add noise to the composition.

The description of how the elements will be organized follows.

We opted for a centered design, within the limits of the shape. It was considered unnecessary to add more text information or appendices outside such limits (Fig. 14).

Regarding the typographic composition, due to the length of the word "vegetarian" (when compared with the word "vegan"), it was decided to divide it into 3 parts. The typographic arrangements of the words in 3 lines, or 1 line, respectively, are yet another differentiating element between the two labels (Fig. 15).

Inside the main body, the letters intertwine with the pictogram in an organic composition. Merging the elements allowed for the text information to grow and occupy a large percentage of the label without taking away from the familiar element that is the pictogram (Fig. 16).

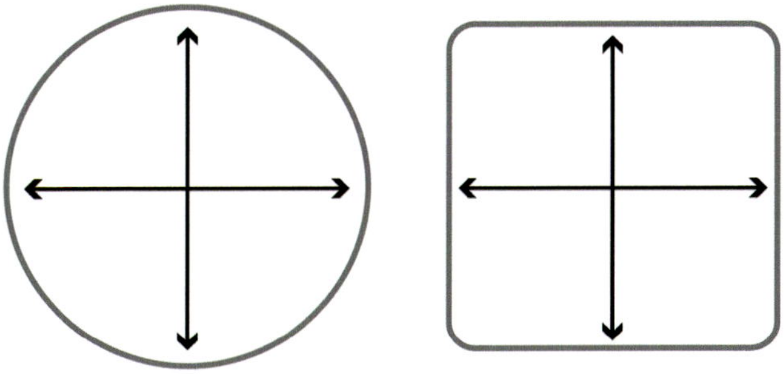

Fig. 14 Centered composition without appendices

Fig. 15 Composition of the text information

Fig. 16 Combination of elements: shape, text information and pictogram

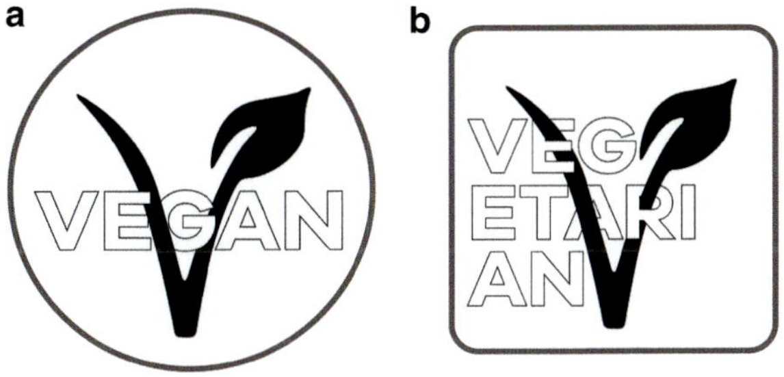

Color

When revisiting the matter of the labels' color, even though it has already been argued that color should not be taken as the only and most important distinguishing factor, it is nevertheless pertinent to pick different colors for the labels. The limitations of basing the distinction on color alone are:

(1) the consumer may suffer from a condition that makes color distinction difficult.
(2) the producer may want to print the labels in high contrast or in just one color and
(3) the perception of color is sensitive to changes in the angle from which a consumer perceives them as well as by the brightness of the environment [14].

However, color combined with other elements of the composition is another available means to reach the objectives of the labels' redesign.

Color, if appropriately selected, may bring inherent and immediate value to the brand, like a carefully chosen name. Colors evoke a variety of associations that, without prior conditioning, can be used to communicate a brand's desired image in the consumer's mind [2].

Next, the results of applying color to the labels are presented.

For the labels to have different colors, the yellow was kept as the dominant color for the vegetarian label and the colors green was assigned for the vegan label for its association with nature and plants. Since the design elements are grouped within the label's limits, it was important to select a neutral color for the text, in this case white. The pictogram was kept in the same shade of green of V-Label's branding, not only for the sake of familiarity, but also for contrasting with the new proposed colors.

On the original V-Label uses primary yellow, in CMYK color mode with 100% yellow. But since the redesign proposal doesn't make use of appendices and concentrates the information within the label's limits, the legibility of white text would be compromised on a background in CMYK color mode with 100% yellow, so it is proposed to add 25% magenta.

A white frame/border It was also added to ensure that the labels always stand out, even when applied on backgrounds with images or similar colors to the ones used (Fig. 17).

Fig. 17 Final proposal for the labels' redesign

4.3 *Evaluation of Design Results*

An online survey was conducted on a platform called Jotform, aiming to demonstrate the efficacy of the redesign proposal. A multiple-choice form was created that contained images of similar vegan and vegetarian products already certified by V-Label and participants were asked to identify the vegan products in the images as opposed to the vegetarian one.

All clues present on the packaging that alluded a product's suitability for a particular diet were eliminated, for example, words like "vegan", "egg" or "cheese". The only indicator that allowed the distinction between vegan and vegetarian products was the label.

The survey consisted of three initial questions related to the age, country, and diet of the participants, followed by 12 questions with product images (6 with the current V-Label and 6 with the redesign proposal) where participants were asked to identify the vegan products. On the final question, participants should state which labels they thought allowed for a better identification, the current or the proposed ones (Figs. 18 and 19).

In the 12 questions aimed at identifying the vegan product, there were images with the products side by side and identified as A and B. The participants could choose between the answer "A", "B" or "non-perceptible". The latter was placed for cases in which it was not possible to identify the vegan product at all. Several examples were presented, such as individual and similar products from the same brand, similar products from different brands, groups of similar products from the same brand, groups of different products and from different brands—to reflect how these could be perceived on a supermarket. The response time of each participant was measured

Fig. 18 Products containing the current label design

Fig. 19 Products containing the proposed redesigned label

in each of the 12 questions with product images, to find out whether the redesign proposal would allow for faster identification of the vegan product.

One of the limitations of this study stems from the fact that the questions do not appear in a random order as the participant is filling out the survey.

The results obtained are presented below. In this analysis the term "current design" refers to questions containing product images with the current V-Label and the term "redesigned proposal" refers to questions containing product images with the labels developed for this study (Figs. 20, 21, and 22).

The survey had 100 participants, the majority aged between 18 and 47 years old. More than half of the participants are in Portugal (58%), followed by Macao (16%) and Germany (13%). Most respondents identify themselves as followers of a flexitarian diet (41%), followed by an omnivore diet (37%) and a pescatarian diet (9%) (Fig. 23).

In the 12 questions aimed at identifying the vegan product, the 100 participants were able to correctly identify the vegan product on average 83.5% of the time.

In the 6 questions that refer to the current design, the sum of the correct answers of all participants is 478, which means that vegan products were correctly identified 478 times. On average, the 100 participants were able to correctly identify the vegan product 79.6% of the time, which is below the average.

In the 6 questions referring to the redesign proposal, the sum of the correct answers of all participants is 524, which means that vegan products were correctly identified 524 times. On average, the 100 participants were able to correctly identify the vegan product 87% of the time, which is above the average.

Still in the 12 questions aimed at identifying the vegan product, the 100 participants said that the difference between a vegan and vegetarian product was not perceptible on average 10.92% of the time.

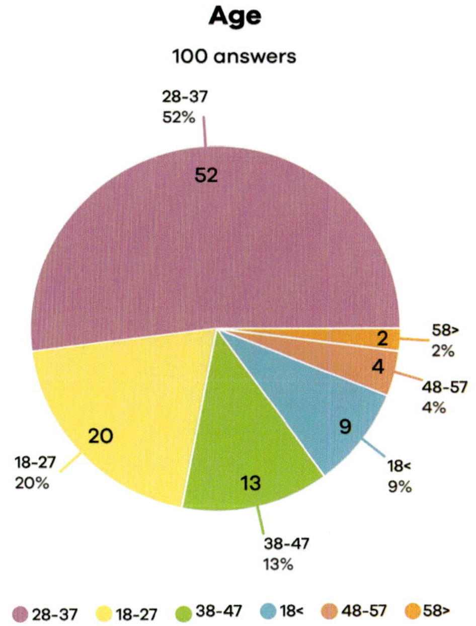

Fig. 20 Participants' age

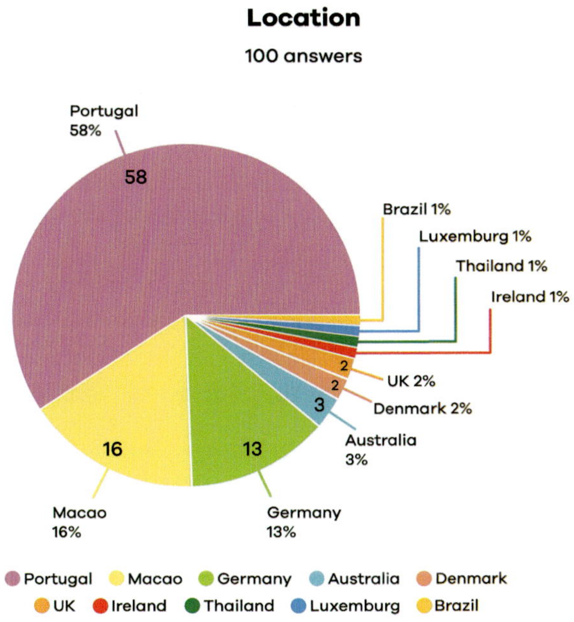

Fig. 21 Participants' location

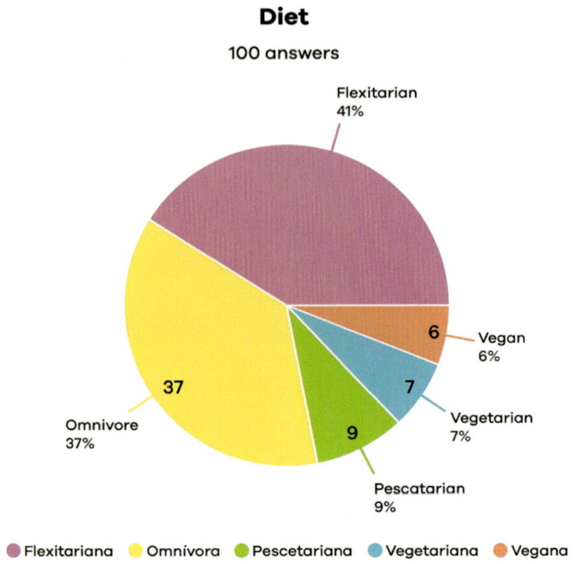

Fig. 22 Participants' diet

Average time		Current design		Design proposal	Global
	Quest. 4	00:02:50	Quest. 7	00:01:41	
	Quest. 5	00:02:20	Quest. 8	00:01:30	
	Quest. 6	00:01:53	Quest. 9	00:01:21	
	Quest. 10	00:01:14	Quest. 11	00:01:01	
	Quest. 12	00:00:52	Quest. 13	00:00:43	
	Quest. 14	00:00:34	Quest. 15	00:00:23	
Average response time		00:01:37		00:01:06	00:01:22
Correct answers		**Current design**		**Design proposal**	**Global**
	Quest. 4	79	Quest. 7	82	
	Quest. 5	86	Quest. 8	90	
	Quest. 6	85	Quest. 9	86	
	Quest. 10	76	Quest. 11	88	
	Quest. 12	83	Quest. 13	90	
	Quest. 14	69	Quest. 15	88	
Total correct answers		478		524	
Average of correct answers		79.66666667		87	83.5
"Non-perceptible" answers		**Current design**		**Design proposal**	**Global**
	Quest. 4	14	Quest. 7	12	
	Quest. 5	11	Quest. 8	5	
	Quest. 6	13	Quest. 9	7	
	Quest. 10	20	Quest. 11	9	
	Quest. 12	11	Quest. 13	5	
	Quest. 14	18	Quest. 15	6	
Total "non-perceptible" answers		87		44	
Average of "non-perceptible" answers		14.5		7.333333333	10.91666667

Fig. 23 Results obtained on the online survey: average response time, correct answers, "non-perceptible" answers

In the 6 questions referring to the current design, the sum of the "non-perceptible" answers of all participants was 87. On average, the 100 participants said that it was not possible to identify the vegan product 14.5% of the time, which represents a number above the average.

In the 6 questions referring to the redesigned proposal, the sum of the "non-perceptible" answers of all the participants is 44. On average, the 100 participants said that it was not possible to identify the vegan product 7.3% of the time, which represents a number below the average.

The average response time recorded for each participant for each of the 12 questions was 01:22 s. The average response time for the 6 questions referring to the current design was 01:37 s while the average response time for the 6 questions referring to the redesigned proposal was 01:06 s. The time that each participant took on average to identify the vegan product is lower when products carry the redesigned labels (Fig. 24).

which label do you think works best to allow for a better identification?

In the final question, participants were asked to express if they had a preference on which labels should be used to identify vegan and vegetarian products. 80% of respondents said they preferred the redesigned labels. 14% of respondents said they preferred the current labels and 6% said they had no preference.

Through this survey, it was possible to conclude that the labels developed for this study were well received by the respondents, with 80% of them expressing their preference for the redesigned version. More importantly, it was possible to verify that the proposed redesign of the labels led to more correct identifications of vegan products or groups of products, and that the identification occurred in a shorter time, when compared to the current label design.

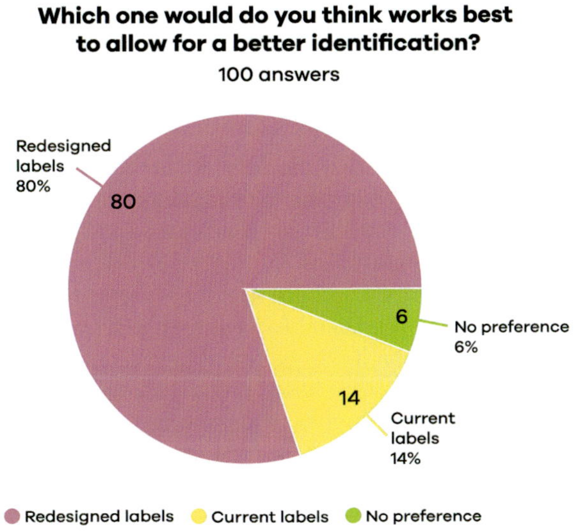

Fig. 24 Results obtained on the online survey final question:

4.4 Final Considerations

This study aimed at redesigning V-Label's vegan and vegetarian labels so that their identification and distinction would be clearer and more efficient. The pertinence of the redesign is premised on understanding the current social context regarding the growth in the number of supporters of plant-based diets, the role played by organizations that advocate for plant-based movement and how the manage certification programs for vegan and vegetarian products. The success of the project stems from the recognition of a need to clearly identify plant-based products and graphic interventions based on theoretical knowledge about branding, shape, typography, color, and composition.

Using V-Label's specific case and its current labels design, it was possible to conclude that the differentiation between them is insufficient, considering their use in a store context, where usually vegan and vegetarian products are found in the same sections, with the labels applied in a small scale the product's packaging. The analysis of the current visual aspect of the labels, made it possible to derive the existing problems and how they could be solved, leading to a design improvement and the creation of communication strategies in accordance with the organization's goals. The solutions presented are the result of a literature analysis, which allowed the construction of a solid project, based on specific methodologies of the discipline.

After the online survey, it was possible to conclude that the presented solutions allow for a faster identification and better distinction between vegan and vegetarian products. The proposed solutions led to better recognition by consumers, regardless of their level of prior knowledge of the labels themselves or the of the certified products. It is highlighted the role of design as a support for the growth of the plant-based movement. In addition to fulfilling the functional requirement of a proper identification of plant-based products, the labels also allow for a clear distinction between the adequacy of the product to a given diet. The proposed labels also reflect the innovative aspect of the organization, which intends to keep up with the current trends, while supporting the plant-based movement with innovative projects and solutions.

It is recognized that the project should be continued in the future, namely in the deepening of communication strategies and standardization of all the company's communication platforms, such as website and social media. This project should also lead to discussions regarding progresses that are being made in the food sector and regarding new products that will emerge soon, that can be an important piece to reduce humanity's environmental footprint without compromising taste. For example, it is expected that soon it will be possible to purchase lab grown meat and fish, which, despite not being plant-based products, could be considered cruelty-free products. It would be interesting to discuss what visual solutions can be found that allow organizations to certify these product categories.

References

1. Airey D (2015) Logo design love: a guide to creating iconic brand identities. Berkeley, Calif. New Riders
2. Bottomley P, Doyle J (2006) The interactive effects of colors and products on perceptions of brand logo appropriateness. Mark Theory 6(1):63–83. https://doi.org/10.1177/1470593106061263
3. Chen C, Vien C, Dian L, Thomas C (2015) Effective simplification for logo design. Design Society
4. Chung-Yun C, Cheung V, Li D, Cassidy T (2015) Effective simplification for logo design. Design Society
5. Cullen K (2012) Design elements, typography fundamentals: a graphic style manual for understanding how typography affects design. Rockport, Beverly, Ma
6. De Lange R, Esterhuizen H, Beatty D (1993) Performance differences between times and helvetica in a reading task. Electron Publ 6 (3):241–48.https://ils.unc.edu/courses/2018_fall/inls161_001/materials/03/Serif.SansSerif.10.1.1.39.6537.pdf
7. Ellfattah M (2014) Web design for color blind persons. Int Des J 4(4):37–46
8. Eurostat (2022) Population on 1 January. Europa.eu. 2022.https://ec.europa.eu/eurostat/databrowser/view/TPS00001/bookmark/table?lang=en&bookmarkId=c0aa2b16-607c-4429-abb3-a4c8d74f7d1e
9. Gerke M, Janssen M (2017) Vegan foods: labelling practice. Ernahrungs Umschau 64(3):54–57. https://doi.org/10.4455/eu.2017.011
10. Henderson P, Cote J (1998) Guidelines for selecting or modifying logos. J Mark 62(2):14–30. https://doi.org/10.2307/1252158
11. Jiang Y, Gorn G, Galli M, Chattopadhyay A (2015) Does your company have the right logo? How and why circular- and angular-logo shapes influence brand attribute judgments. J Consum Res 42(5):709–726. https://doi.org/10.1093/jcr/ucv049
12. Laakso S, Niva M, Eranti V, Aapio F (2021) Reconfiguring everyday eating: vegan challenge discussions in social media. Food, Cult Soc (April):1–22. https://doi.org/10.1080/15528014.2021.1882796
13. Lawo D, Esau M, Engelbutzeder P, Stevens G (2020) Going vegan: the role(s) of ICT in vegan practice transformation. Sustainability 12(12):5184. https://doi.org/10.3390/su12125184
14. Lee H, Deng X, Unnava H, Fujita K (2014) Monochrome forests and colorful trees: the effect of black-and-white versus color imagery on construal level. J Consum Res 41(4):1015–1032. https://doi.org/10.1086/678392
15. Mermelstein N (2019) There's a logo for that—food safety and quality. Ift.org, April 2019. https://www.ift.org/news-and-publications/food-technology-magazine/issues/2019/april/columns/food-safety-and-quality-product-certification-logos
16. Murchie K, Diomede D (2020) fundamentals of graphic design—essential tools for effective visual science communication edited by Marie-Claire Shanahan. FACETS 5(1):409–422. https://doi.org/10.1139/facets-2018-0049
17. NSF (2021) Food trends, changes and challenges. Nsf.org.https://nsfinternational.widen.net/s/fss72qqxsv/ct_food_trends_insight_ereport
18. O'Connor Z (2013) Colour, contrast and gestalt theories of perception: the impact in contemporary visual communications design. Color Res Appl 40(1):85–92. https://doi.org/10.1002/col.21858
19. ProVeg/Smart Protein Project (2021) Plant-based foods in Europe: how big is the market? https://proveg.com/wp-content/uploads/2021/02/Smart-Protein-Plant-based-Food-Sector-Report_-Webinar-slides.pdf
20. Romney C (2005) With serifs or without: which typeface should I use for my materials? Between the Keys (JALT MW SIG) 13(1)
21. SAFE—Safe Food Advocacy Europe (2017) "Vegan Definitions and Standards." https://www.safefoodadvocacy.eu/wp-content/uploads/2020/04/SAFE-Vegan-standards.pdf.

22. Skopos Group (2016) 1,3 Millionen Deutsche Leben Vegan. Skopos-Group.de.November 15, 2016. https://www.skopos-group.de/news/13-millionen-deutsche-leben-vegan.html.
23. Strizver I (2010) Type rules: the designer's guide to professional typography. Wiley, Hoboken, N.J.
24. V-Label (2021) The growing importance of vegan food labels: how do conscious consumers shop in 2021? V-Label. https://www.v-label.eu/case-study-vegan-food-labels
25. V-Label (2022a) Home Page—V-Label. V-Label. May 25, 2022. https://www.v-label.com/
26. V-Label (2022b) FAQ—V-Label. V-Label. May 30, 2022. https://www.v-label.com/faqs/
27. V-Label (2022c) Information for Producers—V-Label. V-Label. May 30, 2022. https://www.v-label.com/info-for-producers/
28. V-Label (2022d) About Us—V-Label. V-Label. September 16, 2022. https://www.v-label.com/about-us/
29. Vegan Action /Vegan Awareness Foundation (2022) Certification. Vegan.org. February 22, 2022. https://vegan.org/certification/
30. Veganz (2020) Veganz Nutrition Study 2020. Veganz.com. October 30, 2020. https://veganz.com/blog/veganz-nutrition-study-2020/
31. World Health Organization. Regional Office for Europe (2021) Plant-based diets and their impact on health, sustainability and the environment: a review of the evidence: WHO European office for the prevention and control of noncommunicable diseases. https://apps.who.int/iris/handle/10665/349086

A Product-Application-Based Residential Cooling System with Zero Emission

Atharva Nikam and Pranita Ranade

Abstract Climate change caused by global warming has recently led to increased temperatures in urban areas. With rising temperatures, the effectiveness of fans and coolers has reduced, and the demand for air conditioners has increased, which is not eco-friendly or cost-effective. This leads to overconsumption of electricity/non-renewable energy, causing increased production of CFCs and GHGs. Due to the global warming threat, there has been an increase in demand for sustainable products or solutions. The objective of the proposed product is to introduce an eco-friendly, cost-effective cooling system, which promotes UNESCO's 13th sustainable development goal, i.e., 'Climate Action'. The proposed product-application-based solution envelopes the "Zero Emissions" idea that will help maintain comfortable temperatures in residential sectors. "Indirect-Direct Evaporative Cooling" technology is employed in the proposed eco-friendly system compared to "Conventional Cooling" technologies. Critical design thinking and various research methods are employed in the proposed concept. The proposed design solution is economical and sustainable, catering to a wide range of consumers.

Keywords Indirect–direct evaporative cooling technology · UX/UI design · SDG · Climate change · Global warming

A. Nikam · P. Ranade (✉)
Symbiosis Institute of Design, Symbiosis International (Deemed University), Pune, India
e-mail: pranitaranade@gmail.com

N. Martins and D. Raposo (eds.), *Communication Design and Branding*, Springer Series in Design and Innovation 32,
https://doi.org/10.1007/978-3-031-35385-7_6

1 Introduction

Due to the increase in global warming and rising temperatures, the use of air conditioners has increased. The effectiveness of fans and coolers has reduced, and the demand for ACs has increased, which is not eco-friendly and cost-effective. India is the 3rd largest polluter as of 2022, with 2.9 gigatons of pollution [1]. This paper addresses the 13th UNESCO Sustainable Development Goal i.e. Climate Action. Due to the rise in CFC (Chlorofluorocarbons) and GHG (Global house gasses) emissions, there has been a need to introduce a product with minimal emissions. Air conditioners account for high electricity bills and aren't pocket friendly. Air conditioners are still a luxury for many.

Large industrial spaces are cooled by natural cooling technologies such as Direct and Indirect evaporative cooling. However, there hasn't been any natural cooling machine introduced for residential purposes. In Indirect Evaporative cooling, the primary air gets cooled without contact with water. Hence in the first stage, the air is cooled without any moisture and then cooled further in the second stage with the direct evaporative cooling process with an extra reduction of 5 °C. Some USPs of this technology are 60–80% lower energy consumption than conventional air conditioners. 100% fresh, clean, and cool air, Eco-friendly: no CFCs involved, thus helping reduce GHGs; zero ODP (Ozone Depletion Potential) and indirect, direct evaporative cooling technology deliver 5 °C more cooling and help in achieving 60% less moisture than direct evaporative cooling. Therefore, due to the global warming threat, there has been an increase in demand for sustainable products or solutions. The introduced product is cost-effective and with minimal emissions. Thus, making it affordable for most economic households in India. All the above content has been discussed in the paper. This study helped determine how an effective system can reduce emissions and impact global warming. The design thinking approach provides a solution that would be helpful to the users.

2 Research and Design Methodology

The user-centered Design approach has been followed in several stages to develop the solution. The research stages include secondary research, such as literature review and global emission statistics, and primary research methods, like identifying user groups, user survey analysis, telephonic interviews, and formulating contextual inquiry models. A detailed literature review was conducted on different keywords related to the topic, such as climate action, problems, AC contributions, cooling methods before air conditioners, alternate options for ACs, progress in the field, indirect and direct evaporative cooling through several online search tools, including Jstor, Google Scholar, SCOPUS, WoS and a few open-sourced articles. The survey, contextual inquiry, insight generation, and empathy mapping were applied to understand the problem and map users' needs. Later, an application and a product have been proposed in this paper. The proposed application helps deliver a seamless experience to the users with the ability to interact with gestures, voice recognition, and application. The product features a natural cooling method like the direct–indirect evaporative cooling method.

2.1 *Literature Review*

A theoretical framework was formed using the design thinking approach. Through brainstorming, a detailed literature review was conducted on the selected domain to get information on various things such as the current scenarios, progress in the field, and old and new methods used to cool houses. Diminutive research and development have focused on minimal emissions after its innovation. The findings of the literature review are discussed below:

Sustainability Development Goals: The United Nations adopted the SDGs in 2015. To make the world a better and more peaceful place to live in. The goals aim to positively impact several humanitarian notes and promote a clean, green, and equal world. The development of these 17 sustainable development goals should achieve a balance in social, economic, and environmental sustenance; the goals are primarily created to end discrimination, poverty, hunger, and AIDS [2]. Goal 13: Climate Action Overview: The official website for the United Nations Sustainability Goals explains the premise of Goal Number 13. The need for the goal, the targets set, and the achievements have been explained in detail. The plans are set to be achieved by the year 2030. "Take urgent action to affect climate change and its impact" is the mission statement for SDG 13 [3]. Importance of Goal 13: As climate change becomes more prominent due to global warming, the author explains that if immediate actions are not taken, it will lead to irreversible consequences, which would cause severe harm to the earth and all living organisms. The increased emission rates of GHGs account for 50% more than in 1990. The economic losses caused by climate-related disasters cost a country millions and billions of USD. The goal was to mobilise USD 100 billion annually by 2020 to address the need of emerging countries to invest in low-carbon development and adapt to climate change [3].

Supporting vulnerable countries would have an impact on various SDGs together at once. Measures such as human security and sustainable natural resource management should be integrated. With urgent action, limiting the increase in global mean temperature to two degrees Celsius can be possible. Factors such as strong political will, increased investment, and use of existing technology could help prioritise development Targets and Indicators: The targets and indicators mark the significant areas to tackle in the climate change crisis [2].

Progress: The United Nations Official Documents System claims there has not been much improvement in the climate action field. The level of pollution and heat has dramatically increased, despite the onset of a pandemic. The scientists also warn that if immediate changes are not made, the temperatures will continue to rise, leading to disturbing consequences for the planet [4].

Significant problems that hinder us from achieving the goal: The author explains that the main reason behind the failure of the goal is the over-dependency on fossil fuels. Actions taken by different world governments are often flawed due to political incapacities or feuds. In developing countries, hesitancy and lack of knowledge also play a huge role. Overpopulation and over-indulgence in lavish comforts are also reasons for the difficulties in achieving the goal [5].

How air conditioners contribute to climate change: Due to rapid industrialisation and growth in the commercial sector, the need for ACs grew. Soon, owning ACs became a status symbol and a necessity in several households. A study projects that the number of ACs and mobile phones is similar. The author explains that the devices consume a lot of energy and produce about 2 billion tons of carbon dioxide yearly, which can deplete resources and cause a massive environmental impact [6].

How households were kept cool before air conditioners: The author has provided an overview of some conventional methods of space cooling that were used before the invention of air conditioners. Although the techniques may not be as effective, some ways are still applied to modern architecture that help keep indoor temperatures comfortable [7].

Alternate methods currently in practice to avoid air conditioners: The article explains how homes can be kept cool without using air conditioners. The ways may not be as effective as ACs, but they help to some extent [8].

Solutions are currently gaining popularity: The Evapoler website explains the process of the cooling methods and how they are more eco-friendly than conventional ACs. The systems use elements such as water and other environmentally friendly refrigerants instead of CFCs or HCFCs [9].

Natural and Evaporative Cooling Systems: Lower environmental temperatures can be achieved through the dissipation of heat from buildings with the help of evaporation, convection, radiation, and conduction is referred to as Natural cooling. Whenever a process does not require renewable energy sources, that's natural cooling. E.g., Motor operated machines use the word hybrid to characterise their operational process. When the partial vapour pressure of water on a wet surface is higher than the adjacent atmosphere, evaporation occurs. By absorption of sensible heat, a change from water from liquid to vapour can be observed [10].

Indian market: With more than 1.3 billion population in India, a rise in the competitive market with numerous opportunities created. India's energy conservation act allows the Indian government to promote energy efficiency. Indian Bureau of energy efficiency (BEE) estimated 60–80 terawatt hours (TWh) for 2014. At the same time, its prediction of a rapid increase in demand could add about 140 GW (1 billion watts)(equivalent to 300 power plants of 500MV each) as peak demand in India by the year 2030 [11]. Indian temperatures range from 32 °C to 45 °C Celsius approximately. A rise in income may lead to demand for comfort and air conditioning. A 15-fold increase in energy consumption only by the use of ACs is predicted. The demand from 2016, 90 terawatt hours (TWh) to 1,350 TWh in 2050 can be noted. Global predictions show that currently, 1.6 billion units of ACs would grow to 5.6 billion units by 2050 [12].

Direct Indirect Evaporative Cooling (DIEC): In DIEC, the hot primary air is processed through an indirect cooling technique, cooled without direct contact with water. The cool air is transferred to direct evaporative cooling, also known as adiabatic or dry bulb cooling. The secondary air is cooled simultaneously with the sprinkled water droplets. This process helps in achieving minimal moisture and humidity in the cooled air. Natural air cooling can achieve 60–80% lower energy consumption than conventional air conditioning systems; 100% fresh, clean air delivers 5 °C more cooling and adds 60% less moisture than DEC [13].

Advantages of two-stage evaporative cooling: 100% fresh air through air conditioners, easy and simple manufacturing, perfectly humidified dry regions, reduction in emissions of air pollutants, and combustion rates of fossil fuels. Design considerations: Testing indirect evaporative cooling (IEC) and direct evaporative cooling (DEC) together. Possibility of independent air conditions, including relative humidity (RH) and temperature for primary and secondary air streams. Air temperature after the IEC unit in direct flow. Air temperature and RH after the IEC and DEC units [14].

2.2 *Competitor Study*

Different competitor types, e.g., air conditioners and coolers, were studied to gain more information regarding currently available technology to understand their characteristics. Natural cooling techniques were considered to analyse their impact. For instance, Direct/ Indirect evaporative cooling technologies were analysed. These evaporative cooling techniques are influenced by renewable resources. The data relating to consistency, cost-effectiveness, sustainability, durability, etc., were formulated into the table. The following Table 1 represents the findings that state evaporative cooling techniques are the most effective in reducing energy consumption and emission, which would help reduce global warming.

2.3 *Primary User Research*

Data gathering methods included a survey with 18 users, including young, older adults, and a few senior citizens, and a telephonic interview with one. A survey was carried out to understand and gain insights into how the usage of cooling systems in

Table 1 Competitor analysis of existing cooling technologies

Features	Air conditioners	Air coolers	Natural systems	Direct evaporative cooling	Indirect evaporative cooling	Direct indirect evaporative cooling
Consistency	✓	✗	✗	✓	✓	✓
Cost-effective	✗	✓	✓	✓	✓	✓
Efficient	✓	✗	✗	✓	✓	✓
Long term	✓	✓	✗	✓	✓	✓
Convenience	✓	✗	✗	✗	✗	✗
Easy operation	✓	✗	✗	✗	✗	✓
Eco-friendly	✓	✗	✓	✓	✓	✓
Sustainable	✗	✗	✓	✓	✓	✓
Uses renewable energy	✗	✓	✓	✓	✓	✓
Used in residences	✗	✓	✓	✗	✗	✗
Total	**6**	**4**	**5**	**7**	**7**	**8**

Indian households impacts climate change. The survey sample contributors are both males and females from different educational backgrounds. The questionnaire aimed to gain insights from the survey on users' preferences and usage. A few importantt questions are; (1) What kind of cooling systems do you have at home? (2) How many AC units do you have at your home? (3) How often do you use ACs and coolers? (4) Do you think temperatures in your residence have risen compared to the last few years? (5) Greenhouse gas emissions (carbon dioxide, carbon monoxide, methane etc.) from air conditioning will account for a 0.5 °C rise in global temperatures by the end of the century. Therefore, would you reduce the regular consumption of ACs to positively impact the environment?

Survey analysis shows that respondents use various products for home cooling besides ACs. Around 83.3% (15 respondents) have ACs, followed by 88.9% (16 respondent) having fans in their houses. About 72.2% (13 respondents) use ACs for three months in a year i.e. summer season, followed by 22.2% (4 respondent) who use them for 4–6 months in a year. Users' opinion on rising temperatures since past years; 88.9% (16 respondents) think temperatures have risen drastically compared to the last few years. and due to which there is increase in usage of ACs. To know the consumers buying preferences and priorities while shopping for a home cooling system, respondents were queried to rate from 1 being least preferred to 4 being most preferred. Twelve respondents answered that they would go for cost-effective cooling systems, 15 respondents rated highly for comfort, 10 would rate high and appreciate eco-friendly cooling systems, and 13 preferred ease of use. From the survey, it is understood that most respondents are aware of the rising global temperatures leading to global warming. 77.8% (14 respondents) would like to reduce emissions by less AC consumption as ACs too impact the environment.

2.4 Contextual Enquiry

A contextual inquiry was conducted to understand the real-life problems of persons using ACs. The objective was to observe users in their natural environment and record the observations. Contextual inquiry models such as the flow, sequence, cultural, and artifact models are developed.

The contextual inquiry has four principles: Context, Partnership, Interpretation, and focus. The partnership is focused on a free discussion between the user and the researcher to generate insights. Interpretation values the feedback the user gives and is marked as a priority to address in the further process. Lastly, the user should know the project's purpose and what information would be relevant. The research was carried out with the user in complete comfort and equal control of the discussion.

The flow Model—Fig. 1 represents the interaction and communication between users in their context while purchasing ACs. It helped in knowing the user's expectations and requirements and what excites them. The 'lightning' symbol represents barriers which also act as key opportunities.

The Sequential Model in Fig. 2 shows the sequence of the steps followed and the associated frustration points. The model states a user journey in the existing scenario initiated by a trigger followed by an intent to that trigger action. The journey helps in understanding users' pain points and frustrations.

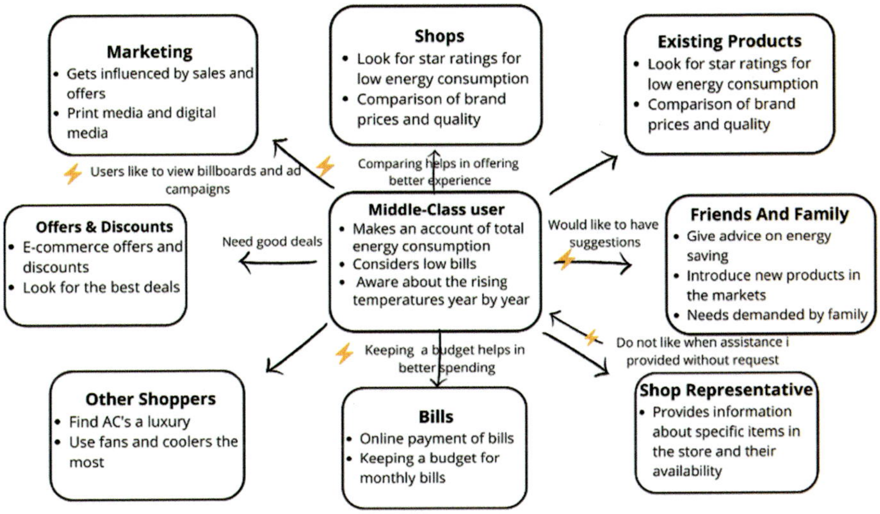

Fig. 1 The flow model for purchasing air conditioner for home

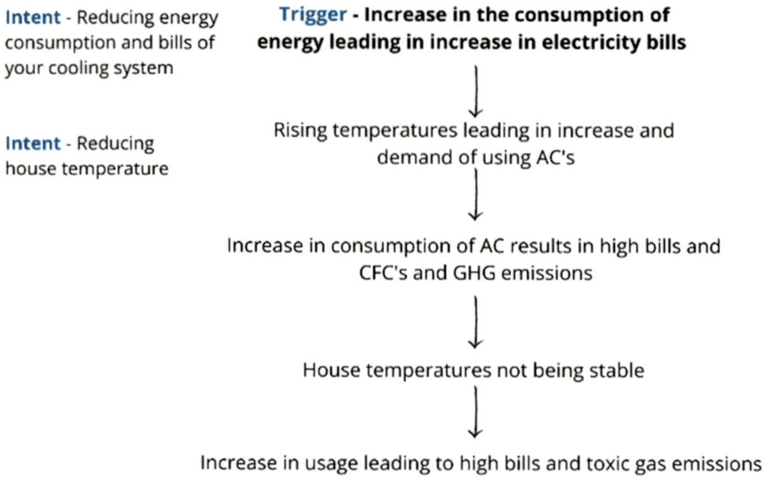

Fig. 2 Sequence model showing user's frustrations

Figure 3 represents the Cultural Model—The culture of the context, meaning the tone, language, and trigger within the context is formulated in a cultural model. This model helps understand the interrelationship between different stakeholders.

The Artifact Model—Fig. 4 represents the working environment in the planning and development stage of the product. It represents the product concepts functionality with Indirect evaporative cooling (IEC) and Direct evaporative cooling (DEC). They are combined to form Direct, indirect evaporative cooling (IDEC). The model helps in understanding the product-concept functionality better.

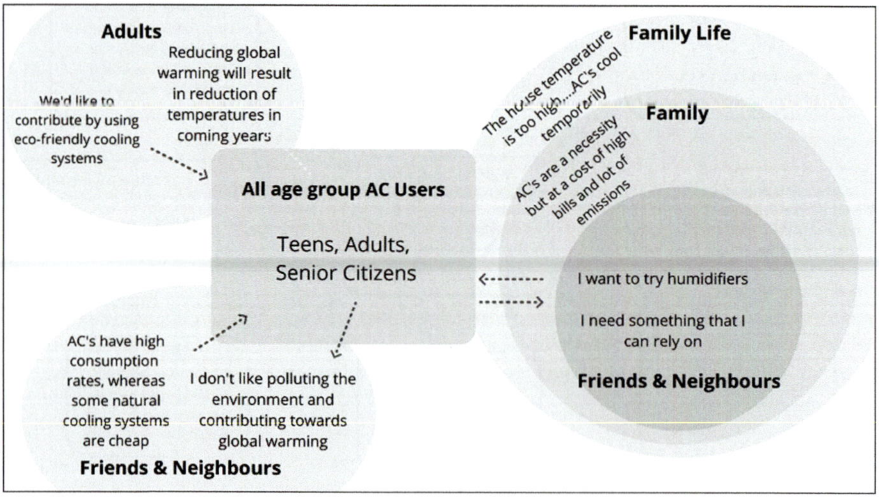

Fig. 3 Cultural model with trigger

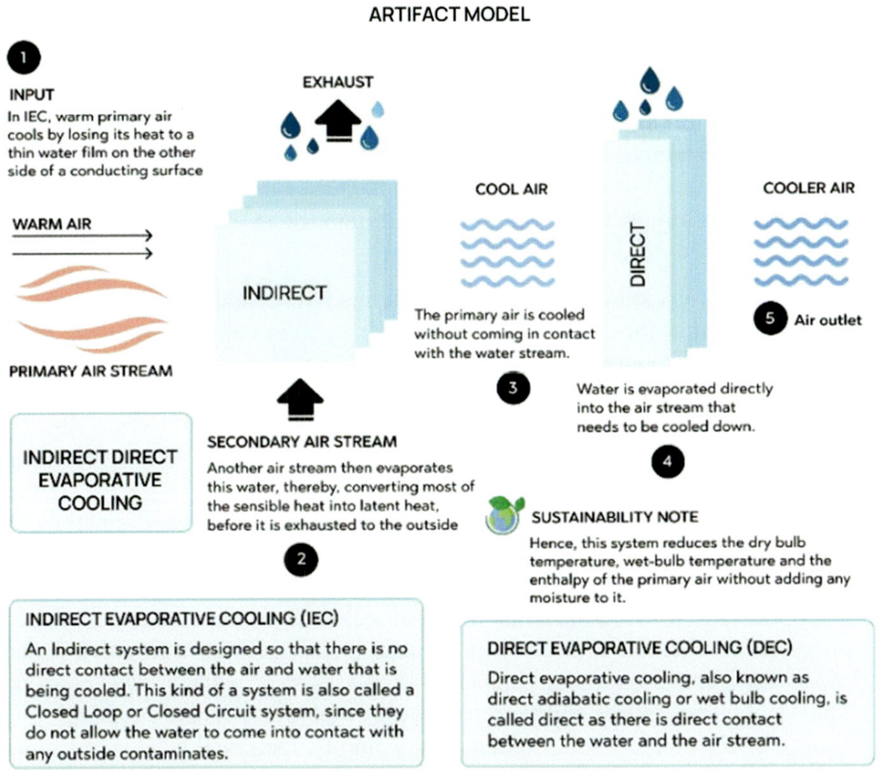

Fig. 4 Artifact model with artifacts with explanation

The above study sheds light on people's thought processes and difficulties, from buying ACs to utilising them. Contextual inquiry helped in understanding users interaction with the product in their natural environment. The methodology is curated by the user's ability to recall and explain the process, where a scope for addressing pain points and introducing new features for enhanced customer satisfaction is created. An application that focuses on offering a seamless experience to its users by creating a perfect ecosystem. This research method helped propose an entirely eco-friendly product prototype introduced with minimal emissions, saving energy and consumption costs. The application and the product help solve most of the problems faced by the users. This system is explained in detail in further sections of this paper.

3 Conceptualization and Ideation of the Entire System

The application introduces an ecosystem of devices available to operate the air conditioner. Users can use the cooling system with a remote, mobile app, google home/ Alexa, voice recognition, or even gestures. This supports providing the user with a sense of total control over the system with which they interact. Issues like dying of batteries at the utmost need won't make a difference as we have introduced an intelligent system with various features such as;

1. The app lets users know about the current temperatures and humidity.
2. Users can control the cooling system in every room in the house, helping them save more energy and money.
3. Families can connect to their homes, access all the rooms with cooling systems, and view detailed usage statistics daily, weekly, and monthly.
4. Users can view their consumption based on 'Switch-on Device' information from their phones.
5. The design proposal introduces an interactive remote, which exerts small touch haptics when the temperature increases or decreases.
6. Users can access sleep mode, fan speed, AI mode, and Eco mode.
7. The home page provides information about real-time temperature and humidity, offers the ability to connect with Bluetooth devices for innovative home capabilities, and also provides impactful success stories by the product concept.
8. The AR mode offers the ability to see real-time temperature and humidity.
9. Users can view the UV index, pollutants, visibility, feels, and wind speed.

The following Fig. 5 show a block model and a Figs. 6, 7 and 8 high-fidelity mock-up of the final visual designs of the cooling system application, which address the problems the users face and try to reduce the cognitive load while interacting with the system.

Figure 5 represents the Sequential model, which explains the application and its usage stage wise. Based on the sequence of usage, further the customer journey, task flows, hierarchical task analysis and information architecture developed. Concept sketches for each task designed. A formative testing of the mobile application helped

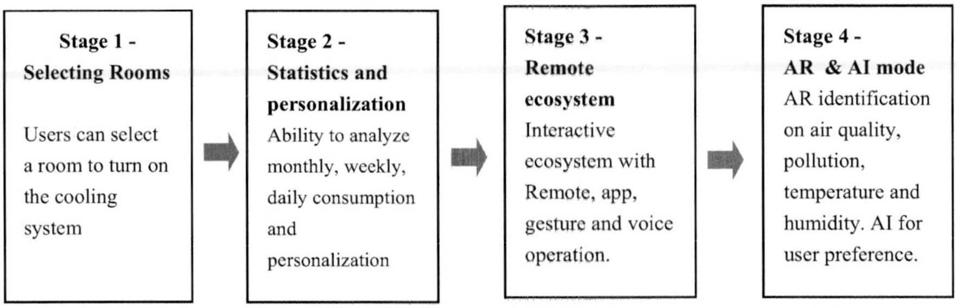

Fig. 5 Sequential Block Model showing the Usage of Application

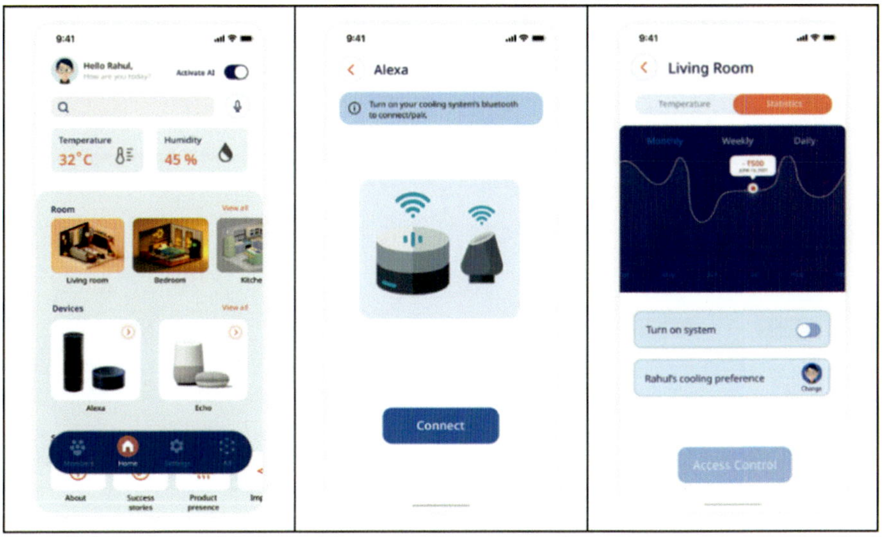

Fig. 6 Home page—visual designs: prototype of home cooling system (Part 1)

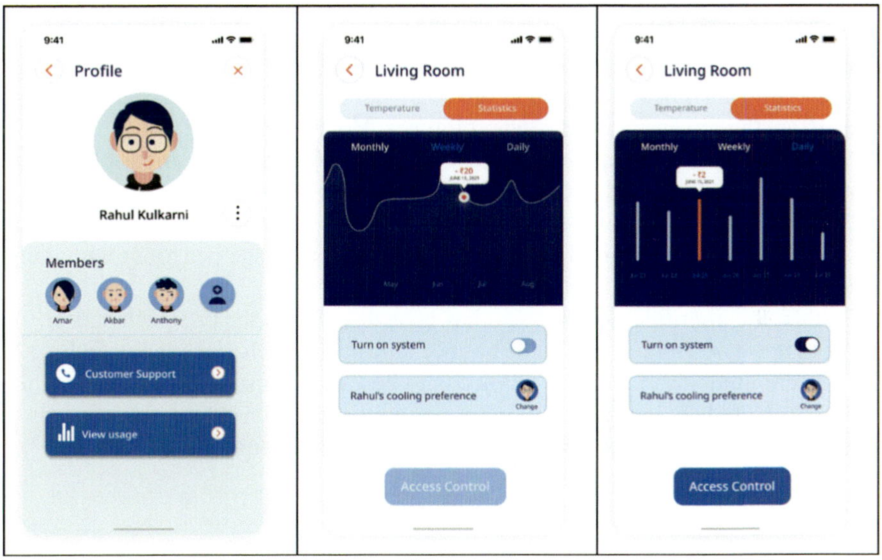

Fig. 7 User profile page—visual designs: prototype of home cooling system (Part 2)

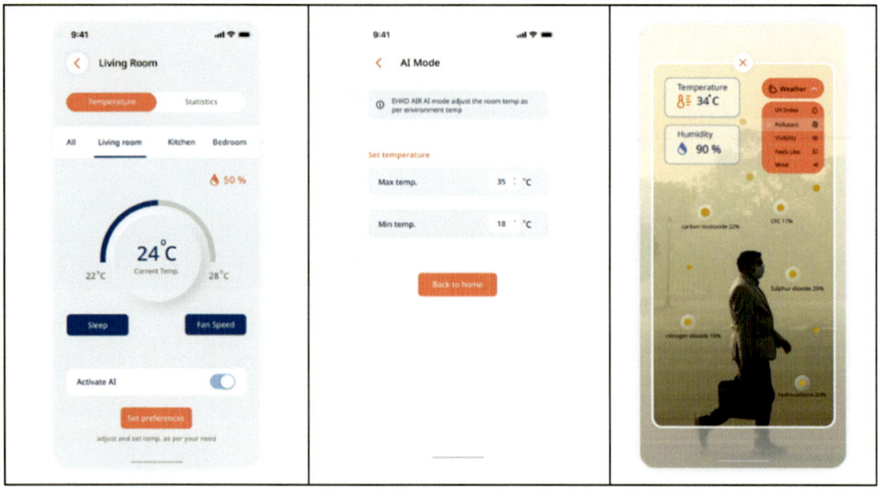

Fig. 8 Dashboard—visual designs: prototype of home cooling system (Part 21)

analyse user journeys, expectations, and pain points. Insights, overall satisfaction, ease of use, aesthetics, and user reactions were assessed for further application development i.e. High fidelity prototypes (visual designs of screens).

The following Figs. 6, 7, and 8 are high fidelity prototypes (visual designs). Figure 6 are the screens represent the prototypes 'Home page' from where users have the ability to view real time temperature, humidity. According to room preference users can select rooms and customize cooling in each and every room.

Figure 7 are the user profile screes, from where they can add members details who can have a control over the system and cooling system usage per room with daily, weekly and monthly consumption graphs.

Further, the high-fidelity prototype has been tested with the prospective user.

A gesture-based interaction guide has been introduced below (as shown in Fig. 9). The gesture guide has potential and needs to be easy for users to interact with the system. The guide is introduced to get a sense of interaction. Moreover, it needs to be tested with the users upon product prototype development.

4 Usability Testing

A system usability scale (SUS) test was employed to conduct the usability test for the proposed concept with users. The purpose of the usability test is to understand user's choices, ease of use while interacting with the system, feelings, thoughts, errors/frustrations and expectations under a free non-biased environment. Users were given about 5–7 min to explore the concept. For usability testing, fixed questions were asked to calculate the system usability scale of the application. The summative

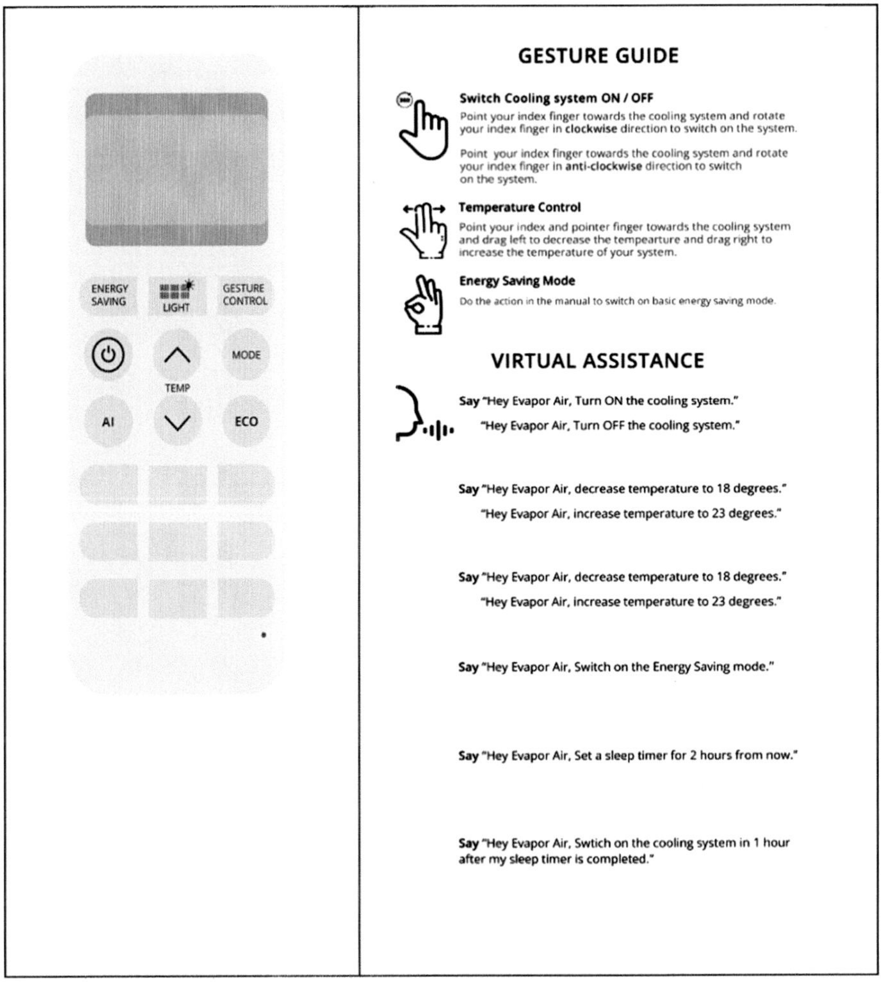

Fig. 9 Remote control and gesture control showing virtual assistance enabled seamless interaction

testing included 5 participants. Insights were generated based on how users felt while interacting with the application. General doubts regarding testing were cleared before the exercise began. It was seen that no information about the actual test i.e., test details which could initiate any kind of biases, was shared.

The system usability scale includes ten questions where participants have to give their opinion on how strongly they agree or disagree with the question based on a Likert scale ranging from 1 to 5. Target group—Youngsters, adults, and senior citizens were considered. It was ensuring that users were comfortable while going on with the test. The following figures show the result of SUS testing. 4 out 5 users felt confident while interacting with the application and rated it high for aesthetics and navigation (Fig. 10).

Participants	Characteristics- Age & Profession	SUS score
P1	21 Yr, BBA student	80
P2	36 Yr, Engineer	85
P3	51 Yr, Medical Professional	67.5
P4	28 Yrs, Business Analyst	77.5
P5	45 Yrs, Designer	85
Total	395/500	
Average	79/100 (68 – 80.3) Top edge of Grade B	

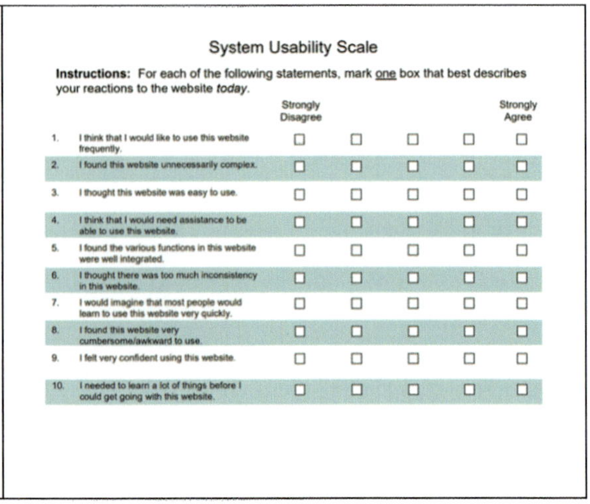
System Usability Scale

Instructions: For each of the following statements, mark <u>one</u> box that best describes your reactions to the website *today*.

		Strongly Disagree				Strongly Agree
1.	I think that I would like to use this website frequently.	☐	☐	☐	☐	☐
2.	I found this website unnecessarily complex.	☐	☐	☐	☐	☐
3.	I thought this website was easy to use.	☐	☐	☐	☐	☐
4.	I think that I would need assistance to be able to use this website.	☐	☐	☐	☐	☐
5.	I found the various functions in this website were well integrated.	☐	☐	☐	☐	☐
6.	I thought there was too much inconsistency in this website.	☐	☐	☐	☐	☐
7.	I would imagine that most people would learn to use this website very quickly.	☐	☐	☐	☐	☐
8.	I found this website very cumbersome/awkward to use.	☐	☐	☐	☐	☐
9.	I felt very confident using this website.	☐	☐	☐	☐	☐
10.	I needed to learn a lot of things before I could get going with this website.	☐	☐	☐	☐	☐

Fig. 10 System Usability Scale questionnaire and SUS Conclusion

SUS Calculation:

- $80 + 85 + 67.5 + 77.5 + 85 = 395/5$ i.e., 79.
- 79 average – (68 – 80.3) Grade B – Good.

5 Business Model Canvas and DVF Matrix

Figure 11 represents the business model canvas and sheds light on the unique value proposition, cost structure, revenue potential, unique selling proposition, and channels for marketing. The proposed concept helps achieve 60 to 80% energy conservation through indirect, direct cooling technology. The cooling system will showcase 5 °C more cooling and 60% less moisture in the desired room. This helps in understanding the viability and feasibility of the proposed solution. Cost structure helps better resource allocation, and revenue streams build a way to monetise the business to maximise profits. Customer segments help know the target audience better to design the product with specific user requirements. Early adopters provide a scope to flourish the business shortly.

Figure 12 shows the desirability, viability, and feasibility matrix help understand how the solution is desirable, viable, feasible, and ethical. It refers to the scope for scalability, accessibility, sustainable solution, and ease of use. The DVF matrix helps determine if the concept is desirable by customers and if you're solving the right problem , feasibility accounts for the operational measures and capabilities.

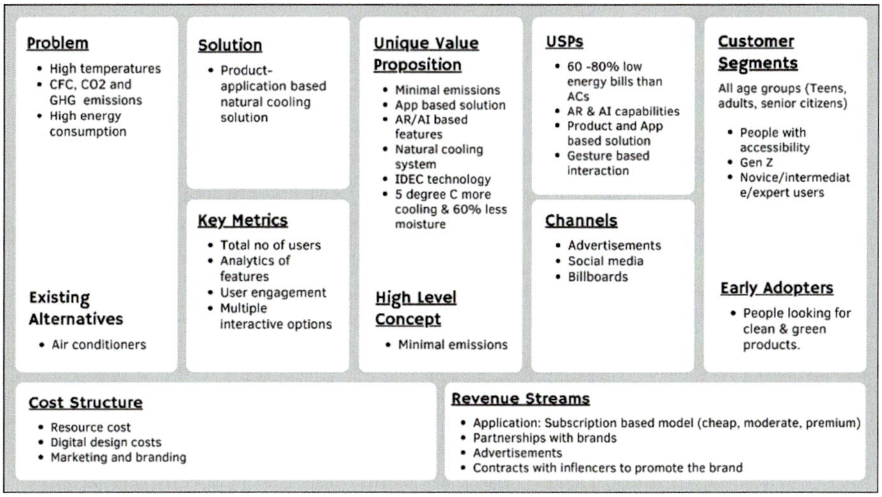

Fig. 11 Business model Canvas

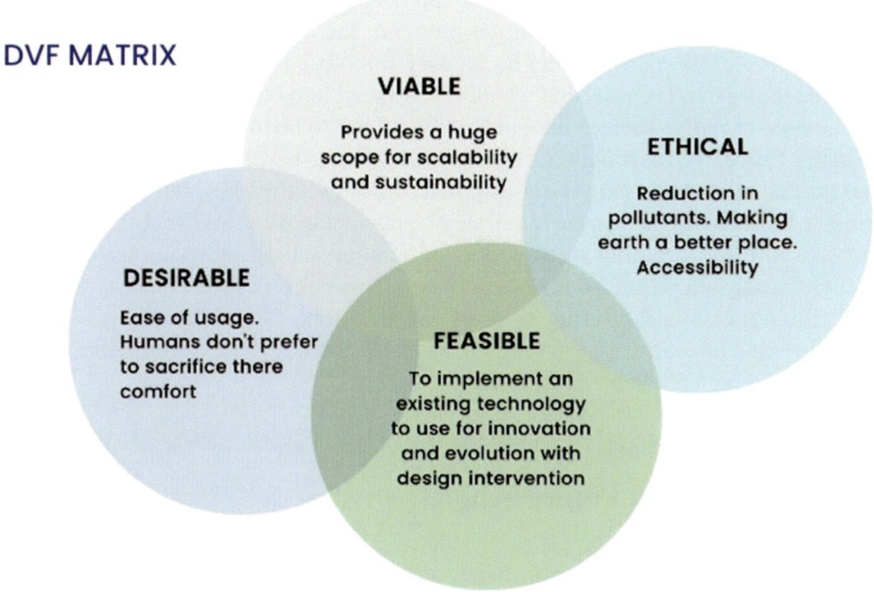

Fig. 12 Desirable-viable-feasible (DVF) matrix

In contrast, viability accounts for a profitable future and sustainability, ensuring a positive social and environmental impact. Ethicality accounts for sustainable growth and accessibility. It aims to reduce pollutants and make a better place to live for humankind.

6 Discussion

The literature review helped to understand the problems, methods of natural cooling solutions, and current progress in the field. There are a few applications in the industry sector where natural cooling is used for large spaces. However, no application is seen in the residential sector. People often face many difficulties while using remotes such as draining/wearing out of battery, buttons not working, tough findability of remote keys in the dark. Considering Indian market and usage, such problems are very common as usage isn't throughout the year. Modern solutions can address these problems—very few cooling devices in the market focus on reducing emissions and energy consumption.

A user survey came with the result that there is a need for a natural cooling system to be introduced, which will impact emission levels and help in reducing global warming. This cooling system will help facilitate users' problems and eventually help save the environment. Hence, this adds to having great scope for the project.

Contextual inquiry helped in understanding users in their natural context. It helped in making the work models. The models were used to comprehend the relationship between various stakeholders. It also analysed user triggers and frustration points.

The usability test conducted to check app's readiness and whether the user's feel the ease of use. The score of usability testing, i.e., the System Usability Scale (SUS) average score of 79, falls into the B category (68–80.3). This indicated that people accepted the design proposal and would recommend it to others. Most of them found it to be user-friendly. The gesture guide in Fig. 9 has to be integrated and tested with the users. Currently, the proposed concept lacks gesture-based testing. The SUS score also suggests that the system is efficient in terms of usability, navigation, and ease of use. The business model canvas is a strategic management canvas for outlining goals, cost structures, key metrics to be addressed, unique selling propositions, customer segments, early adopters, and revenue streams. This helps in understanding the business requirements and catering to users' expectations. The desirability, viability, feasibility, and ethicality matrix state the business characteristic to consider and also creates a "Sweet Spot" for innovation.

7 Conclusion and Future Scope

Recently there has been a massive increase in global warming due to emissions by various devices. Emissions of CFCs and GHGs harm the environment as the need to use ACs has risen because of rising temperatures in recent years. Innovations in cooling systems haven't led to a revolution where a cooling system could replace the current AC system. Global warming is a problem that humans need to reduce as much as possible to save the environment. People have become more aware and interested in using eco-friendly devices with minimal emissions. Therefore, this paper presents a product-application-based concept for the cooling system industry that emphasises intelligent systems and applications for a personalised experience and helps offer the best experience like never before. The virtual assistance and the gestures unlock the ability to interact with such systems in a simpler, easier, and more efficient manner. The solution is tested with users from different age groups. The results show that people are more curious and appreciated the concept. The problem statement was formulated after detailed secondary and primary research. The contextual inquiry provided more data on real-life problems. It can be concluded that this system will make users comfortable and proud by helping to reduce pollution drastically and work just as efficiently as an Air Conditioner with low electricity bills, emissions, and cost-effectiveness. It will be beneficial for futurist lifestyle changes. The product resembles a great scope in achieving a sustainable future and reducing global warming and energy demands in the future. Although the introduced product is still a concept, further testing, research and development are needed.

References

1. Rajat Gupta DMSSNU, This will be a decisive decade. With intentional action, India can accelerate decarbonisation at scale while pursuing economic growth. McKinsey Sustain
2. UNDP (2022) What are the sustainable development goals? https://www.undp.org/sustainable-development-goals. Accessed 21 Apr 2022
3. “Goal 13: Climate Action,”. https://www.undp.org/sustainable-development-goals/climate-action. [ccessed 21 Apr 2022
4. United Nations (2021) Progress towards the Sustainable Development Goals, UN Economic and Social Council
5. “Axios,” 19 August 2019. https://www.axios.com/why-climate-change-is-so-hard-to-tackle-the-global-problem-5035a6ec-2d92-4cf9-9926-f763d4481bb4.html. Accessed 21 Apr 2022
6. Buranyi S, “Buranyi,” 29 August 2019. https://www.theguardian.com/environment/2019/aug/29/the-air-conditioning-trap-how-cold-air-is-heating-the-world. Accessed 21 Apr 2022
7. McFadden C, Uysal C, Gosavi A, Papadopoulos L, Paleja A (2021) https://interestingengineering.com/how-people-kept-cool-before-air-conditioners. Accessed 21 Apr 2022
8. Erickson A (2021) “Erickson,”. https://www.readersdigest.ca/home-garden/home-improvement/how-to-cool-your-house-without-ac/. Accessed 21 Apr 2022
9. “Evapoler,”. https://www.evapoler.com/product/indirect-evaporative-cooling-decool-4/. Accessed 21 Apr 2022
10. Santamouris M (1990) Natural cooling techniques, vol AVIC 10879, pp 143, 144
11. Abhyankar N, Shah N, Park WY, Phadke AA (2017) Accelerating energy efficiency improvements in room air conditioners in India: potential, costs-Benefits, and policies, pp 7–9, April 2017
12. Osunmuyiwa OO, Payne SR, Vigneswara Ilavarasan P, Peacock AD, Jenkins DP (2020) I cannot live without air conditioning! The role of identity, values and situational factors on cooling consumption patterns in India. Energy Res Soc Sci:1–3
13. Navon HAR (1994) Feasibility of direct-indirect evaporative cooling for residences, based on studies with a desert cooler. Build Environ 29(3)
14. Ghassem Heidarinejad MBDE (2009) Experimental investigation of two-stage indirect/direct evaporative cooling system in various climatic conditions. Build Environ

Communication Design and Brand Advertising

Exploring Racial Diversity in Fashion Brand Advertising: An Instagram-Based Study of Three Prominent Brands

Lara Martins, Nuno Martins, Leonardo Pereira, and Daniel Raposo

Abstract Cultural and racial diversity in fashion brand communication has been a growing discussion topic, often associated with either spontaneous or organized by citizens movements advocating for issues of discrimination, exclusion, and even human rights. This article's goal was to investigate the ethnic representation in the communication and promotion content published by three reference clothing brands on the Instagram social media platform: H&M, Lefties, and Zara. The study focused on the analysis of the Instagram pages of these three brands, between January 2020 and January 2022. In this article, we begin with a literature review on the topics of diversity and representation. We then present the methodologies and results of the carried out analysis on H&M's, Lefties' and Zara's Instagram posts. Finally, we discuss the results and their respective conclusions.

Keywords Design and branding · Ethnic diversity · Public interaction · Instagram social media · Clothing brands

L. Martins
School of Design, Polytechnic Institute of Cavado and Ave, Barcelos, Portugal

N. Martins (✉)
Research Institute for Design, Media and Culture, School of Design, Polytechnic Institute of Cávado and Ave, Barcelos, Portugal
e-mail: nmartins@ipca.pt

L. Pereira
DigiMedia, Department of Communication and Art, University of Aveiro, Campus Universitário de Santiago, 3810-193 Aveiro, Portugal

D. Raposo
Research Centre for Architecture, Urbanism and Design, Polytechnic Institute of Castelo Branco, Castelo Branco, Portugal

N. Martins and D. Raposo (eds.), *Communication Design and Branding*, Springer Series in Design and Innovation 32,
https://doi.org/10.1007/978-3-031-35385-7_7

1 Introduction

Culture is an essential component of human identity and plays a significant role in shaping individuals' beliefs, values, and perceptions [6]. In today's globalized world, where people from different cultures come together, advertisers are keen to tap into cultural influences to create campaigns that resonate with specific target audiences. One approach that has gained significant popularity in recent years is the use of models from different cultural backgrounds in advertising campaigns. By showcasing diverse models, companies can appeal to a wider audience and demonstrate their commitment to inclusivity and diversity.

The *Colors of Benetton* campaign is a well-known example of how using models from different cultures can be highly effective in promoting diversity and inclusion. The campaign was highly successful in its efforts to break down cultural barriers and promote unity, with its iconic ads featuring models from various cultural backgrounds, races, and ethnicities. This campaign demonstrated the power of using diverse models to create a connection with audiences and increase brand loyalty.

Therefore, in this article we will explore the use of models from different cultures in advertising, with a specific focus on three well-known fashion brands: H&M, Zara, and Lefties. Each of these brands has used diverse models in their campaigns to appeal to a wider audience and showcase their commitment to diversity and inclusivity. By analyzing the strategies and tactics used by these brands, we hope to gain insight into the effectiveness of using models from different cultures in advertising and its impact on brand image and audience perception.

1.1 The Power of the Consumer

Consumer influence is a widely recognized phenomenon that has gained considerable attention in recent years. Consumers have been found to exert influence on businesses, not only through their purchases but also through their expression of opinions and concerns. This influence has been greatly amplified by the emergence of social media and other digital platforms, which have facilitated the sharing of experiences and opinions, potentially affecting a business's reputation and profitability. As a result, businesses have started to pay closer attention to consumer preferences and needs, taking steps to address concerns and adapt to consumer demands. By virtue of their purchasing power and their ability to shape the market through their actions, consumers hold a significant degree of influence over businesses and industries, making their voices essential in shaping the market's future.

The lack of diversity in advertisements has become a growing concern for the public in recent years, particularly in the wake of events such as the BLM[1] protests in 2020, which highlighted the importance of reaching diverse ethnic groups on a

[1] **Black Lives Matter (BLM)** is a decentralized political and social movement that seeks to highlight the racism, discrimination, and racial inequality experienced by Black people.

large scale. However, addressing this issue is challenging due to the persistence of color-blind racism[2] (Morris & Kahlor, 2014), which slows down progress by denying that racism is still a problem. For instance, a survey conducted by ICS/ISCTE,[3] in Portugal in 2020, showed that 52% of the Portuguese population believes that there is less ethnic-racial discrimination in Portugal than in the rest of Europe. This perception contrasts with the fact that the Commission for Equality and Against Racial Discrimination received more than 408 complaints in 2021.

2 Whiteness Theory

The Whiteness Theory suggests that race and ethnicity are significant factors in shaping our perceptions and experiences, including how we view and respond to advertising. While the term "color-blind racism" refers to a denial of racial discrimination and an attempt to ignore race altogether, the Whiteness Theory postulates that this approach perpetuates racial inequality by failing to recognize the impact of race and ethnicity on individuals and society as a whole.

Despite its relevance to advertising and consumer perception, the Whiteness Theory is not commonly applied in these contexts. This may be due to a lack of awareness or understanding of the theory among advertisers and marketers, or a reluctance to acknowledge the role of race and ethnicity in advertising campaigns.

However, according to [5], there are many missed opportunities for advertisers who fail to consider the implications of the Whiteness Theory in their campaigns. By understanding the impact of ethnic identity on consumer behavior, advertisers can create more effective and inclusive campaigns that resonate with diverse audiences.

For instance, individuals with high ethnic identities are more likely to respond positively to advertisements featuring models of the same ethnicity, as they feel a stronger sense of cultural connection and representation [16]. On the other hand, those with low ethnic identities may have a more positive response to advertisements featuring white models, as they may perceive them as more universal or mainstream (Morris & Kahlor, 2014). By taking these factors into account, advertisers can tailor their campaigns to better reflect the diverse identities and experiences of their target audience.

---

[2] **Color-blind racism** is the belief that racial inequality is no longer an issue that warrants attention because there are now equal opportunities for people of all races.

[3] **ICS/ISCTE surveys** are a collaboration between the Institute of Social Sciences of the University of Lisbon (ICS-ULisboa), the Lisbon University Institute (ISCTE-IUL), and Impresa Publishing Group S.A., namely through SIC and Expresso. This collaboration aims to collect, process, and disseminate data on the attitudes and political behaviors of the Portuguese population by conducting opinion polls (surveys) on representative samples of the population.

2.1 Color of Benetton and Dove "Real Beauty" Campaign

Advertising campaigns play a significant role in shaping societal attitudes toward diversity and inclusivity. Benetton's "United Colors of Benetton" campaign stands out for its bold use of colors to showcase a diverse range of individuals. The use of bright and contrasting colors creates a visual impact that unifies individuals from different races, ethnicities, and cultures, conveying the message that diversity is beautiful and should be celebrated. Similarly, Dove's "Real Beauty" campaign challenges traditional beauty standards by featuring women of different ages, races, and body types in their natural states. This approach promotes body positivity and encourages women to accept themselves as they are, without relying on heavy makeup or retouching.

The impact of both campaigns has been significant in initiating discussions and debates about the need to embrace differences and celebrate individuality. The campaigns have contributed to the efforts toward creating a more inclusive and accepting world. This effort is seen in the reaction to the negative response towards Colors of Benetton made by other retailers, which spurred the audience to create pro-Benetton groups in Germany to fight the backlash and discredit that Benetton received [12]. However, further research is needed to determine the long-term effectiveness of such campaigns in promoting diversity and inclusivity. Future studies can investigate the impact of advertising campaigns on societal attitudes towards diversity and inclusivity, as well as the potential for such campaigns to influence behavior and promote positive social change. Overall, advertising campaigns have the potential to play a significant role in promoting diversity and inclusivity, and their unique approaches can contribute to creating a more accepting and inclusive society.

2.2 Diversity in Social Media

The clothing industry is recognized as one of the most fiercely competitive markets, where clothing brands need to remain adaptive and flexible to the ever-changing trends to remain successful. The increasing accessibility of the internet and the widespread usage of social media have intensified the need for brands to be more responsive to their target audience's needs and preferences.

Diversity and inclusivity are becoming increasingly important values to consumers, and brands need to ensure that they reflect these values. Consumers expect to see more representation of people of color in the fashion industry, and clothing brands are under pressure to feature models from different ethnicities and skin colors in their advertising campaigns and on their runways.

Moreover, the purchasing power of minority groups is rising, particularly in the case of Asian Americans. According to a study by Humphreys [7], the purchasing power of Asian Americans increased by 180% between 2000 and 2014. This demographic represents a growing segment of the market, and brands need to be aware of their preferences and purchasing habits.

However, [4] study found that Asian Americans may not necessarily prefer models of their ethnicity. Social status may play a more significant role in their decision-making process than ethnic identity. Nevertheless, clothing brands should aim to be inclusive and representative of all ethnicities and cultures to appeal to the diverse range of consumers in the market.

3 Case of Study and Methodology

The present study aimed to investigate the stance of international brands on the issue of diversity and inclusivity. To this end, the Instagram accounts of three major brands, namely H&M, Lefties and Zara, were examined as exemplified in Figs. 1, 2 and 3. Specifically, data on the likes, comments, and ethnicity of the models were collected for January, May, June, and December of 2020, as well as January 2022. Given the BLM protests in June 2020, which highlighted the need for ethnic-racial diversity among professionals, we examined whether these brands had already supported non-Caucasian models in January and May 2020, before this public appeal.

The data collected in June 2020 reflected the brands' response to this request, as well as the consumer behavior in response to this fact. Additionally, the data from December 2020 and January 2022 revealed whether the brands continued to present cultural diversity in their posts and whether the public's interaction with the advertising was a result of genuine interest or a perception of social status, provoked by CSR[4] advertising. Notably, previous research suggests that consumers may support CSR propaganda initiatives not because they support the cause, but for selfish reasons such as maintaining a certain social image that is more favorable to them [13].

To analyze the models featured in the posts, we divided them into four categories, with an additional category to indicate posts that solely contained products. The categories were "Black" for models of African or similar descent with black or mulatto skin tones; "White" for Caucasian models; "Asian" for models of Asian origin; and "Mix" for posts that contained multiple models of multiple cultures. Overall, this study sheds light on the approach of major international brands towards diversity and inclusivity and underscores the importance of genuine commitment to promoting diversity in advertising campaigns.

[4] **Corporate Social Responsibility (CSR)** it is the idea that a company should play a positive role in the community and consider the environmental and social impact of business decisions.

Fig. 1 Screenshot of H&M's Instagram feed for January 2020

3.1 *H&M—Results*

Data collected from H&M's posts, shown in Fig. 4, demonstrates that both in January and May 2020, there was a balanced diversity among models of different ethnicities. However, in June, contrary to what would be expected, there was a significant increase in posts featuring white models and a simultaneous decrease in posts featuring models of African descent. In December of that year, there was a restoration of ethnic balance in the posts, with an even greater number of black models than Caucasian models, which remained the case in January 2022. It is worth noting that posts featuring exclusively "Asian" models were scarce, with these professionals being included in the "Mix" category, along with models from other ethnicities.

Figure 5 depicts the average number of likes per publication in each category, with the "White", "Black", and "Mix" categories maintaining a similar level of engagement in January and May 2020. However, in June 2020, the "Mix" category displays a notable increase in likes, surpassing even the "Product" category, which had been the strongest in 3 out of the 5 months analyzed. This suggests a positive audience response to diversity and inclusivity, possibly driven by the BLM movement.

Fig. 2 Screenshot of Lefties' Instagram feed for January 2020

Conversely, a sharp decline in the number of likes is observed in December 2020 and January 2022, particularly in posts featuring non-Caucasian models. This decrease could be attributed to a reduction in H&M's page views among its target audience or some other change on the platform between December 2020 and January 2022.

The findings from Fig. 6, which represents the quantification of publication comments, suggest that there was a notable and consistent increase in user engagement with posts showcasing non-Caucasian cultures during specific months in 2020, specifically January, May, and June. This increase in interaction may imply a positive response from the audience towards diversity and inclusivity. Additionally, this trend occurred before the BLM's event, which further supports the possibility of a genuine interest in diverse content.

However, the sudden decrease in overall numbers observed in December 2020 and January 2022, as seen in Fig. 3, raises questions about the potential reasons for this shift. It could be due to a change in the audience's preferences, a shift in the way the Instagram application promotes content or a combination of both. Further investigation would be necessary to determine the cause of this trend. Nonetheless,

Fig. 3 Screenshot of Zara's Instagram feed for January 2020

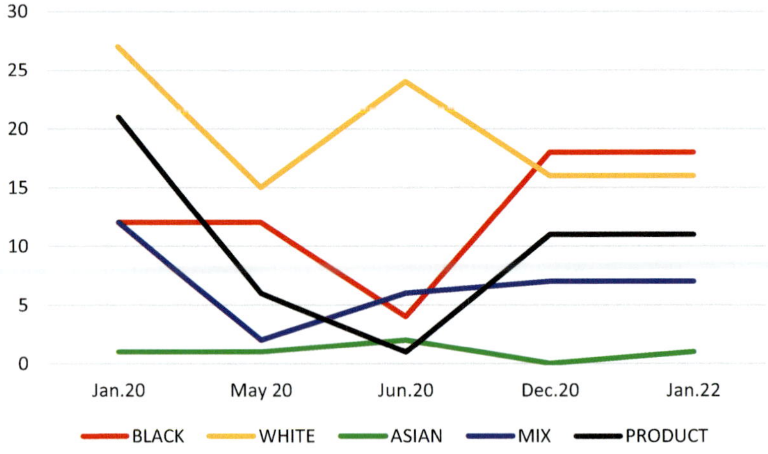

Fig. 4 Number of posts made by H&M on Instagram

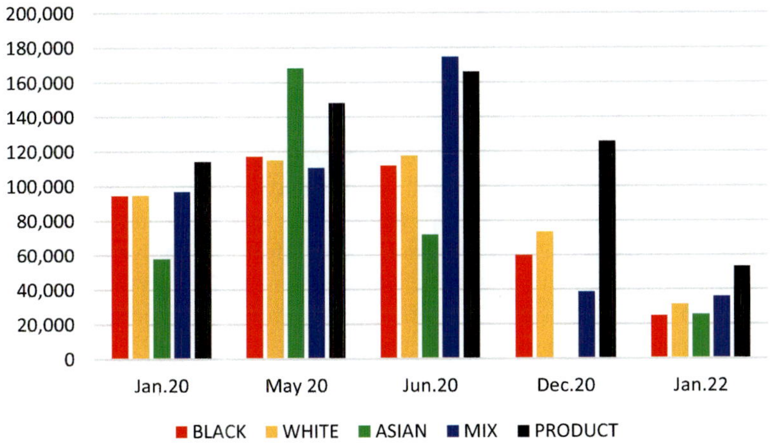

Fig. 5 The average number of likes for each publication category, categorized by the ethnicity of the model, at H&M

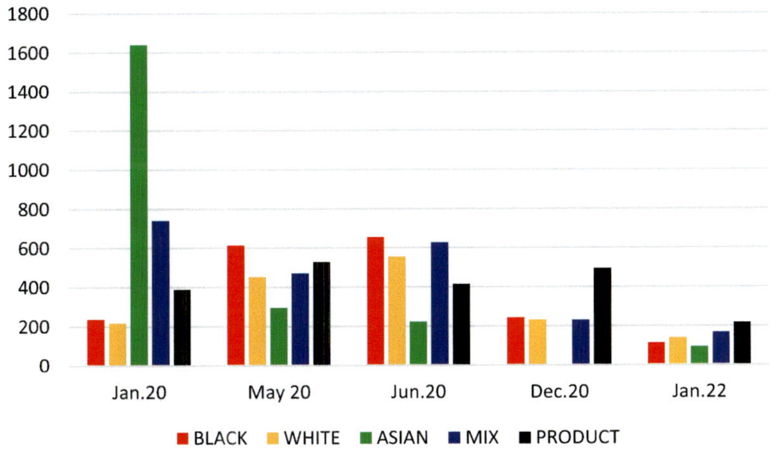

Fig. 6 The average number of comments for each publication category, categorized by the ethnicity of the model, at H&M

these results highlight the importance of ongoing monitoring and analysis of user engagement with diverse content on social media platforms.

Due to the low number of posts in the "Asian" category, it is difficult to conclude from the results presented in Figs. 5 and 6. The low sample size can affect the statistical significance of the data, and as a result, it may be challenging to generalize the findings to the overall population. It is important to keep this limitation in mind when interpreting the results of this analysis.

3.2 Lefties—Results

The findings in Fig. 7, featuring the number of posts by category, suggest that Lefties has struggled with diversity in their representation of ethnic and racial minorities. Specifically, the data shows that in December 2020, only 6 posts featured non-Caucasian models compared to 18 posts with Caucasian models across a combination of 5 categories. While Lefties posted a single image in June 2020 in support of the BLM movement, there was no noticeable effort to improve diversity on its Instagram page. While there was some improvement in January 2022, with more non-Caucasian models appearing in Lefties' posts, they continued to present a lack of cultural diversity in their model selection.

Figure 8 reveals a significant surge in likes from January, May, and June to December 2020 in the "White" category. In December, the average of this category was more than twice that of June, indicating a rise in audience engagement, possibly driven by the increase in diversity in posts. Although the "White" category remained dominant in December 2020, the other categories, except for "Asian", were closely competitive. However, this situation changed drastically in January 2022, which suggests that the interest of many who liked the posts was not genuine but rather resulted from CSR propaganda.

The data presented in Fig. 9, relative to the number of comments, is consistent with the findings in Fig. 7, as both graphs show similar indicators. This reinforces the conclusion that the audience's engagement with the content is related to the diversity of the models represented in the posts.

The lack of data or limited representation of the "Asian" category in the graphs makes it challenging to draw accurate conclusions or make informed assessments about the performance or engagement level of this category in comparison to the other

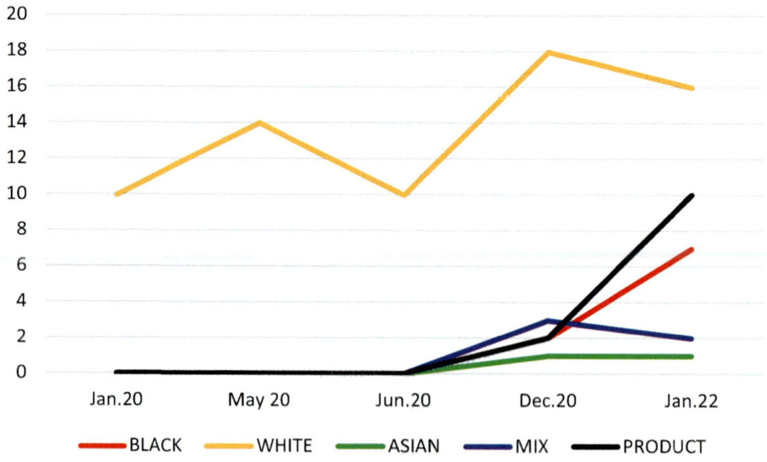

Fig. 7 Number of posts made by Lefties on Instagram

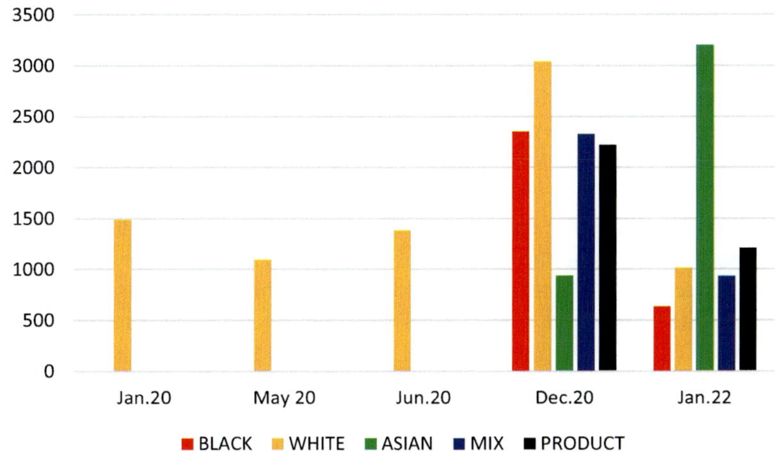

Fig. 8 The average number of likes for each publication category, categorized by the ethnicity of the model, at Lefties

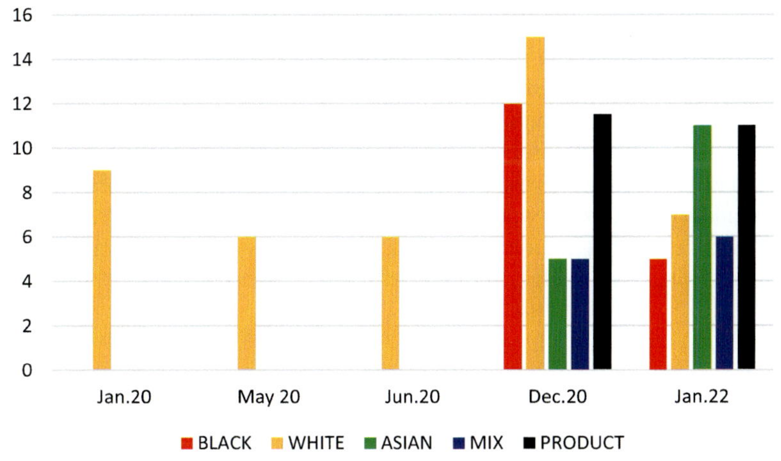

Fig. 9 The average number of comments for each publication category, categorized by the ethnicity of the model, at Lefties

categories. This underscores the importance of including adequate representation of all categories in data analysis to ensure a comprehensive understanding of the trends and patterns observed.

3.3 Zara—Results

Figure 10 illustrates that Zara has the largest number of posts in the "Asian" category, although the overall number remains low. In January, May, and June 2020, the difference between the "White" and "Black" categories remained noticeable. However, diversity increased in December of the same year and January 2022, with greater balance among the different categories. This could be seen as an indicator of Zara's commitment to addressing the need for greater representation of diverse cultures.

Figure 11, representing publication likes, reveals that there was already a strong interest from the audience in seeing posts with diverse ethnicities present in January and May of 2020, even before the BLM protests gained momentum. In June, the "Black" category reached its peak in terms of the number of likes, surpassing posts featuring only Caucasian models. This suggests that there was a growing awareness and appreciation for diversity in fashion. However, in December of that year, there was a significant drop in the number of likes in the "Black" category, which may imply that the audience's choices were influenced by social image rather than a genuine interest in diversity.

By January 2022, the audience's preferences had shifted once again, and there was now a greater interest in the presence of different cultures within the same publication rather than in posts featuring only one category. This indicates a more inclusive and open-minded approach to fashion, in which diversity is celebrated and represented.

Figure 12 shows that in January 2020, the number of comments was considerably lower than in the other months, indicating a lack of audience interaction with the posts. The month with the highest growth in interaction was December 2020. However, once again, in January 2022, there was a sharp decrease in engagement, with all categories, except "Mix", experiencing a decline. This may suggest that there was a change in the Instagram platform or algorithm that affected audience engagement.

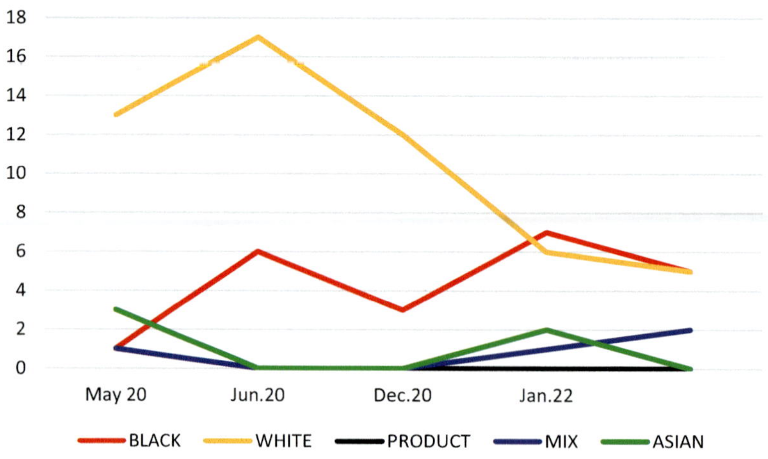

Fig. 10 Number of posts made by Zara on Instagram

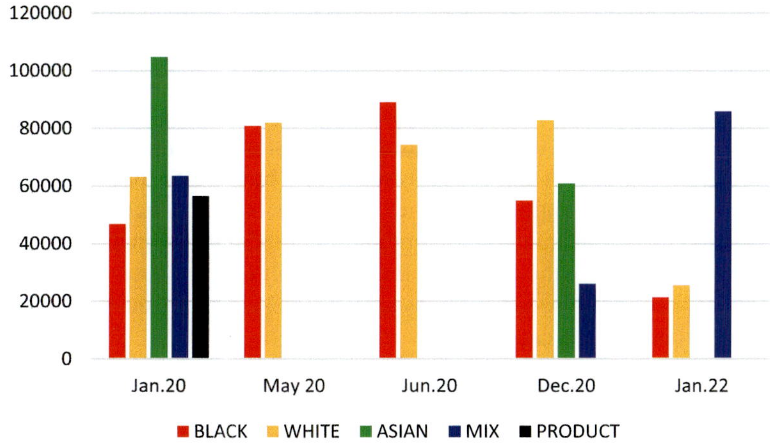

Fig. 11 The average number of likes for each publication category, categorized by the ethnicity of the model, at Zara

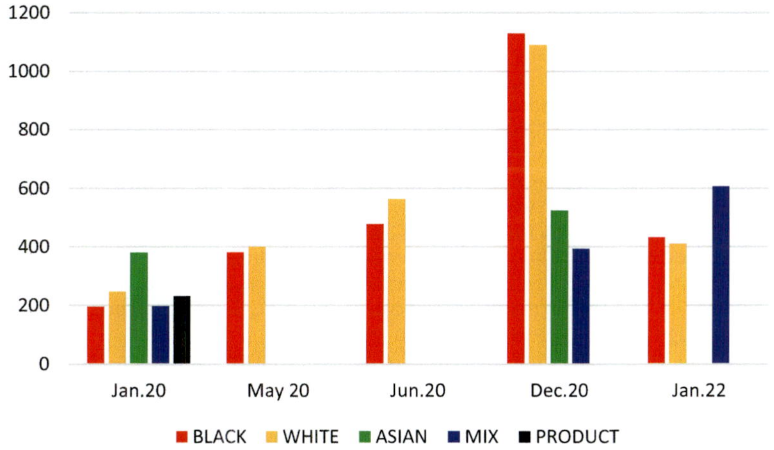

Fig. 12 The average number of comments for each publication category, categorized by the ethnicity of the model, at Zara

4 Conclusion

The data presented across the different graphs shows that the "Asian" category is volatile and unpredictable, making it difficult to draw clear conclusions. This is likely due to the relatively smaller number of posts compared to other categories. To draw more accurate conclusions, additional data such as sales figures, audience reactions, and other factors would need to be considered [15].

Based on the data analyzed, H&M appears to be the brand with the most posts and the highest level of cultural diversity in the models featured. Zara is also notable for its increasing emphasis on diversity in posts from 2022 onwards. Lefties, on the other hand, has the least diversity among the analyzed brands but has shown gradual progress in including more diverse cultures in its posts over time.

Overall, it does not seem that the analyzed brands have based their choices solely on a fashion perspective resulting from the BLM protests. This conclusion is based on the observation that these brands have continuously used professionals from different cultures over time. As for the audience, initial support for the cause at certain times appears to have been motivated more by matters of status and social image, rather than the importance of the cause itself.

References

1. Aaker J, Brumbaugh A, Grier SA (2000) Non-target Market Effects and Viewer Distinctiveness: The Impact of Target Marketing on Attitudes. J Consum Psychol 9(3):127–140
2. Morris, A, Kahlor LA (2014) Whiteness theory in advertising: racial beliefs and attitudes toward ads. Howard J Commun 25(4):415–430. https://doi.org/10.1080/10646175.2014.955929
3. Martin BAS (2004) University of Otago) is an associate pro-, Christina, KwaiChoi, Lee & University of Auckland) is a, se—(2004) the influence of ad model ethnicity and self-referencing on attitudes: evidence from New Zealand. J Advert 33(4):27–37. https://doi.org/10.1080/00913367.2004.10639172
4. Brumbaugh AM, Grier SA (2006) Insights from a "Failed" experiment: directions for pluralistic, multiethnic advertising research. J Advert 35(3):35–46
5. Burton D (2009) "Reading" whiteness in consumer research. Consum Mark Cult 12(2):171–201. https://doi.org/10.1080/10253860902840982
6. Grier SA, Deshpandé R (2001) Social dimensions of consumer distinctiveness: the influence of ssocial status on group identity and advertising persuasion. J Mark Res 38:216–224
7. Humphreys JM (2008) The multicultural economy. Terry College of Business, University of Georgia, Selig Center for Economic Growth
8. Hye Jin Paek & Hemant Shah (2003) Racial ideology, model minorities, and the "Not-So-Silent Partner:" stereotyping of Asian Americans in U.S. Mag Advert, Howard J Commun, 14:4, 225–243. https://doi.org/10.1080/716100430
9. Jacobs Henderson J, Baldasty GJ (2003) Race, advertising, and prime-time television. Howard J Commun 14:2, 97–112, DOI: https://doi.org/10.1080/10646170304267.
10. Jeremy J, Sierra PhD, Michael R, Hyman PhD, Torres IM, Ph D (2009) Using a Model's Apparent Ethnicity to Influence Viewer Responses to Print Ads: A Social Identity Theory Perspective. J Curr Issues Res Advert 31(2):41–66. https://doi.org/10.1080/10641734.2009.10505265
11. Loureiro SMC, Maximiano M, Panchapakesan P (2018) Engaging fashion consummers in social media: The case of luxury brands. Int J Fash Des, Technol Educ 11(3):310–321. https://doi.org/10.1080/17543266.2018.1431810
12. Barela MJ (2003) Executive Insights: United Colors of Benetton—From Sweaters to Success: an Examination of the Triumphs and Controversies of a Multinational Clothing Company. J Int Mark 11(4). ISSN 113–128:1069–2031
13. Ramasamy B, Yeung MCH, Au AKM (2010) Consumer Support for Corporate Social Responsibility (CSR): the Role of Religion and Values. J Bus Ethn 91:61–72
14. Loureiro SMC, Serra J, Guerreiro J (2019) How Fashion Brands Engage on Social Media: a Netnography Approach. J Promot Manag 25(3):367–378. https://doi.org/10.1080/10496491.2019.1557815

15. Suárez-Carballo F, Martin-Sanroman J, Martins N (2021) Analysis of the feminist graphics published in Instagram by Spanish female professionals related to the International Women's Day (2019–2020). Commun Soc 34(2), 351–367. https://doi.org/10.15581/003.34.2.351-367
16. Sierra JJ, Hyman MR, Torres IM (2009) Using a model's apparent ethnicity to influence viewer responses to print ads: A social identity theory perspective. J Curr Issues Res Advert 31(2):41–66
17. White PH, Harkins SG (1994) Race of source effects in the elaboration likelihood model. J Pers Soc Psychol 67:790–807
18. Lee YJ, Kim S (2019) How do racial minority consumers process a model race cue in CSR advertising? A comparison of Asian and White Americans. J Mark Commun 25(3):307–327. https://doi.org/10.1080/13527266.2016.1278256

"So that Kyoto Will Always Remain Kyoto": Reflections on the Impact of Outdoor Advertising Policies in Kyoto City

Ana Seixosa and Maria Cadarso

Abstract Recent changes in the Kyoto City Landscape Plan, have allowed citizens and mayor-certified organizations to proactively work together in creating more sustainable landscapes. In the outdoor advertising context, the system remains geared towards well-established restrictions and communication routes between administration and advertisers. This paper reflects on the current state of communication between the city, the community, and advertisers, speculating on the possibility of creating a more integrated system by analyzing the trends in the "Kyoto Landscape Awards" within the Outdoor Advertising category. The results point to tendencies in the attribution of the awards towards the regeneration and preservation areas of the city, bypassing new urban development and residential areas that constitute an opportunity for innovation and creativity. An integrated system, furthering information exchange and collaboration oriented, could allow the community to be more directly involved in the process of creation and decision-making regarding the outdoor advertising that invades their daily lives, which could, in turn, improve the urban experience and encourage the sprouting of new meaningful places.

Keywords Outdoor advertising · Local identity · Landscape policies · Urban experience · Participatory design

A. Seixosa (✉) · M. Cadarso
Universidade Europeia, IADE, Faculdade de Design, Tecnologia E Comunicação, UNIDCOM/IADE, Unidade de Investigação Em Design E Comunicação, Av. D. Carlos I, 4, 1200-649 Lisboa, Portugal
e-mail: acf.seix@gmail.com

N. Martins and D. Raposo (eds.), *Communication Design and Branding*, Springer Series in Design and Innovation 32,
https://doi.org/10.1007/978-3-031-35385-7_8

1 Brief Overview

From a previous investigation we have determined that Kyoto's outdoor advertising policies have, directly and indirectly, limited qualities such as colors, lights, materials, and visual elements that are often depicted within the city—especially of those that are non-traditional [1]. This study compared outdoor advertising tendencies in three Japanese cities (Kyoto, Tokyo, and Osaka), revealing there are cultural preferences expressed in advertising that disclose the intrinsic nature of each city. At its conclusion, the investigation provided best practice guidelines for western brands looking to enter these local markets, articulating that while more rigorous restrictions imposed on outdoor advertising can be beneficial to the cities, there is still potential in the disposition to adapt and innovate on behalf of brands, rather than focusing on established rules.

As the most prevalent case of following the rules, with the administration's strong desire to protect the city's heritage, the previous investigation found outdoor advertising design in Kyoto is encouraged to denote attributes easily associated with traditional aesthetics and/or portray traditional elements. Although both the city and community of Kyoto have been described as schizophrenic in the way in which they adhere to traditional norms and radical reforms [2], some of these attributes are more representative and more easily connected to the mentality and taste of an ancient Japanese society [1], not often used by people nowadays, particularly in daily conversations. Hence, while the reproduction of traditional components or the insinuation of conventionally Japanese aesthetics in Kyoto's outdoor advertising will often fit within an established local identity and be more conciliatory in relation to the city's traditional surroundings, it is important to consider that different cultural elements—elements of popular culture, alternative culture, mass culture—will be present in every person, albeit in different proportions [2]. The restrictions on outdoor advertising have helped Kyoto to rediscover itself in the past and to better communicate its identity today [3]. However, we found a scarcity and repetition in the tone of communication, in place of adaptation and innovation of advertising techniques which would specially promote and attempt to improve the urban experience in new areas of the city, where it would coincide with contemporary society [1].

Because 'local' is always subject to change, it is important to reflect on local relationships and boundaries, on the alignment of values between different social actors within a common space. As reasoned by Ganseforth et al., localities are up for debate both from within and without, where we must address its ongoing de-institutionalization and re-institutionalization processes and localities as a common, but still underdeveloped, topic of research [4]. Globalization and localization processes require a dialogical conceptualization of self and identity [5], where global and local voices are constantly exchanging and negotiating with each other. This need for balancing both environments within a region, all the while respecting the social fabric in which different agents and systems act, has been a growing area of academic concern, emphasized by Manzini who described contemporary localities as a combination of specific characteristics of places, of their communities, with new tensions and frictions caused and supported by globalization, encouraging interconnectivity and social innovation [6].

2 Contextual Framework

The discussion bellow includes a collection of reflections on the state of the art regarding advertising practices and the impact they may have on the relationships between the space and its community—either online or physical. The points presented bellow mean to introduce a discussion on the overarching themes that involve this investigation, presenting some of the trends, issues and concepts that have emerged through previous studies on the topic, and the societal changes that have been occurring over the years.

2.1 The Evolution of Marketing: Finding Out What People Want

Selling a product and stablishing your brand as a household name, were relatively simpler practices a few decades ago. At that time, the market revolved around the sellers and near monopolies that allowed companies to forgo efforts which involved the marketing philosophy or consumer satisfaction [7]. With the arrival of the digital age, consumers were able to choose from a wide array of products and services, bringing about changes in consumer behavior that could no longer be ignored. Although by then the idea of satisfying consumers' needs was being addressed, both when discussing marketing strategies and product manufacturing itself, the rapidly changing dynamics demanded companies to expand their focus from consumer to human being, highlighting social and environmental problems [8]. Looking at consumers as human beings meant attending needs that went beyond a product fulfilling its function. At last, as most recently stated by Kotler et al., it took marketing roughly seventy years to transition from a focus on products and sales to the idea of human centricity [9].

In today's globalized, saturated market, connectivity and interaction, enabled by the new technologies, have allowed companies to reach the individual and specific groups through new mediums. The concept of big data has made it easier for companies to find out what an individual wants by simply following their digital footprint. Yet, this increased surveillance of potential consumers has led to a lack of personal space [8], which, in the digital touchpoints, manifests itself visually in the advertisements that cover their screens.

2.2 *Online Advertising in the Experience Age: The Digital Touchpoint*

Although curated messages would, in theory, be able to generate a successful communication, the effectiveness of online advertising strategies is still highly depended on its ability to attract visual attention [10]. Consequently, online ads are constantly competing with the surrounding content and disrupting user experience, alike most ads in physical touchpoints. While Higgins cited a number of studies that have suggested manipulating aspects such as location, animation, onset, and even relevance in order to retain the user's attention and detour a lack of engagement with the narrative of the advertisement in question, adblock reports for the year 2021 have revealed that the number of users of digital media who have some type of online ad blocker has continued to increase, with over half a billion users on mobile devices [11]. Aside from that, the growing tendency for websites and applications to offer a premium service that, among other features, would allow consumers to bypass advertisements, have alerted companies for the need to produce more meaningful, sustainable content or risk losing their space on users' screens and, in turn, their minds. This sentiment was echoed by the PageFair Adblock report, which showed an increase of online users' acceptance of the Acceptable Ads program, where adblock users are twice as likely to accept light, non-intrusive ads over ad block walls or pay for content [11]. Ultimately, the reliance on big data, as efficient as it is in tracking potential consumers' interests, has sidetracked advertisers in addressing them correctly—in reaching the human being. As reasoned by Drigo, the effectiveness of advertising is waning because the classic model of advertising—which relied on fixating a message in the consumer's mind and highlighting the functional or psychological benefits of a given product—is no longer as effective as it used to be [12]. Alike Kotler et al. have proposed, principles such as participation, collaboration and co-creation must be addressed [8], where companies need to understand not what people click on, but their desires, what could be incorporated in the communication to add value to their lives.

2.3 *Outdoor Advertising in the Experience Age: The Physical Touchpoint*

As most recently stated by Kotler et al., today's younger generations, with a greater care about societal problems than its previous counterparts, have effectively forced companies to incorporate social impact into their business models [9]. Consequently, when ads move from the digital to the physical touchpoint across customers' journey, advertisers who wish to stand out will often have to consider the discourses around the sustainable development of the localities they wish to engage in face of globalization.

The importance of 'place' and 'local identity' has been debated for a long time, with cities striving to proclaim their differences and emphasize aspects that make them unique and that, traditionally, result in better tourism and investment rates. Following this perspective has led companies to adopt strategies based on the established ideology 'think global, act local' often attributed to a similar concept defended by Patrick Geddes (1854–1932). In his reflections on the evolution of cities, Geddes argued that each new project conceived for a given city should be the expression of the local and regional personality, culminating in a local character that "is attained only in course of adequate grasp and treatment of the whole environment, and in active sympathy with the essential and characteristic life of the place concerned" [13]. Through this work, Geddes attempted to show the ways in which education, conservative surgery and participation between the interested agents could contribute to the socioecological city development. While his vision of the city addressed the importance of articulating both the physical and the social environment in the field of planning, emphasizing the holistic character of city development, his theory was often scorned in favor of, the more popular, differentiation hypotheses of the time [14].

More than a century later, the strong globalization of the market has emphasized mobility and economic progress, global society and global culture, and contributed to the dilution of the concepts of 'place' and 'community' [15]. Moreover, differentiation hypotheses are still regularly employed by local governments as a marketing strategy in the promotion of cities as tourist destinations and investment targets. As criticized by Rebelo et al., these differentiation efforts may validate administrations' hegemonic narratives, amalgamating in the corporate identity of the municipality and its associates, and result in the appropriation of the city's identity by other entities as means of authentication [16]. At last, governments wish to evoke a sense of place, whilst expanding their own visions on the local identity. In the meantime, to integrate a stronger and more participative community, local inhabitants need to experience a greater enjoyment of the place, to nurture a sense of belonging and agency [17].

One element that has disturbed the appreciation of place is outdoor advertising, which, through a global advertising culture, has assisted a growing homogenization of urban spaces. To solve this problem and to rediscover local identity and urban landscape, local administrations have considered a legislative angle, regulating outdoor advertising through restrictive ordinances. This has been the case, e.g., in the city of São Paulo, Brazil, with the creation of the Clean City Law [18]; and Kyoto, Japan, with the restriction and removal of outdoor advertisement objects [3]. Conversely, this focus on law-making to safeguard the urban landscape, may put the enjoyment of the community at risk, whose point of view tends to be considered only after the creation of new policies. In Kyoto city, e.g., private dwellings, such as the *kyo-machiya* (traditional wooden town houses), may be classified as important for the development of the urban landscape, thus falling under the scrutiny of the local government [3]. Furthermore, the implementation of stricter restrictions by some local governments did not necessarily lead to an improvement on city identity and/or the community's well-being. According to Drigo, not only the initial rearrangements made to comply with the Clean City Law still viewed the city of São Paulo as a showroom for brands, the lackluster of the removal of some billboards, as well as of smaller advertisements that used to signalize different market agents and color popular commercial streets, intensified a strangeness in the place now bare of advertisements [18]. Being a part of the urban environment, outdoor advertising can signify different sociocultural contexts, an ability that can contribute to the quality of life and resilience of the community in general.

Regarding urban space and advertising as sign systems, Drigo suggested that they can form a set and achieve functionality if advertisements can be treated as elements of the urban context, both in their production process and in their distribution in that context [19]. Moreover, the traditional city planning methods are gradually being contested and paralleled by more fluid processes, typically led by social actors who see the city as a complex living entity, made up of people (communities) and their places of residence as a network of collaborative projects [20]. For these reasons, it is our belief that greater care in the regulations made on outdoor advertising is necessary, as well as greater support from the brands in the construction of place, becoming relevant to investigate how outdoor advertising, as an object of consumption in itself, could collaborate with communities to truly adapt to and reflect different urban contexts.

3 Relevance and Impact

3.1 The Case of Kyoto: Restrictions to Liberate Landscape

The period that proceeded the end of the Second World War and post-Occupation in Japan was one of rapid economic growth, known historically as the "Japanese miracle" [2]. This scenario of prosperity caused the Japanese market to become saturated and advertisers to increase their efforts in making their product stand out among competitors. In Kyoto's outdoor advertising context, the rapid modernization of the city and the disruptive advertising that had been growing within the urban space, led the policies of landscape preservation and urban planning in Kyoto to acquired greater importance for the local administration [3].

Throughout its history, the scenery of Kyoto city was designated a scenic place, attracting people to temples and shrines for more than religious beliefs, and often being reproduced in a series of everyday objects [21]. The unorganized expansion of the urban area and the intensification of commercial activities during the fifties, was a cause of concern to the local government, who feared losing Kyoto's cultural heritage and traditional landscape. In 1956, the local autonomy law was amended, and Kyoto became a city designed by the government, who later established its own regulations for outdoor advertising. Over the next few decades, restrictions on outdoor advertising were reformed under which the standard of height and size of the objects was revised, including indoor advertisements displayed in windows [21]. Restrictions on the composition and location of advertisements were also imposed according to the characteristics of each region of the city, which, at this time, was divided into a number of different districts with varying degrees of scenic importance (district of scenic beauty; aesthetic district; historic climate prevention district; large structure control district; etc.). By 2005, when new age technology arrived and it's fast-changing pace threatened to expose Kyoto's landscape to new disturbances, the government established the "Council on Landscape Formation of Kyoto Shining Forever" [21]. Following new recommendations from this council, the city of Kyoto created a new landscape policy where, among other projects, was the implementation of even stricter regulations on outdoor advertising. This time, to the restrictions already made on outdoor advertising, the following were added: use of a more restricted color palette, prohibition of bright red and yellow as base colors and/or the use of disruptive colors to the immediate scenario; format standardization of the lateral store signs by the roadside; removal of flickering lights and inappropriate mobile advertising; and complete removal of billboards from the top of buildings [22]. This review aimed to maintain harmony in relation to the local characteristics of height and design of the buildings, especially regarding the urban attributes of the kyo-machiya that carry significant cultural value. Furthermore, the administration created incentives for the design of outdoor advertising that could make each district more attractive. Thus, advertisements with a historical design and intended for the well-being of society, not only could have a monetary gain but also favor from a relaxation in some restrictions [22].

While the restrictions imposed on outdoor advertising were beneficial and still are essential for maintaining and building landscape in Kyoto, at an age of experience, it should be equally essential to consider the thoughts and impressions of its inhabitants who, much like the city, have experienced changes on regards to their identity over the years.

3.2 Problem Statement

Alike online advertisers, outdoor advertisers have, for a long time, been used to finding solutions by thinking of place in generic and spatial terms—where the space is the three-dimensional structure to be used, and to organize the interactions between objects and people [23]. However, it is not the space that manages the interaction; it is the place, a space that is valued and built by its inhabitants, containing different behavioral and cultural expectations that amount in a distinguishing experience [15, 17, 23]. Similarly, the creation of laws and regulations by local governments and urban planners, such as the removal and restrictions of outdoor advertising, although aiming to restore a sense of place to their cities, have generally overlooked extending the conversation towards the party capable of embedding meaning into a space—its people. It is, therefore, necessary to reflect on the way in which advertisers think of urban space in the outdoor advertising world and integrate the community's vision more directly in the process of creation, finding and understanding the place for which advertisements should be designed.

This scenario truly requires thinking of human beings, of understanding their need to contribute, to make a difference in the world, through the sharing of knowledge and technologies that can turn people's experience into something more productive and meaningful [9]. In Kyoto city, the local government acknowledges that the creation and development of the historic urban landscape requires the active participation of various stakeholders, including the local community [24], emphasizing the need to make information available and encourage the community's awareness. While Kyoto's District plan—based on the "City Planning Act" [3] is said to want to improve the development of local communities by the collaboration of the city and its citizens, where the plan is drawn by the residents of each district themselves, "under the "Building Standard Act", the city will have a coercive power over the rules defined by the district plan if such rules takes the status of the city ordinance" [24].

At last, this arrangement exposed the relationships of power that exist within the urban space, where an already established hierarchy will control the narrative and the impact of the contributions of the community. The focus on complying with previously stablished ordinances may also hinder creativity and innovation by discouraging revolutionary consciousness. We recognize the importance of understanding, protecting, and communicating culture and heritage, nevertheless, in maintaining the built environment, we must also recognize that the clash of different agents and cultures is an integral part of contemporary society and should be addressed when asserting identity. A local community will be a part of the global society; hence it is equally important to allow for the renewal of this community, which will not be guided by a constant appreciation for the traditional culture alone. Especially at a time where the focus lays on creating experiences, both the construction of new spaces and interventions in existing ones, should not be projected with a sole intention to preserve or amend, but with the desire to elevate the value built within the physical spaces that make up a city.

As of April 2021, the Kyoto administration recognized the importance of promoting sustainable urban development, confirming changes on the City Landscape Plan accompanying the "Further Evolution of the New Landscape Policy" through the "Evolution of the Landscape Creation Process" [3]. The introduction of plans in accordance with each region's vision, and the evolution of the process of creating landscapes that realize these visions for each region contributed to the enhancement of the plan. Still, in the outdoor advertising context, the creation and implementation processes follow a well-established system that restricts not only physical attributes of the advertisements, but also the negotiations to government and advertisers [3]. The current system structure has the government acting as a middleman in balancing the discussions and propositions around the development of urban landscapes, ultimately reenforcing its position as the agent with the most influence over the built urban environment (Fig. 1).

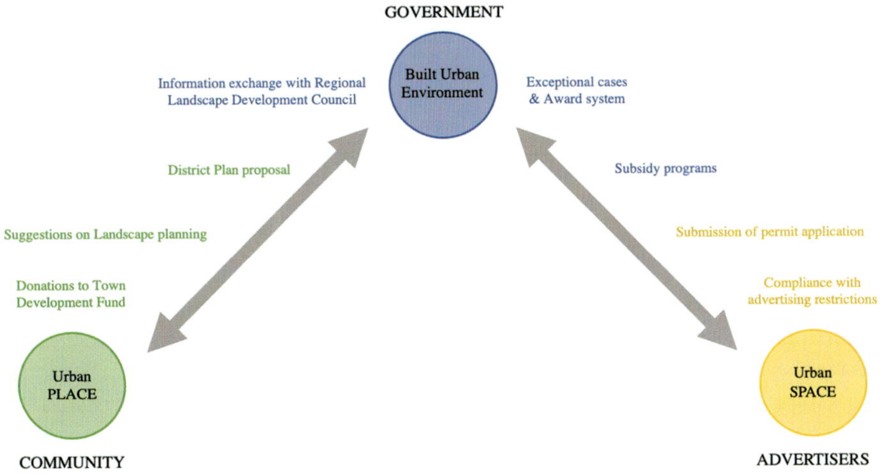

Fig. 1 Current system of communication in Kyoto to maintain the built urban environment

4 Methodology

Considering that one of the most relevant issues to be addressed in this ongoing investigation regards the improvement of places, through outdoor advertising, by elevating the community's input, in this section we set out to explore the existing relations between good outdoor advertising and the city, based on the Outdoor Advertising Awards given by the Kyoto administration and associates over the years [3]. We aim, with this analysis, to investigate tendencies in the outdoor advertising context caused by the current system implemented in Kyoto city. This analysis would serve to substantiate the idea that a change in practices on behalf of the administration and advertisers, to involve the community more directly in the creative process, may be able to improve not only the place but the relationship between these agents and the community.

That said, this section is divided into two stages where the first constitutes the sample whereas the second uses methods of compositional interpretation and content analyses to examine trends.

4.1 Sample Characterization

To make information about landscape more accessible to the public, the administration has made a number of documentations about town planning and landscape development available on the Kyoto City Official Website [3]. As of December 2018, among the documents are four digital booklets regarding the outdoor advertising awards credited in the years of 2012, 2013, 2015 and 2018 in the city. For

Table 1 Sample profile

Year	Number of applications	Number of awards
2012	789	139
2013	1277	209
2015	1207	184
2018	1215	25
Total	4488	557

this study, we examine the outdoor advertising outcomes contained in each of these documents, discarding special awards and commendations given to organizations and businesses without the production of a specific advertising outcome. Thus, the final sample is non-probabilistic in nature, resulting in a total of 557 objects studied, as can be observed in Table 1.

4.2 Procedures

The proposition of this analysis is oriented towards confirming the problem relevance by finding tendencies on the ascription of outdoor advertising awards in Kyoto. In this sense, the hypothesis here is that this study will demonstrate a greater concentration of awards in the Conservation and Revitalization areas of Kyoto city, considered as such by the government [21]. Consequently, the sample was described following the compositional interpretation method, where the variables most relevant to the current stage of the investigation were identified. For this study, we consider the following variables: "Store Name"; "Ward"; "Brand Category"; "Award"; "Award Year"; "Storefront Style"; "Brand Origin"; and "Store Status". These variables were later split into different sublevels (variations), defining a clear and replicable coding sheet that allowed for the content analysis. This coding sheet was discussed with a second evaluator with design knowledge, allowing for the discussion of the relevance of some variables and the discovery of inconsistencies. The final description of the study objects, and findings report, was provided once the coding sheet had been refined. The most suitable tables for the purpose were used to present the outcomes of this confirmatory phase, using the SPSS tool to collect all quantitative data.

The final stage of this study involved the discussion and interpretation of the results based on the framework developed thus far, where we intended to recognize a narrative in the outdoor advertising context of Kyoto city and question the possibility of it not matching the needs of the community—deliberating on possible implications of some trends, as well as solutions to imbalances.

4.3 Results

In content analysis, we considered 8 study variables with 43 sublevels, examining bellow the data of the variables that express pertinent results to this stage of the investigation. To understand the geographical distribution of the awards within Kyoto city, the variable "Ward" (subdivision of the city) was studied (Table 2).

The findings demonstrate that the sample presents a high concentration of awards on the following three sublevels, arranged in the ensuing order of perceived importance: (a) Nakagyō; (b) Higashiyama; and (c) Shimogyō. These three wards are contained within the Conservation and Revitalization areas [25], thus, corroborating our hypothesis regarding the distribution of the awards. In contrast, the sublevel Minami presents the lowest value for the variable, at 1.1% in the sample. This ward is located south of Kyoto Station and is included in the Creation area of Kyoto City [21].

Regarding the origin of the awarded brands' advertisements, the variable "Brand Origin" revealed most of the businesses awarded were Japanese, with the sublevel National brand accounting for 97.7% of the sample value, as shown in Table 3.

The variable "Storefront Style" (Table 4) revealed that the sublevel Traditional is the most frequently awarded among the outdoor advertising styles, accounting for 63.6% of the sample's value.

Table 2 Frequencies for the variable *Ward*

Ward	Frequency	Percent
Nakagyō	179	32.1
Fushimi	17	3.1
Shimogyō	84	15.1
Higashiyama	99	17.8
Kamigyō	50	9.0
Sakyō	61	11.0
Ukyō	18	3.2
Minami	6	1.1
Nishikyō	8	1.4
Kita	26	4.7
Yamashina	9	1.6
Total	557	100.0

Table 3 Frequencies for the variable *Brand Origin*

Brand origin	Frequency	Percent
National brand	544	97.7
International brand	13	2.3
Total	557	100.0

Table 4 Frequencies for the variable *Storefront Style*

Storefront style	Frequency	Percent
Traditional	354	63.6
Modern	114	20.5
Mixed	89	16.0
Total	557	100.0

Table 5 Frequencies for the variable *Store Status*

Store status	Frequency	Percent
Running business	515	92.5
Temporarily closed	10	1.8
Permanently closed	32	5.7
Total	557	100.0

Finally, we examined the results for the variable "Store Status" to determine how many of the businesses awarded were still active (Table 5). Despite occasional changes in location, for the most part, the businesses awarded are still in operation, as evidenced by the high value obtained in the sample for the sublevel Running Business (92.5%). Consequently, business cycles in Kyoto appear to progress slowly, with low business turnover despite the saturated global market and the city's status as a touristic capital.

It should be noted, given the intent of this analysis, that the content of each individual advertising piece awarded was not examined. In the future, this analysis could be revisited, and new variables added and examined to deliver an exploration of trends within the physical attributes of what is considered, by the government and associates, good outdoor advertising in Kyoto city.

5 Discussion

In consideration of the relevancy of the problem stated, this study on the effects of the current system for outdoor advertising creation in Kyoto city, through the analysis of the outdoor advertising awards, has uncovered the administrations and associates' demarking of good outdoor advertising in the city, which corroborate a reprioritization of certain landscapes over others and of which impact will be discussed in this section.

While the protection of the existing landscape in Kyoto is of paramount importance to the administrations, who hope to preserve the traditional landscape for future generations by—among other means—establishing stricter ordinances for outdoor advertising, this study has shown that the less traditional or commercial sites of Kyoto are underprioritized. The Minami ward, e.g., part of the "New Urban Function Concentration Region" [21] is described as a mostly plain area containing many residential areas and apartment facilities, with neighborhoods developing as industrial complexes as well as containing several underdeveloped land lots [25]. This area is a place for opportunity and innovation, where outdoor advertising policies are generally less strict, yet it has the lowest level of perceived relevance within the study sample (Table 2). The results obtained in the sample have revealed a higher frequency of awards in areas within "Natural and Historical Landscape Conservation Region" and "Harmonized Downtown Revitalization Regions" [21], which comprise the city center and historical urban areas containing many temples and shrines, as well as areas framed by historically significant mountain ranges [25]. Noting these are areas with a higher concentration of businesses, they nevertheless contain some of the most notorious Kyoto landscapes and attractions, constituting a hotspot for tourism and administrations' concerns. As we have concluded by the study of the variable "Storefront Style", most of the awarded advertising display a Traditional style (Table 4) that will more directly benefit traditional areas of the city. The high number for the Modern sublevel, on the other hand, will benefit the city center, equally significant as the place where contemporary Kyoto begun to flourish and as a commercial center—once again, located within the most awarded wards.

Yet, even in these prioritized areas, there is a significant difference in the value added (or lack thereof), by the outdoor advertising displayed along popular streets, such as Shijō Street (Fig. 2), and the advertising displayed in, less favored, usually more residential areas. In areas with laxer restrictions, the adaptability of advertising outcomes to the surrounding landscape is often depended on the disposition of the brands, creating an environment where some brands chose to adapt while others search for ways around the regulations to still stand out (Fig. 3). The trends in location for the advertising outcomes studied, expose a strategy of preserving and improving spaces with an already stablished character, which will contribute to strengthen the city's celebrated identity, rather than anticipating its expansion and variations for the future. Areas currently lacking points of attraction or distinctive architectural attributes, will likely also lack in the adaptation and the innovation of such outcomes, and in the improvement of the urban experience through outdoor advertising. In some of these areas, it is possible to find advertising structures that are no longer adequate, as for restrictions in height, placement, color, etc., but that have not yet been properly reorganised or removed.

Through the analyzes of "Brand Origin", this study has revealed advertisements by international brands are not as often perceived as a good addition to the surrounding landscape, propelling the idea that the restrictions are a hinder to globalized brands, who must still change their identity to fit the city's ordinances and forgo established techniques to stand out among competitors. While much like the variable "Ward", an imbalance within this variable is to be expected considering location and distribution, another reason for such disparity may be that while following restrictions may help external agents fit in and preserve the cityscape, they fundamentally will add limited value to the city and the community. Furthermore, brands with no connection to the place will often make just enough changes on their visual identity to meet the demands, or replicate the style used by regional brands. Ultimately, and considering

Fig. 2 Standardization in color and design of outdoor advertising displayed along Shijō Street, Photos by the author

Fig. 3 Different brands' response to the restrictions imposed on outdoor advertising in less prioritized areas of Kyoto city, Photos by the author

how long these restrictions have existed in Kyoto city, the acclimation of their advertisements might be seen as trivial to the local inhabitants, and/or feel less genuine than the regional (sometimes even national) brands', who will often display already agreeable styles and techniques in relation to the city's surroundings and history. The low frequency in which international brands have won awards in the sample, may also reveal a difficulty on behalf of the administration in balancing the global and the local environments, where the global is often seen as a liability to the social fabric of a traditional, but complex and mutable city.

The landscape plan drawn up by the administration, of which the restrictions applied to outdoor advertising are part, aimed at the conservation, revitalization, and creation of Kyoto landscape, so that "Kyoto will always remain Kyoto" [21]. The current system for outdoor advertising implementation operates as to preserve and highlight Kyoto's established values and identity, with a more forceful hand within traditional areas of the city [21, 22]. In areas more subjected to change, these restrictions have allowed for repetition as well as transgressions, sparking the debate on the limited contributions of this system, especially with regards to the community well-being. As stated by Saito, the price paid for the development of appreciation of the aesthetic landscapes, is the neglect of the everyday environment and the experience of the local inhabitants [26]. The author concluded that an inattentiveness for such variables may result in an impoverishment, both aesthetic and ecological, of the everyday landscape where people commute, work and live.

In the end, Kyoto is Kyoto also because of its people. They are the ones whose way of living and crafts have attracted the touristic masses and whose younger generations feel increasingly disconnected from their *furusato* (hometown). As mentioned by Mock, big 'outside' cities such as Kyoto, are not considered to be nearly as 'cool' as the capital, Tokyo, by the media, where young people are encouraged to go to find a more happening lifestyle [27]. On his observations on the depopulation and aging processes of rural Japan, the author noted how "the government has flailed away on a variety of furusato revival plans, mostly white elephant projects, while local entrepreneurs and officials try to figure out what they can offer that affluent Japanese want" concluding that "sustainable businesses and industries remain a hope rather than a reality". In time, the focus on the preservation and the dissemination of the traditional city as a tourist investment target, and a difficulty in creating new meaningful spaces where the contemporary community can feel represented, has regarded Kyoto as a living museum which may upset the development of place and the mischaracterization of the city at a human level.

Similarly, the outdoor advertising ordinances established for Kyoto city seem to have lost their initial distinctiveness, having been utilized as a blueprint for other cities' and countries' own ordinances. In a study on the acceptability of outdoor advertising design in historical urban areas in China and Japan, Yi concluded, within a range of designs that meet the restrictions, there was "no significant difference in acceptability of outdoor advertisings between the Chinese and Japanese buildings, or between different types of Japanese buildings" [28]. Noting that a certain congruity between the visual traits of vernacular architecture of the cities analyzed may be the reason for such perceived uniformity, one could not as readily consider these communities as being uniform among themselves. The restrictions have limited outdoor advertising in Kyoto city to a set of representations and values brands can interpret as guidelines [1] which will lead to homogenization.

Although the restrictions may arise nostalgia, they may equality cause frustration and a sense of claustrophobia for their limiting nature, in the same way that Manzini described closed communities [29]. As explained by the author, this type of community barely exists nowadays—currently in crisis or in the process of changing—while new communities, as a place of opportunity and interaction, are increasing, where less spatial constraints have altered the way they exist and their relationship to places. Going forward, with this type of community in mind, it is believed that establishing local identity and agency should employ methods other than restrictive action. At the same time inhabitants may value a place's nature and recognized identity, regardless of how small and enclosed it may be, the space will consist of a number of diverse sub-spaces, each with its own unique identity and spatial qualities [30]. As the case, it is implied the identity of Kyoto city should not overshadow the identity of Sakyō, Ukyō, Minami, etc., as well as even smaller neighborhoods' individualities. Ganseforth et al. have similarly noted that while the tendency of public policy in Japan is to focus on what people have in common rather than what sets them apart, there have been instances where national attempts to create larger political units, and stronger local identities, were met with resistance and were challenged by the retention of more locally based characteristics [4].

At last, outdoor advertising is itself an object of consumption, an expression of social-cultural context, and a reflection that the city is a living city, that there is a particular community with which it wishes to engage. In a consent for the value of planning-oriented marketing and advertising, Jean Baudrillard, (1929–2007), famous philosopher and sociologist and advertising critic, stated that "if all advertising were abolished, individuals would feel frustrated by the empty hoardings. (…) One of the first demands of man in his progression towards well-being is that his desires be attended to, that they be formulated and expressed in the form of images for his own contemplation".

If we intend to develop 'local' and 'community' in a sustainable manner, making it a source of opportunity for the different agents involved in the urban environment, greater care is needed when developing planning practices, as well as greater appreciation and involvement of the value generated by the community in question. According to Devisch et al., the implementation of more democratic planning practices has been on demand, particularly in Europe, varying from a need for better information clarity to direct participation in decision-making processes [30]. Thus, we believe that a more participatory approach could improve the urban experience of the local community and the role of outdoor advertising within the urban environment, giving the community more authority over how the meaning of the objects that surround them is formulated.

Motivated by this need to defend society driven sustainability innovations regarding place-making activities that involve communities, local governments, and advertisers, we propose an informed outdoor advertising creation system, that could not only save companies and administrations resources and time, but also produce

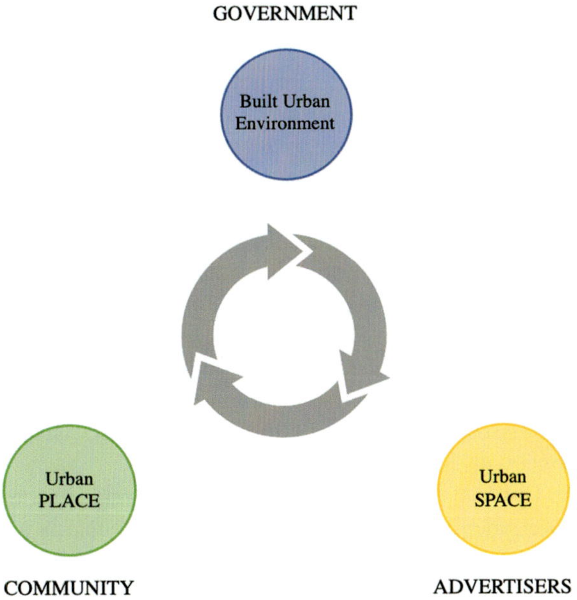

Fig. 4 Proposition of an integrated system for the creation of outdoor advertising

better outdoor advertising outcomes (Fig. 4). Working with individual communities to create solutions for the sustainable development of their dwellings can represent a valuable source of new ideas and innovations for the current system, despite its highly institutionalized nature and resistance to change. Ultimately, we aim at adding to the growing academic debate involving the nature of place and the, perhaps small, but significant contribution a more responsive, sustainable outdoor adverting practice can bring to our cities and communities in the future.

6 Conclusion

The built urban environment plays an essential role in the perception of a region, translating a cultural image which is also reflected in an individual's attitude to convey the impression that their activity in the region maintains certain patterns [32]. City scaping and the urban experience are connected, where a *sense of place* [17] will be a result of how the built environment affects a community.

This study has shown that there are tendencies in the classification of good outdoor advertising that may be validating a narrative on part of the Kyoto government and associates, whilst overlooking certain spatializations of social relations. Although the current outdoor advertising implementation system in Kyoto city has been beneficial for the sustainable development of landscape in the city for many years, the proposition of a more integrated system could represent an incremental change to the system whose impact may add new value to advertising, help develop old and new spaces, and nurture a greater sense of community and cooperation within a living, changing society.

Governments and administrations are gradually emphasizing citizen engagement to increase transparency and involve and empower local communities into working together—demonstrated by Kyoto government's changes in the city development plan, and its past declaration of a need to disseminate among the community the idea that "landscape is their property" [24]. However, implementing this notion without considering existing rules and power dynamics and the hitherto validation of some entities' hegemonic narratives over the local identity, will not provide inclusivity, or the sustainable improvement of the community experience. As stated by Devos et al., certain groups have been and are frequently still marginalized or denied power within the planning process, since planners hold the authority to reject certain publics, ideas, and values [30]. Yet notions regarding place are dispersed among coexisting and occasionally contradicting agents, whose narrative and approach will have an effect within the built urban environment.

This analysis helped us corroborate the importance of a better interaction between governments, community, and advertisers. Thus, as we intend to explore in the future of this investigation, a system geared towards information exchange, promoting the conversation and collaboration between these different agents, could not only help them to better understand the context in which their theories are rooted, but also enable the creation of new meaning within living places, whether traditional and controlled or contemporary and fluid.

Acknowledgements This research is being developed within a Ph.D. investigation funded by the Foundation for Science and Technology (FCT), through UNIDCOM/IADE R&D Unit, under the grant UI/BD/152240/2021.

References

1. Seixosa A (2020) Publicidade como elemento de divulgação da cultura intrínseca de uma cidade estudo de caso nas cidades japonesas de Kyoto, Osaka e Tokyo [dissertation/thesis]. IADE-U Institute of Art, Design and Enterprise, Portugal http://hdl.handle.net/10400.26/32858
2. Sugimoto Y (2014) An introduction to Japanese society, 4th edn. Cambridge University Press, Australia
3. Kyoto City Official Website, https://www.city.kyoto.lg.jp/menu4/index.html, last accessed 2022/12/29
4. Ganseforth S, Jentzsch H (eds) (2022) Rethinking locality in Japan, 1st edn. Routledge, New York
5. Hermans HJM, Dimaggio G (2007) Self, identity, and globalization in times of uncertainty: a dialogical analysis. Rev Gen Psychol 11(1):31–61
6. Manzini E (2014) Making things happen: social innovation and design. Des Issues 30(1):57–66. https://doi.org/10.1162/DESI_a_00248
7. Kotler P, Armstrong G, Saunders J, Wong V (1999) Principles of marketing, 2nd edn. Prentice Hall Europe, Milan
8. Kotler P, Kartajaya H, Setiawan I (2010) Marketing 3.0: from product to customers to the human spirit. Wiley, New Jersey

9. Kotler P, Kartajaya H, Setiawan I (2021) Marketing 5.0: technology for humanity. Wiley, USA
10. Higgins E, Leinenger M, Rayner K (2014) Eye movements when viewing advertisements. Front Psychol 5(210). https://doi.org/10.3389/fpsyg.2014.00210
11. Blockthrough website, https://blockthrough.com/blog/2021-adblock-report/, last accessed 2022/12/29
12. Drigo MO (2016) Alcances e Limites da Publicidade sob a Perspectiva da Teoria social de Niklas Luhmann. Observatório 2(2):280–300. https://doi.org/10.20873/uft.2447-4266.2016v2 Especial2p280
13. Geddes P (1915) Cities in evolution: an introduction to the town planning movement and to the study of civics. Williams & Norgate, London
14. Clavel P, Young R (2017) "Civics": Patrick Geddes's theory of city development. Landsc Urban Plan 166:37–42. https://doi.org/10.1016/j.landurbplan.2017.06.017
15. McClay W. M., McAllister T. V. (Eds.): Why place matters. Geography, identity and civic life in modern America. New Atlantis Books, USA (2014).
16. Rebelo AM, Alvelos H, Domingues Á (2022) The city is not a brand: a critical analysis of the narrative and appropriations of "Porto." In: Martins, N., Brandão, D. (eds) Advances in design and digital communication II. DIGICOM 2021. Springer Series in Design and Innovation, vol 19. Springer, Cham. https://doi.org/10.1007/978-3-030-89735-2_52
17. Tuan Y (1977) Space and place. The perspective of experience. University of Minnesota Press, Minneapolis
18. Drigo MO (2009) Cidade/invisibilidade e cidade/estranhamento: São Paulo antes e depois da lei "Cidade Limpa." Galáxia 17:49–64
19. Drigo MO, Souza LCP (2012) Publicidade de rua em São Paulo e cidades alemãs: dimensões histórica, intercultural e semiótica. Intexto 27:215–235
20. Manzini E, Cipolla C (2019) Design for social innovation and cities. DESIS Network. ISBN: 978-88-941673-0-6
21. Kyoto City Official Website. Chapter 2: The history of landscape formation and town development in Kyoto [PDF]. https://www.city.kyoto.lg.jp/tokei/cmsfiles/contents/0000281/281300/2shou.pdf, last accessed 2022/12/29.
22. Kyoto City Official Website. Chapter 3: Conservation, Revitalization and Creation of Kyoto Landscape [PDF]. https://www.city.kyoto.lg.jp/tokei/cmsfiles/contents/0000281/281300/3shou.pdf, last accessed 2022/12/29.
23. Harrison S, Dourish P (1996) Replacing space: the roles of place and space in collaborative systems. In: Proceedings of the 1996 ACM conference on computer supported cooperative work—CSCW'96. ACM Press, New York, USA. https://doi.org/10.1145/240080.240193
24. Kyoto City Official Website. Chapter 4: Kyoto's Landscape From Now On [PDF]. https://www.city.kyoto.lg.jp/tokei/cmsfiles/contents/0000281/281300/4shou.pdf, last accessed 2022/12/29.
25. Kyoto City Official Website. Chapter 1: Understanding the Landscape of Kyoto [PDF]. https://www.city.kyoto.lg.jp/tokei/cmsfiles/contents/0000281/281300/1shou.pdf, last accessed 2022/12/29.
26. Saito Y (2002) Scenic national landscapes: common themes in Japan and the United States. Essays Philos 3(1)
27. Kingston J (ed) (2014) Critical issues in contemporary Japan, 1st edn. Routledge, London
28. Yi Z (2018) Acceptability of design and color of outdoor advertising in historical urban areas in China and Japan [dissertation/thesis]. 筑波大学 (University of Tsukuba), Japan. https://hdl.handle.net/2241/00152614
29. Manzini E (2019) Politics of the everyday. Bloomsbury Publishing Plc, London
30. Devisch O, Huybrechts L, Ridder R (2019) D: Participatory design theory: using technology and social media to foster civic engagement. Routledge, New York
31. Baudrillard J (1996) The system of objects. Verso, London
32. Goffman E (1959) The presentation of self in everyday life. Doubleday Anchor, New York

What Do #Storytelling and #Marketing Have in Common? A Comprehensive Literature Review from the Web of Science

Henrique Marques, João P. Almeida, Adriana de Fátima Valente Bastos, and Oliva M. D. Martins

Abstract Storytelling is a powerful marketing tool that can be used to attract the audience's attention and influence behavior. However, this investigation seeks to understand more deeply the importance of written narratives in the marketing field. In this sense, the objective of this article is to explore similarities and identify patterns, phases or stages, variables, indicators, and respective relationships (models) to help marketers to create storytelling. In the analogy of the visual methodology analytical process, this literature review created a selection of the sample and developed content to structure storytelling within the marketing framework. Through the analysis of 78 papers published in the Web of Science main collection, this research finds out three clusters: marketing cluster, content cluster, and context cluster. Our results indicate that, in marketing, storytelling elicits brand identification, awareness, and customer engagement, as well as it helps with self-expression, a sense of belonging, and a perception of the value of the product or brand. We find some variables, indicators, and respective relationships (models) that can be used in storytelling in the marketing field to improve value awareness. This review also allowed us to identify factors related to the structuring of marketing storytelling. And we found three key elements of the story construct that are transversal: content, classification, and character.

H. Marques
Instituto Politécnico da Guarda (IPG), Av. Dr. Francisco Sá Carneiro 50, 6300-559 Guarda, Portugal

J. P. Almeida (✉) · O. M. D. Martins
Instituto Politécnico de Bragança (IPB), Campus de Santa Apolónia, 5300-253 Bragança, Portugal
e-mail: jpa@ipb.pt

J. P. Almeida
Research Centre in Digitalization and Intelligent Robotics (CeDRI), IPB, Bragança, Portugal

Laboratório Para a Sustentabilidade E Tecnologia Em Regiões de Montanha (SusTEC), Bragança, Portugal

A. de Fátima Valente Bastos
Instituto Federal de Pernambuco (IFPE), Campus Cabo de Santo Agostinho, 54510-110 Pernambuco, Brasil

N. Martins and D. Raposo (eds.), *Communication Design and Branding*,
Springer Series in Design and Innovation 32,
https://doi.org/10.1007/978-3-031-35385-7_9

Keywords Storytelling · Marketing · Value-Awareness · Behavior

1 Introduction

If on one hand, consumer engagement is stimulated by the narrative nature [1], on the other, building trust, storytelling attracts and holds the audience's attention [2], meaning that marketing already uses this technique to communicate effectively.

In order to connect the story to the reader, Beaufils [3] argued that it is possible to tell a story and get the reader's attention by manipulating experience and immersion in time and space, as well as through the senses (e.g., touch, sight, or smell). Social networks are an example of that. In Instagram, for example, individuals can add a story that is relevant because people are using Instagram as a social media marketing [4] to develop communication with the target audience. Thus, one of the most important objectives of storytelling is to attract and retain people's attention. Because of that, another important observation about storytelling is the power to influence behavioral intentions and generate empathy.

Considering that using features such as narrative esthetics, relevance to readers, and emotions are crucial in marketing applications [5], the main question is: "is there a way to write stories successfully?". Or, in other words, is there a flexible structure (or form) to help marketers create a story?

Indeed, most of the storytelling is subjective, and depends on the object and individuals, as well as the content, or even the competition of the market, for marketing storytelling, which makes it difficult to identify patterns.

Aiming to answer this question, the objective of this article is to explore similarities and identify patterns, phases or stages, variables, indicators, and respective relationships (models) to help marketers to create storytelling.

Considering the relevance of previous works, this research opted to explore this broad field to use variables, indicators, and their relationships (model) for storytelling. Thus, this literature review aims to understand better these two areas of knowledge, the content of storytelling and the marketing field.

The analytical process of the visual methodology used the steps of sample selection, followed by content analysis and semiotic analysis to identify connotative meanings [6], this research created a selection of the sample, developed a content analysis [7] through VOSviewer software [8], and then, exploration and interpretation of the results. The variables were identified to structure storytelling within the marketing framework, to be used.

2 Identifying Topics of Interest

Aiming to understand better, the investigation started with a keyword on the Web of Science platform (https://www.webofscience.com/) [9]. The research began with two keywords: storytelling (topic) and marketing (topic), with no time limit. This search result points out 683 articles. The research interest was centered on these two areas. To refine the search, it was defined that the most appropriate will be articles published in the main collection of the Web of Science, in English and with open access. By applying these filters, 82 articles were selected [10]. Figure 1 shows the association of these articles and their respective most representative themes.

The software identified three clusters, which were interpreted as themes related to marketing, content, and the context in which it would be inserted. The marketing cluster covered the following themes: approach, brand, case study, process, product, social medium, storytelling, and value. Table 1 gives a summary of the clusters.

Storytelling is used in practice in marketing communication [27], and across apps and platforms, brand storytelling can affect consumer-brand relationships [28]. Stories provide no meaningful indication [29]. Concepts are created and, depending on the resources available, the perception of authenticity, the history of the farm, as well as the environment, can be influenced [30].

Behavior-relevant variables such as User experience (UX), brand attitudes, and brand-related behavioral intentions, as well as willingness to pay and empirical

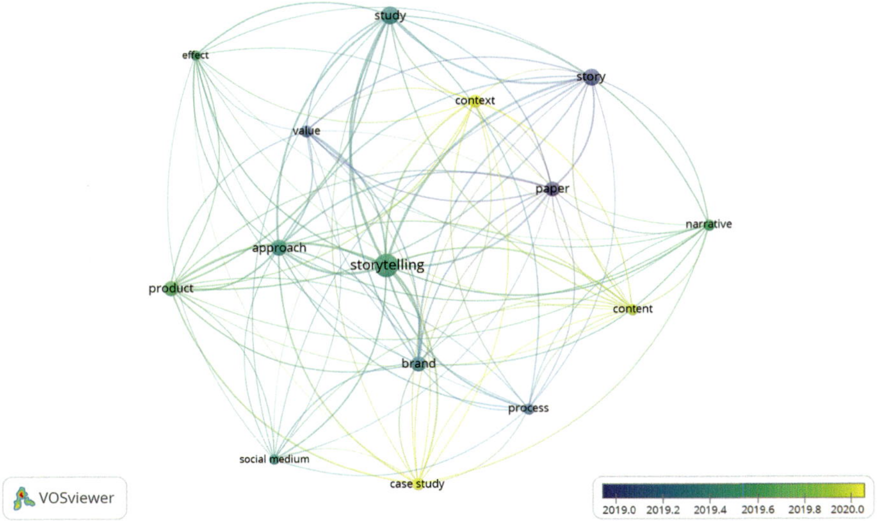

Fig. 1 VOSviewer software clusters analysis of Web of Science data base. *Source* Free version of VOSviewer, version 1.6.18 (created on 22 December 2022) [8]

Table 1 Marketing cluster

Marketing Cluster	Conceptual framework
Approach	E-word of mouth (e-WOM) on social media platforms, strategies of the online community, gift promotion, flagship stores, service from experts, and showbiz marketing can be used to create a meaningful brand experience as well as event marketing, storytelling, and strategies such as free samples and exclusive distribution can be explored to influence consumer perception [11], as well as a "sub-stream of place branding" by approaching a globally relevant socio-cultural phenomenon from a brand storytelling perspective [12]
Brand	Brand Storytelling [13]. Researchers should consider the relevance of emotions [14] as well as explicit and implicit information processing [15] on the development of the brand, which can be developed through stories [11]. Brand value can explore user-generated content [16]. Transferring, dynamically redeploying, and categorizing were considered bran strategies [17]
Case study	Experiential strategy [18] and Game of Thrones reviewers [19]
Process	Immersive experience can be used through technology as a strategy for a virtual shopping or event [11]
Product	Storytelling elicits product story and product demand [20] as well as brand identification, self-expression, a sense of belonging, and a perception of the value of product or brand [21]
Social medium	Influencers are seen as aesthetic and emotional support [22]. Storytelling can be developed through social media marketing [23]
Storytelling	Different story elements encourage emotional, cognitive, and behavioral responses [1]. Storytelling emotionalizes content [15] and reinforce brand image [11]. Rodner et al. [22] suggested creating visual storytelling (visual content and sense-making)
Value	Increasing awareness of the stories' value, for individuals (e.g. psychologically) as well as collectively (in sociology and anthropology research) [24, 25]. Storytelling has been a useful strategy for engagement [26]

Source Our elaboration

evidence on the effects of UX on brand-related measures like online shop attractiveness, were considered relevant by drawing on theories and methods of psychology, marketing, consumer behavior on the brand process [15].

Innovativeness design and product exclusivity can be used as a support to create an impact on experiential marketing [11]. In addition, storytelling is a communication technique that can contribute to the development of brand love [21].

The second cluster was identified as the content cluster. This cluster covered the following themes: content, narrative, paper, and story. Table 2 gives a summary of this cluster.

Finally, the context cluster covered the following themes: context, effect, and study. The following Table 3 gives a summary of the clusters. Table 3 gives a summary of the third cluster.

By analyzing the connections, we found that the themes are interconnected, except for the social medium, which is not connected to either the narrative or the case

Table 2 Cluster of content

Content Cluster	Conceptual framework
Content	Storytelling has an effect that is shaped by brand identity [12, 21]. Content is one element of the story [31] that can be considered central through conversations, listening, and maintaining dialogue, continuously co-creating stories with users [32]
Narrative	The narrative creates value for the product and the brand [21]. Narratives on agriculture, history, and knowledge promote the transference between generations [33]. A myth that is clearly imaginary, can be part of the narrative as well as it is possible to transform the myth into a model of an imaginary-real world [34]
Story	There are three key stages of storytelling: (i) organizational norms and interaction; (ii) the circulation of public relations, marketing, and media messages, and promotion; and (iii) a meaningful consumer experience [35], as well as brand story elements such as story plot, characters, and verisimilitude [1]

Note "Paper" was identified as the fourth keyword. Nevertheless, we considered that there was no sense in the conceptual framework of "paper". Thus, it was associated with content, narrative, or story

Table 3 Cluster of contexts

Context Cluster	Conceptual framework
Context	Traditional stories support the city's branding strategy [36]. The narrative can contribute to raising consumer awareness, differentiate products, and result in symbolic value creation [37]
Effect	Customer loyalty through different meanings [38]. Marketing strategy can promote inclusivity [39]. It is also possible having a cheaper private label [40]
Study	Consumer experiences of people and their narratives and storytelling can explore products and origins [35]. Story plot, characters, and verisimilitude play a different role in activating each dimension of customer engagement [1]

study, which makes us reflect on the convergence of the two dimensions studied. The elements related to the methodological aspects of the selected papers were identified and categorized using a set of criteria explained in the methodology section.

3 Materials and Methods

This literature review aimed to identify common aspects in papers published in the Web of Science platform [9], with no time limit, according to two keywords: "Storytelling" (topic) and "Marketing" (topic) [10]. The search was filtered according to the following assumptions: articles with open access, published in English in the main collection of the Web of Science. The search was conducted on December 13, 2022 [10], which resulted in the initial selection of 82 articles. Before the reading began, the research defined that the final version of the paper would be the only one that mattered. In this sense, articles published in journals were kept, and the others (e.g., conference papers) were eliminated. The exclusion is justified by the fact that only articles published in journals correspond to the final version of the paper. In this case, four more articles were eliminated, leaving 78 to be considered.

With the objective of developing a methodology that would explore similarities and identify patterns, phases or stages, variables, indicators, and respective relationships (models) to help marketers to create storytelling, the research sought to understand the methodology developed in these different studies. The final sample resulted in 78 articles, although there were some that did not fit the focus of interest and, for this reason, were not considered.

These 78 articles were divided by the four researchers to be analyzed, specifically according to the methodology of the investigations on storytelling (topic) that were associated with the scope of marketing (topic).

The methodologies were differentiated into two large dimensions: qualitative and quantitative. An assessment of methodologies defined three types: exploratory qualitative research (E); descriptive (D), and causal (C). Qualitative analysis also identifies literature review (LR). Figure 2 shows the general methodology.

Aiming to analyze the qualitative methodology, the main techniques used in the different articles were grouped into the individual interview (IE), group interview (GI), observation (Obs), visual storytelling method (VS), storytelling workshop (WS), narration storytelling (NS), performance text (PT), and current heterodox analytic narratives (CHAN). The data were analyzed using textual analysis (TA), content analysis (CA), secondary base data analysis (SBDA), images/performances (IP), and content-semiotic analysis (CSA) (Peirce's theory of semiotic analysis). An interpretation of the signal (Mc Kiernan, 2021) [41] may be incomplete. In addition, the location was grouped into national (N) or international (I) studies. Scope and sample were also identified, as well as other aspects that could be considered relevant. Finally, aiming to identify variables, indicators, and their relationships (models), the results were evaluated. Besides, the relevant aspects that don't belong to the initial structure of the frame were also described as notes or observations. Figure 3 shows the qualitative methodology.

The evaluation of quantitative methodology was framed mainly as descriptive (D) or causal (C). Eventually as an exploratory (E). The main techniques used in the different articles were grouped into questionnaires (Q), observations (Obs), and storytelling techniques with parallax scrolling (S). Most of the data were analyzed using statistical techniques such as CB-SEM, PLS-SEM, or ANOVA. In addition, the

Fig. 2 Methodology

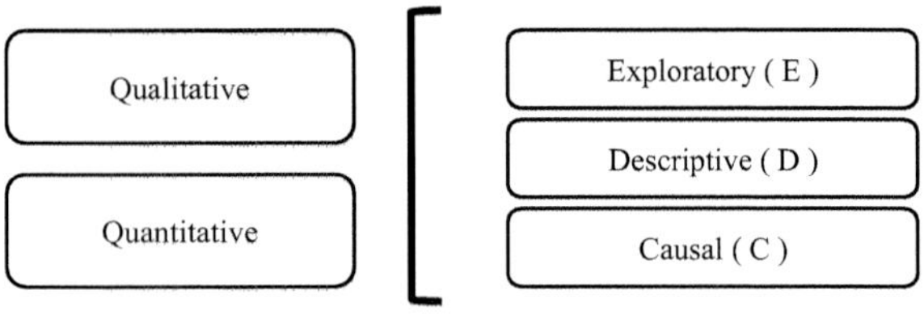

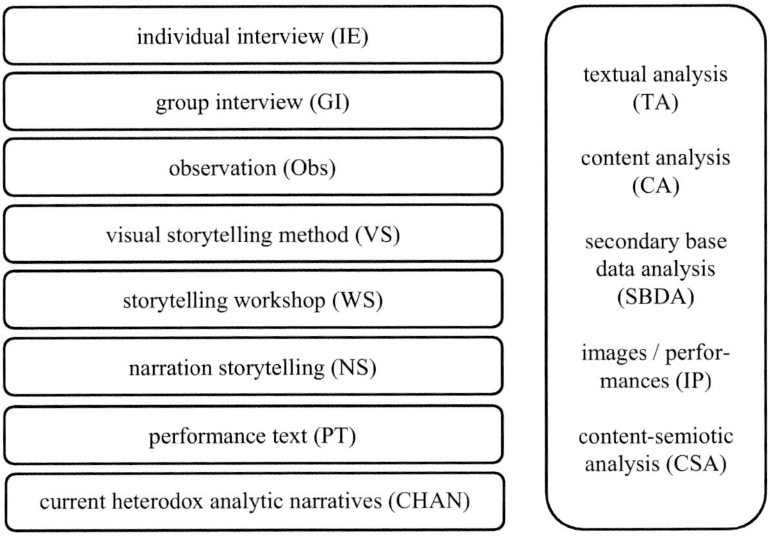

Fig. 3 Qualitative methodology

location was grouped into national (N) or international (I). Scope and sample were also identified, as well as other relevant aspects that could be considered. Finally, aiming to identify variables, indicators, and their relationships (models), the results were evaluated. Besides, the relevant aspects that don't belong to the initial structure of the frame were also described as notes or observations. The models that could be used in marketing, especially by social marketing, to promote healthy behavior, with benefits to individuals as well as the society and environment. This research helps to identify variables, indicators, and relationships that can be used in future studies.

4 Analysis of Methodologies

An assessment of qualitative and quantitative methodologies was developed. However, some studies that limited themselves to mentioning storytelling or provided a superficial and summarized approach to the theme were disregarded. They were disregarded, after the researchers' evaluation.

4.1 Analysis of the Qualitative Methodology

The results point out to 56.41% of exploratory qualitative research (E) 5,13% of descriptive (D), 2.56% of causal (C), and 10.26% of literature review (LR). In addition, 21.79% was considered both, qualitative and quantitative analysis, while 21.79% was not considered as qualitative.

Regarding the techniques, qualitative research found 19.23% of individual interviews (IE), 3.85% of group interviews (GI), 7.69% of observation (Obs), 1.28% of visual storytelling method (VS), 17.95% of narration (N) or performance text (PT), and 5.13% of literature review (LR). In addition, 19.23% was considered as a mix of methods, while 25.64% wasn't evaluated.

In addition, 28.21% of the data analysis used textual analysis (TA), while others 29.49% have chosen to use content analysis (CA), 2,56% decided to analyze images/performances (IP) and 14.10% were considered as a mix of methods. Finally, 25.64% wasn't evaluated.

In relation to "location", 38.46% of the studies were centered on the same country (national (N)) while other 35.90% were not limited to the border (international (I)) and other 25.64% has not been well defined in the paper.

4.2 Analysis of the Quantitative Methodology

The evaluation of quantitative methodology was framed mainly as descriptive (D) or causal (C). However, it is noteworthy that only 7 articles used quantitative methodology (8.97%). Eventually, 2,56% of the article was exploratory (E). The results also point out 3.85% of descriptive qualitative research, compared to 2,56% of causal (C).

The main techniques used in the different articles. The review found that 3.85% of the articles were grouped into questionnaires (Q), 1.28% of the articles were grouped into storytelling technique with parallax scrolling (S) as well as other 2,56% of the articles were grouped into secondary data and 1.28% of the articles were grouped into meta-analysis.

Regarding the data analysis, most of the data were analyzed using statistical techniques such as Structural Equation Modeling. The review identified that 2.56% of the articles used PLS-SEM, 1.28% of the articles used ANOVA, 1.28% of the articles used correlations, or logistic multilevel models, 2.56% of the articles used descriptive statistics, and 1.28% wasn't identified.

In relation to "location", 7.69% of the studies were not limited to the border (international (I). In addition, this research aims to identify variables, indicators, and their relationships (models).

5 Variables, Indicators, and Respective Relationships (Models)

There are models that are used in marketing to attract and retain consumer attention. However, there are three key elements of the story construct that are transversal and should be presented for the first time: content, classification, and character [31].

According to Dias and Cavalheiro [21], in 2008, Woodside, Stood and Miller justified the storytelling through five arguments: (1) we naturally think through narratives; (2) the stories can reinforce memorization; as well as (3) can afford delightful experiences; (4) the products and the brands can appeal to psychological prototypes, to create a strong consumer identification; and (5) stories provide clarity. The story also can use elements such as felt specialness and past identity salience [20].

Storytelling is a method [17] of telling people's experiences that are not often told [42]. Storytelling can also use animated stories, presentations, storyboards, video stories, cartoons, radio series (like podcasts), and mobile games [43].

Moreover, storytelling is a strategy [44] and a methodological approach through the lived experience of our sociocultural engagement through five stages of a Quest Plot Story, according to Booker, in 2015: the call (initial state), the journey (the hero and companions set out by hostile situations (trials, monsters, temptations, etc.), the arrival and frustration (which have to be overcome), the final ordeal (the hero must prove that he is truly worthy of the prize), the goal described as the last exciting escape from death [13]. Nevertheless, storytelling is also just one of the elements that can be simple, unexpected, consistent, and emotional [45].

Product narratives can be considered as a new level of product extension, creating an identity that drives customers to take ownership of products for their own self-expression, increasing engagement and loyalty [46]. In this type of product narrative, we find the story of the company [37], the brand [39], describing places [36], and so on.

The collective narrative in video sharing identifies the importance of the interdisciplinary experience [47]. Through short videos [45], as well as quality, label, traceability trust, and willingness to pay, storytelling shapes consumers' quality and trust perceptions [48]. Linguistic practices, such as storytelling, can improve legitimacy [49], and add evidence of authenticity and familiarity to reinforce the overall consumer experience [50]. And scents with music can be explored in perfect harmony [51]. Cultural and social issues make up half of the story to understand places, origins, and traditions [33].

In addition, storytelling allows us to develop digital literacy, analytical skills, and creativity, as well as teach how to collaborate, help to delegate tasks, and hold shared project responsibility [43].

A contribution that emerged from journalistic storytelling explains that we can be through exploring key players, mapping alliances, or revealing hidden ties, as well as if there are associations around actors and the evolution of these associations over time [52]. According to the authors, forms of storytelling can also explore the interaction between modes such as static, dynamic, or animated diagrams, as well as language, layout, photograph, or pictogram.

Brand stories establish strong relationships with consumers [53]. Thus, a deep understanding of the core values is necessary to increase engagement [1]. In addition, emotions are critical to storytelling advertising, and it has a substantial impact on attitudes, and decision-making behaviors [54]. Collaborative storytelling can be told through different storytellers on social networks [32].

One important piece of information (i.e., the past identity or biographical history of the product) is enough to trigger the perception of the customer, which means that products with histories cause greater demand because they imbue customers with a sense of specialness [20].

Storytelling can also explore Personification (Life), Questing (Location) Phraseology (Language) regarding consumer behavior, allegorically [55], as well as be built on the experiential approach, rise of mobile social media, user-generated content, and gamification [24]. And hybrid structures in strategic communication in general and more specifically in public relations (PR) assume an innovation function in systems and facilitate learning [56].

The campaign aims to identify an emotional response, as well as generate action or behavior [1]. According to the authors, from a managerial perspective, the findings showed how particular branded story elements, properly orchestrated, may stimulate cognitive, emotional, and behavioral engagement.

Finally, experiential strategy framework could be developed through interconnected elements such as framework structure, imagining (e.g., theatre and dramaturgy), imparting (e.g., (hi)storytelling) interpreting (e.g., performances and roles), interacting (e.g., co-creating), initiating (e.g., impromptu encounters), improvising (e.g., adapting); identity (e.g., authenticity and transformation) [18]. Working through the rich details of ethnographic stories helps to reach a deep understanding of market realities [57]. And marketers should help customers by highlighting the products' identities [20].

This study provides insights for researchers and marketers. These insights can help professionals to evoke a good experience, as well as to understand how these factors can be used in the engagement of the customer.

6 Final Considerations

We naturally think through narratives and stories can reinforce memorization as well as delightful experiences. Besides, products and brands can appeal to psychological prototypes, to create a strong consumer identification, which can be provided through stories.

Storytelling elicits brand identification, awareness, and customer engagement, as well as helps with self-expression, a sense of belonging, and a perception of the value of the product or brand. Product narrative is a concept that adds value to the product, as well as to the brand. In other words, storytelling as a communication technique contributes to the development of brand love.

In the construction of branding, storytelling can use emotions and images, as well as innovativeness design and product exclusivity, to create an impact. Another alternative is an immersive experience. Through technology (e.g., implementing strategies such as virtual shopping or event) and social media, marketing can create and build an emotional bond of loyalty and trust. In addition, marketing can explore e-word of mouth (e-WOM) on social media platforms.

Digital marketing strategies could be based on factors of influence such as experience, environmental context, quality, and other factors, and explore lifestyle or cultural aspects. And influencers could be seen as aesthetic and emotional support to provide a real-world with tangible solutions.

Regarding storytelling, there are three good types of stories: 'despair', 'comedy', and 'courage', and five categories to be used: a novel, hedonic, authentic, prestigious, and sophisticated. Besides, linguistic practices, such as storytelling, can improve legitimacy.

Storytelling evokes images of those on the sidelines telling stories. Humor and the way people gather online in communities should be highlighted. In addition, the low cost could be considered a great benefit. For future investigations, this review suggested to explore how incorporating new technologies such as virtual reality and artificial intelligence can affect storytelling and marketing; and how data storytelling can be applied in marketing strategies to convey information in a clear and engaging way and increase engagement and loyalty of the target audience.

6.1 Theoretical Implications

Storytelling is very powerful and helpful in attracting and retaining attention. However, it can be used for different purposes. For example, in the marketing field, storytelling can be used to create relationships, preferably long-term ones, as well as other ways to add value to a product or brand, such as promoting co-creation and stakeholder engagement.

With the rise of digital and the growing availability of large amounts of data, new and innovative ways to communicate effectively to large audiences are needed. For this to happen, it may be necessary to reinvent the way in which narratives can be used with the huge amount of information that is currently available to brands or marketing companies. Developing an attractive narrative from a large amount of data will certainly pose many challenges soon for both Marketing and Storytelling.

In this research, the data storytelling was dispersed. No significant data storytelling applied to the marketing area came up, which means that beyond specific particularities, we can find great challenges. This may represent an excellent opportunity for future research.

Based on this literature review, we see that there are different ways to tell a story. Nevertheless, to structure a narrative, marketing should define phases, as well as the main variables, indicators, and respective relationships (or models) to be used in the Marketing field.

6.2 Practical Implications

This review allowed us to identify factors related to the structuring of the storytelling tool, variables, indicators, and their respective relationships (models), as well as the main phases and stages required to use this tool in the marketing environment.

Through humor and ambiguity (highlighting how people gather online in communities and put forward low-cost remittance as a great benefit), storytelling evokes images of those on the margins telling stories. Social marketing also can explore this tool to promote good behaviors.

In marketing, more specifically in advertising, storytelling can also encourage more engagement between advertisers and the public, for the story and not just for the product. Storytelling in the marketing field can be used to improve value awareness. Our results indicate that storytelling elicits brand identification, awareness, and customer engagement, as well as it helps with self-expression, a sense of belonging, and a perception of the value of the product or brand.

This review also identified three key elements of the story construct that are transversal: content, classification, and character. Applying storytelling concepts on the communication processes can really make a difference in how the public sees the brand and/or the business.

Furthermore, in an era where capturing people's interest is increasingly difficult and traditional sales promotion actions no longer have the same impact, storytelling can, using various techniques (e.g., soundscapes, conversations, angles, and influencers), help to introduce differentiation and compose a narrative that shows a product in a positive way. It is suggested that this allows for better results in attracting and fixing a brand in people's memory.

Therefore, for brands, getting stories generated directly by the public and involving public relations professionals in storytelling construction can be a strength. They can teach the public about the products and use digital realities such as virtual reality or influencers for this.

Acknowledgements This work received funding from the Fundação para a Ciência e Tecnologia (FCT, Portugal) and from national funds FCT/MCTES (PIDDAC) through financial support to CeDRI (UIDB/05757/2020 and UIDP/05757/2020) and SusTEC (LA / P/0007/2021), as well as from the European Social Fund through the Center Regional Operational Program (CENTRO-04-3559-FSE-000162) through financial support to Instituto Politécnico da Guarda (IPG). This research also would like to thank Instituto Politécnico de Bragança (IPB), Portugal, and as Instituto Federal de Pernambuco (IFPE), Brasil.

References

1. Dessart L, Pitardi V (2019) How stories generate consumer engagement: An exploratory study. J Bus Res 104:183–195. https://doi.org/10.1016/j.jbusres.2019.06.045
2. Rufner, S. Using Narratives and Storytelling to Communicate Science with Nonexpert Audiences. Writing and the Sciences: An Anthology (2020).
3. Beaufils, C. Contemporary Text Experiences and Storytelling. InMedia. The French Journal of Media Studies, (8.1.) (2020).
4. Fatanti MN, Suyadnya IW (2015) Beyond user gaze: How Instagram creates tourism destination brand? Procedia Soc Behav Sci 211:1089–1095
5. Akgün AE, Keskin H, Ayar H, Erdoğan E (2015) The influence of storytelling approach in travel writings on readers' empathy and travel intentions. Procedia Soc Behav Sci 207:577–586
6. Chandra Y, Shang L (2017) An RQDA-based constructivist methodology for qualitative research. J Cetacean Res Manag 20(1):90–112
7. Van Eck, N. J., Waltman, L. Visualizing bibliometric networks. In Y. Ding, R. Rousseau, & D. Wolfram (Eds.), Measuring scholarly impact: Methods and practice (pp. 285–320). Springer (2014).
8. VOSviewer Software, version 1.6.18; Constructing and Visualising Bibliometric Networks; Leiden University: Leiden, The Netherlands, 2022.
9. Clarivate. Available online: https://www.webofscience.com/wos/history (accessed on 06 December 2022).
10. Web of Science, Citation Report Marketing (Topic) and Storytelling (Topic) in on 22 December 2022. Retrieved from https://www.webofscience.com/
11. Rivera-Toapanta, E., Kallas, Z., Čandek-Potokar, M., Gonzalez, J., Gil, M., Varela, E., ... Gil, J. M. Marketing strategies to self-sustainability of autochthonous swine breeds from different EU regions: a mixed approach using the World Café technique and the Analytical Hierarchy Process. Renewable Agriculture and Food Systems, 37(1), 92–102 (2022).
12. Rossolatos G (2020) A brand storytelling approach to Covid-19's terrorealization: Cartographing the narrative space of a global pandemic. J Destin Mark Manag 18:100484
13. Glover C (2018) Rapha and its embedded storytelling. Journal of Fashion Marketing and Management: An International Journal 22(1):17–34. https://doi.org/10.1108/JFMM-12-2016-0110
14. CL, C., Elicher, M. J. Literary Cinematic Tourism: New clues of the Brazilian Literature influences on Film Tourism development in Brazil (2022).
15. Karampournioti, E., Wiedmann, K. P. Storytelling in online shops: the impacts on explicit and implicit user experience, brand perceptions and behavioral intention. Internet Research (2021).
16. , N. F., Scarles, C., Cohen, S. A. The brand value continuum: Countering co-destruction of destination branding in social media through storytelling. Journal of Travel Research, 59(8), 1506–1521 (2020).
17. Liu Y, Öberg C, Tarba SY, Xing Y (2018) Brand management in mergers and acquisitions: Emerging market multinationals venturing into advanced economies. Int Mark Rev 35(5):710–732. https://doi.org/10.1108/IMR-01-2017-0011
18. Lund NF, Holst-Beck P, Pine BJ II, Leask A (2022) Hamlet Live: the 7 I's Experiential Strategy Framework for heritage visitor attractions. J Herit Tour 17(2):125–141
19. Irimiás A, Mitev AZ, Michalkó G (2021) Narrative transportation and travel: The mediating role of escapism and immersion. Tourism management perspectives 38:100793
20. Kamleitner B, Thürridl C, Martin BAS (2019) A Cinderella Story: How Past Identity Salience Boosts Demand for Repurposed Products. J Mark 83(6):76–92. https://doi.org/10.1177/0022242919872156
21. Dias P, Cavalheiro R (2022) The role of storytelling in the creation of brand love: the PANDORA case. J Brand Manag 29(1):58–71
22. Rodner, V., Goode, A., Burns, Z. Is it all just lip service?: on Instagram and the lobalization of the cosmetic servicescape. Journal of Services Marketing (2021).

23. Michael N, Fusté-Forné F (2022) Marketing of luxurious gastronomic experiences on social media: The visual storytelling of luxury hotels. Int J Tour Res 24(6):827–838
24. Moscardo G (2020) The story turn in tourism: forces and futures. Journal of Tourism Futures 7(2):168–173
25. Moscardo G (2020) Stories and design in tourism. Ann Tour Res 83:102950
26. Frost W, Frost J, Strickland P, Maguire JS (2020) Seeking a competitive advantage in wine tourism: Heritage and storytelling at the cellar-door. Int J Hosp Manag 87:102460
27. Grębosz-Krawczyk, M. Consumer storytelling as an element of word-of-mouth communication of nostalgic brands: Evidence from Poland. Innov. Mark, 16, 74-84 (2020).
28. Boukis, A. Exploring the implications of blockchain technology for brand–consumer relationships: a future research agenda. Journal of Product & Brand Management (2019).
29. Chen A, Eriksson G (2019) The making of healthy and moral snacks: A multimodal critical discourse analysis of corporate storytelling. Discourse, Context & Media 32:100347
30. Mei XY, Hågensen AMS, Kristiansen HS (2020) Storytelling through experience scape: Creating unique stories and extraordinary experiences in farm tourism. Tour Hosp Res 20(1):93–104
31. Mitchell SL, Clark M (2021) Telling a different story: How nonprofit organizations reveal strategic purpose through storytelling. Psychol Mark 38(1):142–158
32. Lund NF, Cohen SA, Scarles C (2018) The power of social media storytelling in destination branding. J Destin Mark Manag 8:271–280. https://doi.org/10.1016/j.jdmm.2017.05.003
33. Castelló E (2020) Storytelling in applications for the EU quality schemes for agricultural products and foodstuffs: place, origin and tradition. Span J Agric Res 18(2):e0105–e0105
34. Palo T, Mason K, Roscoe P (2020) Performing a myth to make a market: The construction of the 'magical world'of Santa. Organ Stud 41(1):53–75
35. Castelló E (2021) The will for terroir: A communicative approach. J Rural Stud 86:386–397
36. Camprubí R, Planas C (2020) Storytelling in tourism destination branding: the case of lobal. Cuadernos de Turismo 46:617–619
37. Rinallo, D., Pitardi, V. Open conflict as differentiation strategy in geographical indications: the Bitto Rebels case. British Food Journal (2019).
38. Närvänen E, Kuusela H, Paavola H, Sirola N (2020) A meaning-based framework for customer loyalty. International Journal of Retail & Distribution Management 48(8):825–843
39. Brusk J, Engström H (2021) Marvinter: A case study of an inclusive transmedia storytelling production. Convergence 27(1):103–123
40. Krampe C, Fridman A (2022) Oatly, a serious 'problem'for the dairy industry? A case study. International Food and Agribusiness Management Review 25(1):157–171
41. Mc Kiernan DK (2021) Formal qualitative probability. The Review of Symbolic Logic 14(4):882–909
42. Joseph E (2019) Discrimination against credentials in Black bodies: Counter stories of the characteristic labour market experiences of migrants in Ireland. Br J Guid Couns 47(4):524–542. https://doi.org/10.1080/03069885.2019.1620916
43. Semenchenko, T. O. Peculiarities of foreign language teaching to future specialists of financial and credit field in circumstances of eurointegration and lobalization. Financial and Credit Activity Problems of Theory and Practice, 3(26), 510–515 (2018). https://doi.org/10.18371/fcaptp.v3i26.143870
44. Ingenbleek, P. T. M., Zhao, Y. The Vegetarian Butcher: On its way to becoming the world's biggest 'meat' producer? International Food and Agribusiness Management Review, 22(2), 295–307 (2019). https://doi.org/10.22434/IFAMR2018.0051
45. Finkler, W., Leon, B. The power of storytelling and video: A visual rhetoric for science communication. Journal of Science Communication, 18(5), A02 (2019). https://doi.org/10.22323/2.18050202
46. Dias, L., Dias, P. Beyond Advertising Narratives: "Josefinas" and their storytelling products. Anàlisi, 47–62 (2018). https://doi.org/10.5565/rev/analisi.3118
47. Gordon R, Waitt G, Cooper P, Butler K (2018) Storying energy consumption: Collective video storytelling in energy efficiency social marketing. J Environ Manage 213:1–10. https://doi.org/10.1016/j.jenvman.2018.02.046

48. Cao S, Foth M, Powell W, McQueenie J (2021) What are the effects of short video storytelling in delivering blockchain-credentialed Australian beef products to China? Foods 10(10):2403
49. Kašperová E (2021) Impairment (in) visibility and stigma: how disabled entrepreneurs gain legitimacy in mainstream and disability markets. Entrep Reg Dev 33(9–10):894–919
50. Ikäheimo JP (2021) Arctic narratives: brewing a brand with neolocalism. J Brand Manag 28(4):374–387
51. Spence C (2021) Musical scents: On the surprising absence of scented musical/auditory events, entertainments, and experiences. I-Perception 12(5):20416695211038748
52. Bounegru, L., Venturini, T., Gray, J., Jacomy, M. Narrating networks: Exploring the affordances of networks as storytelling devices in journalism. Digital Journalism, 5(6), 699–730. (2017). [43].
53. Sanders, J., van Krieken, K. Exploring Narrative Structure and Hero Enactment in Brand Stories. Frontiers in Psychology, 9 (2018). https://www.frontiersin.org/articles/https://doi.org/10.3389/fpsyg.2018.01645
54. Zhang W, Fesenmaier DR (2018) Assessing emotions in online stories: Comparing self-report and text-based approaches. Information Technology & Tourism 20(1):83–95. https://doi.org/10.1007/s40558-018-0122-y
55. Brown S, Stevens L, Maclaran P (2022) What's the story, allegory? Consum Mark Cult 25(1):34–51
56. Hoffjann O (2021) The innovation function of hybridization in public relations. Media Commun 9(3):155–163
57. Cayla J, Arnould E (2013) Ethnographic stories for market learning. J Mark 77(4):1–16

Applying Eye Tracking Technique to Evaluate Poster Design: A Study on World Peace Poster

Bhaskar Mishra and Anirban Chowdhury

Abstract In recent years, the world has been confronted with a myriad of difficulties as a result of the pandemic and the war conflicts that have broken out between countries. In this scenario, it is important to focus on world peace because world peace might influence the growth and prosperity of the entire global community. On the other hand, eye tracking is a relatively new technique for the study of visual attention and perception in poster design. This research work examines the effectiveness of design elements in world peace poster design using an eye tracking technique used for the measurement of attention, attractiveness, and understanding of the messages conveyed using posters. We designed three novel posters on the theme of world peace (using Photoshop and Illustrator), and the eye tracking was conducted using the GazeRecorder software and a questionnaire survey with 20 participants (age ranged from 23–43 years, 47.4% male, 52.6% female) was conducted to understand the users' reactions to the designed posters. Eye movements are used to provide a comparatively novel source of data about visual attention and evaluation of design elements. Creative poster designs that are eye-catching, have a brief message, and can be understood at a glance are more effective in the context of world peace message communication. The study highlights the use of eye tracking as an active area of research that is being applied to the study of world peace poster design. It was observed that poster 2 (P2) was more attractive as the design was significantly more original, aesthetically pleasing, and communicative to the target audience for the promotion of a world peace-related message. The study reports on people's perceptions of poster design, particularly different design elements, and their effectiveness, as well as people's attention to certain messages or information on design posters, which transmit the message and cause them to think in a certain way.

B. Mishra
University of Petroleum and Energy Studies (UPES), Dehradun, India

A. Chowdhury (✉)
Symbiosis Institute of Design (SID), Symbiosis International (Deemed University), Pune, Maharashtra, India
e-mail: chowdhuryanirban14@gmail.com

N. Martins and D. Raposo (eds.), *Communication Design and Branding*,
Springer Series in Design and Innovation 32,
https://doi.org/10.1007/978-3-031-35385-7_10

Keywords Attention · Cognition · Eye tracking · GazeRecorder · Poster design · World peace

1 Introduction

In recent years, the world has faced several challenges due to the pandemic and the wars that have erupted between countries. The coronavirus pandemic has spread throughout the world, affecting many countries. In December 2019, the virus was discovered and reported in Wuhan, China [1]. Because of this, all countries' governments take action to combat the pandemic and establish rules and regulations, such as a lockdown for a period of time and people staying at home, wearing masks, and keeping a safe distance from one another [2]. Furthermore, there have been human casualties, as well as a global financial crisis [3]. Political tensions between major countries are also rising as a result of the pandemic [4]. The crisis between Russia and Ukraine is also currently involving the rest of the world. The outcome is that the world is dealing with many difficulties. In this scenario, it is important to focus on world peace because world peace might influence the growth and prosperity of the entire global community. The concept of world peace refers to a world free of violence. Peace is a basic requirement for humans and human societies.

Is there any new and interesting way to take more steps toward peace in these difficult times? The poster could be the answer. Before proceeding, it is important to understand what a poster is. A poster is an abstract [5]. It is used to promote the media. It is a single sheet with one face printed in two dimensions [6]. It is also used to communicate information, data, schedules, and offers to the public. Posters include text, graphics, and colour as elements. Posters that succeed in capturing the attention of the audience usually have one dominant and interesting element [7]. Graphics are the most important aspect of poster design. Photographs, designs, and patterns are examples of graphics. The text is the second element. The text contains both the main text and the complement text. The poster's main text is the title. The title should be short and simple [6]. Subtitles or taglines can be used as text complements for posters. Color is an element that should not be overlooked in posters. The use of contrasting colours in typography, designs, and so on is intended to increase the poster's appeal. The purpose of the world peace poster is to promote peace messages. All of the elements work together to support the peace message, causing the target audience to think in a specific way. On the other hand, eye tracking techniques have emerged as a potential way to record individual eye movements and assess visual attention in a number of study areas [9]. It is a relatively new technique for the study of visual attention and perception in poster design. The eye-tracking variables fixation duration and fixation count are more useful for determining visual attention [8].

This research work examines the effectiveness of design elements in world peace poster design using an eye tracking technique used for the measurement of attention, attractiveness, and understanding of the messages conveyed using posters.

2 Literature Survey

Eye movements and fixations were tracked using an eye tracker. A minimum gaze duration of 300 ms reliably indicates interest as a fixation [9]. Frequently, fixation patterns are analysed using heat maps, which depict the length of time participants fixated on each area. Heat maps analyse fixation trends using data from multiple participants [10]. The colour coding system used in heat maps is simple and easy to read. Fixations occurred in the coloured areas; longer fixations in red indicate longer times spent there, while shorter fixations in green and yellow indicate decreasing times spent there. The areas that have no colour are the ones that did not have any fixations performed on them [11–14]. Fixation data can also be used to visualize information for targeted areas. Fixation duration, frequency, timing, and percentage of viewers reveal targeted viewing behaviour. A subject\stimulus is divided into regions in order to generate a map of fixation information for specific areas. These regions are referred to as areas of interest (AOIs), and they can be created in a variety of ways. AOIs in the gaze recorder indicate dwell time, first view, and viewed by. The amount of time respondents spent looking at a specific AOI is referred to as dwell time. The Time to First Fixation (TTFF) indicates how long it takes a respondent (or all respondents on average) to look at a specific AOI after the stimulus is presented [13].

Eye tracking techniques have been used in an increasing number of research studies in recent years, such as interaction design, packaging design, advertising, user experience, media, and so on [15]. It can be used to study selective exposure in all types of media. One of them is the analysis of political posters and advertisements from various parties to determine which elements are highlighted. People also spend more time on political advertisements that reflect their own political beliefs [16]. It is also used in hospitality research to investigate customers' visual attention on the frontage of street vendor stores, restaurant banners, menu labelling, and so on. In this study, performance parameters included (a) average fixation duration, (b) fixation counts, and (c) revisit counts for the area of interest [17]. Another study employs eye tracking to track and analyse the poster for the well-known Korean beverage Jinro Soju. The outcome demonstrates that the advertising model's face received more visual attention than her body. Furthermore, the advertisement image takes precedence over text elements [18]. In addition, the celebrity of the endorser had a significant impact on attention to ad elements [19]. Another research study emphasises the use of eye movement monitoring devices in the education/teaching of students. Students use heat maps and analytics to adapt the viewers' thinking process and learn which element dominates the viewer's choice [20]. An intriguing study in which depressive symptoms are linked to an attentional bias toward socio-emotionally charged memes rather than neutral memes. As a result, there are more fixations with depressive memes than with neutral memes [21].

3 Methodology

This experiment was designed to evaluate the effectiveness of design elements in world peace poster design using an eye tracking technique used for measurement of attention, attractiveness, and understanding of the messages conveyed using posters. Using Photoshop and Illustrator, we designed three novel posters (see Fig. 1) on the theme of world peace for the study. Twenty randomly selected male and female research scholars from a variety of disciplines from the anonymous university at Dehradun, India, volunteered for this experiment. Their ages ranged from 25 to 40. The research scholar's vision was either normal or corrected. The eye tracking was conducted using the GazeRecorder software. Before starting the experiment, participants were asked to sit in front of the system. The distance between the system and the participant was approximately 18 inches. Then click the experiment launch button and begin tracing your eyes. Gaze calibration is the initial stage in eye tracing. So, check a few conditions before beginning the gaze calibration. Your face is visible, your room is well-lit, there isn't a bright source behind you, and there aren't any light refractions on your glasses. Following the calibration process, three posters with the theme of world peace are displayed on the system for 5 s each.

Also, participants in the eye-tracking experiment were asked to complete a basic questionnaire based on a seven-point Likert scale about the three posters with the theme of world peace, including if they were original (indicates that the idea has never been presented or considered before), innovative (consists of coming up with new ideas or things.), aesthetically pleasing (includes color balance, visual balance, graphics, font, size), and whether they effectively conveyed the message. Based on the GazeRecorder software's heat map (Fig. 2) and analytics (dwell time-time viewed, time to first fixation-time to first view at areas of interest, as presented in Fig. 3) the eye tracking data were analysed. In addition, the data is further statistically

Fig. 1 The three novel posters on the theme of world peace were designed using Photoshop and Illustrator

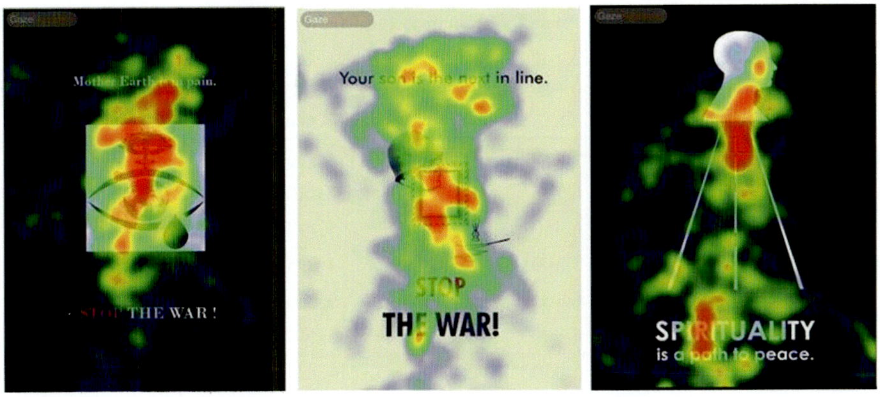

Fig. 2 Depicts three novel posters on the subject of world peace, along with aggregated heat maps from the GazeRecorder

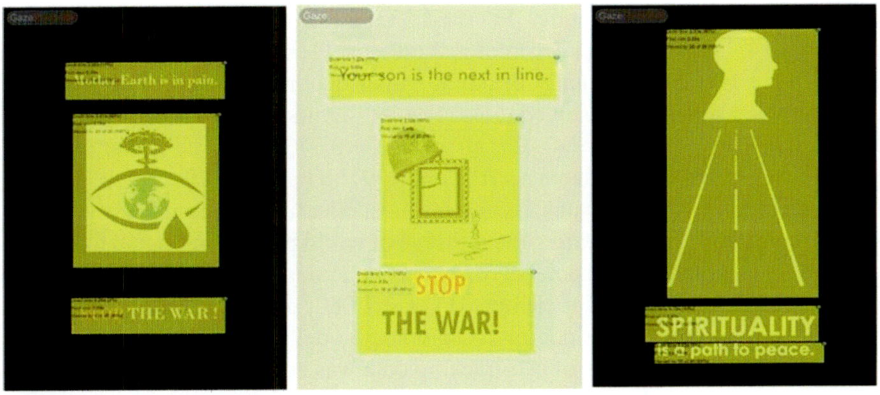

Fig. 3 Depicts three novel posters on the theme of world peace with analytics (dwell time-time viewed, time of first fixation-time to first view) in the GazeRecorder

analysed using SPSS 20.0 software, and the eye tracking data was compared with the questionnaire results.

4 Results and Discussion

From the questionnaire-based user responses, it was observed that Poster 2 is better in terms of Originality, Innovativeness, and Aesthetic Pleasantness Perception as mean values on the seven-point scale were higher for these aforesaid parameters. On the other side, participants perceived Poster 1 as the least original, innovative, and aesthetically pleasing. Please see Table 1 for the detailed results. All the mean

Table 1 Poster wise mean variations of Originality, Innovativeness, and Aesthetic Pleasantness Perception

Measure	Poster	Mean	Std. error	95% confidence interval	
				Lower bound	Upper bound
Originality	1	5.750	0.403	4.906	6.594
	2	6.700	0.105	6.480	6.920
	3	6.350	0.264	5.797	6.903
Innovativeness	1	5.500	0.432	4.595	6.405
	2	6.400	0.134	6.120	6.680
	3	5.800	0.268	5.240	6.360
Aesthetic	1	5.050	0.413	4.185	5.915
	2	6.000	0.290	5.393	6.607
	3	5.600	0.373	4.820	6.380

variations for perceive Originality [$F(1) = 4.333$; $p < 0.05$], perceive Innovativeness [$F(1) = 8.143$; $p < 0.01$], and perceive Aesthetic Pleasantness [$F(1) = 5.651$; $p < 0.05$] were found significantly different as per quadratic model. The univariate analysis (when sphericity assumed) also revealed significant differences in perceive Originality [$F(1) = 3.978$; $p = 0.027$; effect size = 0.173; observed power = 0.678] and perceive Aesthetic Pleasantness [$F(1) = 3.397$; $p = 0.044$; effect size = 0.152; observed power = 0.605]. Poster 2 is also the most effective and significantly [$F(1) = 9.531$; $p = 0.006$] communicating the message of world peace. Among all the design elements (text, graphics, and colour) of the poster, audiences perceived colour as the most important and significant element [$F(1) = 7.080$; $p = 0.015$], when observing the results of within-subjects contrast (Quadratic model of estimate).

When qualitative analysis of eye-tracking data was done through heat-map analysis, it was observed that participants fixated on most of the areas (graphics, text, complement text) for poster 2. This suggests that the clearer visual hierarchy of poster 2 retained more impact in attracting participants' attention. These kinds of results indicate that poster 2 is more attractive. Poster 3 received a more scattered viewing pattern meaning a scattered fixation pattern. This is particularly because poster 3 receives little attention from participants. Poster 1 has a more intense fixation on the graphics, as evidenced by a strong shade of red, but the complementary text is green. Therefore, some areas of Poster 1 receive little attention from participants (see Fig. 2).

All three posters have separate AOIs for their graphics, text, and complementary text areas. The yellow shaded area represents the AOIs area, with dwell time in seconds, dwell time percentage, the first view in seconds, and viewed in numbers. It was observed that the first AOIs for poster 1 are graphics, with a dwell time of 3.07 s and a dwell time percentage of 62%, the first view being 0.35 s, and 20 of 20 participants viewing it. The text then has a dwell time of 0.92 s and a dwell percentage of 11%, a first view time of 0.79 s, and is viewed by 12 of 20 participants. The dwell

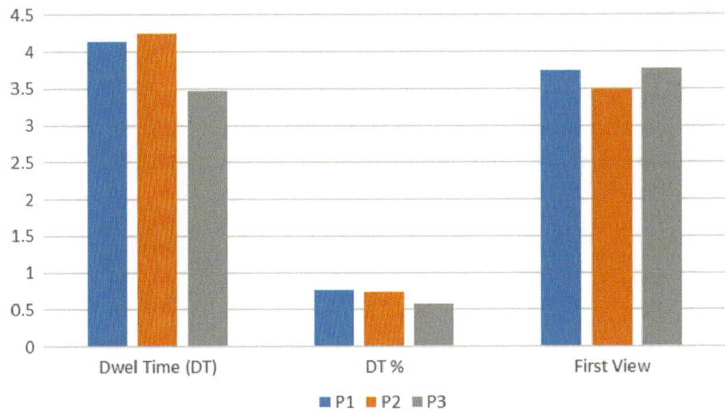

Fig. 4 Poster-wise overall eye-tracking parameters dwell time (DT), DT %, and first view time variations

time for the complement text is 0.24 s and a dwell percentage of 2%, the first view is 2.68 s, and 9 of 20 participants view it. The first AOI for poster 2 is graphics, with a dwell time of 2.32 s and a dwell percentage of 45%, the first view being 0.44 s, and 19 of 20 participants viewing it. The text then has a dwell time of 1.22 s and a dwell percentage of 17%, the first view is 0.85 s, and 14 of 20 participants view it. The dwell time for the complement text is 0.71 s and the dwell percentage of 12%, the first view is 2.2 s, and 16 of 20 participants view it. For poster 3, the first AOI is graphics, with a dwell time of 2.93 s and a dwell percentage of 60%, the first view being 0.08 s, and 20 participants viewing it. The text then has a dwell time of 0.72 s and a dwell percentage of 10%, the first view is 1.53 s, and 14 of 20 participants view it. The dwell time for the complement text is 0.52 s and a dwell percentage of 5%, the first view is 2.04 s, and 10 of 20 participants view it (see Fig. 3).

From the eye-tracking area of interest study, it is revealed that there are poster-wise variations of dwell time, dwell time percentage, and first view time. Overall dwell time (in seconds) and dwell-time percentage were higher for poster two (P2) and the first view (in seconds) was lower for poster two (P2). These results indicate that poster two (P2) was more attractive (Figs. 3 and 4).

5 Conclusion

When we compared the eye-tracking results with the questionnaire-based responses, it proved that poster 2 (P2) was more attractive as the design was significantly more original, aesthetically pleasing, and communicative to the target audience for the promotion of a world peace related message. Therefore, poster two (P2) is communicating the message effectively and can be recommended as an initial material for the promotion of world peace. Furthermore, their distribution would have to be global with extensive reach and the role of social media is significant. In addition, the approach taken in this study can also be applicable for poster design evaluation in near future. There is a limitation to this study; it is possible to achieve some interesting results if a better composition of poster samples is used with the same methodology as used in the study or as used in an eyetracking study by Chowdhury et al. 2013 and 2018 [22, 23].

References

1. Lone SA, Ahmad A (2020) COVID-19 pandemic–an African perspective. Emerg Microbes Infect 9(1):1300–1308
2. Pokhrel S, Chhetri R (2021) A literature review on impact of COVID-19 pandemic on teaching and learning. High Educ Futur 8(1):133–141
3. Syropoulos S, Puschett E, Leidner B (2021) Positive and negative peace as predictors of pandemic preparedness: evidence from a micro-and macro-level investigation during the onset of the COVID-19 pandemic. Polit Psychol 42(5):729–745
4. Tanabe J (2020) Exploring a post-covid-19 sustainable peace model. Soc Ethics Soc J Appl Philos 6(2):73–103
5. Van Dalen J, Gubbels H, Engel C, Mfenyana K (2002) Effective poster design. Educ Health-Abingdon-Carfax Publ Lt 15(1):79–84
6. Utoyo AW, Aprilia HD, Kuntjoro-Jakti RADRI, Kurniawan A (2021) Visual communication design: Poster as an important way to encourage social distance in Jakarta when the epidemic 19. In: IOP conference series: earth and environmental science, vol 729, no 1 IOP Publishing, , p 012140)
7. Patria AS, Kristiana N, Aryanto H (2019) Comedy film posters in the 70's Era: content analysis of changing trends. In: Social sciences, humanities and education conference (SoSHEC 2019). Atlantis Press, pp 172–177
8. Chowdhury A, Karmakar S, Reddy SM, Sanjog J, Ghosh S, Chakrabarti D (2012) Visual attention analysis on mutated brand name using eye-tracking: a case study. World Acad Sci, Eng Technol Int J Soc, Behav, Educ, Econ, Bus Ind Eng 6(8):1132–1135
9. Pan B, Hembrooke H, Gay G, Granka L, Feusner M, Newman J (2004) The determinants of web page viewing behavior: an eye tracking study. In: Proceedings of the 2004 symposium on eye tracking research & applications. pp 147–154
10. Chapman P (2005) Remembering what we've seen: predicting recollective experiences from eye movements when viewing everyday scenes. In: Underwood G (ed) Cognitive processes in eye guidance. Oxford University Press, UK, pp 237–258
11. Rayner K, Liversedge SP, White SJ, Vergilino-Perez D (2003) Reading disappearing text: cognitive control of eye movements. Psychol Sci 14:385–388
12. Djamasbi S, Siegel M, Tullis T (2011) Visual hierarchy and viewing behavior: an eye tracking study. In: International conference on human-computer interaction. Springer, Berlin, Heidelberg, pp 331–340
13. Djamasbi S (2014) Eye tracking and web experience. AIS Trans Hum-Comput Interact 6(2):37–54
14. Punde PA, Jadhav ME, Manza RR (2017) A study of eye tracking technology and its applications. In: 2017 1st international conference on intelligent systems and information management (ICISIM). IEEE, pp 86–90
15. Chamberlain L (2007) Eye tracking methodology; theory and practice. Qual Mark Res: Int J
16. Marquart F, Matthes J, Rapp E (2016) Selective exposure in the context of political advertising: A behavioral approach using eye-tracking methodology. Int J Commun 10:20

17. Jeon, Y., Cho, M. S., & Oh, J. (2021). A study of customer perception of visual information in food stands through eye-tracking. *British Food Journal*.
18. Hwang MK, Kwon MW, Park MH, Kim CY (2020) A study on the visual precautions of soju advertising posters using eye tracking. J Korea Multimed Soc 23(2):368–375
19. Zahmati M, Azimzade M, Sotode MS (2020) Using eye tracking technology to investigation the impact of celebrity athlete endorsement on the attention to advertising. J Adv Sport Technol 3(2):61–70
20. Maravić Čisar S, Pinter R, Kovári A, Pot M (2021) Application of eye movement monitoring technique in teaching process. IPSI Trans Adv Res 17:32–36
21. Akram U, Ellis JG, Cau G, Hershaw F, Rajenthran A, Lowe, M, ... & Drabble J (2021) Eye tracking and attentional bias for depressive internet memes in depression. Exp Brain Res 239(2):575–581
22. Chowdhury A, Karmakar S, Reddy SM, Ghosh S, Chakrabarti D (2013) Product personality rating style for satisfaction of tactile need of online buyers—a human factors issue in the context of e-retailers' web-design. In: 2013 International conference on human computer interactions (ICHCI) 2013 Aug 23. IEEE, pp 1–8
23. Chowdhury A, Chakrabarti D, Karmakar S (2018) Anthropomorphic televisions are more attractive: the effect of novelty. In: Ergonomics in caring for people: proceedings of the international conference on humanizing work and work environment 2015. Springer, Singapore, pp 243–249

Brand Image and User Experience

Between the Experience and the Image of the City: 'New Babylon' and 'Learning from Las Vegas' as Paradigmatic Cases

Víctor Larripa, Javier Antón, Catia Rijo, and Helena Grácio

Abstract This chapter analyzes the existing tension between the experience of the city and the image of it, arguing that the designer is a creative agent that acts as a mediator between both poles. Although the growing primacy of the visual has marked the notion of cities throughout the twentieth century, this investigation presents two paradigmatic cases to illustrate the opposite: The idea that the conception of the city can—and probably should-start from experience, not so much from its image. These cases are the vision of Las Vegas that, as a manifesto, Robert Venturi, Denise Scott-Brown, and Steven Izenour provide in 1972; and New Babylon that Constant Nieuwenhuys devised between the 1950s and 1960s. In the light of these cases, the text concludes by prompting—or rather by asking—what is the role of the contemporary designer in the city now that we are fully immersed in the twenty-first century.

Keywords Experience · Image · City · Las Vegas · New Babylon · Design · Venturi · Scott-Brown · Izenour · Constant Nieuwenhuys

The experience of the city and the image citizens perceive of it are not the same thing. Quite the contrary, there is a powerful tension between experience and image when we face the question of the city, its life, and its design. The present text, therefore, intends to analyze that tension, arguing that the designer is a creative agent that acts as a mediator between both poles. This duality between image and experience, or between the visual and the haptic, or ultimately between the object and the subject, emerges in the theoretical debates on art and aesthetics in the XIXth century. The text, therefore, begins its narrative thread by briefly illustrating those ideas, to then

V. Larripa · J. Antón (✉)
Universidad de Navarra, 31009 Pamplona, Navarra, Spain
e-mail: lncs@springer.com

C. Rijo · H. Grácio
Instituto Politécnico de Lisboa, 1549-020 Lisboa, Portugal

N. Martins and D. Raposo (eds.), *Communication Design and Branding*,
Springer Series in Design and Innovation 32,
https://doi.org/10.1007/978-3-031-35385-7_11

reflect their translation towards other creative fields, that takes place in the spring of the XXth century. Among them is, logically, the design of the city.

Thus, although the growing primacy of the visual, that has dominated architecture and design in the twentieth century, directly marks the conception of cities, this chapter presents two paradigmatic cases to illustrate quite the opposite. The idea that the conception of the city can—and probably should-start from experience, not so much from its image. These cases are the vision of Las Vegas that, as a manifesto, Robert Venturi, Denise Scott-Brown and Steven Izenour provide in 1972; and the New Babylon that Constant devised between the 1950s and 1960s. In the light of these cases, the text concludes by prompting—or rather by asking—what is the role of the contemporary designer in the city, now well into the twenty-first century.

1 Object Versus Subject, Optical Versus Tactile: XIX Century Theories of Perception[1]

The lens through which a space is perceived determines how it engages. This phenomenological understanding holds that our awareness of the objective and subjective stimuli in our environment determines how we interpret our experiences. The idea of tactility has typically been linked to the immediacy of daily experience, while opticality is often associated with a more distant form of perception. The opposing viewpoint between "the near" and "the far" apprehension of the environment is nothing new. This conflict played a major role in aesthetic discourse in the late XIXth century (Vischer, "Optical sense," 91). Particularly at the turn of the XIXth century, German aesthetic discourse offers us a variety of experiential categories, such as the close view versus the distant view, the tactile versus the optical, and distraction versus attention. Various thinkers, including Hildebrand, Wölffin, Riegl, and Benjamin, played a role in creating, defining, redefining, reversing, and even challenging the range of perceptual categories. These theorists studied the modes of artistic perception.

Wölfflin believed that the interpretation of a building's form and character was not solely a function of the eye, but rather a result of a principle of bodily empathy: "So here, too, we must say: Physical forms possess a character only because we ourselves possess a body. If we were purely visual beings, we would always be denied an aesthetic judgment of the physical world" (Wölfflin, "Prolegomena", 151). In essence, he defined perception as a type of empathetic physical interaction with our environment. His argument was that our bodies provide us with insights into

[1] Pieces of this section and the one about Constant's New Babylon were part of a major investigation undertaken in the University of Columbia at the Masters in Critical, Curatorial and Conceptual Practices in Architecture and partially published in Antón, J., Lauter, M., & Reina, T. (2021). "Interference Patterns. Optical vs Tactile Experiments in Spatial Immersion, from Psychogeography to Holograms" in *Espacio Tiempo y Forma. Serie VII, Historia Del Arte,* (9), 211–236. https://doi.org/10.5944/etfvii.9.2021.30488.

the nature of gravity, strength, and contraction, and that this experiential knowledge allows us to identify other forms.

On the opposite end of the spectrum, Hildebrand focused on the optical realm when discussing perceptual categories. He introduced the concepts of the "near view" and the "distant view", which would later be expanded upon by Riegl and Benjamin. According to Hildebrand, there exists a correlation between the tridimensional structure of an object and how it appears as a visual perception (Hildebrand, The Problem of Form, 16). This implies that a single object can generate multiple visual appearances depending on the viewing angle or the circumstances under which it is observed. The perception of an object's spatial attributes is crucial for our orientation in the outer world. Hildebrand believed that our comprehension of the reality of things is primarily dependent on our general spatial concepts and the way we perceive spatial structure.

Hildebrand's viewpoint regarding the concept of a three-dimensional object was that it is partially formed through stereoscopic vision, which creates the impression that certain parts are closer than others: "an idea, namely, that certain parts are nearer than others" (Riegl, Late Roman Art, 22). Nonetheless, when an object is observed at close proximity, its perception is governed by two-dimensional factors such as color variations, light and shadow, and size. Consequently, as one approaches an object, there is a threshold where it becomes challenging to appreciate the object's entirety without continually scanning its surface. Hildebrand recognizes that there is no inherent link between the two-dimensional images we perceive and the three-dimensional objects that we imagine or reconstruct mentally. He, therefore, places more emphasis on the "distant view" as opposed to the "near view." To bridge this gap between perception and mental construction, Hildebrand suggests that artists operate between these two points, not only creating artistic objects but also teaching us how to observe the world itself. This dichotomy between the near and the distant view, the subject and the object, or the experience and the image is also present in Riegl and Benjamin's theories of tactility. Both associate tactile perception with the near view and visual perception with the distant view. This dichotomy can also be compared to the ones used in this chapter to define the perception of the city: the experience versus the image of it (Fig. 1).

Alois Riegl utilized and expanded upon Hildebrand's ideas of perception by incorporating the concepts of tactility and opticality (Riegl, 22). In 1901, he introduced the contrast between these two terms to describe a departure from traditional canons of form, which led to the emergence of the modern spatial concept. Riegl's theory of perception links "subjectivity" with opticality, and "objectivity" with tangibility (Riegl, 22). The perception description is reversed from Hildebrand's:

> "The particular sense organ, which we use the most for the perception of external objects, is the eye. Yet this organ shows us the objects only as colored planes and by no means as impenetrable material individuals; this optical perception especially makes the objects of the external world appear to us in a chaotic mixture. [...] Definite knowledge about the enclosed individual unity of single objects we obtain only with our sense of touch. It alone procures us knowledge about the impenetrability of the borders, which enclose the material individual. These borders are the tactile surfaces of the objects". (Riegl, Late Roman Art, 22).

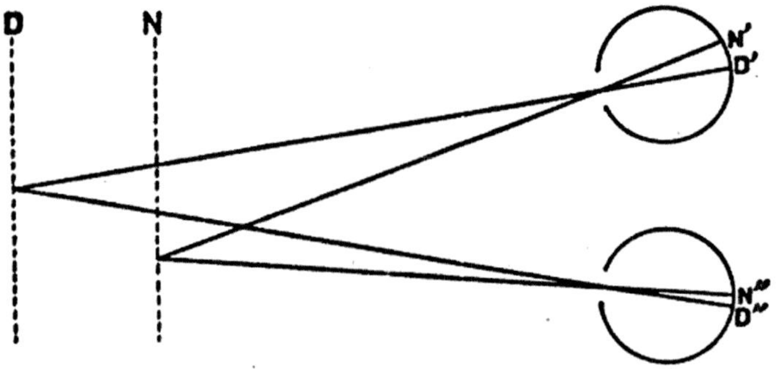

FIG. 3. STEREOSCOPIC VISION.

HOW LIGHT COMING FROM A DISTANT AND A NEAR POINT IS PROJECTED UPON THE RETINA. D' AND N' ARE FARTHER APART THAN D'' AND N''. THE FOLLOWING FIGURE SHOWS HOW THIS RELATIVE DISPLACEMENT APPEARS TO OUR CONSCIOUSNESS AS A VISUAL IMPRESSION.

Fig. 1 Near and Distant view (Hildebrand, 22)

Walter Benjamin presents a distinctive perspective on the connection between architecture and tactility in one of his writings (Benjamin, Technological Reproducibility, 238). The advancements in technology alter how perception works, and as a result, they reorganize both the production and the reception of art. Riegl believed that Hildebrand's notions of "the near and distant" views altered the significance of these categories. In contrast, Benjamin acknowledged the division but reversed its implications. Benjamin put forward a compelling alternative to Riegl's idea of tactility as materiality. He argued that new artforms, such as Dadaism, possessed a tactile quality that hit the viewer like a bullet, resulting in a demand for film. This artform also had a predominantly tactile component based on changes of location and focus that periodically overwhelmed the viewer (Benjamin, 238). Benjamin's concept of tactility is dynamic and relates to movement and distraction. He views the near view positively, unlike Hildebrand who denigrated it. Benjamin sees tactility as connected to use and opticality as connected to perception, positioning the two in opposition to each other.

The way buildings are received can be seen from two perspectives: use and perception, or in other words, tactility and opticality. This type of reception cannot be compared to the focused attention of a traveler standing in front of a well-known building. Tactile reception differs from contemplation in optical reception. It is not achieved through concentrated attention, but rather through habit. This habit significantly impacts the optical reception of architecture, which typically occurs through casual noticing rather than careful observation. (Benjamin, 268).

In his book, the Arcades Project, Benjamin extends his thoughts on perception and tactility to the city, arguing that the city is not actually homogeneous, as even its name sounds different in different districts. He suggests that the experience of boundaries is most apparent in cities, more so than anywhere else except for perhaps in dreams (Benjamin, Arcades, 88).

By adopting this perspective, Benjamin challenges Hildebrand's notion of the 'near view', and redefines Riegl's steady concept of tactility as materiality, turning it into a more fluid concept of tactility as movement. He is not referring to a close and deliberate perception of materials, but rather an unconscious and intimate perception of the environment that can be seen as a dynamic and distracting form of perception.

After exploring these various critical perspectives on perception and the role of the artist in mediating it, we can extend our understanding of this mediator to encompass a broader sense. What the artist was for these aesthetic theorists, could be perfectly applied to the designer at the beginning of the XXth century. The designer, as was the artist, is also a mediator between those two realities, the tactile and the optical, operating in various new fields like industry, architecture, the city, advertisement, etc. Perhaps this is precisely one of the greatest contributions of the Bauhaus: the gathering of all these creative disciplines as the modern concept of this kind of mediator.

If that mediator is now, in a way, the designer, when we talk about the city, the tactile and the optical, could be translated into its perception as experience or as image. In effect, the designer creates the object (the building, the city, the machine, etc.) that brings with it a new way of living-modern life, that has a specific image and that produces certain experiences. It is in this duality, according to which the subject perceives the object from the tension between its image and its experience, that the modern designer consciously operates.

2 Image Versus Experience: The City in the XXth Century

Undoubtedly, the duality between image and experience, and the idea that the designer operates as a mediator between the two, is perfectly applicable to the design of the city throughout the twentieth century. Although the object-subject or image-experience tension was established in the fields of art and thought already in the XIXth century, it would soon infiltrate other disciplines where creativity plays a fundamental role. In this sense, as has been pointed out above, the experiences of the Bauhaus were capital for discovering that, in fields such as industry, architecture, fabric design, theater or the city, a new professional role was necessary. In accordance with the modern Bauhaus approach: the designer is a creative professional that operates between the subject and the object. Consequently, between the object and its image and the experience that the object produces in the subject. Modern Design is precisely born as a discipline that bridges those two poles.

Thus, on occasions, the designer—whether it was the architect, the product designer, the urban planner, etc.—would concentrate on configuring the experience more than the visual issues when facing a design; and on other occasions—the majority of them—the accent would fall on the visual field rather than on the real user experience. In fact, the growing primacy that has been given to the field of image in almost all disciplines during the XXth century is not alien to the world of design. One of the biggest problems of the creative disciplines, not in vain, has been the forgetting of the experiential facet and the linked to the subject. Understanding in those cases—wrongly it seems—that success lies in the image of the designed object, be it an industrial product, a building, a work of art or an urban operation.

> "The ocular bias has never been more apparent in art of architecture than in the past 30 years, as a type of architecture, aimed at a striking and memorable visual image, has predominated. Instead of an existentially grounded plastic and spatial experience, architecture has adopted the psychological strategy of advertising and instant persuasion; buildings have turned into image products detached from existential depth and sincerity (....) As a consequence of the current deluge of images, architecture of our time often appears as mere retinal art of the eye" ([1], 20)

The city, then, is part of this general drift of the creative world. Since Modernity also imbued the design of cities—it is worth remembering experiences such as Hilberseimer's vertical cities, Le Corbusier's ville radieuse, JJP Oud's urban settlements, Bruno Taut's proposals, and many others—the architect, from his drawing board, would play again this conscious role of mediator between the experience and the image of the city. Moreover, through the image of the city, the architect would configure the experience of the inhabitant. Through the design of its shapes, dimensions, aesthetics, organization, orientations, materials, lighting, uses, etc., the modern urban designer would be able to modulate and calibrate the experiences of future citizens. The experience and the image of the city are not then, separate, and stagnant realities; but rather two c connected poles of the creative work.

Kevin Lynch, in his influential text of 1960, "The image of the city" would address, precisely, this tension between the image and the experience of the city. Through the idea of "legibility", Lynch explains the way in which the inhabitant builds his subjective perception of the city and ultimately his experience of it. Despite the title of the text, Lynch's vision focuses on the citizen and advocates a lived city whose design should make it easier for the inhabitant—or the visitor—to understand its basic structure and its references. A "readable" and "understandable" city is a more lived-in and safer city [2].

Through the design of the image, the experience of the city is configured; but also by working on the experience, the designer operates on the image that is being designed. Lynch's text was, perhaps, one of the first steps to understand this bidirectionality of creative work in urban planning and design. Thus, his theories and writings were essential to understand that the design of cities could start from the perception and experience of the future inhabitants and not only from the ideal vision of the designer or architect (Fig. 2).

In any case, the danger posed by the pre-eminence of the image over other parameters of design clearly existed before Lynch, and it exists after. In fact, it is a growing danger despite the contributions of Lynch and many other great theorists who have worked in similar directions; like Jane Jacobs, Jan Gehl, and many others. Unfortunately, the unstoppable development of technology seems to reinforce the exclusively visual sphere of objects and cities.

Thus, the problem lies at the point where the image acquires such primacy in the design process that it ceases to be understood as a means to configure the experience of the inhabitant, and begins to be conceived as the essential goal. In other words, it

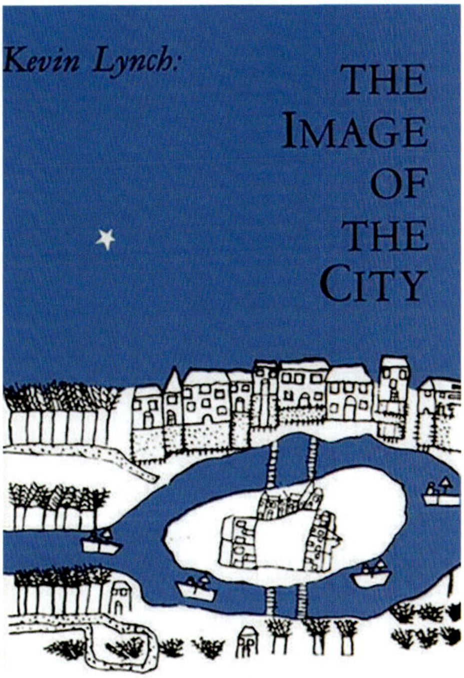

Fig. 2 Cover of "The image of the City" by Kevin Lynch. First edition

is actually understood as an almost personal imposition of the designer, who forgets that the city is always designed to be lived in. Hence, the importance of the experience through the senses that are not sight is annulled or relegated; relations or sensations are forgotten as purposes of design. Once again Pallasmaa perfectly illustrates, in a claiming tone, to what extent the city is lived and experienced:

> "I confront the city with my body; my legs measure the length of the arcade and the width of the square; my gaze unconsciously projects my body onto the facade of the cathedral, where it roams over the mouldings and contours, sensing the size of recesses and projections; my body weight meets the mass of the cathedral door, and my hand grasps the door pull as I enter the dark void behind. I experience myself in the city, and the city exists through my embodied experience. The city and my body supplement and define each other. I dwell in the city and the city dwells in me". ([1], 40)

It is not the object of this article to break down the different theories on urban design that have prevailed throughout the last century; this would be an almost incomprehensible task. Nor is it the intention of the article to account for the most important city experiences or designs [3], much less to account for which fell into the dark limits of visual primacy and which, instead, prioritized the realm of experience in theri design process. The text aims to account for two unique cases that took place in the 1960s: the first is the Las Vegas study that Robert Venturi, Denisse Scott Brown and Steven Izenour carried out; and the second deals with the vision of Paris

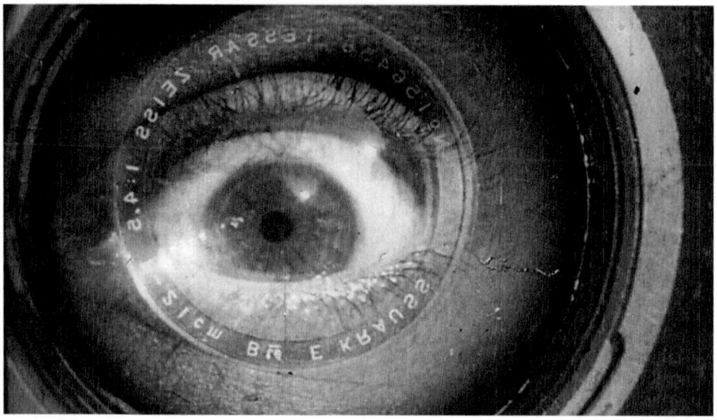

Fig. 3 Dziga Vertov, 1929. *Source* Final shot of the film "Man with a Movie Camera"

provided by the so-called Situationists. Valuing these two visions perhaps reinforces the aforementioned idea that the city, above all, is lived and experienced (Fig. 3).

3 Learning from Las Vegas; Communication and Symbolism in the City

In 1972 Robert Venturi, Steven Izenour and Denisse Scott Brown published a book that was highly influential in the world of architecture: Learning from Las Vegas. The book, which is a kind of manifesto, would change the way of understanding the role of buildings in the urban landscape and would even open new ways of understanding many phenomena related to the conception of cities: the influence of commercial fervor on the cities, the city lived at night, the city lived from the car, the realm of the artificial and fictitious, etc.

The text, in fact, is the result of a study that the aforementioned architects carried out in the fall of 1968 with their students at the Yale School of Art and Architecture [4]. In addition to the usual research work in classrooms and in the university library, that academic work was based on a stay of 4 days in Los Angeles and 10 days in Las Vegas. In other words, the analysis they carried out was largely founded on an experience of the city itself. The book, then, has a first part where the results of the research are presented, using numerous and interesting graphics, drawings, and photographs made by the students. And it also has a second, more relevant section, where the aforementioned manifesto is produced. A proposal that is based, logically, on the urban reality of the then already fervent Las Vegas (Fig. 4).

The entire book distills a certain taste, sometimes exaggerated, for the Pop aesthetics of the moment: elements such as posters, advertisements, signs, lighting and other devices that come from popular culture are highlighted and emphasized; the purely commercial and even deliberately capitalist side of the city is highlighted.

Fig. 4 Denise Scott Brown in Las Vegas. 1966. Venturi, Scott Brown and Associates. *Source* University of Pennsylvania Architectural Archives Camera"

And the authors consciously try to build a particular aesthetic out of all this: in their own words, they defend "an architecture of the ugly and the ordinary" [5]. But, behind this reading of the book and the work, perhaps superficial, there is a powerful message—the manifesto—that has two very clear objectives: the first objective might be to subvert the already old idea of "form follows function" inherited from modern architecture and modern design, and emphasize the symbolic role of architecture in the city. The second objective, more pertinent to this article, is none other than, once again, to underline the role of the designer as a mediator between the experience and the image of the city. For Venturi, Scott Brown, and Izenour, such mediation takes place essentially through the symbolism of architectural form. Not surprisingly, the subtitle of the book is "the forgotten symbolism of architectural form".

Las Vegas is then a city based on the domain of the car. It is a city designed to be lived, at least initially, from the vehicle. Thus, the entire city emerges and is organized around a large central road-not so much a street-called the Strip. The sides of the Strip are gradually being colonized by casinos and hotels whose appearance is configured by a gigantic advertising billboard, normally placed strategically above the body of the building and positioned obliquely towards the road. The mission of the posters is none other than to capture the attention of the visitor—Las Vegas is, above all, a city for visitors. Driving at the speed allowed by the vehicle, the latter has little time to scrutinize the architecture of hotels and casinos, and will probably stop at the one whose sign is more attractive and striking. Once the visitor stops, a second stage of the process will begin, which consists of experiencing an artificial world, which does not distinguish between day and night, and which occurs exclusively inside the casino-hotel. In short, this experience of the citizen, quickly summarized

Fig. 5 The Las Vegas Strip. 1968. Venturi, Scott Brown and Associates. *Source* University of Pennsylvania Architectural Archives

here and perfectly illustrated in the book, would directly condition the formation of the city from the 1960s.

> "The sign for the Motel Monticello, a silhouette of an enormous Chippendale highboy, is visible on the highway before the motel itself. This architecture of styles and signs is antispacial; it is an architecture of communication over space; communication dominates spaces as an element in architecture and landscape", the authors explain. ([5], 8)

From this research Venturi, Izenour and Scott Brown unfold their theoretical contribution. For this, they define a new type of building: The decorated Shed. It is basically a reinterpretation of the casinos and hotels that make up the city. The decorated shed is made up of a simple and prismatic body that contains the entire program and the necessary functions; and on that structure a gigantic poster is placed that contains, instead, the whole layer of meaning and symbolism of the building. It is the sign with its huge inscription that reveals the function of the building, not so much the shape of the building itself. An iconic sketch is born here that, today, is part of the history of recent architecture: "I am a Monument". Venturi and his companions, ironically, draw a decorated shed whose giant sign says that it is a monument. That is, the building no longer needs to have the visible form of a monument because its sign can announce it (Figs. 5 and 6).

In reality, the authors propose disaggregating two aspects that Modern Architecture[2] had indissolubly united up to now, form and function. For the architects who

[2] Modern Architecture refers to the movement that took place during the 20 s and 30 s in architecture, and whose greatest achievement was the overcoming, or even elimination, of the traditional idea

Fig. 6 Bid Donut Drive-In. Los Angeles. 1970. Venturi, Scott Brown and Associates. *Source* University of Pennsylvania Architectural Archives

defended Modernity, the form should arise and emanate from the function in such a way that it transmitted or reflected it. This question, in the opinion of Venturi, Scott Brown and Izenour, made sense in the 1920s and 1930s, when it arose, but by the 1960s it had lost its *raison d'être*. They explain that, given that architectural form has a very relevant symbolic dimension in the city, architects who staunchly defend "form follows function" end up deforming their buildings in an attempt to convey meaning. And as a result, their works are not correctly covering the communicative layer, nor are their functions properly housed. The extreme case, almost in a humorous tone, they explain, would be the "Duck": a building that, to symbolize that roast duck is sold inside, takes on the literal form of a duck (Fig. 7).

> "We shall emphasize image in asserting that architecture depends in its perception and creation on past experience and emotional association and that these symbolic and representational elements may often be contradictory to the form, structure and program with which they combine in the same building—explain Venturi, Scott Brown and Izenour—Where systems of space and structure are directly at the service of program, and ornamente is applied independently of them, this we call the decorated shed". ([5], 7)

Their proposal then is the opposite: by separating a pavilion from the facade-sign, which contains the signifying layer, said pavilion, already freed from its symbolic

---

of ornament and decoration, in favor of architectural forms that were born from the function or the need. Among its champions are names like Le Corbusier, Walter Gropius, Bruno Taut, J.J.P. Oud, Mies van der Rohe, etc., etc. Robert Venturi, in his ideas and writings, does not discredit the values of this movement and emphasizes its necessity and logic at the time it emerged. Instead, he is critical of the architects who, 30 years later, were still anchored in the same postulates and, above all, in the aesthetics that derived from that movement.

Fig.7 "I am a Monument" sketch. Venturi, Scott Brown, and Associates. *Source* University of Pennsylvania Architectural Archives

load, can perfectly resolve its program and its functions. And in parallel, the sign is the perfect device to visually convey a message; Especially at a time when the car is the method of transportation par excellence in North America. The poster is, in short, the device that the architect now must transmit a visual and symbolic meaning to the citizen; and therefore, it is the tool to generate a city.

In the book, after all, there is a very clear call for the architect to reconnect with the citizen's urban experience and forget about the architectural object as such. Thus, the large billboard, understood as the main façade of the building, is a communication interface between designer and citizen, between architecture and city. Communication, although clearly visual, arises as a mediation between the experience of the citizen (who circulates in this case in his vehicle) and the architectural object. At first glance, it might seem that Venturi, Scott Brown and Izenour emphasize a conception of the city centered on the visual realm, through the book's powerful images and their idea of an illuminated billboard as the building's façade. But, in reality, a deeper reading reveals that its intention is instead to emphasize the experience of the citizen, who is ultimately the recipient of the visual messages that emanate from the building. The city is not designed from its image, but from visual communication, or—in Lynch's words—from its legibility.

4 New Babylon

The Situationist International (SI), an avant-garde group influenced by Dadaism and Surrealism, explored urban environments through psychogeography and *dérivé* (drift). They subverted conventional urban approaches with the development of the idea of unitary urbanism, thus disabling centralized authority. Cartographic methods were often used to represent situations within the city. The concept of *Dérivé*, which translates as "drift," referred to an experimental behavior associated with the urban environment. It involved quickly moving through different surroundings and was linked to the psychological effects of the city's visible layout. The SI coined the concept of psychogeography, or "unitary urbanism," for mapping out the fading delineation of different atmospheres or environments. Psychogeography was defined by their founder, Guy Debord, as the examination of the precise laws and specific effects of the geographical environment on individuals' emotions and behavior. They sought to create a new vision of the future city by changing people's perceptions within the already constructed urban landscape, getting to a tactile experience rather than an optical representation. Through these processes they created maps that were not intended to impose logic on the city but to offer a different mode of mobility and interaction that was closely tied to emotions.

One of the founding members of the SI, Constant Nieuwenhuys, left the group in 1960 due to conflicting ideals about the use of cartography, instead preferring an experience more nomadic and playful of the future city he was envisioning. His vision was concentrated and catalyzed in an all-encompassing city called New Babylon that sought to establish a harmonious relationship between the built environment and the human sensorium. Its design was immense and intended to have freedom at the core of it, with work located underground and play suspended in the air. However, Nieuwenhuys encountered a paradox—while striving to create a utopia of pure perception-, his models of that city eventually turned into "depictions" of the future. He was trapped in a pre-presentation of a non-existing reality. Despite their tactile nature, the outcome of this pre-presentation was a transmission of a view of the city to the mind, resulting in a pure intellect emphasis, rather than interpellant to the entire sensorium. The group he rejected, the SI, on the contrary, was more focused on corporeal perception of existing cities like Paris, and their practices were based on movement and a tactile approach. However, their project was unsuccessful in practice since it was implausible for every person in a city to partake in the time shift of the *dérivé* simultaneously. Conversely, Benjamin connected tactility with movement and distraction, and these concepts can be seen in the development of psychogeographic practices in art and experience architecture.

For Constant, the models on New Babylon were intended to establish a new, world-wide, understanding and function as a technique for encountering new urbanism. In 1956, he began working on this ambitious architectural vision of the future that consumed most of his life. For over two decades, he created an extensive collection of scale models, manifestos, pictures, photographs, drawings, essays, conferences, exhibits, and movies related to New Babylon. The project was a sort of provocation as well as a representation for what could be called "the creative city". Constant's idea was to conceive New Babylon as the consequence of the masses' creativity, that had yet to be totally harnessed. Behind its conception remains the idea that creative work would withdraw due to mechanization and automation, thus generating a transformation in thinking and morality, and conducting humans to the beginning of a new society.

Constant's efforts to design for what he considered the "creative man" was somehow based on the notion of *homo ludens*, asserted in 1938 by the writer Johan Huizinga. Huizinga explained the prominence of the element of play in society and culture, and identified the theoretical space in which it should occur. The writer defends that psychology must address, observe, and describe play; and, at the same time, play is a sort of function that generates culture.

Also, Constant found a source of inspiration in the work of Yona Friedman, a Hungarian architect known for his megastructure conceptions. Friedman's *Ville Spatiale* can be described as a utopian design that reflects his theories in a very accurate way: it is a spatial metal grid of tetrahedral pieces superimposed over a city, which works as a matrix and allocates constructions, volumes, functions… Although Friedman's megastructures seem to be very similar to the ones proposed afterwards by Constant at a first glance, it can be said that Constant's ones are far more architectural in their conception. Friedman published a manifesto called "Mobile Architecture" in 1958, where he described a new mode of mobility, not of the constructions but rather for inhabitants who are given a new freedom; while Constant proposed a more intricate idea of freedom based on the evasion of labor and the fullness of creativity.

Furthermore, Constant's models were not only architectural representations of his utopian city, but also, they were three-dimensional drawings that challenged traditional models and perspectives. They were designed to be perceived as aerial drawings, but when observed from a different angle, they would convert into fully 3D representations. This amalgamation of perspectives was further emphasized by the manner the models were displayed, alternating between vertical and horizontal planes. He created his own cartography by blending "aerial photographs" of his maquettes to form new maps. According to Mark Wigley, Constant's models propose a new way of living that is being drawn in three dimensions through multiple layers of transparency. ([6], 28) (Figs. 8 and 9).

Fig. 8 Spatiovore, 1960. Metal and Plexiglass, Groondplaat 65 × 65 cm, 90 × 65 cm. Model by Constant Nieuwenhuys

Fig. 9 Construetie Met Dooraiehtige Vlakken, 1954. Aluminum and Plexiglass, 76 × 76 × 50cm. Model by Constant Nieuwenhuys

These New Babylon models were conceived and constructed with different materials, metal wire, transparent plastics, timber, etc. Constant applied these models and designs on the whole Netherlands territory, since he considered them as a design for a new culture. One that was characterized by an extremely creative lifestyle and a nomadic attitude which he emphasized by means of gigantic labyrinths. The form of that utopian megastructure was generated by a horizontal skeleton built basically with steel and concrete. The skeleton, in fact, created a sort of network over the globe in which there were no limits, boundaries, no centrality or impositions of any kind. To reinforce here the concept of mobility, the artist gave extraordinary relevance and

Fig. 10 Interior Red Sector, Ruimtecircus, 1956. Ijzeerdraad, Groondplaat 110 × 90 cm., 69 × 59 × 59cm. Model by Constant Nieuwenhuys

a certain omnipresence to programs such as airports, ports, intermodal stations, etc. The general grid was split by sectors, which were the smallest elements, the basic units of this Babylonian arrangement (Fig. 10).

The units in this utopia were devised to have hotels, autonomous rooms, health centers and schools, libraries, and research facilities that could be easily customized to meet the needs of the inhabitants. The movable and adjustable systems allowed for walls, floors, and supplies to be easily mounted or dismounted to create different zones of attraction. Inhabitants could adjust lighting, sound, and temperature at any time, promoting a sensuous and creative way of life. Constant envisioned the New Babylonians as the true builders of this utopia, reinforcing the principle of disorientation with labyrinthian structures and a nomadic way of life without borders. Early exhibitions primarily showcased models, but later photographs and films gained prominence. The films, shot over several years, offer a meandering perspective that blurs the constructions together into a single picture, reinforcing the movement inherent in the intended use of the space.

In his vision, New Babylonians had a variety of technical implements at their disposal to customize and renew their environment without delay. He made them aspired to create a world in which their freedom through play was realized, and it was their responsibility to create it through a continuous process of recreation. And then, New Babylon, was meant to be a product of their culture and served as a model of reflection and play for others. The use of evolving techno-space allowed for free actions that are not hindered by capital or labor. In the end, the legibility of the city was not based on its image but on experience and communication.

5 Closing Remarks

This research has sought to highlight the role of the designer as a creative intermediary between the object and the subject, the visual and the haptic, and the image and the experience. Nineteenth century theories allowed us to trace the origin of these dualities, starting from the world of art. And Modernity at the beginning of the XXth century, in a way, translates them for the first time into creative worlds beyond the role of the artist himself: the architect, the urban planner, the engineer who operates for industry, the designer of products and services, etc. However, throughout the century, the polarization between image and experience was exacerbated until the almost total dissociation between the two that we are experiencing today.

Although many designers have prioritized—and still prioritize—image over experience, there are cases that allow us to understand that the scale of values in the design process should be almost the opposite. As Pallasmaa and many other authors have claimed, it is convenient to prioritize experience over image, since the latter could be superficial, fleeting, deceptive, partial and, above all, emerges from the designer and not so much from the subject. The examples of Las Vegas and New Babylon allow us to recover visions of the city where the protagonism returns to the field of experience, play, freedom as exemplified in these two paradigmatic cases.

However, the twenty-first century still demands a step further. It seems that it is not enough for the designer to focus on modulating the citizen's experience by being the sole agent of the creative process. Instead, the complexity of today's world inexorably demands that the designer must rather be a catalyst of a whole participatory process where numerous issues and prior questions come "into play". The current role of design in the city should therefore not focus so much on providing specific solutions that aim to directly improve experiences, but rather to look beforehand at the major complex problems that affect the contemporary city, where the real challenge is to understand better the whole ecosystem as was suggested by Constant.

From the understanding of these problems, the possible and multiple solutions that can be provided will always be more appropriate to intervene, act and improve the urban phenomena of today. We could state with Robert Dilts that "Flexibility comes from having multiple choices, wisdom from having multiple perspectives" ([7], 47).

Thus, designers today are faced with the need to incorporate into the creative processes as many agents as possible of the complex reality or their field of action. In the case of a city the involvement of the citizen is an unnegotiable must. It is not so much a matter of creating "for" the citizen as of creating "with" the citizen, so that their inputs trigger a richer, more intelligent and fruitful creative process. The designer, then, is a sort of facilitator whose know-how orchestrates these complex processes. And in any case, the central position in such processes is always held by people; after all, they are the ones who think, live, experience, and enjoy the city. As Jan Gehl points out "a good city can be compared to a good party—people stay for much longer than really necessary, because they are enjoying themselves". ([8], 117).

References

1. Pallasmaa J (2008) The eyes of the skin. Wiley, New York
2. Lynch K (1960) The image of the city. The MIT Press, Cambridge
3. Ordeig JM (2004) Diseño Urbano y pensamiento contemporáneo [Urban Design and Contemporary Thought]. Instituto Monsa de Ediciones, Barcelona
4. Venturi R, Scott Brown D, Izenour S (1968) A significance for A&P parking lots, or learning from Las Vegas. Architectural Forum 128(2):36–43
5. Venturi R, Scott Brown D, Izenour S (1977) Learning from Las Vegas. The forgotten symbolism of architectural form, 2nd edn. The MIT Press, Cambridge
6. Wigley M (2001) Paper, scissors, blur. In: De Zegher MC, Wigley M (eds) The activist drawing: retracing situationist architectures from constant's new Babylon to beyond. Drawing Center, New York
7. Jha S (2022) The path to ease and glow. Notion Press, Chennai
8. Gehl J (2010) Cities for people. Island Press, Washington
9. Benjamin W (2005) The work of art in the age of its technological reproducibility. In: Jennings MW, Eilar H, Smith G (eds) Selected Writings, Walter Benjamin. Harvard University Press, Cambridge, p 4
10. Benjamin W (2002) The arcades project. Harvard University Press, Cambridge
11. Hildebrand A (1907) The problem of form in painting and sculpture. G.E. Stechert & CO, New York
12. Riegl A (1985 [1901]) Late roman art industry, trans. Rolf Winkes. Bretschneider, Rome
13. Riegl A (1985 [1901]) Late roman art industry. Giorgio Bretschneider, Rome
14. Vischer R (1994) On the optical sense of form: a contribution to aesthetics. In: Mallgrave HF, Ikonomou E (eds) Empathy, form and space. Problems in German aesthetics. 1873–1893. Chicago University Press, Chicago, pp 91–123
15. Wölfflin H (1994) Prolegomena to a psychology of architecture. In: Mallgrave HF, Ikonomou E (eds) Empathy, form and space. Problems in German aesthetics. 1873–1893. Chicago University Press, Chicago, pp 91–123

Destination Image Through TripAdvisor´s Reviews Analysis

Elaine Scalabrini, Jessica Ferreira, Senka Borovac Zekan, and Paula Odete Fernandes

Abstract Tourists' satisfaction and motivation have been recurrent themes in tourism literature. In recent years these themes have also been addressed based on online evaluations carried out by tourists, TripAdvisor is one of the most used sites. In this context, this study aims to analyse the image of *Bragança*'s tourism destination based on TripAdvisor reviews during the pandemic period (2020–2022). To this end, 1444 quantitative and qualitative reviews of attractions, hotels, and restaurants in *Bragança*, Northern Portugal, were analysed. Based on the Latent Dirichlet Allocation Algorithm three dimensions were determined for the attractions, two dimensions for the hotels and two dimensions for the restaurants. The descriptive statistics made it possible to establish that the municipality has a positive tourist image. Given results, theoretical and practical implications of this important Marketing theme are presented.

Keywords Destination image · TripAdvisor · Travellers

E. Scalabrini (✉) · J. Ferreira · P. O. Fernandes
UNIAG, Instituto Politécnico de Bragança, Bragança, Portugal
e-mail: elaine@ipb.pt

J. Ferreira
e-mail: jessica.ferreira@ipb.pt

P. O. Fernandes
e-mail: pof@ipb.pt

S. B. Zekan
University Department of Professional Studies, University of Split, Split, Croatia
e-mail: sborovac@oss.unist.hr

N. Martins and D. Raposo (eds.), *Communication Design and Branding*,
Springer Series in Design and Innovation 32,
https://doi.org/10.1007/978-3-031-35385-7_12

1 Introduction

The constant challenges that tourist destinations face make necessary the creation of several strategies to maintain competitive advantage [1]. In the process of destination selection and choice, tourists search for advice and recommendations from others and trust the perception and opinion of those who have already tested the tourism product [2].

The increasing amount of user-generated content disseminated through social media services and travel websites has made a wealth of information available online. On the one hand, tourists access this information to support their decision-making process [3]. Alternatively, tourism enterprises see these online services as appealing promotional mediums.

For decades, some researchers have been trying to study motivations and interpretations derived from this online information, furthering study on the image of the destination, the trustworthiness of the comments, the impact of the rating and the reactions of travellers, highlighting, in the last three years, the pandemic trends [1, 2, 4–8].

Considering the world's largest travel website, TripAdvisor [9, 10], this study aims to analyse the image of *Bragança*'s tourism destination based on TripAdvisor reviews during the pandemic period (2020–2022). The definition of an attraction on TripAdvisor includes a wide range of groups and categories; each has a geographical locator [9] and presents additional comments and quotations. In this prism, the methodological process explores the reviews and quotations of *Bragança*'s attractions, hotels, and restaurants in the Northern Portugal region. *Bragança*'s tourism is promoted by its culture, heritage, gastronomy, and rurality. As support tools for this analysis, the Knime Analytics 4.6.4 platform was used to prepare and process the data, and IBM SPSS software, for descriptive statistics. Based on TripAdvisor´s reviews, the Dimensions of analysis of the tourist destinations´ components (attractions, hotels, and restaurants), are supported by the Latent Dirichlet Allocation (LDA) Algorithm. The quantitative data allowed to determine the image of *Bragança* as positive, negative, or neutral during the analysed period.

This study's thinking and logical structure followed some steps, filtering the field of research. Specifically, this research started from a bibliometric analysis that allowed knowing the development and impacts of the existing literature until then. Using the bibliometrix R tool, this analysis was compiled in a database of the open access papers under the search equation: "Tourism" and "TripAdvisor", considering the SciVerse Scopus and Web of Science (WoS) databases. Then, the literature was discussed by analysing the most cited, most recent, and most relevant productions.

Continuously, as a methodological process, the descriptive analysis of the data and the relationship tests of the comments are exposed. After the pre-processing of the comments, the LDA algorithm modelling was used, which determines dimensions based on the existence of a hidden structure between the words. Finally, tables are presented to complement and expose the data obtained in the presentation and discussion of the results. The number of comments, the components of the evolution and development of the destination of the different dimensions under analysis, divided by attractions, hotels, and restaurants, were analysed.

At the end of the study, future suggestions are also presented, which relate the field of study to further research.

2 Framework

2.1 Bibliometric Framework

Bibliometrics is a field in biblioteconomics and information science that applies statistical and mathematical methods to analyse and build indicators on the dynamics and evolution of scientific information. Many studies explain the need to use bibliometric tools for more quantitative analysis of scientific production [11–13]. The Bibliometrix R Package is an open-source tool for quantitative research in scientometrics and bibliometrics that includes all the main bibliometric analysis methods. Bibliometrix is more than a statistical tool, becoming a community of international creators and users who exchange questions, impressions, opinions and examples with an open-source project [14].

Accordingly, to quantitatively analyse the scientific literature's behaviour, it was considered, firstly, carrying a bibliometric analysis, using the Bilbiometrix R Package tool.

Intending to know the development and impacts of literature in the field of research, this analysis collects in a database the open access papers according to the search equation: "Tourism" and "TripAdvisor", considering the SciVerse Scopus and Web of Science (WoS) databases.

The filtering process of the compiled database involved some necessary steps until the final database was obtained. In the search for the equation, only open-access papers were considered.

From the Scopus databases, 190 results were considered, and WoS 233 results. In the compilation process of both databases, 140 repeated papers were excluded, resulting in a final database of 283 papers.

A descriptive database reading highlights the scientific production between 2012 and 2022, with 165 sources, 737 authors and more than 950 keywords. The annual growth rate was 49.29%, and the average citations per document were 16.38 citations.

Once the scientific production of the field under research was analysed, a gradual growth was observed from the appearance of the first scientific paper in 2012, until 2020. In 2021, scientific production decreased slightly, growing again in the last months. On the other hand, when observing the citation rate of the scientific papers by year, the analysis turns out to be the opposite. There was a gradual increase in citations until 2015, followed by a sharp decline until 2018. In the following years, until 2021, there was a slight growth, but it was from 2021 onwards that there was a peak in citations, with a current growth trend.

This growth stands out in the journals Tourism Management, and International Journal of Hospitality Management highlighted as the sources with the most significant citations influence in the research field. The journal Sustainability stands out in the publication of scientific papers in the field of research.

The origin of these researches highlights some international co-authorship and co-citation relationships. Specifically, the relationship between Europe and North America, collaborating in some studies, is distinguished. Besides, it was interesting to understand that the most prominent affiliations belong to the Iberian Peninsula, emphasising the University Institute of Lisbon (ISCTE-IUL) and the Complutense University of Madrid. Spain and Portugal are among the TOP3 countries of the authors who contribute most to this scientific production, also highlighting the United Kingdom.

In evidence of this bibliometric analysis, the authors' keywords are analysed, which show the topics worked so far. With a higher occurrence, it stands out the words: TripAdvisor; tourism; online reviews; social media; sentiment analysis.

The coupling authors' study reveals some clusters that show the relation of the keywords with their development and relevance. Specifically, with extraordinary relevance and development, it was categorised into three niches: tourism, satisfaction, and tourism development; online reviews, sentiment analysis and hotels; hospitality, word-of-mouth and impact. TripAdvisor, online reading systems and online platforms form a group at the centre of development and relevance. On the other hand, the clusters of big data, regression analysis and tourists are topics to emerge or decline. From this list of topics, tourism development and satisfaction, sentiment analysis through online reviews, and the impact of word-of-mouth on hospitality are in the spotlight of scientific research.

Finally, to leave topics for future studies, it was considered interesting to study the research trends. Observing sentiment analysis, machine learning, the hotel industry, online reviews, satisfaction, and marketing are featured as keywords of tendency.

Considering these results in the bibliometric analysis and the scientific papers with greater relevance in the research field, the next session is dedicated to the literature review of the scientific papers in the database.

2.2 *Literature Review*

This session presents some studies on the topics and the conceptualisation of some important concepts. The database under analysis was used for this discussion, specifically the most cited, recent, and relevant scientific papers.

The first paper registered in this database was in 2012, by Matthias Fuchs and Markus Zanker, entitled "Multi-criteria Ratings for Recommender Systems: An Empirical Analysis in the Tourism Domain". In this study, the authors sought to analyse TripAdvisor's multi-criteria ratings and the structuring of reviewers' overall satisfaction with the help of a Penalty-Reward Contrast analysis [15].

Henceforth, studies in the research field have followed different directions. Considering the list of the most relevant scientific papers obtained from the bibliometric analysis, it is understood that the authors have worked on themes associated with: the interpretation of the destination image by visitors [1]; the creation of decision support models using social information [4]; the trustworthiness of positive and negative comments, and the analysis of companies' responses to negative comments [2, 5, 6]; the impact of traveller ratings on hospitality [7]; and, most recently, traveller reactions during pandemic trends [8]. Place branding and place reputations are also themes related to image studies [16, 17].

Standing out from the most cited scientific papers in the research field, different concepts are understood. Destinations must deal with various new challenges to gain and maintain a competitive advantage. Smart destinations, which emerged from the concept of smart cities, particularly highlight the significance of synergies between stakeholders and addressing travellers' needs before, during and after their trip [1].

When choosing a tourist destination, people must often rely on the advice and recommendations of other people. Other people's opinions can be accessed through direct word of mouth, books, journalists, or even writings on social media [2].

The increasing amount of user-generated content disseminated through social media services, such as reviews, comments, and past experiences, has made a wealth of information available. Tourists can access this information to support their decision-making process. This information is freely accessible online and generates so-called "open data". Studies show that tourists can consider adopting open data analytics to make better predictions about the attractiveness of a particular destination [3].

New data could be acquired now by analysing tourists' interactions on social media sites or their use of mobile apps that enhance their travel experience. Big data analysis can provide new insights into destination choices and support strategic decision-making in tourism destination management. In this context, social media and online analytics play a significant role as they support information search, decision-making and knowledge exchange for tourists. For companies operating in the tourism sector, social media represent a means of communication with customers and a place for implementing a good part of the marketing strategy. Travel websites are utilised by tourists who have specific questions, which are usually not answered in common reviews of tourist attractions: forums reveal specific information needs and their connection with potential destinations [18].

TripAdvisor is the world's largest travel website. Founded in 2000, it was used by 390 million unique visitors every month at the end of 2016. It hosts user-generated content and reviews of destinations worldwide, and different language and nationality versions offer access to information in multiple settings. The global, multilingual reach and widespread use of TripAdvisor offers a potential opportunity to overcome some difficulties of studying geographically dispersed activities [9, 10].

TripAdvisor's efficiency as a collaborative recommendation medium depends mainly on several factors: the extent to which the problem can be easily represented;

the extent to which its solution requires self-motivated people and context-specific, distant and pervasive knowledge; and the extent to which its evaluation includes a large number of experienced internet users. While false and paid online reviews can negatively affect TripAdvisor's efficiency [6], the extent to which the crowd is efficient can also produce the antibodies that safeguard against this opportunistic conduct [19].

The definition of an attraction on TripAdvisor includes various groups and categories, including venues, tours, operators, events and activities. Each has a geographical locator [9] and features different reviews.

Online reviews provide additional information about the product to reduce uncertainty. Thus, consumers often rely on online reviews to form purchasing decisions. However, an explosion of online reviews brings the problem of information overload to individuals. Identifying reviews containing valuable information from many reviews becomes increasingly important for consumers and businesses, especially for experiential products such as attractions. Unlike consumers, businesses want to detect potential valuable reviews before they are rated to avoid or promote their negative or positive influence, respectively [7, 20].

The most recent scientific papers show the impacts of the pandemic and customer satisfaction with restaurant service quality during the outbreak of COVID-19 [21, 22]. The research trends also highlight studies on linguistic interpretation, text and sentiment analysis of reviews [23–25].

3 Methodology

3.1 Data Collection and Pre-processing

To achieve the aim of this study, TripAdvisor the major tourism review platform was used. Other studies have been dedicated to this analysis, using the same platform in different tourism components [26, 27]. Thus, the scope of this study was the attractions, hotels, and restaurants of *Bragança*, located in the Northern region of Portugal, in the sub-region of *Terras de Trás-os-Montes*, on the Spanish border with approximately 34,582 residents [28]. In terms of tourism, *Bragança* is a town where tourists can visit and know the heritage, and natural landscapes, in the Natural Park of *Montesinho* and diversified gastronomy.

Therefore, the data, corresponding to quantitative ratings, the titles and the reviews written in all languages were collected in October 2022. The top ten attractions, the top seventeen hotels and fifteen restaurants presented on TripAdvisor in the month were considered, totalling 1,444 reviews and quantitative evaluations (Table 1). In addition, the period considered for analysis was the reviews posted during 2020–2022.

In the data collection period, the best attractions, hotels, and restaurants on TripAdvisor are those presented in Table 2. Considering the total number of existing reviews

Table 1 Number of reviews

Destination components	Number of reviews
Attractions	241
Hotels	230
Restaurants	973
Total	1,444

Source Authors' own elaboration

Table 2 Destination components and number of reviews (n) on TripAdvisor

Attraction	n	Hotels	n	Restaurants	n
Castelo de Bragança	73	*Pousada de Bragança*	26	*Solar Bragançano*	210
Aldeia de Rio de Onor	52	*Ibis Hotel*	24	*O Abel*	159
Domus Municipalis	15	*São Lázaro*	26	*Bela Época*	63
Cidadela de Bragança	10	*A. Motesinho*	41	*G Pousada*	28
Igreja de Santa Maria	16	*Tulipa Hotel*	8	*O Careto*	53
Centro de Arte Contemporânea	7	*Glamping Hills*	7	*O Batoque*	21
Igreja da Sé	7	*Candeias do Souto*	11	*Tasca do Zé Tuga*	145
Museu Ibérico da Máscara e do Traje	11	*Estalagem*	14	*Poças*	66
Museu Abade de Baçal	7	*Pousada da Juventude*	4	*Geadas*	41
Parque Natural Montesinho	8	*Informal*	10	*Casa Nostra*	13
Centro de Ciência Viva	9	*Moleiro de Bacal*	2	*Rosina*	80
História e Arte	0	*Arado*	3	*O Javali*	54
Centro de Interpretação da Cultura Sefardita do Nordeste Transmontano	2	*Nordeste Shalom*	6	*Alma Lusa*	31
Galeria George Dussaud	3	*Santa Apolónia*	8	*Emiclau*	6
Museu Militar de Bragança	21	*O Abel*	16	*Quinta das Queimadas Panorama*	2
		Baixa Hotel	18		
		Santa Maria Solar	6		
Total reviews	**241**	**Total reviews**	**230**	**Total reviews**	**973**

The original names in Portuguese presented on TripAdvisor
Source Authors' own elaboration

on TripAdvisor, the number of reviews collected in the period proposed in this study corresponds to 11.1% of the attractions, 12.8% of the hotels and 17.3% of the total reviews of the restaurants.

In the first step, Knime Analytics Platform 4.6.4 was used to prepare and analyse de data. This software was previously used in other tourism studies [26, 27]. This open-source software uses modular pipelining to analyse analytics data [26]. The data pre-processing consists of a punctuation eraser, removing all punctuations from the text, followed by a case converter, changing the text to lowercase. After this, all the numbers and the reviews with less than three characters (N Chars filter) were removed. The next step was to apply the stop word filter to remove no significant words. Considering the reviews were all translated into Portuguese, a list of common stop words in this language was used. Using the Porter algorithm all words were stemmed.

Related to quantitative evaluations, a descriptive analysis was performed to determine the means, standard deviations, and distributions of the evaluations. Based on a previous study [29], the positive image was considered with scores of 4–5, the neutral image with a score of 3 and the negative image with scores of 1–2.

3.2 Data Analysis

Different methods have been used to analyse TripAdvisor's reviews, which extract and model the topics and establish the image of destinations or the feeling towards the visit. One of the most used is LDA modelling which determines dimensions based on the existence of a hidden structure. Considering a large number of reviews, LDA dimensions according to the co-occurrence of the terms. The dimension is considered a latent construct of the total corpus of comments [30].

Hence, following previous studies, the steps below were performed to complete the LDA analysis. i) determine the number of dimensions; ii) extract the dimensions; iii) appoint the dimensions; iv) determine the number of reviews in each dimension. Next, on SPSS, the mean scores, and the distribution of reviews in each dimension were established. This step was performed to determine the destination's positive, neutral, and negative image.

The optimal number of dimensions was determined by performing the Elbow Method, based on sum squared errors. The Elbow bend is confirmed as ideal 3 dimensions for the attractions, two for the hotels and two for the restaurants. Following the dimensions were extracted using the LDA algorithm, each of the dimensions contained 10 terms and then were nominated according to the experience of the researchers and based on previous studies related to the image of destinations and TripAdvisor ratings [26, 27].

Next, evaluations' means, standard deviations and frequency distribution were calculated. TripAdvisor allows a quantitative classification from 1 to 5, 1 is the lowest score and 5 is the highest. Thus, based on these evaluations it was possible to determine whether the image of the tourism components of *Bragança* presented a positive or negative image, in the analysed period.

4 Findings

As aforementioned, the number of dimensions in each component of the tourist destination was determined using k-means clustering. Calculating the sum squared errors was delimited by the Elbow Method to confirm the number of dimensions. Thus, three dimensions were determined for attractions, two dimensions for hotels and two dimensions for restaurants.

Subsequently, the LDA algorithm was used in Knime to extract the number of dimensions and the terms that were a component of each dimension, as also the weight that each of the terms represents in the dimension; the higher the dimension, the more representative that term is in that dimension. Some terms are repeated in the dimensions; however, the weights are different. The labels of each dimension were determined by the authors of this research, based on previous studies. Tables 3, 4 and 5 present the dimensions and the prevalent terms and their respective weight.

Attractions have three dimensions: heritage, regional characteristics, and culture. The heritage dimensions are characterised by elements that represent the heritage of *Bragança* such as a castle, museum, tower, and military. The second dimension was named regional characteristics once representing locals where tourists can see the regionality aspects such, as the villages, houses and typical. Although the terms of the third dimension are similar to the first one, culture was the name of this dimension, since it presents aspects related to this, such as churches and paintings municipality.

There are two dimensions related to the hotels: quality and infrastructure. The first dimension, quality, includes terms related to the perception of the services and this is indicated with terms such as good, excellent, clean, and comfortable. The second dimension is the infrastructure, which connotes analysis regarding the structure used during the staying in hotels in *Bragança*, such as pool, place, and farm.

Table 3 Dimensions of attractions

Heritage		Regional characteristics		Culture	
Term	Weight	Term	Weigh	Term	Weigh
Castle	204	Village	135	Church	77
Museum	121	House	36	Interior	32
Military	70	Centre	26	Castle	28
Tower	57	Exhibition	24	Beautiful	20
Fortress wall	55	Typical	22	Building	20
Interior	44	Pretty	22	Painting	16
Interesting	40	Beautiful	20	Public	16
Entrance	33	Excellent	20	Monument	16
Art piece	32	Museum	20	Saint	15
Space	31	Art	10	Municipality	15

Source Authors' own elaboration

Table 4 Dimensions of hotels

Quality		Infrastructure	
Term	Weight	Term	Weigh
Good	179	Pool	50
Excellent	116	Stay	37
Clean	106	Local	32
City	95	Place	31
Enjoyable	83	Space	30
Kindly	78	Clean	29
Centre	77	Enjoyable	29
Comfortable	66	Kindly	26
Quality	65	Farm	25
Big	64	Good	23

Source Authors' own elaboration

Table 5 Dimensions of restaurants

Quality		Gastronomy	
Term	Weight	Term	Weigh
Excellent	552	Meat	260
Quality	357	Pieces of meat	246
Service	345	Potato	178
Price	340	Service	157
Menu	297	Price	136
Attendance	282	Wine	136
Ambience	247	Menu	119
Wine	216	Codfish	119
Enjoyable	199	Excellent	114
Kindly	179	Nuts	112

Source Authors' own elaboration

Like hotels, restaurants also have two dimensions. The first dimension is named quality with a similar term cited in hotels. The main terms are excellent, quality, attendance and ambient. The second dimension is gastronomy where are cited the principal ingredients used in gastronomy in the region of *Terras de Trás-os-Montes*. The meat is recognised as a product of excellence in the region, and this is demonstrated in this dimension.

After determining the dimensions, the tourism image components were divided into positive, neutral, or negative based on TripAdvisor quantitative evaluations. Tables 6–8 present the means, standard deviations, and absolute and relative distribution of the scores for each dimension, determining the image.

Table 6 Evaluation of attractions

Score	Global		Dimension 1		Dimension 2		Dimension 3	
	4.16 ± 0.979		4.21 ± 0.092		4.33 ± 0.110		3.84 ± 0.128	
	n = 241	%	n = 99	41.1%	n = 81	33.6%	n = 61	25.3%
1	6	2.5	1	1.0	3	3.7	2	3.3
2	12	5.0	6	6.1	2	2.5	4	6.6
3	27	11.2	9	9.1	6	7.4	12	19.7
4	89	36.9	38	38.4	24	29.6	27	44.3
5	107	44.4	45	45.5	46	56.8	16	26.2

Note Dimension 1 = Heritage; Dimension 2 = Regional Characteristics; Dimension 3 = Culture
Source Authors' own elaboration

The global media of attractions (Table 6) was 4.16 points (±0.979), where 81.3% was positive (scores 4 and 5 points). The evaluation of each dimension follows the same trend, and the dimension with the highest average was Regional Characteristics (4.33 points ±0.110), this is also the dimension with the highest percentage of evaluations with a score of 5 points (56.8%). A positive evaluation written in August 2022 by a tourist from Amora (Portugal) concerns the beauty and the differential of the village of Rio de Onor:

> Aldeia de Rio de Onor is a beautiful community village. Upon entering the village, the first thing you notice is the typical village houses built in schist. What incredible beauty combined with the friendliness of its inhabitants. Well worth a visit.

On the other hand, Dimension 3—Culture presented a mean between neutral and positive images (3.84 points ±0.128) and the highest percentage of evaluations 1, 2 and 3 were presented in this dimension (29.6%). The evaluations with lower scores were related to the churches, with comments stating the churches were not open for visitation, as can be observed in the following review, written in October 2021 by a tourist from Brazil:

> Unfortunately, I realize that here in the region they do not like us to visit the churches, because 80% of them were closed to the public even with the hours described on the signs of operation. The churches that I went to were open because I went to mass on Sunday.

Related to the evaluation of hotels (Table 7) the global mean is 4.07 points (±1.173), representing a positive image, also corroborated with 76.5% of the evaluations with scores 4 and 5 points. Dimension 1 presented a mean (4.20 points±1.016) over the global mean, representing 79.8% of positive evaluations (4 and 5 points). One of the best-evaluated aspects was cleanliness and quality of services, as can be observed in the comment made in September 2020 by a tourist from *Viana do Castelo* (Portugal):

> The truth is that we loved everything: cleanliness, facilities, location, decoration, and friendliness. We went on a greenway promotion, but we didn´t feel the difference in treatment, they were impeccable. The room was beautiful, the view unforgettable and the service 5 stars, I do not understand why it does not have more stars. The best!.

Table 7 Evaluation of hotels

Score	Global		Dimension 1		Dimension 2	
	4.07 ± 1.173		4.20 ± 1.016		3.73 ± 1.473	
	n = 230	100%	n = 168	73%	n = 62	27%
1	16	7.0	7	4.2	9	14.5
2	8	3.5	2	1.1	6	9.7
3	30	13.0	25	14.9	5	8.1
4	66	28.7	51	30.4	15	24.2
5	110	47.8	83	49.4	27	43.5

Note Dimension 1 = Quality; Dimension 2 = Infrastructure
Source Authors' own elaboration

Table 8 Evaluation of restaurants

	Global		Dimension 1		Dimension 2	
	4.45 ± 1.080		4.78 ± 0.532		3.75 ± 1.507	
	n = 972	100%	n = 655	67.4%	n = 317	32.6%
1	45	4.7	0	0	45	14.2
2	42	4.3	6	0.9	36	11.4
3	51	5.2	19	2.9	31	9.8
4	132	13.5	85	13.0	47	14.8
5	702	72.3	544	83.2	158	49.8

Note Dimension 1 = Quality; Dimension 2 = Gastronomy
Source Authors' own elaboration

On the opposite side, Dimension 2—infrastructure, presented a mean (3.73 points ±1.473) lower than the global mean, presenting a higher percentage (32.3%) of negative or neutral evaluations (1, 2 and 3 points). The comment that best demonstrates the disappointment with the infrastructure was made in January 2020:

> Disappointing! Terrible service, I was assigned the worst room in this hotel! A back, side room with a tiny, claustrophobic window, it was probably a storage room that they remodelled to be a room! When I complained about the Wi-Fi and that there was not enough network in these rooms (number 34) the reception simply said they would send "someone" to fix it and until the day I left nobody came to see the case! They promise something and simply ignore me, the hotel with many empty rooms and make me wait for someone to fix a weak Wi-Fi signal? This room is tiny, the bathroom leaks water from the shower to the entire floor! The kettle to make tea only has tea! The coffee that appears in the photos is a lie! The mini bar is locked! Bath towels, although perfume, don't dry! The so-called Spa, they charge for everything and is outside the hotel, Turkish bath is closed for work (new detail). But the most regrettable in this inn is the disregard for the customer ... and the absurd price for what it is! Not even worth €30!.

Regarding the *Bragança* destination´s components, the restaurants were the ones that presented the highest mean 4.45 points (±1.080), with 85.8% of positive evaluations. When each dimension is analysed, Dimension 1—Quality had a high mean (4.78 points ± 0.532), with 96.2% of positive evaluations. The quality can be proven in the review written in December 2021 (Table 8):

> Restaurant with a very welcoming atmosphere. I found the food very good, well-served portions, with adequate quality and price. The staff was very friendly and attentive.

Gastronomy, with its ingredients (Dimension 2), presented a mean lower than the global mean (3.75 points ±1.507) and 35.4% of negative or neutral evaluations. Although the region of *Terras de Trás-os-Montes* is recognised for its unique gastronomy, some comments evidenced displeasure with the services and the products, as is observed in the review written by a tourist from Madrid, in September 2020:

> We were surprised at the low quality of the product seeing the number of good references this place has. We did not feel that our experience was like many reviews. The dishes were sad and not very tasty. The mushrooms were very tough. The rice was oily, and the tomatoes were nice but tasteless. The service was slow for the few tables there were. The only decent thing was the homemade chocolate cake. A shame.

5 Discussion and Conclusion

5.1 Research Implications

Related to the bibliometric analysis, the results obtained in this study highlight the scientific production between 2012 and 2022, with an annual growth rate of 49.29% and average citations per document of 16.38 citations, showing a high evolution from 2017 to the present day, demonstrating a continuous interest in this subject and introducing new approaches to analyse the image of tourist destinations.

The countries that contribute most to scientific production in the research field are Portugal and Spain, showing higher production and affiliations ratios. About 80% of the comments in the database under analysis are of Portuguese and Spanish origin.

The increasing amount of user-generated content disseminated through social media services and travel websites has made available a large amount of online information, where, in the process of destination selection and choice, tourists take advice and recommendations from others and rely on the perception and opinion of those who have already tested the tourism product [1–3].

Several studies show the positive evaluation of destinations and services from the analysis of comments on the TripAdvisor platform [1, 26, 31]. Using the same methodology, the present study can positively assess *Bragança*'s global destination, underlining distinctive ratings for the different components. Similar studies have also revealed this positive image of destinations such as Thailand [26] and also tourist equipment such as train stations [27] and airports [31].

Extensive data analysis can provide new perceptions of destination choices and support strategic decision-making in tourism destination management. In this context, for companies operating in the tourism sector, TripAdvisor represents a means of communication with customers and a place to implement a good part of the marketing strategy [9, 10, 18].

It is worth noting that studies analysing TripAdvisor are important when related to place branding and place reputation since positive reviews such as those found in this study demonstrate a good reputation of the destination and reinforce the place branding.

The definition of an attractive on TripAdvisor includes many groups and categories. For the present study, three dimensions were determined for attractions, hotels, and restaurants.

Attractions are segmented into heritage, regional features, and culture. The heritage dimensions are characterised by elements that represent the heritage of *Bragança*, such as the castle, the museum, the tower and the military. The second dimension was named regional characteristics, representing places where tourists can see regional aspects, such as villages and typical houses. Although the terms of the third dimension are similar to the first one, culture was the prominent name in this dimension since it presents aspects related to art, churches, painting and municipality. This result is directly related to the historical and cultural characteristics of *Bragança.*

There are two dimensions related to hotels: quality and infrastructure. The first dimension, quality, includes terms related to the perception of services and this is indicated with terms such as sound, excellent, clean, and comfortable.

The second dimension is the infrastructure which contains the analysis regarding the structure used during a stay in hotels in *Bragança*, such as the swimming pool, venue, and farm.

Like hotels, restaurants also have two dimensions. The first dimension is called quality, with similar terms cited in hotels. The main terms are excellent, quality, service, and atmosphere.

The second dimension is gastronomy, where the main ingredients used in the gastronomy of the *Terras de Trás-os-Montes* region are cited. Meat is recognised as a product of excellence in the region, which is demonstrated in this dimension.

The results related to hotels and restaurants did not differ from similar studies, as these are clear attributes presented in the evaluations related to these tourism destination components [26].

The most recent scientific papers show the research trend on the impacts of the pandemic and customer satisfaction with the quality of restaurant service during the outbreak of COVID-19 [21, 22]. From the analysis obtained, which considered the pandemic period, there was no disturbance caused by the pandemic, noting only a lesser influence in the lockdown months, a more significant impact on domestic tourism and a new category of analysis associated with sanitation and safety.

5.2 *Practical Implications and Contributions*

After determining the dimensions, the image of the tourism components was divided into positive, neutral, or negative based on the quantitative evaluations of TripAdvisor. In general, the hotels are well-evaluated, but it is necessary to pay attention to their infrastructure. One of the points to be highlighted is that some comments refer that the images presented on booking websites do not represent reality. They are considering the need to pay attention to what is disclosed on the websites.

Regarding restaurants, the most positive component demonstrated by the average was the image. It was analysed that it is necessary to maximise this positive image by offering quality services and products, preferably of local origin.

The global average for attractions was equally positive, and the evaluation of each dimension followed the same trend. On the one hand, culture presented an average between neutral and positive images and the highest percentage of evaluations. On the other hand, the evaluations with lower scores were related to churches, with comments stating that churches were not open to visitors.

Regarding the evaluation of the hotels, the same positive image is observed. One of the underscored aspects with a better evaluation was the service's cleanliness and quality. On the opposite side, the infrastructures presented a higher percentage of negative or neutral evaluations. As for the components of the *Bragança,* restaurants were the ones that presented the highest average with 85.8% of positive evaluations.

Comparing all the analysed dimensions, quality had a high average. Gastronomy, with its ingredients, presented a lower average than the global.

It was highlighted that the region of *Terras de Trás-os-Montes* is recognised for its unique gastronomy, but some comments showed dissatisfaction with the services and products.

It was also important to analyse that the attractions must have determined the opening hours and their compliance since the main negative comments related to this component. Strengthening regional aspects is essential to make *Bragança* a differentiated destination.

Lastly, the analysis of TripAdvisor reviews can contribute to managers and planners identifying and minimising destination weaknesses as well as maximising strengths in their marketing strategies.

5.3 *Limitations and Future Studies*

TripAdvisor's efficiency as a collaborative recommendation medium depends mainly on several factors. Although false and paid online reviews can negatively affect TripAdvisor's efficiency, as the crowd is efficient, it can also produce the barriers that safeguard itself from these opportunistic behaviours. Still, it stands out, as a significant limitation of this project is the reliability of the comments and the influence of possible conditions in the period under study. A limitation of the study may be the period of analysis. Since only the pandemic timeframe was determined, the image may be differentiated in an analysis of a longer period.

Specifically, in the bibliometric analysis, TripAdvisor; tourism; online reviews; social media; sentiment analysis stands out with a higher occurrence. In this sense, future studies should extend the analysis period and follow new lines of research within the field of sentiment analysis and regional tourist profiles.

Acknowledgements UNIAG, R&D unit funded by the FCT—Portuguese Foundation for the Development of Science and Technology, Ministry of Science, Technology and Higher Education. Project no. UIDB/04752/2020.

References

1. Kladou S, Mavragani E (2015) Assessing destination image: an online marketing approach and the case of TripAdvisor. J Destination Market Manage 4(3): 187–193. https://doi.org/10.1016/j.jdmm.2015.04.003
2. Sparks BA, Bradley GL (2017) A "Triple A" typology of responding to negative consumer-generated online reviews. J Hospital Tour Res 41(6): 719–745. https://doi.org/10.1177/1096348014538052
3. Pantano E, Priporas CV, Stylos N (2017) 'You will like it!' using open data to predict tourists' response to a tourist attraction. Tour Manage 60:430–438. https://doi.org/10.1016/j.tourman.2016.12.020
4. Zhang HY, Ji P, Wang JQ, Chen XH (2017) A novel decision support model for satisfactory restaurants utilizing social information: a case study of TripAdvisor.com. Tour Manage 59: 281–297. https://doi.org/10.1016/j.tourman.2016.08.010
5. Filieri R (2016) What makes an online consumer review trustworthy? Ann Tour Res 58:46–64. https://doi.org/10.1016/j.annals.2015.12.019
6. Filieri R, Alguezaui S, McLeay F (2015) Why do travelers trust TripAdvisor? Antecedents of trust towards consumer-generated media and its influence on recommendation adoption and word of mouth. Tour Manage 51:174–185. https://doi.org/10.1016/j.tourman.2015.05.007
7. Banerjee S, Chua AYK (2016) In search of patterns among travellers' hotel ratings in TripAdvisor. Tour Manage 53:125–131. https://doi.org/10.1016/j.tourman.2015.09.020
8. Uğur NG, Akbıyık A (2020) Impacts of COVID-19 on global tourism industry: a cross-regional comparison. Tour Manage Perspect 36(April):100744. https://doi.org/10.1016/j.tmp.2020.100744
9. Spalding M, Parrett CL (2019) Global patterns in mangrove recreation and tourism. Mar Policy 110(April):103540. https://doi.org/10.1016/j.marpol.2019.103540
10. Mkono M, Tribe J (2017) Beyond reviewing: uncovering the multiple roles of tourism social media users. J Travel Res 56(3): 287–298. https://doi.org/10.1177/0047287516636236
11. Raan AFJV (2003) The use of bibliometric analysis in research performance assessment and monitoring of interdisciplinary scientific developments. TATuP—Zeitschrift für Technikfolgenabschätzung in Theorie und Praxis. 12(1): 20–29. https://doi.org/10.14512/tatup.12.1.20
12. Guilera G, Barrios M, Gómez-Benito J (2013) Meta-analysis in psychology: a bibliometric study. Scientometrics. 94(3): 943–954. https://doi.org/10.1007/s11192-012-0761-2
13. Benckendorff P, Zehrer A (2013) A network analysis of tourism research. Ann Tour Res 43(xx): 121–149. https://doi.org/10.1016/j.annals.2013.04.005
14. Dervis H (2019) Bibliometric analysis using bibliometrix an R package. J Scientometric Res 8(3): 156–160. https://doi.org/10.5530/jscires.8.3.32

15. Fuchs M, Zanker M (2012) Multi-criteria ratings for recommender systems: an empirical analysis in the tourism domain. In: Huemers C, Lops P (eds) E-commerce and web technologies EC-Web 2012 lecture notes in business information processing. Springer Berlin Heidelberg
16. Skinner H (2021) Place branding—the challenges of getting it right: coping with success and rebuilding from crises. Tour Hospital 2(1): 173–189. https://doi.org/10.3390/tourhosp2010010
17. Cleave E, Arku G, Sadler R, Kyeremeh E (2017) Place marketing, place branding, and social media: perspectives of municipal practitioners. Growth and Change. 48(4): 1012–1033. https://doi.org/10.1111/grow.12189
18. Colladon AF, Guardabascio B, Innarella R (2019) Using social network and semantic analysis to analyze online travel forums and forecast tourism demand. Decis Support Syst 123(January):113075. https://doi.org/10.1016/j.dss.2019.113075
19. Ganzaroli A, De Noni I, van Baalen P (2017) Vicious advice: analyzing the impact of TripAdvisor on the quality of restaurants as part of the cultural heritage of Venice. Tour Manage 61:501–510. https://doi.org/10.1016/j.tourman.2017.03.019
20. Fang B, Ye Q, Kucukusta D, Law R (2016) Analysis of the perceived value of online tourism reviews: influence of readability and reviewer characteristics. Tour Manage 52:498–506. https://doi.org/10.1016/j.tourman.2015.07.018
21. Zibarzani M, Abumalloh RA, Nilashi M, Samad S, Alghamdi OA, Nayer FK et al (2022) Customer satisfaction with restaurants service quality during COVID-19 outbreak: a two-stage methodology. Technol Soc 70(April):101977. https://doi.org/10.1016/j.techsoc.2022.101977
22. Rita P, Moro S, Cavalcanti G (2022) The impact of COVID-19 on tourism: analysis of online reviews in the airlines sector. J Air Transp Manage 104(August): 1–11. https://doi.org/10.1016/j.jairtraman.2022.102277
23. Kastenholz E, Cunha D, Eletxigerra A, Carvalho M, Silva I (2022) The experience economy in a wine destination—analysing visitor reviews. Sustainability. 14(15): 1–19. https://doi.org/10.3390/su14159308
24. Chu M, Chen Y, Yang L, Wang J (2022) Language interpretation in travel guidance platform: text mining and sentiment analysis of TripAdvisor reviews. Front Psychol 13:1–8. https://doi.org/10.3389/fpsyg.2022.1029945
25. Colantonio C (2022) TripAdvisor reviews: a new genre in the tourism discourse? Textos en Proceso 8(1): 42–59. https://doi.org/10.17710/tep.2022.8.1.3colantonio
26. Taecharungroj V, Mathayomchan B (2019) Analysing TripAdvisor reviews of tourist attractions in Phuket, Thailand. Tour Manage 75:550–568. https://doi.org/10.1016/j.tourman.2019.06.020
27. Taecharungroj V (2022) An analysis of tripadvisor reviews of 127 urban rail transit networks worldwide. Travel Behav Soc 26: 193–205. https://doi.org/10.1016/j.tbs.2021.10.007
28. INE I.N. de E (2021) Censos 2021. https://censos.ine.pt/xportal/xmain?xpgid=censos21_populacao&xpid=CENSOS21
29. Ali T, Marc B, Omar B, Soulaimane K, Larbi S (2021) Exploring destination's negative e-reputation using aspect based sentiment analysis approach: case of Marrakech destination on TripAdvisor. Tour Manage Perspect 40(January):100892. https://doi.org/10.1016/j.tmp.2021.100892
30. Guo Y, Barnes SJ, Jia Q (2017) Mining meaning from online ratings and reviews: tourist satisfaction analysis using latent dirichlet allocation. Tour Manage 59:467–483. https://doi.org/10.1016/j.tourman.2016.09.009
31. Gitto S, Mancuso P (2017) Improving airport services using sentiment analysis of the websites. Tour Manage Perspect 22:132–136. https://doi.org/10.1016/j.tmp.2017.03.008

Hospitality Branding: Expressing the Brand Through Design and Transferable Experiences

Marina Peres

Abstract A brand is a powerful corporate asset. A brand is much more than a name or logo. A brand, while a representation of personality, refers to the values, and experiences of its customers and the way the brand is perceived by the public and client. Design is an obvious and practical way for organizations to make their products and services more distinctive (Best, K.: Design Management. (2016).). The branding process and brand position are important factors for differentiating a brand in the market. In turn, brand identity is a crucial element of communication with the public. We are emotional beings. We like stories and stories are important to how we as humans understand the world around us. Stories make us feel good, make us explore the senses and revive memories. Stories activate brain and body regions and stimulate emotional and biological brain responses that encourage sharing experiences. The human ability to recall a story increases, as it becomes incorporated into sensory areas. Strong emotions and feelings retain more vivid and lasting memories. Brands should be able to tell stories capturing the public's attention, stimulate empathy and create emotional connections that move the public in their actions and attitudes. A brand story needs to resonate with potential consumers and form a strong bond and loyalty moving forward. The best stories stimulate action by offering our mind simulation (knowledge about how to act) along with inspiration (motivation to act). Hospitality branding uses stories to build empathy with the public and the public with the brand. The development of an emotional brand culture allows for greater connection with the public and therefore a greater loyalty to it (Aaker in Managing Brand Equity, The Free Press, New York, 1991). Combining brand strategy with consistent brand communication and storytelling—the good narrative is with the brand's vision, mission, and corporate culture—with extensive knowledge of the brand's sector, it offers innovative and differentiating design solutions. This, in turn, will be a lever of creativity that applies the design and the brand to create different experiences for its audience and brand followers.

M. Peres (✉)
Media and Culture, Research Institute for Design, Dubai Institute for Design and Innovation (DIDI), Dubai, United Arab Emirates
e-mail: mperes1@gmail.com

N. Martins and D. Raposo (eds.), *Communication Design and Branding*,
Springer Series in Design and Innovation 32,
https://doi.org/10.1007/978-3-031-35385-7_13

Keywords Brand strategy · Visual identity · Visual communication · Customer experience · Immersive experience

1 Hospitality Branding

1.1 Brand-Led Emotional Experiences

Hospitality branding "is the collection of elements that express your unique value proposition to each potential client. It encompasses aesthetic features such as logos and color schemes and the ideals, values, and type of experience that clients expect from you." [1]. According to one study[1] developed by scholars focusing on sustainable luxury brands and products, the hospitality industry clearly dominates in parallel with the fashion industry. Since the fashion industry is "the second largest cause of pollution worldwide" [2].

Design Management offers strategies to design products and service development, from the initial research [3] until desirable by the customers. Aligning brand values and brand beliefs to images of lifestyle.

As a design-led and decision-making process, customers are at the center of the business offer and design process. Firstly, the role of design in business is to help to create a brand aligned with the mission and vision, visually and experientially. Furthermore, develop products and services that address the needs and ambitions of the customers.

Empathy is a method that allows the design team to know about customers' needs and ambitions. Brands operate in the "emotional territory of people´s hearts and minds" [4]. Providing customer experiences through emotional experiences. The brand experience went even further when aligned with consistent brand communication.

A brand communicates to the public. A brand conveys its key ideas, personality, promises, purpose, aspirations, and corporate values to the public through visual representations. One of its main objectives is to transform the public into potential customers, and customers into brand ambassadors. The stronger, more targeted, and more effective this narrative is, the more likely the product or service will be successful.

A strong brand strategy transforms assets, making them more livable, more visible, more inspiring and in turn valuable. Developing a brand strategy with that end goal in mind is critically important. Customers' experience extends beyond a large room and large and comfortable bed. It is an integral part of consistent and continuous brand communication.

Strategy typically focuses on outcomes and sustainability, whereas design is often concerned with the process of creating those outcomes. Despite this distinction,

[1] Springer–Business Research (2020) 13:541–601.

it is possible to align design with business strategy using measurable tools. By establishing a common language, businesses can facilitate effective communication between their design and strategy teams, ultimately resulting in a more cohesive approach to achieving organizational goals [5].

Through the use of metrics and other quantifiable measures, businesses can assess the impact of design decisions on their overall strategy. This not only ensures that design decisions are aligned with business goals but also provides a framework for evaluating the success of those decisions.

In essence, a measurable approach to design helps bridge the gap between strategy and design by providing a common language that enables effective communication and collaboration between the two. This ultimately leads to better outcomes and increased sustainability, as design decisions are made with a clear understanding of their impact on the broader business strategy.

Brand communication needs consistently communicate brand personality. Communicate brand personality is like tell a story. A story is not just a series of facts, but a narrative with a clear purpose to capture the audience interest in the most effective way possible. And nothing captures our interests more than a question, what happens next? The story has a beginning, a middle and an end. The story needs to be share with the right language and channel. Furthermore, storytelling is not just about telling literal narratives, but about evoking a feeling, and emotions, and creating empathy.

Creating the right brand language and signature elements with a brand-focused approach sharing its DNA with a deep understanding of the values, attitudes and behavior of the target customer to create strong customer emotional connection and loyalty.

1.2 Enhancing the Customer Experience in the Hospitality Industry

Brand loyalty is described as a behavioral response and as a function of psychological processes [6]. A customer-first approach is paramount to success in hospitality branding. Customer satisfaction and happiness are always a core goal and the first commitment. Customers purchase products and services based on emotions and their desire for the experiences.

The connection between our emotions and our experiences is an important aspect of hospitality branding. By understanding the role that emotions play in shaping our experiences, hospitality brands can work to create more meaningful connections with guests and build a stronger, more positive reputation over time.

In the hospitality industry, happy guests will generate two critical phenomena that are directedly linked to word-of-mouth referrals: more memorable, create trust and an emotional connection. Brand and design decisions should be made in conscience with the responsibility a brand and its products have. Promising a comfortable, valuable, and unique experience for the customers is one of the main goals of the brand. It is fundamental to work on the relationships between the brand and the customer to deliver the brand´s vision.

Consistency helps to bridge trust. Consistency in design has a huge influence on customer experience. As designers, we need to ensure the customers received the same message at any given touchpoint. Design strategies can increase the customer experience by exploring initiatives that go through listening to the customer's voice.

Stories as part of the brand strategy talk about the mission, brand values, the brand relationship with customers, and brand social initiatives related to sustainability and well-being.

Brand and design strategies significantly increase the likelihood of the guest's connection to the brand and in turn the likelihood of a long-term relationship with the brand, when aligned with the needs and ambitions of its guests. Brand communication should be consistent and focus on guest experiences and loyalty. The first step toward loyalty begins with the customer's becoming aware of the product [7] and brands need to provide open channels for brand relationships with the customer to enhance brand loyalty. For a clear and open communication process, brands need to be sure all touchpoints are strategically aligned. Consistent experiences build trust. And as your organization grows and you add more and more features and elements to your product, this becomes harder and harder to keep a handle on.

2 Hotel Brand Sector

2.1 Cities as Ecosystems of Hospitality Brands and Social Well-Being

Urban centers are developed by people for people. And cities are human-constructed environments designed to cater to the needs and ambitions of their inhabitants. These environments offer diverse experiences and opportunities for the creation of personal memories. Regardless of the degree of cosmopolitan character, cities are prepared to receive human populations and offer access to a range of products and services for their use and enjoyment.

The displacement of people makes the hospitality sector invest more and more in brand recognition through customer relationships and the emotional experiences they can provide. This practice, in a chain, helps to increase the quality of life in cities by bringing more tourists.

Hotels are part of the city's ecosystems. The hotel belongs first to the place where it is built, and then to the people that will work and stay in it.

The covid-19 pandemic had a huge impact on the hotel industry. Beyond the negatively influencing of an extremely saturated market, was the need to adapt to the new challenges and measures imposed by the market and healthy organizations.

During COVID, the hotel industry has taken extreme measures to ensure their guests were safe, tested and comfortable during the entire service experience.

The big challenge for hospitality brands was to retain customers and make the way for new customers and guests. Society relearned to socialize face-to-face after a long period of restrictions and human physical interactions.

Health and sanitation concerns emotionally affected how customers buy a hotel product or service and as guests, how they experience it. Drastic hotel occupancy limits have dampened ambitions for many, and hotels started rethinking their products and services to provide safe and happy experiences to customers.

Likewise, it became necessary to rethink the services and brand strategies to create new and meaningful stories reinforcing the well-being and safe experiences provided by hotels in a post-covid era.

3 Sustainable Luxury

3.1 Sustainability and Luxury in Hospitality

Hospitality is one of the largest consumers of resources such as energy, water, and other natural resources. And consumers are becoming more conscious of their environmental impact and are looking for companies that align with their values. Hospitality brands that demonstrate a commitment to sustainability can improve their reputation and appeal to environmentally conscious customers.

Additionally, governments and other entities and NGOs around the world are implementing regulations aimed at reducing the environmental impact of industries, including the hospitality sector. By adopting sustainable practices, hospitality brands can ensure they comply with these regulations and avoid potential penalties.

The luxury sector has been constantly growing. Luxury products and services have attracted the interest of many. From a social perspective, the luxury industry through mass products to a broad scope has a big chance to create connections between luxury and corporate social responsibility[2] (CSR) and sustainability.

Luxury experience goes beyond material things, it is about spirituality and balance [8]. The values linked to sustainable luxury and the perception of eco products, circular systems or sustainable practices as part of the luxury experience are topics hospitality brands need to be aware of as they have a significant impact on brand reputation and loyalty implications.

How far is a sustainable luxury experience from a luxury and consumerism experience?

Sustainability and luxury in the hospitality industry refers to the integration of environmentally friendly and socially responsible practices into the operations and culture of luxury hotels, resorts, and other types of hospitality businesses. This can

[2] Corporate social responsibility (CSR) is a company's commitment to strive for profitability whilst acting as a good citizen (Freeman and Velamuri 2006),

include many actions and tactics by reducing energy and water usage, implementing waste reduction and recycling programs, sourcing sustainable food and products, and offering eco-friendly amenities and activities for guests.

Nowadays talking about luxury is not only referring to a single product or service but relates to creating desirable moments with a focus on corporate social responsibility and sustainability [9]. The compatibility between luxury and sustainability is a paradox of consumerism, as the sustainable development has become persistent problem for luxury brands [10]. In the current business landscape, sustainable development has emerged as a pivotal issue for all business. Even the luxury industry, has become a focal point in discussions about sustainability. This is because luxury represents a form of consumption that prioritizes motivations beyond functionality [4].

Beyond the moment we walk into the luxury hotel lobby, a Michelin star restaurant, or a business flight company, we appreciate every single detail about the interior design, the colors and the textures inside the room, the service, even the sound and smell of the place. The way we see and perceive those elements is fundamental to create a customer brand image and in consequence brand loyalty. However, there is so much more to how you feel than what you see.

By embracing sustainability, luxury hotels can enhance their reputation and attract guests who are increasingly conscious about the impact of their travel on the environment and their social responsibility to protect the planet for future generations.

The hotel industry has a major impact on sustainability "due to its consumption of natural resources, its effect on the environment, and its economic and social impact on the communities in which such establishments are located" [11]. On the other hand, more than ever, consumers search for information about hotels' sustainability, as they are more aware of sustainability global concerns and global procedures.

Balancing sustainability and luxury can be challenging, as some guests may have different expectations and perceptions of what constitutes luxury. However, incorporate sustainability into their branding efforts, highlighting their commitment to environmental and social responsibility should be part of their overall offering and to provide guests with an exceptional experience while also reducing the negative impact of tourism on the environment and local communities.

Hospitality brands need to be aware and brand strategy should include tactics and activities to increase their footprint and the planet's responsibility. It is time to implement sustainability and circularity, in the operations and brand strategy.

The study [11] about sustainability and hospitality developed in 2020 provides crucial information for hotel managers and for society which stands to benefit if this sector improves its environmental, social, and economic performance. The paper shows consumers WTPM[3] in luxury hospitality when businesses are values-driven or more conscious about sustainability and impactful practices. On the other side, it shows how the hotel industry could establish brand operation strategies to retain more responsible consumers in improving their sustainability practices.

[3] Willingness to pay more for green products.

Hospitality brands must prioritize sustainable practices in their operations, such as minimizing waste, conserving energy, and reducing carbon emissions. This can be achieved through the adoption of eco-friendly technologies and materials, as well as the implementation of sustainable supply chain practices. On the other hand, hospitality brands can communicate their commitment to sustainability through their branding efforts. This includes incorporating sustainability into their marketing campaigns, showcasing their sustainable practices on their website and social media platforms, and partnering with sustainability-focused organizations to demonstrate their dedication to responsible business practices.

3.2 *Soneva Fushi Eco-Resort. A Success Story*

The Maldives is a coral island nation located in the Indian Ocean. Spanning 600 miles with 26 atolls, which are made up of more than 1,000 coral islands, 200 of which are inhabited by local populations while the remaining 120 are reserved exclusively for tourist resorts [12].

The Maldives faces several challenges, including climate change and rising sea levels, which threaten its low-lying islands. The country has taken steps to address these challenges, including setting ambitious targets for renewable energy and working with international partners on climate adaptation measures.

Soneva Fushi (Fig. 1) is an eco-resort located in the Baa Atoll, Kunfunadhoo Island, one of the largest islands in the Maldives. Set in 1995 the resort is situated on a UNESCO-protected 'Biosphere Reserve' meaning flora, fauna and sea life all feel completely uncompromised by the constant human interaction with the island, in fact.

As an example of how luxury brand strategy can be aligned with sustainability and planet responsibility, they have been reducing their environmental impact and increasing biodiversity, implementing sustainable and circular practices all over the years.

According to Soneva's Sustainability Achievements in 2019, the Soneva group banned imported bottled water in 2008 and filters, mineralises, alkalises and bottles its water on-site. Based on the same source, Soneva "has averted the production of 1,500,000 plastic bottles in the last 10 years by using reusable glass bottles. A percentage of revenues from Soneva Water funds over 500 clean water projects in more than 50 countries. It provides clean water to over 750,000 via charities such as Water Charity and Thirst Aid."

The eco-resort has developed a sustainable and circular system called "Eco Centro Waste to Wealth". Following the circular principles to Reduce—Reuse—Recycle, it turns most waste into value and nutrients for the soil, such as compost. Soneva Fushi's main objective was to challenge peoples' perception of waste and tackle waste issues on an island like the Maldives [12].

Fig. 1 Soneva Fushi. Eco-resort is situated in the Maldives (*Source* The air design)

In 2015 the resort brought a new glass recycling centre, "which blows fresh glass tumblers for Soneva Fushi and Soneva Jani, and even invites master glassblowers to create one-of-a-kind pieces of art" [13] (Fig. 2).

Fig. 2 Soneva Fushi's art and glass studio, launched in 2015 [14]

The eco-resort has been building collaboration with Makers' Place as the British artist Alexander James Hamilton,[4] founder of the Distil Ennui Studio™. The artist in an advocate for sustainability at a community, island, and governmental level for over 35 years. He is a passionate ambassador for circular design, "his art engages with the broader public sphere through interventions within natural landscapes and civic spaces alike, arts education, policymaking, issues of sustainability and ecocide" [13].

"Scientific research findings suggest that sustainability has become an element of quality expected by luxury customers" [15]. Designing models of cooperation for luxury experiences also provide responsible and sustainable practices within the hotel industry and other entities to drive real change. That means more and better cooperation with civil society, public entities, NGOs, and the private sector to collaborate, is needed.

To ensure resilience in hotels and hotel groups, a systemic change approach is needed. Design managers and business leaders are responsible for innovating and developing processes and best practices to offer sustainable, environmentally, and socially impactful brand solutions. They always need to work together through a systemic way of thinking. Incorporating circularity before engaging with suppliers, purchases from bio-based and locally sourced suppliers, and plastic alternatives. And in addition, benefits local communities and the environment.

4 Brand Identity and Hospitality

4.1 Creating Hospitality Brands Through Consistent Brand Identity

One of the principal offerings within the hospitality industry is the hotel. As a brand, a hotel serves as a symbol of its unique identity and, as a group, it encompasses a collective of shared characteristics and values under a unified brand umbrella. The perception and evaluation of a hotel by its customers are continuously influenced by the mental and emotional connections established with its branding. The branding of a hotel encompasses the visual representation and image that the hotel conveys to its guests or customers.

A brand strategy needs to be clear on the branding, and whom it aims to serve, and most importantly, gain a clear understanding of what makes it unique. Just at the beginning of the process, designers should have a clear understanding of the brand's mission, vision, and values to ensure the brand identity will be aligned with the customer's goals and ambitions.

Brand designers are storytellers. They can tell a brand story through visuals and create brand concept options supported by research. Designers have the skills and

[4] Sculpture, painting, photography, film, lighting and installation.

background and a clear understanding of the business to conduct a hospitality brand identity program align with the brand purpose and target audience.

Brand identity includes a group of components that comprise hotel branding. There are some aspects designers need to consider when creating a Brand Identity: consistency, authenticity, and the ability to communicate the mission, vision and brand corporate culture through visual references all over the brand touchpoints.

Brands need to have a straight relationship between satisfaction and brand loyalty. One of the first steps in maintaining customer brand loyalty is to build and sustain a positive brand image. A strong brand image is important to brand owners because the brand name distinguishes a product from the competitor's products. Brand image should be a truthful, enlightening, insightful and beautiful message to eye-catch customer attention.

Design management is linked to design, innovation, and technology to provide a competitive advantage across economic, social/cultural, and environmental factors. Design management empowers design to enhance collaboration and synergy between "design" and "business" improving design effectiveness.

The scope of design management ranges from tactical management of corporate design functions and strategies across the organization as a key differentiator and driver of brand success [16].

Design management refers to the continuous processes, strategic decisions, and business practices that facilitate innovation and the creation of well-designed products, services, communications, environments, and brands. The aim of design management is to improve the quality of life for individuals while also achieving organizational success.

Moreover, design management involves the utilization of effective communication channels, teamwork, and leadership to ensure that design processes run smoothly and efficiently. By aligning design efforts with broader business objectives, design management supports both organizational success and the enhancement of individual quality of life.

The design process to develop a brand identity is a systemic process, as it combines different areas to cover the "ongoing processes, business decisions, and strategies that enable innovation and create effectively-designed products, services, communications, environments, and brands that enhance our quality of life and provide organizational success" [17].

As a systemic process it follows a series of design activities, using methods and tools along the four main stages: understanding, ideation, concept development and delivery. And to ensure the collection of elements express a brand unique value proposition to each potential customer.

A brand identity aims to create shared value and build long-term relationships, creating a meaningful role in customers' lives. And consistency is key and brand purpose aligns customer needs with the brand offer and the emotional experience. There are some key advantages to having a brand purpose: brand purpose adds value to society as a whole; it helps to build an emotional relationship between a brand and its consumer (brand loyalty); a unique brand purpose can differentiate the brand from competitors,

The brand purpose is more than, making a profit or driving shareholder value. The higher reason for being a brand is to exist. Furthermore, brand purpose engages customers through living brand experiences, creating ecosystems to make people's lives better. For example, what makes the Nike brand personality so unique, is that the company can appeal to almost anyone that wants the best, the company can attract almost everyone who wants the best and anticipates the customer experience by highlighting human strengths: "To bring inspiration and innovation to every athlete in the world. If you have a body, you are an athlete."[5]

A Brand Identity includes the visual aspect of the brand such as logos, symbol, visual system including the color schemes and typography rules but also the values and type of experience that customers expect from the brand.

Considering we are visual beings and more than ninety per cent of our perceived communication comes from non-verbal cues, and only a small percentage of our perceived communication comes from words, a brand identity must have a strong visual image linked with the brand personality, purpose, and reason for coming into existence in the first place. Together these factors have a powerful influence on accelerating growth and impacting the world and creating brand customer loyalty to achieve the commitment level with customers: have an intense and emotional attachment, receive self-expressive benefits, and have a customer experience that goes beyond merely functional benefits.

A design audit is an opportunity to check the quality of the designs, the visual aspect of the brand, the products, and the user experience, and ensure the visual elements are consistent use across all brand materials. Basically, a design audit is a checkup to make sure the company is expressing itself consistently across all communication channels. By analyzing the consistency of the brand or business visual references and core messages, it is possible to compare to other brands and businesses and identify and fix any inconsistencies. By conducting a design audit there´s a chance to strengthen the brand once again.

At its core, a design audit requires gathering and assessing all brand references, written, and verbal communication, from the business card to website or other social media, from products to services—including any workshops or webinars the brand host, from staff operations to customers feedback channels or even from uniforms to interior design or retail. Many questions can be asked regarding a design audit analysis: is the same logo file always used across assets? Do they use the correct logo and colors? Is the navigation on the website always the same? Is the same logo file always used across assets? Is the typography the same throughout? Does it too follow branding guidelines?

A design audit helps systematically analyze the internal factors of the brand identifying its strength, such as the brand's advantage of improving competitiveness or its disadvantage compared with its competitors, such as its weakness. On the other hand, design audit as a framework, also provide information about the external factors, as the opportunity to improve, but also identify the brand's unfavorable factors in a certain environment or company's competitive position, such as threats. The external

[5] Nike Vision Statement.

factors are not something the company or the brand can control or change but can identify or develop strategies to take advantage of them or minimize their impact.

5 Airlines Brand Sector

5.1 TAP Portugal and the Retro Flight Success Story

Nowadays, travel is more accessible, and each customer has the power to start their own brand experience handling their own booking and looking for recommendations without any intermediary. More than ever, brands must empower brand identity and touchpoints through visual communication and strategic design process to enhance customer brand image and loyalty.

With the ambition to expand its capacity opens new routes, and as part of the celebrations of the 72nd anniversary in the flying business, in 2017 the company invited passengers on board its retro-styled "Portugal" aircraft headed to Toronto, Canada.

The brand strategy was to develop a Retro Flight customer experience using a brand communication campaign providing a back-in-time visual and emotional experience to the customers [18].

The design strategy was to develop a temporary brand image retro look back. The classic image chosen recreates the original 'Transportes Aéreos Portugueses' with typography in the colors which were first displayed on a Lockheed Super Constellation aircraft, received by TAP in July of 1955.

Travelling through time was a glamorous and glorious experience provided to the customers. The main story was based on a 70 s scenario, exploring the communication channels' touchpoints to create a consistent narrative and enhance the customer's experience. The aircraft, an Airbus A330, named "Portugal"[6] was repainted with TAP's 1970s branding (one of the most iconic TAP corporate logos). Crew and staff uniform design takes into consideration many factors: the working environments including varied climates, versatility, durability and practicality, security, health and safety regulations, cost-efficiency, and cultural and religious sensitivities as well (Figs. 3, 4 and 5).

The brand experience went even further, with some partnerships including films from the 1970s via inflight entertainment, as well as a golden oldies music channel, Portuguese products, beyond others, the Sagres beer, the 1928 chocolate brand Regina, bringing back its classic Regina fortune chocolate box, and Ach Brito lavender cologne. All to enhance the customer's experience. Exploring the excellent Portuguese gastronomy, an original menu of the time was developed, and a Michelin chef joined the flight, providing high-level Portuguese dishes with famous red and white wine.

---

[6] This was the second time a TAP aircraft has received the name of the country. As the first one was a Boeing 747–200, delivered to TAP in February of 1972.

Fig. 3 and Fig. 4 Aircraft A330, "Portugal" with TAP's iconic logo from the 70 s. The emblematic company uniforms, designed by French stylist Louis Féraude, for the Retro Flight experience (*Image Source* The air design)

The retrojet[7] is all about branding and connecting emotionally with customers/ passengers. TAP, as a business goes all out with jet-age service to speak to customers'

[7] Retrojet is civil airliner painted in a historic livery.

Fig. 5 Portuguese products from the 70 s (*Image Source* The air design)

nostalgia for the 70 s. According to TAP co-owner on the time, David G. Neeleman[8]—in the end, that main objective has been firmly achieved with not just an Airbus A330 retrojet, but a full historical experience from a golden age of flying for the airline. In addition, a very important cultural and pollical time for the Portuguese nation.

6 Branding and Technology

6.1 Experimental Design as a Technological Approach to Hospitality Branding

With the technological advances and the opportunities of digital channels for sharing online, brands have more visibility and are more exposed to new opportunities. New customers, and new rivals as a competing brand in a market even more global.

Many companies use stories for organizational purposes. Creating empathic relations with the public to create a strong connection with the company and the brand.

[8] Brazilian-American businessmen and entrepreneurs, and former majority shareholders of the TAP Air.
Portugal Group.

People can mimic brain patterns and link them to events they haven't experienced firsthand. According to Uri Hasson,[9] storytelling fosters deep social interactions through brain-to-brain connection and transport people into your experiences and make them live in their memories. This phenomenon is called "brain coupling".

Brain coupling has been investigated using various neuroimaging techniques, such as functional magnetic resonance imaging (fMRI). In this context, studies from Hasson's laboratory have shown that when individuals are affected by the same experience or similar patterns of brain activity, their brain activity becomes synchronized or "aligned." This can happen even if they are not in the same place [10].

In the context of brand communication, when success stories are shared, they allow potential customers to perceive the brand, emotionally deeply and in a positive way, which in turn evokes other regions of the brain favorably. Experimental Design puts the customer at the heart of the experience, as part of the Brand's Purpose.

At the beginning of 2023, Louis Vuitton Brand takes over Harrods Façade to mark the Launch of the Yayoi Kusama Collaboration. Using a projection mapping technique has the brand projected a colorful, moving Yayoi Kusama polka dot design onto the façade of Harrods (Figs. 6 and 7).

Beyond to bringing art to the streets Louis Vuitton x Yayoi Kusama uses the Harrods iconic exterior as a vast canvas, to tell a story of the brand at the heart of London community. Mapping the façade and the 27 windows at street level, with the iconic Yayoi Kusama's visuals elements to create an immersive experience to customers.

Similar brand actions started to be applied to hospitality brands. Even more, branded hotel experiences are popping up across the world, the challenge is to give the customers what they really want—a memorable experience. An immersive experience in a branded hotel is something that is not so common. Offering an immersive experience is a powerful way to give potential guests a way to explore hotels, and to give brand loyalists a way to explore locations and amenities they aren't familiar with.

A collaboration with Rotana Hotels in Dubai and the design academy has been developed for a proposal rebranding of the iconic Villa Rotana Hotel in Business Bay. A dynamic visual grammar inspired by local artefacts that generate a systemic language through a series of abstract or geometric shapes is being developed. This theme aims to explore an open dialogue among motion graphics and brands with the common goal of building stronger relationships between the customer and the place through an immersive and emotional but also sensory experience.

Another example of using technology to express brand personality and create an immersive experience is the Dot Hotel, as the new chic and basic hotel in the heart of Madrid. Starting with the brand proposition of "Find you Dot", the dot is the visual connection on all communication channels (Fig. 8).

It uses "dot" as part of its bold and iconic visual identity representing the center of Madrid. The hotel explores a creative narrative to 'dot', combining the place, culture

[9] Professor of Psychology and Social Neuroscience at the Department of Psychology Princeton University.

Fig. 6 and Fig. 7 Lighting up the entire Harrods building façade with Louis Vuitton and Yayoi Kusama polka dot design (*Image Source* Retail focus)

Fig. 8 Visual references of the bold and iconic visual identity of the dot hotel (*Image Source* Chic and basic hotels)

and hospitality in a system of immersive installations. According to the brand: "dot is a wake-up call, a point to stop and start a new experience".

7 Conclusion

Effective hospitality branding through design is a multifaceted process that involves careful consideration of various factors such as user experience, brand identity, and transferable experiences. By creating an environment that is consistent with the brand's values and identity, and by offering experiences that are unique, memorable, and transferable, hospitality businesses can establish a strong connection with their customers and create a loyal following. Through a strategic and thoughtful approach to design, hospitality brands can effectively communicate their message and differentiate themselves in a crowded market, ultimately leading to increased customer loyalty and business success.

As humans, our emotional experiences are heavily influenced by unique situational factors. Our collective and personal histories play a significant role in shaping our expectations and reactions to life events. The concept of emotions being experienced by our whole selves applies to hospitality branding as well. In the hospitality industry, creating a strong emotional connection with guests is critical to establishing brand loyalty and building a positive reputation. Hospitality brands can create emotional connections with guests by providing personalized experiences, paying attention to their needs, and fostering a welcoming and inclusive atmosphere.

With a welcoming atmosphere by creating an environment that is both physically and emotionally comfortable, the brand can help guests feel have a stronger emotional connection and a more positive brand experience.

Overall, the connection between our emotions and our experiences is an important aspect of hospitality branding and one that should not be overlooked by those in the industry. By understanding the role that emotions play in shaping our experiences, hospitality brands can work to create more meaningful connections with guests and build a stronger, more positive reputation over time.

Guest experience is also related to how hospitality brands adopt sustainable practices, from reducing their environmental impact, as hospitality is one of the largest consumers of resources such as energy, water, and other natural resources. By adopting sustainable practices, hospitality brands can reduce their environmental impact and contribute to the preservation of the planet.

Additionally, storytelling in hospitality branding can serve to foster empathy between the brand and its target audience. Narrative techniques can serve as an effective means of transporting individuals into the experiences of others, thereby allowing them to vicariously live through the memories of the storyteller.

By establishing an emotional brand culture, a deeper connection can be established, leading to increased brand loyalty. To accomplish this, it is imperative to integrate a sustainable brand strategy with consistent brand communication, aligned with the brand's vision, mission, and corporate culture, and it can provide unique and differentiated design solutions that can serve as a catalyst for hospitality brands.

Incorporating sustainability into hospitality branding is an increasingly crucial aspect of creating a competitive edge in the industry.

Consumers are becoming increasingly aware of environmental and social issues and are placing a greater emphasis on sustainability when making purchasing decisions. Hospitality businesses that demonstrate a commitment to sustainability are more likely to attract and retain environmentally conscious customers, which can lead to increased customer loyalty and a competitive advantage.

Incorporating sustainability into branding can also lead to cost savings for businesses. By implementing sustainable practices such as reducing waste, conserving energy, and using eco-friendly materials, businesses can reduce their environmental impact while also reducing operational costs.

Sustainable branding can improve a business's reputation and enhance its image as a responsible corporate citizen. This can lead to increased trust and credibility among stakeholders, including customers, investors, and employees.

Overall, incorporating sustainability into hospitality branding is a crucial aspect of creating a competitive edge in the industry, as it not only meets the expectations of environmentally conscious consumers but also leads to cost savings and improved reputation.

Brands that prioritize sustainability in their operations and marketing efforts can foster a positive brand image, engender customer loyalty, and differentiate themselves in a crowded market. To achieve these outcomes, hospitality brands must take a comprehensive and integrated approach that involves not only sustainable operational practices, but also effective communication and engagement with customers to promote sustainable behaviors. By doing so, hospitality brands can position themselves as leaders in the industry and contribute to a more sustainable future.

References

1. De Pino F (2023) Hospitality branding—stand above the rest. https://mediaboom.com/news/hospitality-branding
2. Woodside AG, Fine MB (2019) Sustainable fashion themes in luxury brand storytelling: the sustainability fashion research grid. J Global Fashion Market
3. Best K (2016) Design management
4. Olins W (2004) Wally olins. Thames & Hudson
5. Lockwood T, Walton T (2008) Building design strategy. Allworth Press
6. Jacoby J, Kyner DB (1973) Brand loyalty versus repeat purchasing behavior. J Market Res 10(1)
7. Aaker DA (1991) Managing brand equity. The Free Press, New York
8. Perez ME (2021) Sustainability & luxury in hospitality
9. Rubini L, De Chiara F (2015) Luxury and sustainability: a common future? The match depends on how consumers define luxury. J Bus Res 68(9):1833–1838. https://doi.org/10.1016/j.jbusres.2015.03.028
10. Gardetti MA, Torres AL (2019) Sustainable luxury: bridging the paradox. In: Handbook of sustainable luxury textiles and fashion. Routledge, pp 3–13
11. Boronat-Navarro M, Pérez-Aranda JA (2020) Willingness to pay more to stay in a sustainable hotel. J Sustain 12(9): 3730. https://doi.org/10.3390/su12093730
12. Shivdasani E, Shivdasani, https://www.agroecology-pool.org/portfolio/sonveva_fushi/
13. Slow Life Magazine. Makers' place: transforming waste into works of art. https://soneva.com/soneva-fushi-launches-makers-place/
14. The Design Air Homepage. https://thedesignair.net/2016/09/27/hot-hotel-soneva-fushi-maldives/
15. Holson D (2012) The strategic designer. How Books, Tools and techniques for managing the design process
16. DMI Homepage. https://www.dmi.org/page/What_is_Design_Manag
17. Kunz J, May S, Schmidt HJ (2020) Sustainable luxury: current status and perspectives for future research. Business research, Springer, Heidelberg, vol 13, no 2, pp 541–601. ISSN 2198-2627https://doi.org/10.1007/s40685-020-00111-3
18. The Design Air Homepage. https://thedesignair.net/2017/07/17/tap-portugal-commences-retro-flight-on-special-retrojet
19. Chic&Basic Homepage. https://www.chicandbasic.com/en/hotel-dot-madrid/services-facilities/
20. Hasson H (2020) Q&A with Professor of Neuroscience Uri Hasson. The future of storytelling. https://medium.com/future-of-storytelling/q-a-with-professor-of-neuroscience-uri-hasson

Legacy of the Reactivation: Communication and Media at the Service of the Business Movement and Resilience to the COVID-19 Pandemic in Spain

Fernando Olivares-Delgado and María Teresa Benlloch-Osuna

Abstract It is interesting to share an initiative that we consider relevant from a business and social point of view. It is a business "activism" movement that emerged on the first day of the lockdown decreed in Spain in response to the COVID-19 pandemic. The movement was structured in several phases: the initial phase, *Esto no tiene que parar*; the intermediate phase, *Actívate*; and the final phase, *Legacy of the Reactivation*. This text describes how an entrepreneurial initiative that arose almost spontaneously, in a context of unprecedented uncertainty and lack of information, such as that experienced during the initial phase of the pandemic, evolved into a powerful tool for business and social resilience in Spain. Through the analysis of a case study, the role of communication management for the activation of projects is mainly detailed. The results lead to affirm that strategic communication and the activation of the appropriate media and supports, mainly textual and audiovisual social networks, were decisive for the success of the project. *Legacy of the Reactivation* represents the beginning of a new era in which companies are called upon to act with determination, through the allocation of economic and intangible resources, to seek the solution to the great global challenges, in the exercise of the role that corresponds to them. One of the main conclusions is that the pandemic has also been, despite everything, an opportunity to reshape trust in the business world and its legitimacy for the future.

Keywords Strategic communication · Business movement · Covid-19 · Crisis communication · Corporate social responsibility

---

F. Olivares-Delgado (✉)
University of Alicante, 03690 Alicante, Spain
e-mail: f.olivares@ua.es

M. T. Benlloch-Osuna
Jaume I University, Castellón, Spain
e-mail: benlloch@uji.es

N. Martins and D. Raposo (eds.), *Communication Design and Branding*, Springer Series in Design and Innovation 32,
https://doi.org/10.1007/978-3-031-35385-7_14

1 Introduction

In this space, it is interesting to share an experience with the rest of the world which we consider unheard of until now: a business movement emerging on the first day of the strict confinement declared in Spain as a response to the COVID-19 pandemic. This paper tells the story of how an unplanned business initiative, arising from the general lack of information about an uncertain and unprecedented situation such as that experienced during the initial phase of confinement due to a pandemic, led to a powerful tool for the resilience of a whole country. It is also an intangible resource of incalculable value for managing learning and current and future social innovation. The symbolic value lies in the leadership and influence of those who did not hesitate to share their actions, learning, concerns, visions and confidence in Spanish society as a whole.

On 14 March 2020, Spain declared a state of emergency due to COVID-19, which entailed the confinement of the whole population. On the same day, 200 business-people, employees, entrepreneurs, freelancers and professionals from diverse production sectors and business sizes from all over Spain decided not to stop so that the wheels of the Spanish economy would keep turning. Essential sectors and services in Spain showed a high capacity for resilience [16]. Resilience, applied to mental health [9] (Bonnano et al. 2009), is the ability to overcome adversity. Supply chains in Spain remained active and there were no shortages of essential products in shops. Supply chains in Spain remained active and there were no shortages of basic necessities in shops, according to the main associations of the sector, such as AECOC and ASEDAS, and the different Ministries.

The important role of the "essential" sectors has been one of the key elements for the country's productivity. 51.2% of Spanish companies maintained face-to-face work during the state of alarm, according to the report *The Future of Work post-COVID-19* [1]. As global consultancy The Addeco Group Foundation states in its study *The Future of Work post-COVID*, "business leaders, governments and workers must seek to better understand each other's labour market needs to jointly develop inclusive policies and innovative human-centred solutions to enhance the seamless transformation of the workforce towards a post-pandemic economy".

2 Spanish Business Leaders, United Around One Idea: #ThisdoesNOThavetoSTOP

#ThisdoesNOThavetoSTOP was the hashtag acting as a link to clearly communicate its purpose. The movement also sought to publicly recognise the work of business people, employees, entrepreneurs and freelancers. The companies of #ThisdoesNOThavetoSTOP continued working and partially prevented the collapse of the Spanish economy, as well as enabling its quick recovery. After 2 months, the community consisted of over 3,000 companies from various production sectors, representing over 4% of GDP and over 1 million jobs. The main objective of #ThisdoesNOThave-toSTOP, in the words of Paula Llop (*coordinator of the initiative*), was "to support companies, recognition and visibility, and ultimately it was very important to thank them for their effort to be more productive than ever at one of the most difficult times".

3 The Strategy of the #ThisdoesNOThavetoSTOP Movement

Extensive media coverage and visibility was achieved at a national level. Over 132 million people were reached (with duplication). Over 120 companies described their experience, which served to inspire citizens around the whole country. Practically all conventional and unconventional forms of media were used: 771 articles in the main press; 461 cases explained on the internet; 800,000 views of videos of companies on own channels used.

3.1 The Evolution of the Movement: From #ThisdoesNOThavetoSTOP to #EActíVate

On 24 May 2020, after two and a half months of activity, supported by over 3,000 companies of all sizes, businesspeople, freelancers, entrepreneurs and employees, "#ThisdoesNOThavetoSTOP" began a new phase oriented toward economic reactivation and transformed into "#EActíVate". This initiative was created to address a greater challenge: accelerating and activating the Spanish economy, bringing visibility to and highlighting initiatives driven by different sectors, and which inspired the activation of others with their actions, to overcome the social and economic consequences of the impact of the health crisis on the economy and the country's business and industrial structure. "#EActíVate is the logical evolution of #ThisdoesNOThavetoSTOP; a step further. Now it's not only about not stopping, it is about accelerating. We are focusing all our action on driving economic activity, on staying active, because the best way to predict the future is by creating it, and in this project we are all united. It is time to do what we know best: take risks, undertake projects, work, be creative and generate well-being," stated the coordinator of the business initiative, Paula Llop, before the launch of the new #EActíVate platform.

Fig. 2 "Today we say "(E)ActíVate: it is not only about not stopping, it is about accelerating. This is no time to limit ourselves"

3.2 The #EActíVate as a Digital Platform for Audiovisual Content

In addition to highlighting the cases of companies whose actions show how to help society, the online space includes sections with dialogue between businesspeople, recommendations for notable professional training events and programmes, graphic reports, studies, and an extensive list of the latest information to inspire others not to stop and to accelerate.

The new digital space soon became a meeting point for businesspeople, freelancers, entrepreneurs and employees. It is an online platform for continuing to be present, giving visibility to their ideas and actions, with the added aim of honouring their work and paying tribute to them, inspiring others, and above all serving as an incentive for reactivating the country's economy together. In this way, in just 6 months, 2,000 new companies joined #EActíVate, allowing the initiative to reach the total of over 5,000 members. Over 1,400 audiovisual content items were posted, which generated one and a half million visits to the page and almost 7.5 million users to be reached on all social networks (see Fig. 2).

3.3 The #EActíVate Comes to Life in Person, Through Business Events

In September #EActíVate took the leap from digital to an in-person format, collaborating at different events to present the initiative and share some inspiring actions of the participating companies throughout the country. The main business associations of Spain also increased their in-person events and had the presence of #EActíVate. Also notable was the *Gran Acto del Corredor Mediterráneo*, held in November 2020, which became one of the first large events to commit to being in person, attended by numerous businesspeople and representatives from civil society, as well as being broadcast in hybrid format, as it could also be followed by *streaming*. Additionally, business fairs, conferences and cultural events at a national level were also in person during autumn of 2020.

The push by business to reactivate the economy and recover commercial values as soon as possible was, according to authoritative voices, key to accelerating the recovery of the Spanish economy.

4 *Legacy of the Reactivation*: A Service for Social Learning and Literacy

In February 2022, after two years of activity, and with over 5,500 member companies of the #ThisdoesNOThavetoSTOP and #EActíVate initiatives, *Legacy of the Reactivation* emerges as the most powerful hub for social knowledge and learning in situations of maximum uncertainty, such as those experienced during the pandemic. Legacy of the Reactivation is the largest source of documents and audiovisual content, setting out how businesspeople, employees, entrepreneurs and freelancers have reactivated the economy during one of the greatest crises experienced in society. The stories of more than 5,500 Spanish companies and their work since the beginning of the COVID-19 crisis are documented in the *Legacy of the Reactivation*, an initiative that compiles their teachings, facts, advice and experiences so that they can serve as a teaching tool for companies, business schools and universities in the face of future crises (*La Vanguardia*; *Europapress*, 15/02/2022). It contains over 3,000 articles of great business and historic interest. Authoritative and influential voices, over 500 inspiring videos about large companies, SMEs, entrepreneurs and freelancers, who despite the difficult situation that the global economy has experienced, have been active, have innovated, have digitised, have reinvented themselves, and have committed to sustainability during the last two years, to drive and accelerate the economic recovery of the country.

The purpose of *Legacy of the Reactivation* is to continue inspiring future generations and to become a memory resource so as not to forget what was learned from one of the greatest crises we have experienced (see Fig. 3). It does so through a valuable source of knowledge so that society in general, businesspeople, employees, entrepreneurs, freelancers and university students and researchers have a permanent record of this difficult period experienced, and the resilience of the business fabric, key for recovering confidence and a positive course in the Spanish economy.

> After two years of the project, we must highlight what companies have achieved, because the largest database of cases of business reactivation during the pandemic has been built," states Paula Llop, manager of the #EActíVate initiative, adding that "we have transformed

Fig. 3 "Discover the inspiring actions of over 5,500 companies", the message on the website

the initiative into a centre for historic documentation which leaves a business Legacy with what has been learned from #ThisdoesNOThavetoSTOP and #EActíVate.

Additionally, she wished to highlight the great work carried out by all professionals and companies that are members of the project. "The initiative is proud to have had the involvement and support of so many companies since its creation. This legacy is a great way of paying homage to all their efforts. Thank you for all of the learning you have shared, which will serve as an inspiration for future generations."

4.1 *Content of* Legacy of the Reactivation

Legacy of the Reactivation can be defined as a digital hub for social and business inspiration. The content is divided into 5 sections (see Table 1):

Archive: more than 3,000 reactivation news items and more than 500 audiovisual contents are available. Contents: FIVE AXES OF THE REACTIVATION (Employability, Infrastructures, Productivity, Reinventing oneself or Sustainability). CATEGORIES (News, Activating Facts, Dialogues, Council, Graphic Report or Visual Report). GEOGRAPHICAL LOCATION (Autonomous Community, province or city). COMPANY SIZE (Large Companies, SMEs, Professionals, Self-Employed or Entrepreneurs). SECTOR (Commerce, Agrifood, Supermarkets, Finance, Industry, Energy, Construction, Health, Science, Technology, Culture, Education or Tourism). NAME OF INDIVIDUAL OR COMPANY. All contents were published between March 2020 and February 2022, being a historical value of the exceptional moment.

Table 1 The legacy of the reactivation content structure

Sections of *legacy of the reactivation*	Description
"The movement"	The evolution of the initiative, from March 2020 to February 2022. A timeline of how the business fabric was activated to recover the country's economy. Through articles, videos, reports and graphics which show some of the key moments
"Expert voices"	The keys to economic reactivation through the testimonials of 250 businesspeople and representatives from civil society, which have the historic value of having been recorded during the two years of the health crisis
"Reactivation stories"	Businesspeople respond to a series of key questions to hear first-hand what the health crisis meant for their companies and what they have learned. Their answers serve as an inspiration and example for the future
"Archive"	Containing over 3,000 articles on reactivation and over 500 audiovisual content items. The search categories are: – Keys to the reactivation – Geographic location – Company size – Production sector – Name of the natural or legal person
"Acknowledgements"	List of 5,500 companies, businesspeople, entrepreneurs, freelancers, employees, associations and organisations which are members of the initiative, sharing their actions to inspire others in economic reactivation

4.2 The Challenges of Legacy of the Reactivation Regarding Its Stakeholders

- Designing and positioning it in society as a hub essentially for business, of a virtual nature, for social learning and innovation, emerging in the exceptional context of the COVID-19 pandemic. Its consideration as a Hub should promote connection with new business and entrepreneurial experiences and with the regenerative values and ethic for the immediate future. Humanity had never before experienced such circumstances, and in *Legacy of the Reactivation,* there is a credible record of what many influential and inspiring businesspeople said, as well as what their companies did, at a crucial moment in recent history. *Legacy of the Reactivation* may undoubtedly promote a substantial improvement of the reputation of businesspeople and their legitimacy in the new era.
- Designing and positioning *Legacy of the Reactivation* among the business collective as a business hub for connection with real experiences of businesspeople, inspiring figures from civil society, entrepreneurs, freelancers and companies during the pandemic and drawing conclusions for highly uncertain environments and circumstances. It may promote the recycling of managers, as well as promoting new leadership for highly uncertain, high-tension environments. Its

content promotes strategic, sectoral approaches, based on the nature or type of company (family or non-family), the region, from a gender perspective, or based on the extent of disruption, innovation or social responsibility.

- Designing and positioning it among the education community as the largest centre of audiovisual content, of experiences narrated in first person by renowned businesspeople and their companies. This content is highly valuable for undergraduate and postgraduate teaching, especially in the fields of social and life sciences and in subjects which allow case studies. *Legacy of the Reactivation* is an endless source for learning values, for example. Likewise, it allows the study of leaders, owners and managers of companies from psychosocial, anthropological, leadership and communication perspectives.

4.3 The Results of the Initiative, from March 2020 to February 2022

One of the most interesting approaches of this initiative is the success in terms of repercussion and notoriety in the media and social networks, as indicators of its public impact. In Google, for example, more than 189,000 results appear when entering "Legado de la Reactivación" and more than 8,250 videos, as of 3 March 2023 (see Table 2).

Table 2 Use of communication in *legacy of the reactivation*

Total members of the initiative	Companies, businesspeople, entrepreneurs, freelancers and employees	5,523
The initiative in the media	– Articles published – Total people reached with appearances in the news (paper, digital, TV and radio)	2,872 462,514,425[a]
The initiative online		
Website	Content posted Visits received Pages viewed	7,177 1,077,676[a] 2,036,706[a]
Social networks	Content viewed Interactions Video plays	59,114,235[a] 285,168 1,784,634[a]
Total website + social networks + newsletter	Times that the content has been viewed	62,980,481[a]

[a] *With duplication*

5 Conclusions

In contexts of uncertainty, it has become clear that communication plays an essential role in the service of collective interests. Companies, through successful and innovative management of personal and media communication, as we have seen through their collective project, *Legacy of Reactivation*, have promoted common and social interests. In summary, we can draw several conclusions from our analysis of the case. For the first time, CEOs of major companies stood in front of their home cameras and filmed messages with little or no control from their homes. The pandemic encouraged spontaneity and communication that was not (overly) scripted or premeditated. *Legacy of Reactivation* has generated a corpus of videos of this nature and content that should be analysed in future work. First, *Legacy of the Reactivation* can be seen as a collectively owned intangible resource, born out of an entrepreneurial movement at a unique moment in recent history. Second, we are convinced that this case has a high value for learning and social innovation. Thirdly, the case demonstrates the need for strategic and professional management of communication, media and networks and design, as has happened with this collective movement. And finally, it can serve for the literacy of business managers and entrepreneurs in contexts of crisis, as well as to enhance business and personal resilience, for new situations of extreme uncertainty that will surely come in the future.

Acknowledgements We would like to thank the people and companies that have made #EactíVate and *Legacy of the Reactivation* possible.

References

1. AA. VV (2019) El Futuro del Trabajo tras el COVID-19. Informe de Robert Walters
2. AA. VV (2020) Futuro del trabajo post-COVID: Reducir las divisiones para la prosperidad compartida, Informe de The Addeco Group Foundation. p 1
3. ADECCO INSTITUTE Homepage. https://www.adeccoinstitute.es
4. AECOC Homepage. https://www.aecoc.es/articulos/el-impacto-del-covid-19-en-la-cadena-de-suministro-sanitaria/
5. AECOC Homepage. https://www.aecoc.es/articulos/c84-el-reto-del-gran-consumo-ante-el-covid-19/
6. ASEDAS Homepage. https://www.asedas.org/la-distribucion-en-la-pandemia-fortalezas-estructurales-para-garantizar-la-alimentacion/
7. Bonanno GA, Gupta S (2009 Resilience after disaster. In: Mental health and disasters. Cambridge University Press, New York, pp 145–160
8. Cyrulnik B (1999) Un Merveilleux Malheur. Odile Jacob, Paris
9. EUROPAPRESS Homepage. https://www.europapress.es/catalunya/noticia-eactivate-convierte-legado-reactivacion-incluye-mas-700-empresas-catalanas-20220215153722.html
10. EActíVate Homepage. https://www.youtube.com/watch?v=Sq23JdgYzxU
11. EActíVate YouTube. https://www.youtube.com/@eactivate6531/videos
12. LA VANGUARDIA Homepage. https://www.lavanguardia.com/vida/20220215/8057905/historias-5-500-empresas-documentadas-legado-reactivacion.html

13. MERCADONA Homepage. https://info.mercadona.es/es/actualidad/estonotienequeparar-acelera-para-apoyar-a-las-empresas-e-impulsar-la-actividad-economica-con-una-nueva-fase-eactivate/news
14. MERCO Homepage. https://www.merco.info/es/
15. ROBERT WALTERS Homepage. https://www.robertwalters.es
16. Olivares-Delgado F, Iglesias-Sanchez PP, Benlloch-Osuna MT, Heras-Pedrosa CL, Jambrino-Maldonado C (2020) Resilience and anti-stress during COVID-19 isolation in Spain: an analysis through audiovisual spots. Int J Environ Res Public Health 17(23): 8876.https://doi.org/10.3390/ijerph17238876

Effects of Animation Types on Visual Search Behavior: A Study on Mobile Icon Search

Anirban Chowdhury and Surabhi Rohankar

Abstract Smartphones usage tremendously increased from being only calling device to a tool that facilitates all personal tasks. The number of applications increased with increased usage of smartphones. As mobile app icons are the basic way to access the applications installed, it becomes difficult to search desired app hidden across a vast number of pages of smartphone menu. This paper attempts to explore if animations have effect on visual search of icons and acceptability of animated icons. Different animated icons were created and evaluated for search behavior in the eye tracking experiment. Results of the current study showed that the vibration animation (out of the ten selected animations) the most positive effect on icon search behavior and was preferred by most of the users. These findings can be used by designers for mobile operating system interface design and in scenarios where search task is crucial in complex and enormous information cloud presented together in a single screen. Similarly, animated icons can also help in promoting apps as they are getting noticed repeatedly on mobile screen.

Keywords Animation · Cognitive ergonomics · Eye-tracking · Icon · User experience

1 Introduction

Smartphones has tremendously increased from being only calling device to a tool that facilitates all personal tasks. With the increase of smartphone usage, the number of smartphone applications has increased. The number of smartphone users in the

A. Chowdhury (✉)
Symbiosis International (Deemed University), Symbiosis Institute of Design, Pune, Maharashtra 411014, India
e-mail: chowdhuryanirban14@gmail.com

S. Rohankar
Excellarate, Pune, Maharashtra, India
e-mail: surabhi.rohankar@gmail.com

N. Martins and D. Raposo (eds.), *Communication Design and Branding*, Springer Series in Design and Innovation 32,
https://doi.org/10.1007/978-3-031-35385-7_15

world are more than 2 billion. People spend more time on the mobile. As availability of smartphones increased, more apps have been developed and incorporated into people's lives. There are about 1.6 million mobile applications available on the leading app store

- Google play store. The worldwide mobile applications downloads were recorded as approximately 2.52 billion in 2015, the expected to rise to 268.69 billion in 2017. Now, the number of app downloads is around 230 billion in 2021 [1].

As the available number of applications on user's phone is rising day to day (average number of applications per mobile is about 22 in 2012 [2] and 44 in 2020 [3]), it sometimes becomes difficult by an individual to find a particular application that is hidden across the vast available menu pages. More similar mobile apps mean more competitor, from business point of view. Now, the questions is whether animated icons help to stand out among competitors when searching for similar app based services like Swiggy, Zomato etc.? Also, the display size of smartphones is small compared to the amount of information that is to be displayed. Thus, there is a need for a tool that will aid users search task of applications.

To address this above-mentioned issue, many researchers have tried to implement predictive models that have adaptive interface which will speed up access to few applications. Shin et al. (2012) studied two techniques to the access to predicted icons over the distractor icons: static highlighting, changing color of predicted icons, and copying predicted icons to different part of the menu to have quick access [2]. None of the above techniques have proved to improve the search performance of icons in the menu.

This paper investigates attention or search time of smartphone menu icons are affected by animation effects and how these possible effects can be explained by the changes in eye movement parameters. Further, what is the preferred animation that is suitable for icon search behaviour.

2 Literature Review

2.1 Animation and Icon Search

In the context of search performance using transition effects, Ponsard et al. (2015) studied two effects- twist (rotation) and Pulse (scaling) on icons and concluded that these effects improved search performance by 8–10% [4]. In 2006, Baudisch et al. stated in their study that animation effects will help user perceive changes in the display [5]. Taking proper design decisions, the applied animation effects can be designed and implemented in such a way that they do not cause any delay or disturb the task performance. In study by Hong et al. they show how flashing animation aids users to find target within a larger amount of information displayed on the screen.

Shanmugasundaram and Irani (2008) in their study proved show that animated transitions have more benefits on user performance [6]. Their study also said, users with animated conditions performed task twice as faster than non-animated condition. In a study with controlled experiments on statistical data (pie charts, bar graphs, etc.), Heer and Robertson (2007) proved how animation transitions improve users' graphical perception [7].

Although animation transitions have benefits, it also has some drawbacks. Firstly, these transitions take more time to complete than static targets. Bartram, Ware, and Calvert (2003) said in their study that, this additional time may not benefit the users who are already familiar with the interface and does not need animated guidance [8]. Also, if animations become too much it may create distraction, disrupting the task at hand. From technological point of view, display refresh rate, hardware support, and algorithmic complexity should be taken in consideration before implementation of animation-based interfaces.

Noting these drawbacks of animated transitions, it becomes more important to prove benefits of animations that will overpower these drawbacks. If there is enough proof provided, designers can then use it to outweigh these drawbacks.

2.2 *Visual Search Behavior*

In the smartphones, the menu screen has grid layout, thus the users always face an icon grid interface when they are interacting with smartphone, and this refers that the visual search is a main method to reach a specific application icon target. As the users install more apps, the app screen gets updated and becomes lengthier making search task more complex. Fleetwood and Byrne (2002) found that icons in small displays (e.g., mobile phones, PDAs) are more difficult to search as compared with desktop-based screens [9]; hence, the study search task on small screen is necessary. Furthermore, van Schaik and Ling (2001) argued that visual search task is also a crucial task in human-computer interaction allied fields like military target achievement, industrial investigation or review, and information recovery activities [10].

In relation with menu selection, Findlater et al. (2009) analysed the issue of visual search task by introducing a concept called ephemeral adaptation, which has an adaptive interface, it first displays predicted items and then non-predicted items fade in gradually [11]. After a certain time, the system goes back to its normal state, maintaining spatial consistency throughout. They used time-based dimension to appeal to predicted items. This concept showed better results for search performance over static highlighting of icons.

2.3 Eye Tracking to Study Visual Search

Eye tracking is a technique in which a user's eye movements are measured to understand both where the user is looking at any given point of time and the sequence in which his eyes shift from one point to another. The eye movements tracking help researchers to study user interfaces and the complexity of user information processing.

Eye tracking studies have greatly benefited as it provides fruitful insights in various domains- problem solving, web design elements, mental imagery, search tasks, etc. [12–15]. Eye-tracking studies have also been conducted for visual attention analysis on brand image study [16], attractiveness and novelty of design evaluation [17]. In an eye-tracking study, the general search patterns of icons were evaluated and it is evident that users search for an icon in a typically crowded screen of other icons might vary in similarity to the target [18]. It was reported in resent studies that icon color and icon border shape are two crucial reasons that affect user search efficiency and experience [19]. There are possibilities to improve cognitive performance of digital interface if designers could optimize the icon semantics and text semantics [20].

In eye tracking experiment various metrics are involved, entry time, scan path, fixations, blink rate, etc. In this experiment 3 parameters were more important and were more focused on.

- Entry time—Time it took for user's attention to shift to the noted area of interest. Lesser entry time means particular area grabs instant attention.
- Fixation time per area of interest—increase in fixations on a particular area in the environment or screen indicate that it is more noticeable or more interesting to the viewer than other areas.
- Fixation Count—Higher numbers of fixations on target indicate that it is more engaging for the user.

3 Hypotheses

In particular, the goal was to aid visual search of icons in the menu. For this we selected different animation effects of icons.

H1: Users will love to prefer or pursue the animated icons for their smartphone menus.

H2: There is a variation between attention related parameters (entry time, fixation time and fixation count) due to icon animation type and its position on the screen.

4 Experimental Study

The experiment was conducted in two parts. Part I: Evaluation of animation effects on icons and Users preference and linking towards three selected animation types using questionnaire survey. Part II: Attentional evaluation of animated icons. Based on results on the first part, stimuli for the next part were prepared. Study was conducted on users who used an android phone for not less than one year.

4.1 Study Part I

This study was conducted to understand preferences to have animated icons in smartphones and identify the best animation type based on preference ratings by users to prove the hypothesis 1 (H1).

4.1.1 Stimuli Preparation

Initially we selected 10 animation effects (Table 1). A flash mock-up of these animations was created for Google Chrome and Facebook icon. A dummy mobile screen layout of smartphone menu was selected. Two animated icons were shown per page of the menu screen, a total of 10 menu pages of mock-up was created. The total working time of all the animations was kept 3 sec.

Table 1 Type of animations considered under the experiment

S. no	Animation type	Description
1	Rotate	The icon rotates 360 degrees completing 2 cycles of rotation
2	Heart beat in	The icon scales down in size about 20% smaller its original size and grows back to original state
3	Skew	The icon skews about 15% to left and right alternatively twice
4	X-rotate	The icon rotates about x axis twice and comes back to original state
5	Heart beat	The icon scales about 20% its original size and shrinks back to original state
6	Fill	The colors of the icon are gradually loaded into the skeleton of the icon
7	Appear	The icon would start from blank to slowly growing to its original size, from 0 to 100%
8	Blur	A blurred icon gradually takes original state from blur effect
9	Load	Gradually elements of are loaded to form the complete icon
10	Vibration	The icon would show a vibrating effect, moving slightly in left to right direction in fast speed

Experts from animation department were shown the animations and were asked to rate on scale of 0-9 based on animation suitability for the smartphone menu. Based on Friedman's test on ratings, 3 animation effects were chosen for further experiment.

From google play store, 4 different app icons were selected based on their number of downloads. 2 were more popular than the other two.

1. Popular—Google Chrome, Facebook
2. Not Popular—IRCTC, Words Game app

A dummy menu screen of Android phone was created, in which all the icons were static and only one icon per screen was animated. A video mock-up of all these screens for 3 animations on 4 selected icons was made. A total of 12 mock up screens was prepared.

4.1.2 Participants

There were 60 voluntary users who participated in the study (Mage = 24.266 years SD = 2.08 years; Male = 55%, Female = 45%). Users between the ranges of 19-30 years of age who used mobile phones with android operating system regularly were selected.

4.1.3 Apparatus

The mock-up was presented on the same apparatus as mentioned above in Sect. 4.1.1.

4.1.4 Measures

Questionnaire was prepared including demographic details, users' ease of search, liking toward the animation and overall satisfaction. Questions related to individual animation rating and preference were also included.

4.1.5 Procedure

Before showing the mock-up, users were first asked to fill the demographic details. They were then shown the mock-up and simultaneously their answers for the ratings were recorded.

4.1.6 Results and Discussion

Friedman's test was conducted considering ease of search, use intention and overall satisfaction as independent variables for each animation individually. It was observed that there was significant variance in mean values for preference ratings for heart beat animation [$\chi^2(2) = 21.65$; $p < 0.05$], Appear animation [χ^2 (2) = 16.88; $p < 0.05$] and Vibration animation [χ^2 (2) = 15.99; $p < 0.05$]. From the mean ratings for the variables, it was observed that users preferred vibration animation more as compared to other animations. From the above study, it was seen that users preferred animations in their smartphone menus. It was now necessary to check whether this animation grabbed users' attention.

4.2 *Study Part II*

The objective was to see whether the animations selected by experts and preferred by the users actually grab their attention when they appear in the smartphone menu and also to establish hypothesis 2 (H2).

4.2.1 Stimuli Preparation

The stimulus used for the previous part was used for eye tracking experiment as well. In these 12 more mock-up screens were added, showing animation on each icon in 2 different positions in the smartphone menu. Mock-up was divided in 4 trials based on different app icons.

4.2.2 Participants

There were 20 voluntary users (Mage = 26.45, SD = 2.94; Male = 75%, Female = 25%). All the users were regular user of mobile phones with android operating system. All are Indian citizens, familiar with selected mobile app icons and are young users. Participants those who have looking glasses for corrected near vision were excluded in this study as eye-tracking errors might be found when using desktop mounted eye-tracking device.

4.2.3 Apparatus

The mock-up application was run on the desktop mounted eye-tracking device. User's eye movements were recorded against the prepared mock-up. The eye tracking device consisted of two parts, head part having camera with IR sensor to detect and record eye movements and a laptop to store and analyze the recorded data. Users' eye movements were recorded software IviewX50, Be-gaze 3.0 and Experiment center 3.1. The apparatus required calibration of eye-tracking glasses. A five-point marker calibration was done for each user before the experiment. Users were asked to sit in a constant position of about 1 meter from the screen, they were instructed to follow the marker on the screen.

4.2.4 Measures

The experiment was a within-subjects design and had two independent variables-animation type and position of icon. Animation type had 3 variations- Heart Beat, ap- pear and Vibration effect, shown in 2 different positions.

In this experiment, entry time, fixation count and fixation time were the primary dependent variables measured for each animated icon in each position. Questions related to animation rating, preference and satisfaction ratings were included in the questionnaire.

4.2.5 Procedure

Before the experiment users were presented with pre-experiment questionnaire with demographic details, android phone usage, icon arrangement preference, etc. Then the users were asked to sit in a particular position so that the sensors of eye-tracking device could detect movement of the users' eyes. Users were shown the trials in random order. After the experiment, users were asked to fill a questionnaire. Then eye tracking video data was analysed fixing AIO for all the screens (Fig. 1).

4.2.6 Results

Repeated measure ANOVA was conducted considering entry time as a dependent variable; and, animation and position of animation as independent variables. There was significant variation observed entry time due different animations

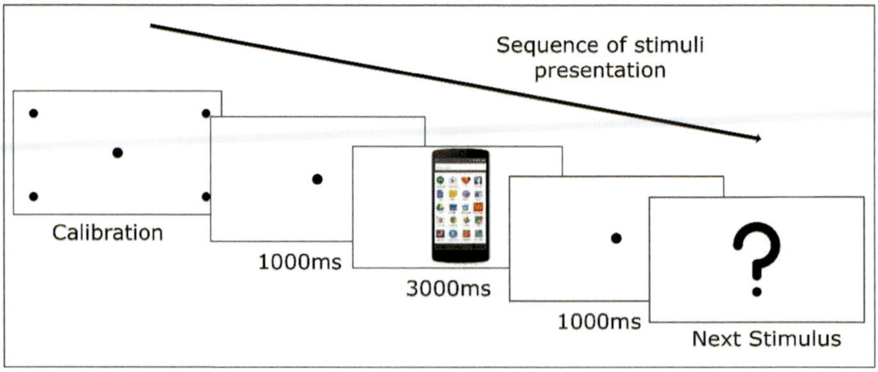

Fig. 1 Stimulus presentation for eye tracking

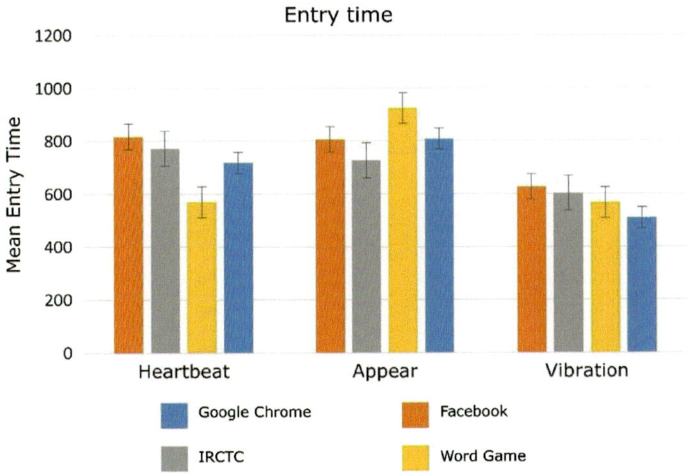

Fig. 2 Changes in mean entry time due to changes in animation type

for chrome [F (2,57) = 4.807; p <0.05], IRCTC [F (2,57) = 12.49; p <0.05], Word Game [F (2,57) = 14.702; p <0.05]. It was found that the animations grab attention irrelevant of where they are placed on the screen for icons- chrome [F (1, 57) = 0.017; p>0.05], Facebook [F (1, 57) =0.209; p>0.05], IRCTC [F (1, 57) = 1.360; p > 0.05]. Also, there is no position (icon placement on screen) wise significant variation in entry time; even if different animation effects were applied for chrome icon [F (2,57) =0.950; p>0.05], Facebook icon [F (2,57) = 0.047; p > 0.05], IRCTC [F (2,57) =0.880; p>0.05], and Word Game icon [F (1,57) = 0.188; p > 0.05]. This means all the animations grabbed users' attention. The graph (Fig. 2) shows that the entry time for vibration animation for all the icons is less as compared to other animations (Table 2).

Similarly, repeated measure ANOVA test was conducted to check variations in fixation time, it was observed that fixation time was significantly different for different animations- Chrome [F (2,57) = 4.520; p <0.05], Facebook [F (2,57) = .280; p>0.05], IRCTC [F (2,57) = 1.756; p>0.05], Word Game [F (2,57) = 3.170; p<0.05].

It was found that the users fixated on animated icons irrespective of where they are placed on the screen for icons- Facebook [F (1,57) = 0.209; p <0.05], word game [F(1,57) = 10.39; p <0.05]. Graph shows (Fig. 3), mean fixation time for vibration animation is more than other animations which means that users' attention fixated on vibration animation more as compared to other animations (Fig. 4).

From the mean ratings for the variables, it was observed that users preferred vibration animation more as compared to other animations. Figure 5 shows users' preferences towards different animations, vibration animation proved to be better across all three parameters. Users' found vibration animation easy to search and said they will love to use this animation.

Table 2 Variations in entry time

Icons	Variables	df	F	Significance	Observed Power
Chrome	Animation	2	4.807	0.012	0.776
	position	1	0.17	0.898	0.052
	Animation*position	2	0.95	0.393	0.207
	Animation	2	1.736	0.185	0.349
Face- book	Position	1	0.209	0.649	0.073
	Animation*position	2	0.047	0.954	0.057
	Animation	2	12.490	0.000	0.995
IRCTC	Position	1	1.360	0.248	0.209
	Animation*position	2	0.880	0.420	0.194
	Animation	2	14.702	0.000	0.999
Word Game	Position	1	13.554	0.001	0.951
	Animation*position	2	0.188	0.829	0.078

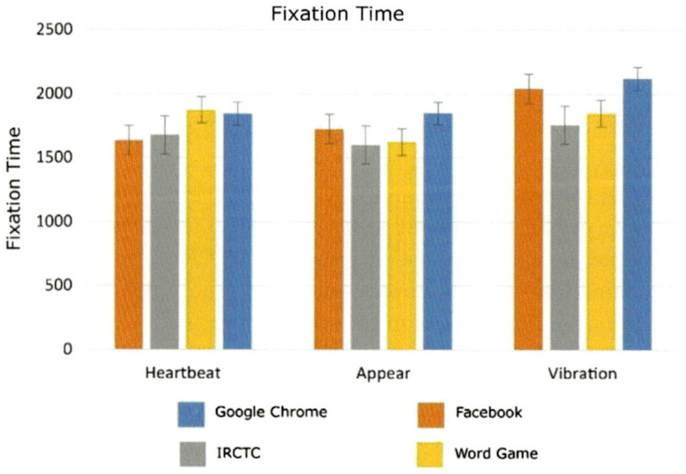

Fig. 3 Variations in fixation time due changes in animation type

4.2.7 Discussion

Fixation time every area of interest (AOI) is well-defined as the entire time spent on a specific AOI. Various studies have already proved that if fixation time is more, the object of interest (on which AOI was fixed) is more attention grabbing. Fixation counts per AOI signifies that the total number of occurrences of fixation on a particular AOI. Hence, more fixations on an AOI means that the particular area of interest is more visually appealing and easy for visual search.

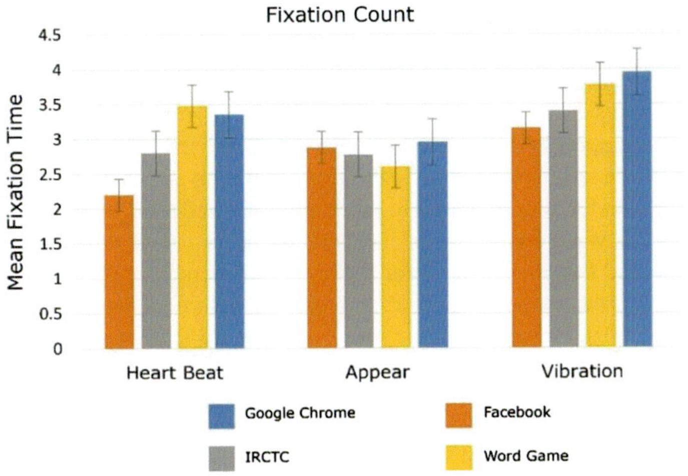

Fig. 4 Fixation count varies with animation type

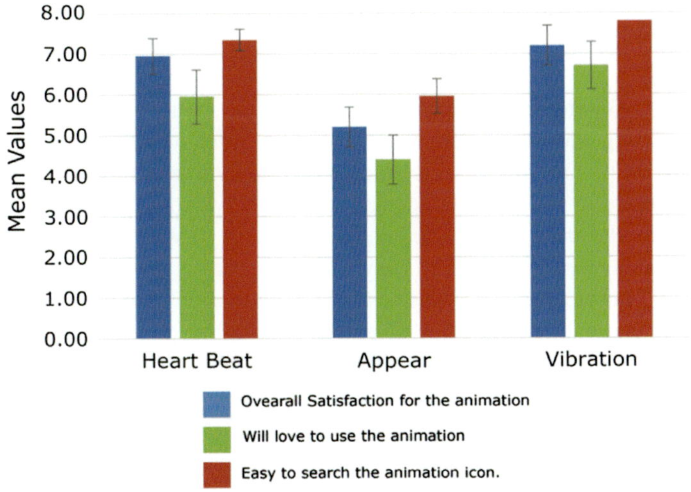

Fig. 5 Mean preference ratings for animations

Studies by Lee et al. (2005) have already established that more fixation durations and fixation counts will mean there is more attention [21]. The similar findings were reported by Chowdhury et.al. 2012 in the context of packaging evaluation experiment [17]; Chowdhury et al. 2014 in the context of bike headlamp design [22]; and, Chowdhury, Chakrabarti and Karmakar (2018) in the context of television design study [18]. Similar results were obtained in our study, fixation time and fixation counts were more for vibration animation. Also, Hong et al. [23], Jacob and Karn

[24], studied that lesser entry time is associated with quicker attention to particular area of interest. In our study, vibration animation had lesser entry time than other animations. It means vibration animation not only grabbed quick attention compared to others but also users' attention was fixated on that animation for more time. Results suggest that animation grabs user attention and can be used for search task.

Out of the three tested animations, vibration animation proved to have more effect on visual search behavior compared to other animation effects. Also, from the questionnaire data, it was observed that most of the users found vibration animation easy to search and that they will prefer it over other animations. It evident that icon color and icon border shape are two crucial reasons that affect user search efficiency and experience [19]. However, in our study, all selected icons were colorful but no borders. Hence, the effect of animation on visual search behaviour was prominent as the effect was probably not due to icon colours or borders. Users were familiar with all icons selected in our study and had prior semantic associations. Therefore, probably no effect on semantic association of icons on visual search in our study; but semantic association might have effect on visual search; and; thus, in cognitive performance in digital interface as reported by other researcher in other context [20].

5 Conclusion

In the constantly changing grid layout of smartphone menu, it is necessary to help users to searching the desired icon with ease in order to launch an app. In this study, the effects of animations were studied on app icon search. Questionnaire data analysis was done to determine the relationships between easily searchable icons with animation and user preferences and satisfaction. It was observed that all the animations grabbed users' attention. Hence, hypothesis 1 is proved. Further, analysis showed that vibration animation was best suited animation type for icon search as it received quicker attention than others selected icons in this study. Hence, the vibration type animation for icon search is preferred more by most of the users. As there were no significant difference observed in attention for same icon when place in different location in the mobile screen. Therefore, hypothesis 2 is also established. However, this study could not explore the effect of age and gender on icon search behaviour, which could be pointed as limitation of the current study, but can be studied in inter future with similar experimental set-up. Designers should use the vibration animation for icon design to get competitive advantages for icon search and can plan to enhance a particular mobile app usage. The current study might be helpful for improving the understanding of icon design and can contribute to improved user experience and effectiveness in brand communication.

References

1. Ceci L, Number of mobile app downloads worldwide from 2016 to 2021. https://www.statista.com/statistics/271644/worldwide-free-and-paid-mobile-app-store-downloads/
2. Shin C, Hong JH, Dey AK (2012) Understanding and prediction of mobile application usage for smart phones. In: Proceedings of the 2012 ACM conference on ubiquitous computing, pp 173–182
3. Kataria M (2022) App usage statistics 2022 that'll surprise you (updated). https://www.simform.com/blog/the-state-of-mobile-app-usage/#:~:text=Normally%2C%20an%20average%20person%20has,is%20split%20between%2018%20apps
4. Ponsard A, Ardekani K, Zhang K, Ren F, Negulescu M, McGrenere J (2015) Twist and pulse: ephemeral adaptation to improve icon selection on smartphones. In: Proceedings of the 41st graphics interface conference, pp 219–222
5. Baudisch P, Tan D, Collomb M, Robbins D, Hinckley K, Agrawala M, Zhao S, Ramos G (2006) Phosphor: explaining transitions in the user interface using afterglow effects. In: Proceedings of the 19th annual ACM symposium on User interface software and technology, pp 169–178
6. Shanmugasundaram M, Irani P (2008) The effect of animated transitions in zooming interfaces. In: Proceedings of the working conference on advanced visual interfaces, pp 396–399
7. Heer J, Robertson G (2007) Animated transitions in statistical data graphics. IEEE Trans Visual Comput Graphics 13(6):1240–1247
8. Bartram L, Ware C, Calvert T (2003) Moticons: detection, distraction and task. Int J Human-Comput Stud 58(5):515–545
9. Fleetwood MD, Byrne MD (2002) Modeling icon search in ACT-R/PM. Cognit Syst Res 3(1):25–33
10. van Schaik P, Ling J (2001) Design parameters in web pages: frame location and differential back- ground contrast in visual search performance. Int J Cognit Ergon 5(4):459–471
11. Findlater L, Gajos KZ (2009) Design space and evaluation challenges of adaptive graphical user interfaces. AI Mag 30(4):68
12. Poole A, Ball LJ, Phillips P. In search of salience: a response-time and eye-movement analysis of bookmark recognition. In: People and computers XVIII—design for life 2005. Springer, London, pp 363–378
13. Just MA, Carpenter PA (1976) Eye fixations and cognitive processes. Cogn Psychol 8(4):441–480
14. Yoon D, Narayanan NH (2004) Mental imagery in problem solving: an eye tracking study. In: Proceedings of the 2004 symposium on eye tracking research applications, pp 77–84
15. Zelinsky G, Sheinberg D (1995) Why some search tasks take longer than others: using eye move ments to redefine reaction times. In: Studies in visual information processing, vol 6. North-Holland, pp 325–336
16. Chowdhury A, Karmakar S, Reddy SM, Sanjog J, Ghosh S, Chakrabarti D (2012) Visual attention analysis on mutated brand name using eye-tracking: a case study. World Acad Sci, Eng Technol Int J Soc, Behav, Educ, Econ, Bus Indus Eng 6(8):1132–1135
17. Chowdhury A, Chakrabarti D, Karmakar S (2018) Anthropomorphic televisions are more attractive: the effect of novelty. In: Ergonomics in caring for people: proceedings of the international conference on humanizing work and work environment 2015. Springer Singapore, pp 243–249
18. Fleetwood MD, Byrne MD (2006) Modeling the visual search of displays: a revised ACT-R model of icon search based on eye-tracking data. Human-Comput Interact 21(2):153–197
19. Liu W, Cao Y, Proctor RW (2021) How do app icon color and border shape influence visual search efficiency and user experience? Evidence from an eye-tracking study. Int J Ind Ergon 1(84):103160
20. Jin T, Wang W, He J, Wu Z, Gu H (2023) Influence mechanism of icon semantics on visual search performance: evidence from an eye-tracking study. Int J Ind Ergon 1(93):103402
21. Lee TR, Tang DL, Tsai CM (2005) Exploring color preference through eye tracking. AIC Colour 3(5):333–336

22. Chowdhury A, Sahu, SP, Chakrabarti D, Karmakar S (2014) Designing of anthropomorphic bike headlight using cognitive ergonomics approach. In: User centered design and occupational wellbeing. Tata McGraw Hill, New Delhi, pp 228–233
23. Hong W, Thong JYL, Tam KARYAN (2005) The effects of information format and shopping task on consumers' online shopping behavior: a cognitive fit perspective. 21(3): 149–184
24. Jacob RJ, Karn KS (2003) Eye tracking in human-computer interaction and usability research: ready to deliver the promises. In: The mind's eye. North-Holland, pp 573–605

Impact of the E-brand on the Consumer's E-trust, Reliance and Resistance Towards the Chatbot

Moez Ltifi

Abstract Currently, corporations are finding a lot of interest in the usage of chatbots for various tasks across a range of industries. The future of interfaces looks bright for chatbots. In order to give customers a better experience, retailers must understand how they engage with their interfaces. To formulate our research hypotheses in this chapter, we draw on two theories, namely the Stimilus-Organism-Response theory and the Social Presence theory. By concentrating on text chatbots, a new interactive technology, we have made significant contributions to the literature on interactive marketing and artificial intelligence. One of the first empirical studies on the causes and effects of consumer trust in text chatbots is the one we conducted. Just the utilitarian usage of chatbots for online customer care has been examined in prior studies. The emotional component of the human-chatbot relationship is added by our study (1). As far as we are aware, no research has yet been done to evaluate how brand experience and behaviour are affected by online brand equity. Our study adds and investigates yet another connection between brand experience and chatbot user trust (2). Our study examines the consequences of trust in the employment of chatbots as well as the attitudes of reliance and resistance (3). Our research is original because of these three contributions. By incorporating the emotional component of this contact, we hope to examine the characteristics (antecedents and repercussions) of customer trust in text chatbots in this chapter. Ultimately, the results add more valuable data for e-service providers and chatbot developers to enhance their capabilities, comprehend the consequences on user experiences, and provide a roadmap for relationship development and strategy creation.

Keywords Artificial intelligence · Chatbots · Digital marketing · e-trust · Online brand equity · Brand experience · Consumer behavior · Structural equation method

---

M. Ltifi (✉)
College of Science and Humanities, Al-Duwadmi Shaqra University, Kingdom of Saudi Arabia, Duwadmi, Saudi Arabia
e-mail: ltifimoez2007@yahoo.fr

Higher Business School, Sfax University, Sfax, Tunisia

N. Martins and D. Raposo (eds.), *Communication Design and Branding*, Springer Series in Design and Innovation 32,
https://doi.org/10.1007/978-3-031-35385-7_16

1 Introduction

Nowadays despite the fact that the applications of artificial intelligence are still in their conceptual stage and have not generated much added value. Some initiatives have been adopted by several companies in various sectors. Intelligent customer relationship management is a main mission of digital marketing that should take advantage of chatbot technology [1].

Instant messaging services like WhatsApp, Facebook Messenger, Snapchat, and Skype have seen a significant surge in digital communication, which creates a business opportunity. Businesses should seize this chance to use chatbots to enhance their current services. The use of chatbots has increased and demonstrated their value in the customer-company interaction over the past few years [1].

Currently, one of the conversational agents that has gained a lot of traction is chatbot technology [2]. Chatbots may imitate human interactions through text conversations or voice commands in a variety of fields, opening up hitherto unimaginable economic opportunities [1, 3].

Chatbot technology is being used more and more frequently. This is supported by the simplicity and accessibility of creating chatbots, significant advancements in artificial intelligence, and growing use of email applications [4].

"*A machine dialogue system that communicates with human users through conversational language*" is the definition of a chatbot [5], p. 489). The chatbot market will be worth more than $9 billion by 2024 [6]. One of the most promising automated methods of contact in retail is chatbots. A chatbot is a computer software powered by artificial intelligence that mimics an interactive human conversation using pre-programmed user phrases and audio or visual inputs [4].

Simply put, chatbots are software applications that mimic human communication and let users communicate with digital gadgets as if they were speaking with a real person [4, 7].

Numerous businesses and brands, like eBay, Facebook, Amazon, and Apple, have embraced this technology. Several businesses have employed chatbots to take orders, make product recommendations, or assist other clients [8]. Artificial intelligence, particularly chatbots, provides complete assistance for a significant percentage of customer services [1, 9].

Customer involvement is crucial in the retail industry to encourage interaction, teamwork, and value co-creation. This interaction is a component of the complete customer experience. This interaction's result triggers cognitive, emotional, and behavioural reactions [4, 10].

Text chatbots are one of many commercial benefits offered by artificial intelligence that have benefitted digital marketing. Chatbots usually operate without negative emotions and always engage with customers in a cordial way as compared to a human [1, 3]. Chatbots automate customer care and effectively address customers' needs by comprehending them [11]. Chatbots can easily handle a high number of consumer communications simultaneously in order to improve customer service efficiency. Chatbots have the advantage of interacting with customers in a more friendlier way than traditional customer support provided by employees [12]. Human psychological states are shifting, yet using chatbots is always beneficial. The use of text chatbots can help businesses in a number of ways. But, a customer's discomfort in speaking with a computer about their unique wants or purchase decisions could be the issue [1].

Consumers may also believe that text chatbots are less trustworthy than people and that they lack empathy and human emotions when communicating with them [1]. This negative perception can damage the brand image of the company in question. To overcome this problem, companies are encouraged to judiciously apply text chatbots to provide better customer service. It is required to facilitate complex tasks and increase the efficiency of chatbots to easily respond to customer queries.

Studies in the commercial sector based on artificial intelligence are recent and rare. We can cite examples of studies on bots [13], others on machines [14] and on chatbots [1, 3].

According to the findings of these studies, computer programmes' characteristics are consistent with empathy and usability [13], which significantly affect consumers' perceptions and decision-making [15], purchase intention [16], and usage intention [13].

There are other attributes that were dropped such as chatbot dependency, chatbot resistance, chatbot disclosure, and task complexity. These studies also neglected the social and emotional aspect of the customer relationship.

The emotional connection of the customer-user occurs when the customer feels social pleasure (feelings of being listened to, feelings of being understood, and feelings of being considered) as a result of a human–computer interaction [4]. This feeling is achieved when the retailer provides social support that matches the motivations of its customers through a quality electronic service. The customer has an emotionally connected experience that shows a sense of belonging that progresses to the engagement stage. This cooperation leads to positive interaction, value co-creation, good retailer performance, and subsequent consumer intent and behavior [4].

The customer experience has been completely reimagined as a result of artificial intelligence's quick development, and businesses now have a tonne of opportunities to engage with their clients via chatbots.

Despite the positive view of chatbot applications in digital marketing in previous studies, there is still a dearth of empirical data on consumer behaviour.. an of At the time of the During the. As for the During the. As for the During the. As for the During the. As for the. the renunciation of some chatbots' ramifications and causes. We address these gaps in theory and practise in our work.

By concentrating on text chatbots, a new interactive technology, our study significantly adds to the literature on interactive marketing and artificial intelligence. One of the first empirical studies on the causes and effects of consumer trust in text chatbots is the one we conducted. Just the utilitarian usage of chatbots for online customer care has been examined in prior studies.

The emotional component of the human-chatbot relationship is added by our study (1). As far as we are aware, no research has yet been done to evaluate how brand experience and behaviour are affected by online brand equity. Our study adds and investigates yet another connection between brand experience and chatbot user confidence (2). Our study examines the consequences of trust in the employment of chatbots as well as the attitudes of reliance and resistance (3). Our research is original because of these three contributions.

The emotional component of the human-chatbot relationship is added by our study (1). As far as we are aware, no research has yet been done to evaluate how brand experience and behaviour are affected by online brand equity. Our study adds and investigates yet another connection between brand experience and chatbot user confidence (2). Our study examines the consequences of trust in the employment of chatbots as well as the attitudes of reliance and resistance (3). Our research is original because of these three contributions.

(1) ***How does brand equity affect the brand experience online?***
(2) ***How does a consumer's online brand experience affect their level of confidence in chatbots?***
(3) ***How does e-trust affect a consumer's reliance on chatbots?***
(4) ***How does e-trust affect customer reluctance to use chatbots?***

The following is a summary of this chapter. A review of previous research on the key ideas covered comes first. The theoretical foundation, justifications for the research hypotheses, suggested technique, and discovered results are then provided. A concluding statement with ramifications will then be made.

2 Review of the Literature, Theoretical Framework and Development of Hypotheses

2.1 Theoretical Framework

We used two theoretical frameworks, such as the "Stimulus-Organism-Response" theory and the "theory of the social presence," to create our study hypotheses in order to address our problem and explain our conceptual model of research.

First, the Stimulus-Organism-Response (S.O.R.) hypothesis, which [17] first proposed and Jacoby later modified (2002). Individuals respond to environmental stimuli and exhibit particular actions, according to this hypothesis [18]. Individuals' reactions and behaviours can be categorised into two categories: approach behaviours with acts like choosing, exploring, and acting, and avoidance behaviours with opposing actions like resisting, seeking, and negatively reacting [19].

The Stimulus-Organism-Response (S.O.R) hypothesis has been demonstrated in a number of contexts, including the web experience [20, 21], online shopping [22], retail [23], the tourism sector [19], and e-commerce [4]. The "S.O.R" idea has strong support in the latter area. In this context, this idea has been embraced as a psychological theory to research consumer behaviour [4, 24–26].

In a similar vein, we can point to the research done by [22], which demonstrates that the environment or atmospheric signals of an online platform (S-stimuli) can have an impact on consumers' cognition or emotions (O-organism), which will then have an impact on their behavioural outcomes (R-response). Also, our study supports this methodology. In order to describe the thought process and consumer behaviour surrounding the use of text chatbots in the context of e-retail, we utilised the S.O.R. theory.

The three parts of the "S.O.R" theory are stimulus, organism, and response [4, 18]. These three elements can be swapped out for others that function similarly, such as "Input-Response-Output" (Stimulus = input/Organism = response/Response = output), in order to make things simpler. According to [27], stimuli are defined as ambient elements that lead people to pay close attention and subsequently get aroused [28]. The "stimulus" in our study is defined as the distinctive characteristics of the text chatbot that would pique consumers' interest, such as empathy and friendliness. According to our research, the text chatbot's distinctive features that would pique customers' interest, such as its online brand equity and e-consumers' brand experiences, are referred to as the "stimulus."

The emotive and cognitive states of people and their process of unintentionally interfering between stimuli and reactions might be described as the "agency" component [4, 27]. In this scenario for the consumer the agency encompasses cognitive functions and affective perceptions of their experience with the text chatbots. The consumer's trust in the text chatbots served as the agency in our study for these cognitive processes and affective judgements.

The "response" is the last element of the S.O.R. theory. It has been defined as the consequences or behavioural outcomes of individuals to their environment [29]. These consequences, responses and behaviours can be positive or negative. In the positive sense individuals respond to their environment positively such as the willingness to stay, explore and interact [4, 30]. In the negative sense can refer to the willingness of individuals to react negatively. In our study, we will test consumers' positive and negative responses toward text chatbots by considering task complexity, chatbot dependency, chatbot resistance, and chatbot disclosure.

Second, the theory of social presence. Since social presence influences how people behave, we have used this social theory to investigate how human warmth is lacking in online operations [1, 31]. Human warmth may still be important despite the possibilities of technology and artificial intelligence capabilities [32]. There is presently little information on how social presence affects interactions between humans and chatbots [1, 2].

To our knowledge, no study has looked at how consumers' behaviour is affected by whether or not text chatbots have a social online presence that they prefer. Our study closes this knowledge gap. The intimacy and promptness of the response are used in our study to measure the consumer's view of the text chatbot as a real person using the social presence theory. We make an effort to comprehend how the conversational design's closeness and immediateness impact customer perception.

2.2 Chatbots Fundamentals

We start by defining chatbots. Chatbots are defined by [33] as "*software agents that simulate an entity, usually a human counterpart that is vague or specifically, with which the user can interact in a conversation (written, spoken, or mixed")*.

Artificial intelligence-based chatbot programmes incorporate one or more human languages into their designs [34]. It is a human-chatbot dialogue and interaction [35]. Dialogues and interactions are considered inputs from the user that are subsequently processed by specific business rules and techniques. Then "bots" are practices of users focused on using artificial intelligence. The capital of the global automation, robotics and computing market is growing exponentially [35]. Companies may design a bot in roughly 25% less time than it takes to produce a typical mobile application, which is advantageous given that cost conservation is a goal for all firms. By utilising robust platforms, bots may be built and maintained for roughly 50% less than mobile applications because they do not require expensive servers [35, 36].

Our study adds to existing studies on chatbots used for commercial purposes [2, 35, 37]. We evaluate prior research on user engagement, perception, and behaviour using text chatbots [38]). According to Brandtzaeg and Flstad [39] and Dandison et al. [35], text chatbots can be viewed as a more intimate source of connection that carries and communicates social value. Our study is based on this relationship approach. Our study takes into account the causes and effects of text chatbot trust.

As previously noted, we base our conceptual research approach on the Stimulus-Organism-Response hypothesis. A text-based chatbot's distinctive qualities are taken into account as stimuli. To draw customers, a chatbot powered by an electronic device can be recognised as realistic and human [40]. Yet, the perceived utility of the chatbot will be significantly impacted by realistic and human-like chatbots. Companies have used artificial intelligence in the form of text-based chatbots that can automatically reply to customer queries in digital marketing and e-commerce [41]. This kind of chatbot is increasingly popular in online buying. A text chatbot's customer service may be perceived by some users as friendlier than that of a typical human customer service representative.

Consumers will feel more satisfied when dealing with human-like machines, claims the social presence theory [42]. Other customers, however, believe that chatbots are too impersonal and always provide inflexible or conventional responses. In this study, we primarily examine how these two antecedents—online brand equity and e-consumer brand experience—affect consumers' perceptions of chatbot reliability.

2.3 Online Brand Equity

First off, the idea of e-brand equity has significant ramifications for both online and offline vendors when determining how to place their products. [43] suggested e-brand equity as a multidimensional construct. The construct is made up of the following five components: emotional connection, fulfilment, trust, and responsive service nature [44].

a. **Emotional connection**

"Emotional connection is a measure of the affinity between consumers and the online business/service brand" [43], p. 805). Because it has been demonstrated to have a favourable effect on consumer behaviour, word-of-mouth, and repurchase intentions, an individual's emotional response is typically voluntarily and strategically significant [45].

b. **Online experience**

With the help of new technologies, e-retailers may employ a variety of mobile and offline channels to provide seamless and ongoing consumer experiences [46]. Through overcoming obstacles like managing customers across channels and unifying the distribution mix, this sort of multichannel commerce has expanded in breadth [44, 47].

Consumer experiences with the brand happen every time they see things, every time they buy these products and receive services, and every time they use them, claim the research [43].

c. **Nature of the responsive service**

It must be easier to understand how the experience relates to the brand. This holds true regardless of whether the corporation has a website or if an intermediary is involved. There needs to be more investigation in this area [44, 48].

The level of contact between the service provided to the customer by the online business and the processes for responding to and aiding customers in physical stores is referred to as "responsive service nature" [43].

Businesses are expected to influence their staff to modify how they behave in direct interactions with customers. Examples of these behaviours include tailoring the service offer to address client needs or addressing a client by name [49].

In order to gain a competitive edge, a company's capacity to deliver quality services and a helpful client experience is crucial [44, 45].

d. **Trust**

According to Christodoulides et al., trust is "consumers' sense of assurance and expectation of constant brand excellence when consumer risk is involved [43].

Due to the fact that differentiation and trust continue to be the fundamental pillars of e-commerce and online branding, these practises are largely identical to those of offline branding [44, 48].

E-retailers can benefit from various distribution methods to give their target customers a convenient and even secure buying experience [46].

Because electronic transactions are inherently uncertain and risky, several studies have examined transactions and payment methods in the context of e-commerce and emphasised the level of various hazards for e-consumers during the transaction process [44, 50].

One important factor that significantly affects trust is the degree of connectedness between customer connections. E-sellers need to make sure that they give e-consumers sincere help and accurate information in order for them to view it as a resource and to benefit from this already built trust [51].

e. **Fulfillment**

Christodoulides et al. [43] assert that fulfilment connects offline and online encounters by extending into both the physical environment and the electronic context of trade. While choosing a certain market channel, marketing communications are crucial [52].

Consumers are appreciative of businesses that demonstrate their value to them and result in positive interactions. E-buyers place a high importance on these businesses. To facilitate resource integration operations, the contact process between businesses and online consumers needs to be competent and well-organized. This focus on providing good service can lead to highly appreciated experiences and results [45].

Studies have shown that the relationship between the company's interactions with customers, such as the navigational and interactive features of its website, has an effect on those interactions' brand dimensions [44, 48].

H1. E-brand equity positively influences the brand experience.

2.4 E-brand Experience

Product branding, shop branding, and private labelling have all been used to the concept of branding in marketing research [53]. Information technology has altered how companies and consumers interact today, resulting in a new sort of commerce [54, 55].

Many conventional businesses have entered the internet marketplace because of e-commerce to create new online retail brands (Melis et al., 2015). Even if e-commerce offers potential customers more and more chances, it also presents a number of challenges for marketers to comprehend the online shopping habits of e-consumers [56].

The e-context is particularly concerned with making website navigation easier, personalising offers, accessing information about products and services, maintaining healthy client relationships, and generating favourable brand word-of-mouth (Mollen and Wilson, 2010; [57].

Many research on the idea of experience in a virtual context are included in the literature review [58–60]. Few research, nevertheless, have looked into the idea of brand experience with online retailers. This gap will be filled by our investigation.

Experiences that are extremely relevant to e-consumers help build brand confidence. People have faith in the company since it can fulfil its commitments [55].

An online customer's interaction with a business serves as a crucial source of first-hand information for building trust [61]. This means that people's perceptions of a brand are shaped by their interactions with it [62].

The idea of trust is mostly found in social psychology literature and has its roots in theories of interpersonal relationships [63]. Theories of personality and social psychology contend that prior encounters and experiences shape how trust is developed in individuals [64].

In the context of electronic commerce, building brand trust involves both information-seeking and the experiences that customers have when they interact with the company [55, 65]. With the theoretical justifications presented above, we may state the following as our premise:

H2. Online brand experience positively influences trust in the chatbot.

2.5 Trust in the Chatbot

The agency, the second part of the "S.O.R." hypothesis, is what we will now discuss. When it comes to trust in the text chatbot, the organism stands in for the people's cognitive and emotional states. Individuals' sentiments and emotions cause us to develop trust in them. [66] assert that trust is founded on how others perceive us. The customer decides whether or not to trust the text chatbot, which is referred to in this study approach as the "agency," after going through a process of developing trust based on their feelings.

"The willingness of the individual or group to be vulnerable to another party", is another definition of trust [1, 67, 68]. Trust has generally been researched in relation to human contact. Many disciplines, including economics, sociology, psychology, and information systems, have studied the subject of trust [1, 69, 70].

E-trust plays a crucial part in describing how people interact with technology at the moment because of the rise in human–robot connection [1, 66]. Our research primarily focuses on consumers' trust in the text chatbot during the e-purchasing process in order to close this gap.

Capability, honesty, and compassion are a few of the antecedents of electronic trust that existing research has adopted [71]. The relationship between people and autonomous robots affects users' perceptions of trust [72]. According to the social presence idea, most interactions between people and computers are social [1, 73, 74].

Consumers nevertheless frequently see these computers as social agents, despite the fact that they do not share human emotions or experiences. As a result, consumers will react to these machines with characteristics similar to how they react to humans [73, 75]. Users' perceptions of robots, according to [42], boost pleasure and enhance human–robot interaction. Lastly, Cheng et al. [1] shown that consumer perception explains trust in chatbots.

We focus primarily on two effects of customer trust in text chatbots, namely dependence on artificial intelligence and resistance to artificial intelligence, as was already mentioned.

2.6 Avoidance/Approach Behaviour Towards the Chatbot

We now turn to "Response", the third component of the "S.O.R" theory. According to this theory, the behavioral response of consumers can take two forms: approach behavior or avoidance behavior [19].

Previous studies on this topic deal with consumers' intention towards automated robots, i.e. approach behaviors only. To address this gap, our study considers both forms of consumer responses, avoidance behavior (resistance) and approach behavior (dependence) to the text chatbot.

a. **Dependency on artificial intelligence**

In general, users would rather depend on a person than an algorithm for behavioural actions [76]. Consumers' fear of automated algorithms grows despite the fact that they cannot influence or explain their conclusions like people can.

A few research examine customers' potential use of bots in the future [13, 77]. Yet, research that support realistic strategies for e-service providers to boost consumers' trust in automated computers rather than a human being are extremely scarce [1]. Our study makes an effort to offer empirical evidence on the use of text chatbots powered by artificial intelligence. According to research on trust, cognitive trust involves people's belief in the abilities and reliability of others. Based on this, we suggest that consumers will be more inclined to rely on the text chatbot to solve their problems and make decisions if they believe the chatbot to be trustworthy during the interaction process. Thus, we state our hypothesis as follows:

H9: E-trust positively influences consumers' reliance on text chatbots.

b. **Resistance to artificial intelligence**

In a few research on consumer reactions to artificial intelligence [76–79, 38] the primary question is whether consumers will accept or utilise robots in the future. Despite the significance of customer resistance, there have been relatively few studies that specifically address consumer opposition to robots powered by artificial intelligence [1, 80].

The marketing literature demonstrates that artificial intelligence suppliers are less likely to take into account specific requests or distinctive qualities of customers, for instance, in the healthcare industry. Customers may demonstrate resistance behaviour towards e-service providers as a result of this circumstance, making them appear to be less reliable [1].

Consumers will logically stop utilising text chatbots in business settings if they discover them to be unreliable or incapable of satisfying their needs, and instead

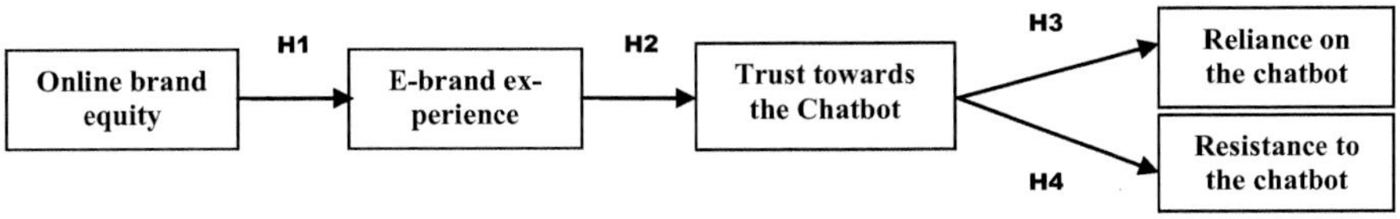

Fig. 1 The study's conceptual framework

turn to more conventional human-based customer support [1, 80]. In light of this, we declare the following to be our hypothesis:

H10: E-trust negatively influences consumer resistance to text chatbots.

Our conceptual model, which is comprised of several theories, is shown in Fig. 1 as a summary.

3 Design Methodology

3.1 Sample and Data Collection Method

We ran a test to validate our conceptual research model. Online telecommunications companies are more likely to use text chatbots because of the repetitive duties involved. In order to explore how brand equity and electronic brand experience affect consumer e-trust of the chatbot, we chose an experimental methodology. Studying how trust in the text chatbot affects reliance on and opposition to artificial intelligence is another important topic (chatbot).

Convenience sampling was used to find participants [81]. Students enrolled in undergraduate programmes at a Saudi university made up our sample. Having a WhatsApp account was a necessity in order to participate (necessary to start interaction with the text chatbot).

To select any of the services offered by the text chatbot, participants were required to communicate with it. The participants responded to questions regarding how they felt about their interactions with the text chatbot after finishing the task and communicating with it. The questionnaire is made up of demographic inquiries, questions on the use of the text chatbot, and lastly inquiries regarding the research constructs. There were 265 participants in all, of which 251 completed usable questionnaires. 14 surveys in all could not be used because of insufficient data. A pre-test was performed before the main experiment to make sure the alteration worked as intended. The demographic details of the participants are shown in Table 1.

Table 1 Demographic characteristics of participants

Measuring elements	Category	Frequency	%
Gender	Male	194	77.29
	Female	57	22.70
Age	<25	221	88.04
	26–30	23	09.16
	31–35	7	02.80
	>36	0	00
Experience with the text chatbot	No experience	8	03.18
	Low experience	182	72.50
	Medium experience	52	20.71
	High experience	09	03.58

3.2 Instruments for Measurement

To ensure the validity and reliability of the measurements, we employed multi-item scales of the 5-point Likert type (1 = strongly disagree, 5 = strongly agree) to measure the variables in our model [82]. The variables in this study were measured using scales that have been used before in the literature and have been tested in a variety of situations and languages, ensuring their reliability. In order to make several measurement scale items more relevant to the topic of our study, we modified them.

Rezaei and Valaei's investigations served as the foundation for developing the assessment of the online brand equity variable [44]. The study by Morgan-Thomas and Veloutsou served as the source for the measurement of the electronic brand experience variable [83]. The measure of resistance was evaluated using the measure of [1]. The reliance index was created using earlier autonomy indexes from Edwards et al. [84].

4 Results

4.1 Construct Validity and Reliability

We used a principal component analysis to determine the structure of the correlations between the items we used in our survey (PCA). PLS 3.0 was the programme we employed. We opted to preserve all of the measuring scale items because all of the commonalities are less than 0.5 [85], based on the analysis of the various similarities and the factorial weight of each item.

Likewise, the Cronbach's alpha values are above the recommended value of 0.7, confirming the validity of our metrics (Table 2). Similar to this, the average variance extracted (AVE) values are above the suggested value of 0.05, which guarantees the

Table 2 Reliability and convergent validity of measures

Constructs	Items	VIF (<10)	Factor loadings (>0.7)	Cronbach's α (>0.7)	Average variance extracted (AVE) (>0.5)
E-brand equity	E1	2.603	0.895***	0.836	0.785
	E2	2.501	0.845***		
	E3	2.125	0.841***		
E-brand experience	F1	3.051	0.961***	0.745	0.823
	F2	3.421	0.914***		
	F3	3.054	0.987***		
Trust toward the chatbot	T1	2.587	0.825***	0.845	0.716
	T2	2.125	0.853***		
	T3	2.014	0.852***		
Reliance on the chatbot	RC1	4.259	0.963***	0.925	0.714
	RC2	4.236	0.915***		
	RC3	4.023	0.984***		
Resistance to the chatbot	RTC1	5.874	0.843***	0.847	0.963
	RTC2	5.987	0.826***		
	RTC3	5.641	0.817***		

VIF—Variance inflation factor. ****p* < 0.001

model's convergent validity [86]. Moreover, Table 3's AVE values are greater than the squares of the inter-construct correlations, ensuring the constructs' discriminating validity [87].

The variance inflation factor (VIF) values are all below the recommended values at the threshold of 10, indicating an acceptable reliability, and the study revealed there was no issue, therefore the multi-linearity was checked [88]. The findings of the VIF test demonstrate that multi-colinearity is not a serious issue in this study [89] (Table 4).

Table 3 Discriminate validity of the constructs

Constructs	E-BE	E-BEX	TC	RLC
E- brand equity	**0.785**[a]			
E-brand experience	0.781	**0.823**[a]		
Trust toward the chatbot	0.706	0.710	**0.716***[a]	
Reliance on the chatbot	0.671	0.705	0.713	**0.963**[a]
Resistance to the chatbot	0.656	0.708	0.710	0.712

[a] *Values on the diagonal represent the AVEs and the other values represent the squares of the inter-construct correlations*

Table 4 Research hypothesis testing results

Hypothèses	R^2	Coef. (β)	Std. error	t-value	p-value	Supported (Y/N)
E- brand equity → E-brand experience	0.52	0.450	0.082	20.69	0.003	Y
E-brand experience → Trust toward the chatbot	0.58	0.510	0.014	18.54	0.001	Y
Trust toward the chatbot → Reliance on the chatbot	0.53	0.490	0.056	16.34	0.002	Y
Trust toward the chatbot → Resistance to the chatbot	0.51	- 0.440	0.084	14.27	0.001	Y

We observe that online brand equity explains 61% of the e-brand experience (R2 = 0.61) and demonstrates the validity of our assumptions. Online brand equity in particular has a favourable impact on the e-brand experience (β = 0.560, t = 24.41, p 0.005). These findings corroborate hypothesis H1 by showing that online brand equity is a significant antecedent for e-brand experience.

Second, the e-brand experience also contributes significantly (R2 = 0.54) to the consumer's e-trust in the chatbot. This demonstrates their potent explanatory abilities. Consumer e-trust of the chatbot is particularly positively and significantly impacted by the e-brand experience (β = 0.480, t = 19.23, p 0.005). Our findings confirm hypothesis H2 by showing that e-brand experience is a strong predictor of consumer e-trust in the text chatbot.

Last but not least, we discover that customer e-trust of the chatbot accounts for 53% of dependence on artificial intelligence and 51% of resistance to it (R2 = 0.53). This demonstrates their profound explanatory capacity. In particular, the degree to which a customer trusts a chatbot has a favourable impact on that customer's dependence on artificial intelligence (β = 0.490, t = 16.34, p 0.005) and a negative impact on that customer's resistance to artificial intelligence (β = −0.440, t = 14.27, p 0.005). These findings show that the consumer's level of e-trust in the chatbot is a key predictor of both his dependence on and resistance to artificial intelligence. As a result, the H3 and H4 hypotheses are verified.

5 Additional Tests: The Mediating Effects of Consumer Trust in the Chatbot

We examined the mediating impacts of online brand experience and customer e-trust towards the text chatbot, with 4,000 bootstrapping resamples to emphasise indirect effects between the variables, in order to completely grasp the link between the variables in our study model.

Table 5 Mediating effects of consumer trust in the chatbot

Mediation path	Indirect effect with bootstrap estimate	Bootstrap confidence intervals	
		Lower 95%	Upper 95%
E-brand equity → E-brand experience → Trust	0.189***	0.045	0.142
E-brand experience → Trust → Reliance on the chatbot	0.398***	0.286	0.187
E-brand experience → Trust → Resistance to the chatbot	0.392***	0.361	0.294

Consumer trust in the text chatbot has statistically significant mediating effects across the board. We first come to the conclusion that the relationship between online brand equity and customer e-trust in the chatbot is mediated by the online brand experience. The relationship between online brand equity and reliance on and aversion to artificial intelligence is mediated, according to our second conclusion, by consumer e-trust. The following results are shown in Table 5 in more detail.

5.1 *Robustness Test*

It is necessary to do additional analysis in order to guarantee the reliability of the primary conclusions drawn. In order to further validate and confirm our obtained results, we therefore want to conduct a second analysis. This action has been done mostly as a result of the intricacy that our study model's variable relationships exhibit. We intend to use the "blindfolding" test to evaluate the importance of the exogenous variables on the performance of the model in order to achieve this goal and for an efficient examination of the robustness of the results generated from our model. Using changes in the criterion estimations (Q2), this method evaluates the predictive utility of each construct [90]. According to the Stone-Geisser blindfold test results (Q2), consumer e-trust of the chatbot (Q2 = 0.231), e-brand equity (Q2 = 0.174), e-brand experience (Q2 = 0.362), dependence on artificial intelligence (Q2 = 0.352), and resistance to artificial intelligence (Q2 = 0.283), all have satisfactory predictive relevance as their values are significantly above 0. [91].

6 Discussion and Conclusion

This chapter has examined the function of text chatbots in illuminating e-commerce customer behaviour. We have also emphasised how e-brand equity affects the e-brand experience. Aside from that, the impact of e-brand experience on consumer e-trust of the text chatbot is also discussed. Last but not least, how consumer e-trust of the text chatbot affects AI dependence and resistance. For the purpose of developing our study model's assumptions and the connections between its many variables, we deployed two theories, namely the Stimilus-Organism-Response theory and the social presence theory.

This study aims to investigate the causes and effects of consumer e-trust in text chatbots. Also, to evaluate the chatbot's mediating impacts on consumer e-trust and electronic brand experience.

We discuss the key findings of our study and draw comparisons with those found in the literature to address our research concerns. The findings of our research are summarised as follows.

First, the e-brand experience is positively impacted by e-brand equity. This result particularly supports Rezaei and Valaei's findings [44]. This discovery demonstrates how significant this effect is. So, the e-brand experience is favourably correlated with how the e-consumer perceives e-brand equity. A strong e-brand experience is therefore dependent on e-brand equity.

Second, the consumer's e-trust in the text chatbot is influenced favourably by the e-brand experience. Particular conclusions from Arauj [2], and Khan and Rahman [55], are supported by this result. This discovery supports the significance of this effect. Our findings demonstrate that a pleasant e-brand experience raises consumer e-trust of the text chatbot. It is feasible and advantageous to enhance the human-chatbot interaction in an e-brand experience.

Finally, we took into account two different types of customer behaviour, including approaches that depend on the text chatbot and avoidances that are resisted by the text chatbot. According to the findings, consumer e-trust in the text chatbot is favourably correlated with their reliance on it, and conversely, it is negatively correlated with their resistance to it. This indicates that there is a stronger positive relationship between e-trust and consumer dependence than a negative relationship between e-trust and consumer resistance. Yet, consumers' approach behaviour has a higher impact due to their trust than their avoidance behaviour does.

Finally, we took into account two different types of customer behaviour, including approaches that depend on the text chatbot and avoidances that are resisted by the text chatbot. According to the findings, consumer e-trust in the text chatbot is favourably correlated with their reliance on it, and conversely, it is negatively correlated with their resistance to it. This indicates that there is a stronger positive relationship between e-trust and consumer dependence than a negative relationship between e-trust and consumer resistance. Yet, consumers' approach behaviour has a higher impact due to their trust than their avoidance behaviour does.

7 Theoretical Implications

Our research offers a number of new theoretical insights in this regard. First off, while the Stimilus-Organism-Response theory and the social presence theory are typically applied in traditional commercial situations, our study did so while using textual chatbots.

The Stimilus-Organism-Response hypothesis is used in the e-commerce setting to examine how the characteristics of the text chatbot affect the development of consumer trust.

Lastly, the research's theoretical framework adds to the body of knowledge on information systems, e-commerce, and digital marketing.

Fourth, this study takes into account the consumer's e-brand experience and e-trust in the chatbot as a way to explain consumer behaviour.

Finally, by taking into account both two forms of consumer behaviour, such as approach behaviour through dependence on the text chatbot and avoidance behaviour through resistance to the text chatbot, this research offers a deeper understanding of how consumers react to AI-based automated chatbots. Chatbots powered by artificial intelligence are a new, developing technology that can improve the future of e-commerce by providing a wide range of advantages to both consumers and businesses. As a result, this research advances knowledge of the constraints and limitations of the consumer behavioural responses that were also noted.

8 Managerial Implications

This research has a number of management ramifications for corporate technology developers and electronic customer service suppliers in particular. The employment of automated robotics and artificial intelligence by businesses is essential in the e-commerce industry. To enhance the customer and/or brand experience, online shops, virtual stores, and e-service providers are all required to engage with their customers automatically. The company in question and the client can communicate automatically through a text chatbot.

Our research helps to clarify views, intentions behind resistance, and behavioural reactions to the text chatbot in the business setting. The company improves its ability to compete with rivals thanks to the thoughtful design and deployment of the text chatbot on its part. Focusing on the human element during a human-chatbot encounter is highly advised because it affects the customers' pleasure, intentions, and future behaviour.

We recommend that technology developers and electronic customer service providers streamline and personalise the use of text chatbots in accordance with the findings of our study. Particularly, the difficulty of the work has a negative impact on how customers view the text chatbot. Strive to maintain effective customer-company communication while adopting chatbot technology. This interaction must simultaneously meet the needs of the customers (information requests, availability, orders, payments, etc.) accurately and promptly, while also providing a warm and welcoming experience for the user. Text chatbot technology enables the user company to provide a helpful response to customer inquiries in order to enhance the e-brand experience and capital.

Finally, businesses should adopt a social and pleasant relationship viewpoint through increasing customer involvement if they want to make a good impression on customers. To improve the social presence and human warmth touch of the human-textbot interaction that leads to consumer e-trust and, subsequently, their reliance and approach and adoption behaviour of artificial intelligence, it is advised to create engaging conversations that include small talk, emoticons, exclamatory comments, and GIFs.

For large firms who have the financial means, they can construct intelligent chtbots specific to their activities by integrating a sentiment analysis algorithm utilising NLP for example. Through their different text interactions, these technologically advanced chatbots can discern the emotional states of their customers. Intelligent chatbots can automate the request if they determine that the clients' emotional states are neutral or favourable. On the other hand, intelligent chatbots have the ability to switch the conversation to a human in the event of the identification of negative emotional states, preventing a problem or customer loss by undermining the value of the customer's engagement with the firm through text chatbot technology.

9 Limitations and Potential Research Directions

Nonetheless, despite these contributions, this study has flaws that should be fixed in follow-up investigations. The survey data that was gathered and the sample size that was employed are related to the first constraint. Students exclusively make up the sample for this study. The sample size employed for analysis using the structural equation method is fairly tiny. To corroborate the findings that would offer valuable hints, it would be intriguing to repeat the study with a larger representative sample size and a different technique of data collecting.

The second restriction relates to the field of the survey. Only a simulated purchase was required of the participants in addition to a made-up task. It would be fascinating to duplicate this research using data from interactions with real businesses to increase the validity of the results.

The adoption of just two antecedents of chatbot technology, such as e-brand equity and e-brand experience, is the third research restriction. It would be fascinating to test additional antecedents, such as the chatbot's level of intelligence, for instance.

The fourth restriction is that we can only test our research methodology in the e-commerce industry, specifically the telecommunications industry. This implies the necessity for additional research using several data sources in fields such as economics, health, agribusiness, etc. in order to generalise the findings.

We have investigated mediating effects in our research. To observe if the consumer's attitude towards the chatbot fluctuates, for example, according to the different levels of involvement, we propose integrating moderating variables such as the type of product, the level of involvement, etc.

Also, the conceptual model that has been proposed does not purport to be exhaustive and might be enhanced upstream and downstream by additional factors, such as the perceived legitimacy of the chatbot and the co-creation of value for the business by leveraging chatbot technology.

References

1. Cheng X, Bao Y, Zarifis A, Gong W, Mou J (2021) Exploring consumers' response to text-based chatbots in e-commerce: the moderating role of task complexity and chatbot disclosure. Internet Res Vol. ahead-of-print No. ahead-of-print
2. Araujo T (2018) Living up to the chatbot hype: the influence of anthropomorphic design cues and communicative agency framing on conversational agent and company perceptions. Comput Hum Behav 85(2):183–189
3. Luo X, Tong S, Fang Z, Qu Z (2019) Frontiers: machines vs humans: the impact of artificial intelligence chatbot disclosure on customer purchases. Mark Sci 38(6):937–947
4. De Cicco R, Silva SC, Alparone FR (2020) Millennials' attitude toward chatbots: an experimental study in a social relationship perspective. Int J Retail Distrib Manage 48(11):1213–1233
5. Shawar BA, Atwell ES (2005) Using corpora in machine-learning chatbot systems. Int J Corpus Linguist 10(4):489–516
6. Pise R (2018) Chatbot market size is set to exceed USD 134 billion by 2024—ClickZ. available at: https://www.clickz.com/chatbot-market-size-is-set-to-exceed-usd-1-34-billion-by-2024/215518/ (accessed 6 Janaury 2023)
7. Oracle (2019)0 What is a chatbot? https://www.oracle.com/solutions/chatbots/what-is-achatbot/
8. Go E, Sundar SS (2019) Humanizing chatbots: the effects of visual, identity and conversational cues on humanness perceptions. Comput Hum Behav 97:304–316
9. Mitchell V (2018) Gartner: why humans will still be at the core of great CX. https://www.cmo.com.au/article/642649/gartner-why-humans-will-still-core-great-cx/
10. Lemon KN, Verhoef PC (2016) Understanding customer experience throughout the customer journey. J Mark 80(6):69–96
11. Daugherty PR, James Wilson H, Michelman P (2019) Revisiting the jobs artificial intelligence will create. MIT Sloan Manage Rev 60(4):1–8
12. Froehlich A (2018) Pros and cons of chatbots in the IT helpdesk. https://www.informationweek.com/strategic-cio/it-strategy/pros-and-cons-of-chatbots-in-the-it-helpdesk/a/did/1332942
13. De Kervenoael R, Hasan R, Schwob A, Goh E (2020) Leveraging human-robot interaction in hospitality services: incorporating the role of perceived value, empathy, and information sharing into visitors' intentions to use social robots. Tour Manage 78:104042
14. Seeber I, Bittner E, Briggs RO, de Vreede T, de Vreede GJ, Elkins A, Maier R, Merz AB, Oeste-Reiß S, Randrup N, Schwabe G, Sollner M (2020) Machines as teammates: a research agenda on AI in team collaboration. Inf Manage 57(2): 103–174
15. Duan Y, Edwards JS, Dwivedi YK (2019) Artificial intelligence for decision making in the era of big data—evolution, challenges and research agenda. Int J Inf Manage 48:63–71

16. Mende M, Scott ML, van Doorn J, Grewal D, Shanks I (2019) Service robots rising: how humanoid robots influence service experiences and elicit compensatory consumer responses. J Mark Res 56(4):535–556
17. Mehrabian A, Russell JA (1974) An approach to environmental psychology. The MIT Press, Cambridge, MA
18. Kamboj S, Sarmah B, Gupta S, Dwivedi Y (2018) Examining branding co-creation in brand communities on social media: applying the paradigm of stimulus-organism-response. int J Inf Manage 39:169–185
19. Kim MJ, Lee CK, Jung T (2020) Exploring consumer behavior in virtual reality tourism using an extended stimulus-organism-response model. J Travel Res 59(1):69–89
20. Mollen A, Wilson H (2010) Engagement, telepresence and interactivity in online consumer experience: reconciling scholastic and managerial perspectives. J Bus Res 63(9–10):919–925
21. Mollen A, Wilson H (2010) Engagement, telepresence and interactivity in online consumer experience: reconciling scholastic and managerial perspectives. J Bus Res 63(9):919–925
22. Eroglu SA, Machleit KA, Davis LM (2003) Empirical testing of a model of online store atmospherics and shopper responses. Psychol Mark 20(2):139–150
23. Rose S, Clark M, Samouel P, Hair N (2012) Online customer experience in e-retailing: an empirical model of antecedents and outcomes. J Retail 88(2):308–322
24. Chang HJ, Eckman M, Yan RN (2011) Application of the stimulus-organism-response model to the retail environment: the role of hedonic motivation in impulse buying behavior. Int Rev Retail, Distrib Consumer Res 21(3):233–249
25. Fiore AM, Kim J (2007) An integrative framework capturing experiential and utilitarian shopping experience. Int J Retail Distrib Manage 35(6):421–442
26. Wu YL, Li EY (2018) Marketing mix, customer value, and customer loyalty in social commerce: a stimulus-organism-response perspective. Internet Res 28(1):74–104
27. Jacoby J (2002) Stimulus-organism-response reconsidered: an evolutionary step in modeling (consumer) behavior. J Consum Psychol 12(1):51–57
28. Eroglu SA, Machleit KA, Davis LM (2001) Atmospheric qualities of online retailing: a conceptual model and implications. J Bus Res 54(2):177–184
29. Donovan R, Rossiter J (1982) Store atmosphere: an environmental psychology approach. J Retail 58(1):34–57
30. Bitner MJ (1992) Servicescapes: the impact of physical surroundings on customers and employees. J Mark 56(2):57–71
31. Hassanein K, Head M (2005) The impact of infusing social presence in the web interface: an investigation across product types. Int J Electron Commer 10(2):31–55
32. Hassanein K, Head M (2007) Manipulating perceived social presence through the web interface and its impact on attitude towards online shopping. Int J Hum Comput Stud 65(8):689–708
33. Hatwar PN, Patil A, Gondane D (2016) AI based chatbot. Int J Emerging Trends Eng Basic Sci 6:85–87
34. Khanna A, Pandey B, Vashishtal K, Kalia K, Pradeepkumar B, Das T (2015) A study of today's A.I. through chatbots and rediscovery of machine intelligence. Int J u- e- Serv, Sci Technol 8(7): 277–284
35. Ukpabi DC, Aslam B, Karjaluoto H (2019) Chatbot adoption in tourism services: a conceptual exploration "in" robots, artificial intelligence and service automation in travel, tourism and hospitality, pp 105–121
36. Waxer C (2016) Get ready for the bot revolution. Computer World. https://www.computerworld.com/article/3126438/emerging-technology/article.html
37. Chung M, Ko E, Joung H, Kim SJ (2018) Chatbot e-service and customer satisfaction regarding luxury brands. J Bus Res 117:587–595
38. Ciechanowski L, Przegalinska A, Magnuski M, Gloor P (2019) In the shades of the uncanny valley: an experimental study of human–chatbot interaction. Futur Gener Comput Syst 92:539–548

39. Brandtzaeg PB, Følstad A (2017) Why people use chatbots. In: International conference on internet science, Springer, Cham, vol 10673, pp 377–392
40. Gilbert RL, Forney A (2015) Can avatars pass the Turing test? Intelligent agent perception in a 3D virtual environment. Int J Hum Comput Stud 73:30–36
41. Kaplan A, Haenlein M (2019) Siri, Siri, in my hand: who's the fairest in the land? On the interpretations, illustrations, and implications of artificial intelligence. Bus Horiz 62(1):15–25
42. Blut M, Wang C, W€underlich NV, Brock C (2021) Understanding anthropomorphism in service provision: a meta-analysis of physical robots, chatbots, and other AI. J Acad Market Sci 1–27
43. Christodoulides G, De Chernatony L, Furrer O, Shiu E, Abimbola T (2006) Conceptualising and measuring the equity of online brands. J Mark Manag 22(7–8):799–825
44. Rezaei S, Valaei N (2017) Branding in a multichannel retail environment: online stores versus app stores and the effect of product type. Inf Technol People 30(4):853–886
45. Karpen IO, Bove LL, Lukas BA, Zyphur MJ (2015) Service-dominant orientation: measurement and impact on performance outcomes. J Retail 91(1):89–108
46. Cao L, Li L (2015) The impact of cross-channel integration on retailers' sales growth. J Retail 91(2):198–216
47. Verhoef PC, Kannan PK, Inman JJ (2015) From multi-channel retailing to omni-
48. Chen H-L, Mathews S (2013) The effects of portal website attitude and e-services on branding of e-stores. Australasian Market J (AMJ) 21(3):155–160
49. Aguirre E, Mahr D, Grewal D, de Ruyter K, Wetzels M (2015) Unraveling the personalization paradox: the effect of information collection and trust-building strategies on online advertisement effectiveness. J Retail 91(1):34–49
50. Mohseni S, Jayashree S, Rezaei S, Kasim A, Okumus F (2016) Attracting tourists to travel companies' websites: the structural relationship between website brand, personal value, shopping experience, perceived risk and purchase intention. Curr Issues Tour
51. Schaefer-McDaniel NJ (2004) Conceptualizing social capital among young people: towards a new theory. Child Youth Environ 14(1):153–172
52. Pauwels K, Neslin SA (2015) Building with bricks and mortar: the revenue impact of opening physical stores in a multichannel environment. J Retail 91(2):182–197
53. Davies K (2010) From the retail brand to the retail-er as a brand: themes and issues in retail branding research. Int J Retail Distrib Manage 38(11/12):865–878
54. Kennedy A, Coughlan J (2006) Online shopping portals: an option for traditional retailers? Int J Retail Distrib Manage 34(7):516–528
55. Khan I, Rahman Z (2016) Brand experience anatomy in retailing: an interpretive structural modeling approach. J Retail Consum Ser 24: 60–69
56. Konuş U, Verhoef PC, Neslin SA (2008) Multichannel shopper segments and their covariates. J Retail 84(4):398–413
57. Rowley J (2004) Online branding. Online Inf Rev 28(2):131–138
58. Bridges E, Florsheim R (2008) Hedonic and utilitarian shopping goals: the online experience. J Bus Res 61(4):309–314
59. Insley V, Nunan D (2014) Gamification and the online retail experience. Int J Retail Distrib Manage 42(5):340–351
60. Petre M, Minocha S, Roberts D (2006) Usability beyond the website: an empiricallygrounded e-commerce evaluation instrument for the total customer experience. Behav Inf Technol 25(2):189–203
61. Ha HY, Perks H (2005) Effects of consumer perceptions of brand experience on the web: brand familiarity, satisfaction and brand trust. J Consum Behav 4(6):438–452
62. Ramaseshan B, Stein A (2014) Connecting the dots between brand experience and brand loyalty: the mediating role of brand personality and brand relationships. J Brand Manage 21(7–8):664–683
63. Morgan RM, Hunt SD (1994) The commitment-trust theory of relationship marketing. J Mark 58(3):20–38

64. Rempel JK, Holmes JG, Zanna MP (1985) Trust in close relationships. J Pers Soc Psychol 49(1):95–112
65. Lee SA, Jeong M (2014) Enhancing online brand experiences: an application of congruity theory. Int J Hospital Manage 40: 49–58
66. Hoff KA, Bashir M (2015) Trust in automation: integrating empirical evidence on factors that influence trust. Hum Factors 57(3):407–434
67. Hoy WK, Tschannen-Moran M (1999) Five faces of trust: an empirical confirmation in urban elementary schools. J School Leader 9(3): 184–208
68. Mayer RC, Davis JH, Schoorman FD (1995) An integrative model of organizational trust. Acad Manag Rev 20(3):709–734
69. Breuer C, Huffmeier J, Hertel G (2016) Does trust matter more in virtual teams? A metaanalysis of trust and team effectiveness considering virtuality and documentation as moderators. J Appl Psychol 101(8):1151–1177
70. Ert E, Fleischer A, Magen N (2016) Trust and reputation in the sharing economy: the role of personal photos in Airbnb. Tour Manage 55:62–73
71. Jarvenpaa SL, Knoll K, Leidner DE (1997) Is anybody out there? Antecedents of trust in global virtual teams. J Manage Inf Syst 14(4):29–64
72. Złotowski J, Yogeeswaran K, Bartneck C (2017) Can we control it? Autonomous robots threaten human identity, uniqueness, safety, and resources. Int J Hum Comput Stud 100:48–54
73. Adam M, Wessel M, Benlian A (2020) AI-based chatbots in customer service and their effects on user compliance. Electron Mark 31:427–445
74. Nass C, Steuer J, Tauber ER (1994) Computers are social actors. In: Proceedings of the SIGCHI, conference on human factors in computing systems: celebrating interdependence. ACM, Boston, MA, pp 72–78
75. Ischen C, Araujo T, Voorveld H, van Noort G, Smit E (2019) Privacy concerns in chatbot interactions". In: Følstad A, Araujo T, Papadopoulos S, Law EL-C, Granmo O-C, Luger E, Brandtzaeg PB (eds) Conversations 2019: chatbot research and design. Springer, Cham, pp 34–48
76. Onkal D, Goodwin P, Thomson M, Gonul S, Pollock A (2009) The relative influence of advice from human experts and statistical methods on forecast adjustments. J Behav Decis Mak 22(4):390–409
77. Heerink M, Krose B, Evers V, Wielinga B (2010) Assessing acceptance of assistive social agent technology by older adults: the Almere model. Int J Soc Robot 2(4):361–375
78. Piçarra N, Giger JC (2018) Predicting intention to work with social robots at anticipation stage: assessing the role of behavioral desire and anticipated emotions. Comput Hum Behav 86:129–146
79. Wirtz J, Patterson PG, Kunz WH, Gruber T, Lu VN, Paluch S, Martins A (2018) Brave new world: service robots in the frontline. J Serv Manag 29(5):907–931
80. Longoni C, Bonezzi A, Morewedge CK (2019) Resistance to medical artificial intelligence. J Consum Res 46(4):629–650
81. Zikmund WG (2000) Business research methods, 6th edn. Harcourt College Publisher, Orlando, FL
82. Peter JP (1979) Reliability: a review of psychometric basics and recent marketing practices. J Mark Res 16(1):6–17
83. Morgan-Thomas A, Veloutsou C (2013) Beyond technology acceptance: Brand relationships and online brand experience. J Bus Res 66(1):21–27
84. Edwards JC, Rust KG, McKinley W, Moon G (2003) Business ideologies and perceived breach of contract during downsizing: the role of the ideology of employee self-reliance. J Organ Behav: Int J Ind Occup Organ Psychol Behav 24(1)1–23
85. Évrard Y, Pras B, Roux E (2003) Market: Etudes et Recherches en Marketing. Dunod. B, Paris
86. Hair JF, Black WC, Babin BJ, Anderson RE, Tatham RL (2010) Multivariate data analysis. Upper Saddle River, Pearson, New Jersey

87. Fornell C, Lacker D (1981) Evaluating structural equation model with unobservable variable and measurement error. J Market Res 18(1):39–50
88. Hua Y, Cheng X, Hou T, Luo R (2020) Monetary rewards, intrinsic motivators, and work engagement in the IT-enabled sharing economy: a mixed-methods investigation of internet taxi drivers. Decis Sci 51(3):755–785
89. Thatcher JB, Wright RT, Sun H, Zagenczyk TJ, Klein R (2018) Mindfulness in information technology use: definitions, distinctions, and a new measure. MIS Q 42(3):831–847
90. Hair JF Jr, Sarstedt M, Ringle CM, Gudergan SP (2017) Advanced issues in partial least squares structural equation modeling. Sage Publications, Thousand Oaks, CA
91. Thakur R (2018) The role of self-efficacy and customer satisfaction in driving loyalty to the mobile shopping application. Int J Retail Distrib Manage 46(3):283–303
92. Fridin M, Belokopytov M (2014) Acceptance of socially assistive humanoid robot by preschool and elementary school teachers. Comput Hum Behav 33:23–31
93. Abashev A, Grigoryev R, Grigorian K, Boyko V (2016) Programming tools for messenger-based chatbot system organization: implication for outpatient and translational medicines. Bio Nano Sci 7(2):403–407
94. Ajzen I, Fishbein M (1977) Attitude-behaviour relations: a theoretical analysis and review of empirical research. Psychol Bull 84(5):888
95. Alnawas I, Hemsley-Brown J (2018) The differential effect of cognitive and emotional elements of experience quality on the customer-service provider's relationship. Int J Retail Distrib Manage 46(2):125–147
96. Birnbaum GE, Mizrahi M, Hoffman G, Reis HT, Finkel EJ, Sass O (2016) What robots can teach us about intimacy: the reassuring effects of robot responsiveness to human disclosure. Comput Hum Behav 63:416–423
97. Bjørn P, Ngwenyama O (2009) Virtual team collaboration: building shared meaning, resolving breakdowns and creating translucence. Inf Syst J 19(3):227–253
98. Calvert P (2017) Robots, the quiet workers, are you ready to take over? Public Library Q 36(2):167–172
99. Channel retailing: introduction to the special issue on multi-channel retailing. J Retailing 91(2):174–181
100. Chattaraman V, Kwon WS, Gilbert JE, Ross K (2019) Should AI-Based, conversational digital assistants employ social-or task-oriented interaction style? A task-competency and reciprocity perspective for older adults. Comput Hum Behav 90:315–330
101. Chen CC, Lin SY, Cheng CH, Tsai CC (2012) Service quality and corporate social responsibility, influence on post-purchase intentions of sheltered employment institutions. Res Dev Disabil 33(6):1832–1840
102. Chen CC, Olfman L, Harris A (2005) Differential impacts of social presence on the behavior modeling approach. Int J Technol Human Interact 1(2):64–84
103. Chen LD, Tan J (2004) Technology adaptation in e-commerce: key determinants of virtual stores acceptance. Eur Manage J 22(1):74–86
104. Cheng X, Bao Y, Zarifis A (2020) Investigating the impact of IT-mediated information interruption on emotional exhaustion in the workplace. Inf Process Manage 57(6):102–281
105. Cheng X, Fu S, de Vreede GJ (2018) A mixed method investigation of sharing economy driven car-hailing services: online and offline perspectives. Int J Inf Manage 41(10):57–64
106. Childers TL, Carr CL, Peck J, Carson S (2001) Hedonic and utilitarian motivations for online retail shopping behavior. J Retail 77(4):511–535
107. Cyr D, Hassanein K, Head M, Ivanov A (2007) The role of social presence in establishing loyalty in e-service environments. Interact Comput 19(1):43–56
108. Cyr D, Head M, Larios H, Pan B (2009) Exploring human images in website design: a multimethod approach. MIS Q 33(3):539–566
109. Czaplewski AJ, Olson EM, Slater SF (2002) Applying the RATER model for service success. Market Manage 11(1):14–17
110. Das G (2016) Antecedents and consequences of trust: an e-tail branding perspective. Int J Retail Distrib Manage 44(7):713–730

111. Davenport TH (2019) Can we solve AI's 'trust problem? MIT Sloan Manage Rev 60(2):18–19
112. Davis FD, Bagozzi RP, Warshaw PR (1992) Extrinsic and intrinsic motivation to use computers in the workplace. J Appl Soc Psychol 22(14):1111–1132
113. Dayan M, Di Benedetto CA (2010) The impact of structural and contextual factors on trust formation in product development teams. Ind Mark Manage 39(4):691–703
114. Etemad-Sajadi R (2016) The impact of online real-time interactivity on patronage intention: the use of avatars. Comput Hum Behav 61:227–232
115. Everard A, Galletta DF (2005) How presentation flaws affect perceived site quality, trust, and intention to purchase from an online store. J Manage Inf Syst 22(3):56–95
116. Fan SC, Fought RL, Gahn PC (2017) Adding a feature: can a pop-up chat box enhance virtual reference services? Med Ref Serv Q 36(3):220–228
117. Gefen D, Straub D (2003) Managing user trust in B2C e-services. e-service J 2(2): 7–24
118. Ha S, Stoel L (2009) Consumer e-shopping acceptance: antecedents in a technology acceptance model. J Bus Res 62(5):565–571
119. Hassanein K, Head M, Ju C (2009) A cross-cultural comparison of the impact of social presence on website trust, usefulness and enjoyment. Int J Electron Bus 7(6):625
120. Holotescu C (2016). MOOCBuddy: a chatbot for personalized learning with MOOCs. In: Iftene A, Vanderdonckt J (eds) RoCHI--International conference on human-computer interaction, vol 91, pp 91–94. Matrix Rom, Bucharest, Romania
121. Holtgraves T, Han TL (2007) A procedure for studying online conversational processing using a chat bot. Behav Res Methods 39(1):156–163
122. Horzyk A, Magierski S, Miklaszewski G (2009) An intelligent internet shop-assistant recognizing a customer personality for improving man–machine interactions. Recent Adv Intell Inf Syst 13–26
123. Hsu P, Zhao J, Liao K, Liu T, Wang C (2017) AllergyBot: a chatbot technology intervention for young adults with food allergies dining out. In: Proceedings of the 2017 CHI conference extended abstracts on human factors in computing systems. ACM, Denver Colorado, USA. pp 74–79
124. Imrie P, Bednar P (2013) Virtual personal assistant. In: Martinez M, Pennarolaecilia F (eds) ItAIS 2013. Proceedings of 10th conference of the Italian chapter of AIS, 'Empowering society through digital innovations', Università Commerciale Luigi Bocconi, December 14, Milan, Italy
125. Jensen ML, Yetgin E (2017) Prominence and interpretation of online conflict of interest disclosures. MIS Q 41(2):629–643
126. Jiang C, Rashid RM, Wang J (2019) Investigating the role of social presence dimensions and information support on consumers' trust and shopping intentions. J Retail Consum Serv 51:263–270
127. Kelley SW, Davis MA (1994) Antecedents to customer expectations for service recovery. J Acad Mark Sci 22(1):52–61
128. Koufaris M (2002) Applying the technology acceptance model and flow theory to online consumer behavior. Inf Syst Res 13(2):205–223
129. Lasek M, Jessa S (2013) Chatbots for customer services on hotel websites. Inf Syst Manage 2(2):146–158
130. Lee S, Dubinsky A (2003) Influence of salesperson characteristics and customer emotion on retail dyadic relationships. Int Rev Retail Distrib Consumer Res 13(1):21–36
131. Li D, Chau PYK, Lou H (2005) Understanding individual adoption of instant messaging: an empirical investigation. J Assoc Inf Syst 6(4):102–129
132. Lombard M, Ditton T (1997) At the heart of it all: the concept of presence. J Comput-Mediat Commun 3(2):1–43
133. Lu B, Fan W, Zhou M (2016) Social presence, trust, and social commerce purchase intention: an empirical research. Comput Hum Behav 56:225–237
134. McKenna KYA, Green AS, Gleason MEJ (2002) Relationship formation on the internet: what's the big attraction? J Soc Issues 58(1):9–31

135. Ming-Chi L (2009) Factors influencing the adoption of internet banking: an integration of TAM and TPB with perceived risk and perceived benefit. Electron Commer Res Appl 8(3):130–141
136. Moon J, Kim Y (2001) Extending the TAM for a WorldWideWeb context. Inf Manage 38(4):217–230
137. Morgeson FP, Humphrey SE (2006) The work design questionnaire (WDQ): developing and validating a comprehensive measure for assessing job design and the nature of work. J Appl Psychol 91(6):1321–1339
138. Murray J, Elms J, Curran M (2019) Examining empathy and responsiveness in a high-service context. Int J Retail Distrib Manage 47(12):1364–1378
139. Negi S, Joshi S, Chalamalla AK, Subramaniam LV (2009) Automatically extracting dialog models from conversation transcripts. In 2009 Ninth IEEE international conference on data mining, 2009 (ICDM'09). IEEE, Miami, FL, pp 890–895
140. Podsakoff PM, MacKenzie SB, Lee JY, Podsakoff NP (2003) Common method biases in behavioral research: a critical review of the literature and recommended remedies. J Appl Psychol 88(5):879–903
141. Powell PA, Roberts J (2017) Situational determinants of cognitive, affective, and compassionate empathy in naturalistic digital interactions. Comput Hum Behav 68:137–148
142. Pugh SD (2001) Service with a smile: emotional contagion in the service encounter. Acad Manage J 44(5):1018–1027
143. Qiu L, Benbasat I (2009) Evaluating anthropomorphic product recommendation agents: a social relationship perspective to designing information systems. J Manage Inf Syst 25(4):145–182
144. Shen J (2012) Social comparison, social presence, and enjoyment in the acceptance of social shopping websites. J Electron Commer Res 13(3):198
145. Siau K, Shen Z (2003) Building customer trust in mobile commerce. Commun ACM 46(4):91–94
146. Starzyk KB, Holden RR, Fabrigar LR, MacDonald TK (2006) The personal acquaintance measure: a tool for appraising one's acquaintance with any person. J Pers Soc Psychol 90(5):833–847
147. Suh B, Han I (2002) Effect of trust on customer acceptance of Internet banking. Electron Commer Res Appl 1(3–4):247–263
148. Tsai WC, Huang YM (2002) Mechanisms linking employee affective delivery and customer behavioral intentions. J Appl Psychol 87(5):1001–1008
149. Van der Heijden H (2003) Factors influencing the usage of websites: the case of a generic portal in The Netherlands. Inf Manage 40(6):541–549
150. Van der Heijden H (2004) User acceptance of hedonic information systems. MIS Q 28(4):695–704
151. Van Doorn J, Lemon KN, Mittal V, Nass S, Pick D, Pirner P, Verhoef PC (2010) Customer engagement behavior: theoretical foundations and research directions. J Serv Res 13(3):253–266
152. Wang W, Benbasat I (2008) Attributions of trust in decision support technologies: a study of recommendation agents for e-commerce. J Manag Inf Syst 24(4):249–273
153. Whang C, Im H (2018) Does recommendation matter for trusting beliefs and trusting intentions? Focused on different types of recommender system and sponsored recommendation. Int J Retail Distrib Manage 46(10):944–958
154. Wood SL (2001) Remote purchase environments: the influence of return policy leniency on twostage decision processes. J Mark Res 38(2):157–169
155. Wu I-L, Chen J-L (2005) An extension of trust and TAM model with TPB in the initial adoption of on-line tax: an empirical study. Int J Hum Comput Stud 62(6):784–808
156. Wu WY, Ke CC (2015) An online shopping behaviour model integrating personality traits, perceived risk, and technology acceptance. Soc Behav Personal: An Int J 43(1):85–97
157. Yu J, Ha I, Choi M, Rho J (2005) Extending the TAM for a t-commerce. Inf Manage 42(7):965–976

158. Zalama E, García-Bermejo JG, Marcos S, Domínguez S, Feliz R, Pinillos R, López J (2014) Sacarino, a service robot in a hotel environment. In: Armada MA et al (eds) ROBOT2013: First Iberian robotics conference, advances in intelligent systems and computing 253. Springer International Publishing, Switzerland, pp 3–14
159. Zhang M, Jin B, Wang GA, Goh TN, He Z (2016) A study of key success factors of service enterprises in China. J Bus Ethics 134(1):1–14

Design, Innovation, and Brand Management

Speculative for Strategic Design

Theories and Contributions of Speculative for Strategic Design

Maria João Gamito Caixas
and Fernando Jorge Matias Sanches Oliveira

Abstract This paper analyzes the concepts of speculation, strategy, and strategic design. Seeking to observe the dynamics of strategic design thinking and how we can apply scenarios as a tool and method for strategic innovation and testing existing strategies, products, and services. This investigation is a literature review primary study in the emerging field, that focuses on fusing speculative design practice and strategic design. The importance of questioning the future in a fast and complex changing world, rewilding the ways of thinking and the nature of the problems, and the responsibility as designers to social change as shapers of society. While most strategies and innovation methods focus on meeting needs, influenced by the market, there is still little understanding in organizations to deal with unpredictability. Recognizing the complexity of today's socio-technological systems, and innovation, stakeholders can work together to achieve more orderly but also more sustainable and innovative solutions that seek greater long-term social, economic, and cultural benefits. This paper serves as an entry point for design practitioners and researchers interested in understanding the connection between speculation, strategy, and long-term thinking.

Keywords Design · Strategic design · Strategy · Speculative design · Design thinking

M. J. Gamito Caixas (✉) · F. J. Matias Sanches Oliveira
IADE-Faculty of Design, Technology and Communication of the Universidade Europeia, Avenida D. Carlos I, 4, 1200-649 Lisboa, Portugal
e-mail: mariacaixas94@hotmail.com

F. J. Matias Sanches Oliveira
e-mail: fernando.oliveira@universidadeeuropeia.pt

N. Martins and D. Raposo (eds.), *Communication Design and Branding*, Springer Series in Design and Innovation 32,
https://doi.org/10.1007/978-3-031-35385-7_17

1 Introduction

In a world of complex and profound changes, full of new technologies, everyone has to constantly design and redesign their existence, whether in an individualistic or collective way, such as companies, associations, organizations, and public entities, among others [17]. As human beings, we determine our identity and our life project. Creating this identity, whether individual or collective, implies putting design capacity into action and consequently implies strategic thinking and reflection in the way of doing things. Most definitions talk about strategy as a balance between ends, ways, and means, focusing on goals, and finding the right resources and methods to achieve those goals, but several theorists consider that strategic thinking is related to emotional aspects affected by social complexity, cultural and economic dynamics, and power games rather than a purely rational logic [28]. We live in an extremely complex world, our social relations, fantasies, aspirations, and fears are quite different from those that emerged in the early twentieth century, yet the ideas present in design theory and practice, in general, reflect issues of this period. [8] state that society has evolved, but the design has not, which probably means that designers need to rethink their processes.

Most people, when they think of design, essentially think of problem-solving, and improving services, equipment, and objects [30]. Deyan [29] argues that design shapes perceptions of how objects can and should be understood and Ezio [17] adds that designers can act as social actors, inducing ideological change. One of the aspects often referred to as intrinsic to the role of design today, is changing social behaviors [17]. Taking this responsibility to the strategic design practice, the emphasis can be placed not only on the realization of a product or service but rather on the prevention of undesirable consequences and on changing mindsets [6]. Through the experience gained from designed products, we can think strategically and reflect on complex problems, the so-called wicked problems, which due to their high complexity do not allow concrete and definitive answers. In fact, in the contemporary age design approaches unlogic problems where diversity and complexity take place [8].

Speculative design is a critical design practice and one of the many ways in which design remains relevant in the face of the complex technological, social, political, and economic changes we are experiencing in the twenty-first century, as a catalyst for change [6]. The speculative design aims at the intellect and the search for questions, urging humans to self-reflect and use their imagination, expanding the boundaries of how to use design and think about objects, far beyond their basic utility. Authors such as [6], propose speculative design as a teaching method that can allow immersion into the unknown, by increasing our predisposition to fix knowledge, whether in the application of design as something structural or in the design elements themselves, where various areas of expertise can contribute. A similar idea from [12] proposes a macro view in the way that institutions teach design with a multidisciplinary approach and a mix of fields such as Communication theory, Understanding of society; Rhetoric; Semantics; Storytelling and narrative, among others.

In a world where design begins to move into complex problem-solving, the exploration of new methods can be useful to generate creative capabilities that can complement a company's organizational and structural strategies, exploring the concepts of speculation and innovation. The main objective of this research is to investigate the contribution of speculative scenario tools for strategic design. The research question addressed in this paper is: Can speculative design methods be implemented in innovation strategy?

2 Theoretical Framework

With globalization and the concentration of people in large urban centers, the concern with problems and challenges such as sustainability, overpopulation, climate change, water shortages, safety, and accessibility has increased. Designers today are increasingly required to respond to these complex problems and social changes in a connected world, in more system-conscious and shifting ways [17], which go far beyond the ability of a single discipline to respond. Social transformation is a complex problem to design complex social systems, social situations, policymaking, and the designing community. According to a commonplace definition, a system is a set of interconnected elements that is organized in a coherent way to achieve a goal [18]. As systems become more interrelated, complexity increases [15], Sevaldson [27]. For [8], complexity is interconnected with unpredictable variables and non-linear, chaotic problems. In strategy, a complex problem, means that the goal of the problem has encountered obstacles along the way, very dynamic and diverse which do not allow its resolution, they are unclear and it's difficult to trace a path to find one right solution [28].

It's becoming clear that many of these challenges we face today are unfixable, and the only way to cross them is by changing our behavior, beliefs, values, and attitudes. Complexity has increased with the high networking capacity and decentralization caused by technological advances, the Internet, the rise of China and India, trends in healthy living, energy crises, and more. As a result of a decentralized and complex world, large-scale experiments in political, social, self-organization, and technological domains are increasingly challenging all dominant market structures, orthodox, centralized corporations, command structures, and even the designer as an author. Markets are more dynamic than ever before and these dynamics and changes affect strategy. Strategy development and implementation today are quite different from a few decades ago when markets were more stable, fixed, and simple [1]. As a result, organizations need to adapt strategically to remain relevant. Strategists need to embrace new perspectives and new ways of thinking, new concepts, and tools. In environments shaped by these new realities, Aaker (2010) suggest the development of five competencies that the strategist needs for the development of tasks, which are, strategic analysis, innovation, developing sustainable advances, control of multiple business units, and the development of growth platforms.

As society changes its values that go far beyond the traditional corporate objectives and purposes of surviving in the market and increasing profits, a new strategy is required and a new framework of understanding that considers the sustainable development of society and the complex range of social relationships. Thinking creatively about the future requires sensibility to the complex world, and the capacity to anticipate scenarios could be a challenge, the objective of speculation is to think and consider different possibilities through future scenarios building, this allows the decision-makers at the strategic end of innovation, envisage different future possibilities and outcomes. Futures are a means to help us think imaginatively and speculate, they are not just a destination or something to be sought. They are not just about the future but also the present, and this is where they become critical, especially when the focus is on limitations [6].

3 Strategy and Strategic Design

'Tactics is knowing what to do when there is something to do, strategy is knowing what to do when there is nothing to do' [3, 22].

A frequent metaphor used to represent the concept of strategy is the game of chess, where the player closely and rationally analyzes and evaluates all the options available at the time to anticipate and outsmart the opponent [28]. This analytical view has been quite influential since the first studies on strategy, but besides these considerations, there is no agreed-upon definition of the concept [14]. Most of the definitions emphasize how strategy is about a balance between ends, ways, and means, about analyzing opportunities and problems and setting up goals, and about the methods and resources available for achieving those goals [9]. Basically, in other words, strategy is defined to discover a critical factor/situation and design the resources and planning properties, to coordinate and focus the actions to deal with those critical situations [28]. A logical, rational, and analytical structure are considered the key elements of a strategy [26] allied to coherence as a descriptor.

Strategic thinking most of the time is focused on the strategic goals of a company, those goals are defined and approved by the board committee and should be supported by the management. Is related to results-oriented, profitable, and being disruptive in the activity. Anna [19, p. 33] described strategy as "any action that takes a direction and moves, making a system evolve with success, according to some flexible but clear rules, and adapting to changes in the environment". In the design field, the goal of the strategy is to promote the efficiency and performance of a company, in the eyes of designers, competitors, and consumers. Strategic design is based on the articulation of an internal and external orientation. Internal orientation is generally how the organization promotes internal knowledge, communication, and understanding. The external orientation is affected and guided by the market and focuses on how design can reach the target market, promoting a consistent brand identity and providing the company with a competitive edge [8].

Many authors have recognized the importance of methodical planning while executing a task or strategy, the use of reactional frameworks of analysis from corporate companies such as SWOT and PESTEL or other quantitative research methods is considered a crucial component for the practice of strategy in design. Strategic design processes are seen as based on sequences of analytical moves [28]. Besides all this, a variety of thinkers considered that human decisions about strategy depend in large scale on emotional aspects and are affected by complex social, cultural dynamics, economic, and power games than purely rational and logical [28]. In this sense, we can say that strategy is a paradoxical and complex process in which the more organizations plan for success (e.g., committing resources, narrowing their focus, and developing specific capabilities toward this specific focus), the more they may increase their chances for failure as the future is uncertain and unpredictable [24]. Therefore, a strategy needs constant adaptations, rather than seeing it as an "attack" planning, organizations should focus on being prepared to perform in a variety of future scenarios and environments and building responses to new and unanticipated situations [25].

4 Critical, Speculative Design

Over the last couple of years, foresight and design have become closer, and practitioners of both disciplines started to become interested in how the two could augment and complement each other's knowledge [10, 13]. In the case of the design field, interest in the future has led to emerging practices such as Critical design, design fiction, or speculative design [21]. These practices emphasize design more as an inquiry-oriented mindset that encourages critical thinking and debate and less as a problem-solving approach [2].

Critical design exists for decades and uses speculative design proposals to challenge preconceptions. One of the main goals of critical design is to question the limited range of experiences that we can obtain through already-designed products and reflect on this design, to recognize the psychological and emotional aspects of people and contribute to solving complex problems. The concept of speculation has been explored and popularized by Anthony Dunne, professor, head of the design interactions program at the Royal College of Art, and Fiona Raby, professor of industrial design at the University of Applied Arts in Vienna. They propose an approach to design that focuses on the creation and the idea of possible futures as a tool to better understand the world we live in and the present to discuss the kind of future people want and don´t want [6]. In this sense, we can say that Speculative design is based primarily on a critical discursive practice/thinking and dialogue, and to this end, it can even use negativity to draw attention to bad possibilities and realities [6].

The authors [16], argue that the term speculative design does not refer to a specific style or movement, but rather encompasses practices from a range of disciplines, including futurists and visionary forms of design fiction, architecture, and critical design. Architecture is the most traditional and developed history of speculative design, more than just diagrams these unbuilt structures are considered a space of interaction between technology, culture, and the built environment. However, these future-oriented projects should not be mistaken as futuristic and dismissible and should be part of the exploration of the space of environmental possibilities [6]. This exploration can take a variety of forms such as creature creation, 3D art and digital, writing and audio storytelling, film, performing experience creation, theatrical staging, and so on. The "what-if" questions that arise from the props are used to initiate discussion and debate. Although it differs from the traditional future trend forecasting methodologies, with the creation of these scenarios and speculative future props, the odds of achieving desirable futures increased [6].

5 Discussion/Results

The concept of strategy primarily depends on a clear and centralized definition of intentions and goals. This deliberate strategy can be successfully executed when there is no interference from external forces, such as the market or the advance of technology, and other events than can occur [1]. One of the reasons why traditional methods of strategy are failing is the fact that we are living in an extremely complex world, of uncertainties and rapid technological development, and this instability in society means a change in the market dynamics. In this highly interconnected world, it's hard to explore implications and find new developments, when situations are unpredictable and when external factors are quite significant, the strategy can emerge from a context-dependent sequence, this means that individuals and managers make the decisions trying to respond to these problems imposed by the external factors. The fact that these decisions are made influenced by external forces, means that central control can be lost.

Design can help integrate new resources and capabilities in organizational departments and functions [28]. Design as a discipline has evolved from not just designing objects and services but also designing systems and strategies and building scenarios. It is used as a tool to drive innovation, strategy, and management in companies, and this makes strategic design an emerging and future-oriented field in the evolution of design. Design practice can materialize scenarios, making them more credible, reflectable, and relatable, and can create the intangible future into a tangible one for human comprehension and engagement. Examples of tools applied to this scenario-building concept can include filmmaking, live-action, science fiction, 3D rendering products, exhibitions, advertisements, storytelling, and more. By doing this, the future scenario can create more impact because it is through design experience that thinking can change and create real action. The interest in the design and construction of possible futures has been emerging, and one of the future-oriented fields in design, as a practice and method, is speculative design [6].

The idea of speculation is not focused on predicting the future or trying to find a resolution to all problems in the world, its focus is on possibilities, guiding us to consider our interests over a set of future probabilities [6]. Speculative design provokes thinking by fostering ambiguity while still grounding ideas in real life and time conditions, in contrast with other design approaches, it aims to question common values and beliefs to rewild ways of innovation and future developments [6]. Speculative design is motivated primarily by curiosity and questions rather than needs. Although speculative design may require some knowledge of technical content and equipment, such as computers, networks, or sensors, the focus is an approach to design that emphasizes experimentation, usability, utility, investigation, or even desirability. Since is not driven and influenced by the market or dictated by engineering principles, it emerges as an opportunity to imagine and explore possibilities without being burdened by the need for deliverables to implement actions or construction plans [16].

Speculative design can be methodically introduced into the strategic design practice, as a form of innovation and construction of possible and probable scenarios, and as a testing and complementing method to rethink existing strategies and artifacts, as a catalyst for new decisions. Scenarios are considered a tool for framing strategic innovation, in fact, strategic foresight has been used and incorporated into innovation and strategy [4]. The field of strategic foresight develops practices and perspectives that anticipate future situations, stress-testing existing strategies, and prepares organizations to evaluate and navigate through them. The strategy has found value in exploring the relationship between companies and their futures, especially when they are confronted with external changes [18]. Speculative design is also often addressed as "functional fiction", which serves a social purpose. It is intrinsically linked to the discipline of critical design [8], which consists of critiquing the present through artifacts already designed and implemented. This artifact is considered a means to rethink what might be wrong in the consumer society, providing insight and reflection for public discourse.

The annual magazine Life at Home research at IKEA from 2021, can be a case study of the implementation of speculative design as a tool for communication and management. In the magazine they ask questions like, what will our homes look like? What will happen next? And will our attitudes towards them and the planet we live on remain the same? And after they offer some optimistic possibilities for" designing the future of life at home", exploring artifacts, probs possibilities, and design fiction. Ludvig Liljeqvist the Global Sustainability Insights and Innovation Leader, at IKEA Retail (Ingka Group) says that "The moment humans leave; nature will come back to cities. It will break the concrete and rewild our urban spaces,". He offers a new perspective, working with insights and foresight, and argues that in the uncertain world that we live in, sustaining a positive future vision requires radical collective, action, and imagination. The home farm advertisement is not a product for sale, but a possible scenario of a garden utility at home.

From a management point of view, Scenario planning can provide systematic methodologies that help organizations develop a strong mindset approach, by confronting the unknown and thinking the unthinkable, plausible futures can expose new patterns of exploring strengths, weaknesses, opportunities, and threats. The construction of these scenarios can be used to simplify complexity and create dialog across stakeholders. Scenario planning embraces the unknown, it´s not a qualitative method as it considers non-linear trajectories. One of the biggest motivations for using this type of approach is to change people's mindsets and behaviors in communicating ideas and visions to the audience. However, despite the enormous amount and new knowledge about future studies, there is very little impact of these on real-life decision-making. With the high complexity, researchers in the design and designers themselves, have increasingly recognized the importance of these factors and future studies, as a need to address the most impactful issues in the world through their practices, thus recognizing new methods for such interventions.

6 Conclusion

This study aimed to understand and clarify emerging and innovative concepts through a literature review analysis in the field of strategy and speculative design. The idea of this approach to design was to suggest, propose, offer, and contribute to the field, and define meaningful insights. Exploring through a literature review the possibilities of the introduction of speculative design in the field of strategy (as a complemented method) and how the two topics are evolving, reveals a growing interest to merge both. The focus of the investigation was to discover value in the use of speculative design in strategic thinking as a tool for organizations and for the development and rethinking of objects that already exist.

In an era, in which complexity increases and competing demands intensify, we believe that methodologies and approaches that more deliberately focus on competing demands in terms of paradoxes are needed. In this introductory article, we have sought to build bridges between speculative design and strategy, in a way to contribute to organizational behavior, innovation, and long-term thinking. Through the literature review, it was possible to consider that Speculative Design consists of a very diverse set of approaches and thrives to combine different disciplines, to achieve critical, engaging, inclusive, and though reflections on the future.

Design can sketch new possibilities and allied to strategy can be a tool for the construction and exploration of scenarios for organizations, exploring new patterns and future possibilities for the companies. Taking into account the list entitled "A/B Manifesto" [6, p. vii], for example, we can consider that by changing the persona, from a consumer perspective to the citizen, we can introduce changes in strategic thinking, and also we can switch our mindset from "change the world to suit us" to "change the us for suit the world" [6, p. vii], to improve strategic processes. Emphasizing design less as an oriented problem-solving approach, to a more inquisitive-oriented mindset can encourage critical thinking, and debate around what could be, using design artifacts.

The future scenarios can be an orientation to analyze the relationship between organizations, their futures, and the public to help in the decision-making process. A critical capability can be a relevant practice for renewing and aligning organizational resources to external changes, putting speculative design as a complementary approach to innovation and management strategy. Critical, future forecasting and speculative design could benefit from a greater view of human nature and the ability to make abstract issues more tangible. It could be applied as a role in public debates, ethical impact on everyday life, social and emerging and future technologies, and as a tool for management and innovation strategies.

References

1. Aaker D, Mclunghlin D (2010) Strategic market management: global perspectives. Wiley
2. Auger J (2013) Speculative design: crafting the speculation. Digital Creativity 24(1):11–35. https://doi.org/10.1080/14626268.2013.767276
3. Boyer B, Cook JW, Steinberg M (2011) Recipes for systemic change. Helsinki (Finland): Sitra/ Helsinki Design Lab
4. Buehring J, Bishop PC (2020) Foresight and design—new support for strategic decision making. She ji—The J Design, Econ, Innov 6(3)
5. Dorst K (2019) Design beyond design. She Ji: The J Design, Econ, Innov 5(2): 117–127. https:/ /doi.org/10.1016/j.sheji.2019.05.001 ebrun J-L (2007) Scientific writing: a reader and writer's guide. World Scientific
6. Dunne A, Raby F (2013) Speculative everything: design, fiction, and social dreaming. MIT Press LTD.
7. Ehls D, Gordon A, Herstatt C, Rohrbeck R (2022) Foresight in strategy and innovation management. IEEE Trans Eng Manage 69:483–492. https://doi.org/10.1109/TEM.2021.307 7342
8. Erlhoff M, Marshall T (2007) Design dictionary: perspectives on design terminology. Birkhäuser, Germany
9. Freedman L (2013) Strategy: a history. Oxford University Press, Oxford
10. Gordon A, Rohrbeck R, Schwarz J (2019) Escaping the "Faster Horse" trap: bridging strategic foresight and design-based innovation. Technol Innov Manage Rev 9(8)
11. Hasson F, Keeney S, McKenna H (2000) Research guidelines for the Delphi survey technique. J Adv Nurs 32(4):1008–1015
12. Heller S (2005) The education of a graphic designer. Allworth, 2nd edn
13. Hines A, Zindato D (2016) Designing foresight and foresighting design: opportunities for learning and collaboration via scenarios. World Futures Rev 8(4):180–192. https://doi.org/10. 1177/1946756716672477
14. Kenny G (2018) Your strategic plans probably aren't strategic, or even plans. Harvard Business Review. https:// hbr.org/2018/04/your-strategic-plans-probably-arent-strategic-oreven-plans
15. Leadbeater C, Winhall J (2020) Building better systems: a green paper on system innovation. The Rockwool Foundation
16. Lukens J, Disalvo C (2011) Speculative design and technological fluency. Int J Learn Media 3:23–40. https://doi.org/10.1162/IJLM_a_00080
17. Manzini E (2015) Design, when everybody designs: an introduction to design for social innovation. MIT Press LTD, Cambridge, Massachusetts
18. Meadows D (2008) Thinking in systems (Wright D, ed) Chelsea Green Publishing
19. Meroni A (2008) Strategic design: where are we now? Reflection around the foundations of a recent discipline. Strategic Des Res J 1(1):31–38. https://doi.org/10.4013/sdrj.20081.05
20. Muratovski G (2016) Research for designers. A guide to methods and practice. SAGE Publications Ltd, Los Angeles, London, New Delhi, Singapore, Washington DC, 2016
21. Neuhoff R, Simeone L, Holst Laursen L (2021) Exploring how design-driven foresight can support strategic thinking about sustainability and circular policy making. In: 14th European academy of design conference: safe harbours for design research the European academy of design

22. Oliveira F (2018) Brand´s identity and visual culture. In: Raposo D (2018) Communicating visually. The graphic design of the brand. London, UK, Cambridge Scholars Publishing. ISBN:(10):1-5275-1336-X. ISBN:(13):978-1-5275-1336-5
23. Olsen W (2004) Triangulation in social research: qualitative and quantitative methods can really be mixed. Dev Sociol 1–30
24. Raynor ME (2007) The strategy paradox: why committing to success leads to failure. Doubleday, New York
25. Reeves M, Haanaes K, Sinha J (2015) Your strategy needs a strategy: how to choose and execute the right approach. Harvard Business Review Press, Boston, MA
26. Rumelt R (2011) Good strategy, bad strategy. Crown Business, New York
27. Sevaldson B (2013) Systems oriented design: the emergence and development of a designerly approach to address complexity 22
28. Simeone L (04 de Maio de 2020) Characterizing strategic design processes in relation to definitions of strategy from military, business and management studies, p 21
29. Sudjic D (2010) A Linguagem das Coisas. Intrínseca, Rio de Janeiro
30. Tharp B, Tharp S (2019) Discursive design: critical, speculative, and alternative things. The MIT Press
31. The Life at Home Magazine (2022) Future home (1): 95–115. https://lifeathome.ikea.com/wp-content/uploads/2021/12/IKEA_LifeatHome_Magazine2021.pdf
32. Yin RK (2015) Estudo de caso: planejamento e métodos. Bookman, Porto Alegre

The Existing Gap Between Design Management and Management—Contributions on How to Bridge It Successfully

Sara Gancho

Abstract Design Management has been successful in connecting the knowledge areas of Design and Management. Companies, services, products, brands, and customers/users are now using design, marketing, and technology to create customer/brand interactions. Design Management has enabled Design to become more business-oriented, while Management has embraced Design and Human-centered approaches for a more strategic output. In the world of business, Design is recognized for its strategic value and is sometimes used as a synonym for innovation, research and development of products and services. To hold its place in the industry, Design Management must embrace a wide range of concerns such as marketing and management, innovation, quality control, training and development. Design is also criticized for lacking a thorough theoretical base, but its practice and theoretical discourse draw on a wide and diverse field of knowledge and skills. Design Management is a critical component of a company's expertise, as it is based on the design process and the creative capacity of designers to visualize solutions. It is also leaning towards prospective methods in a co-design process, which use skills like observation, dialogue, and empathy to improve both the products and services, as well as the processes themselves. Design Management is an ongoing conversation between the company and its environment, which can help to reinforce the credibility of design, improve customer orientation, and develop the creative aspects of corporate culture. This paper documents design management contributions to management such as: user orientation, market research, aesthetic value, brand, collaboration, system thinking, creativity, autonomy, prospective research on environment and vision. In the form of a literature review this paper highlights how management can reinforce their brands, products and services, the credibility of the design function, design strategy, performance indicators, research and experimentation by applying design management at its core., providing a synthesis of the existing research, highlighting the major findings and themes that emerge from the literature on design management.

S. Gancho (✉)
Faculdade de Design, Universidade Europeia, IADE, Tecnologia E Comunicação, UNIDCOM/IADE, Unidade de Investigação Em Design E Comunicação, Av. D. Carlos I, 4, 1200-649 Lisboa, Portugal
e-mail: sara.gancho@universidadeeuropeia.pt

N. Martins and D. Raposo (eds.), *Communication Design and Branding*, Springer Series in Design and Innovation 32,
https://doi.org/10.1007/978-3-031-35385-7_18

Keywords Design management · Design thinking · Business · Management

1 Contextualization

1.1 Bridging the Gap Between Design Management and Management

This paper provides us with a literature review, which provides a comprehensive and critical evaluation of existing research on Design Management. The purpose of this literature review is to identify gaps in the current knowledge, synthesize and analyze the existing research, and provide a context for the research being conducted. Focusing on the themes and issues related to the research area, and providing a synthesis of the existing research, highlighting the major findings that emerge from the literature. It then summarizes the key findings and themes, and highlights the implications of the research for further work.

Design Management has been able to bridge the gap between the Design and Marketing/Management areas of knowledge. Nowadays the way companies, services, products, brands, and customers/users communicate and generate costumer/brand interactions is undergoing rapid and transformative changes with the aid of design, marketing, and technology. Marketing and Design can come together to better plan and implement new solutions for these new, upcoming challenges, with the use of human centered tools and with a Design Management approach. When we focus on digital products and services and the future of technology, the key players are User Interface designers and User Experience Designers. They both work with creating empathy with the users and all the stakeholders involved in the design process, both develop a collaboration and articulateness in their work, and both use design thinking approaches for prototyping their ideas into fully functional products and services. While UI designers' knowledge is around color theory, typography, design systems and the interactions of user interface the UX designers are more focused on product strategy, user research and analysis, visualizing the information architecture and testing and iterating between the different stages of the process. In the context of sustainability, design and design management encompass all processes, objects, and design services, including UI and UX design, as well as digital technology. Designers can use sustainable design principles to create products and services that are environmentally friendly and socially responsible, and this applies to all areas of design, including digital design. Design thinking plays a crucial role in sustainable design by encouraging designers to think holistically about the problem they are trying to solve. It involves considering the environmental and social impacts of the design decisions, as well as the user experience. By taking a human-centered approach, designers can create products and services that meet the needs of users while also being sustainable. Overall, design and design management, including UI and UX design and digital technology, play a significant role in promoting sustainability. By using sustainable design principles and design thinking, designers can create products and services that meet the needs of users while also being environmentally and socially responsible. Together with engaging marketing practices it is possible to combine it into real business opportunities. This paper will focus on understanding how Design became more business focused through Design Management and how Management can improve on that knowledge by embracing Design and Human-centered approaches in a more strategic way. Design management and management science are two different fields of study, with different approaches and objectives. Design management is focused on creating, managing, and improving the design of products, services, and processes. Management, on the other hand, is focused on the development of models, methods, and tools to help organizations manage their operations and make better decisions. The gap between design management and management science can be bridged by recognizing the need for both disciplines to work together to achieve better results. Design managers need to understand the principles of management to effectively use management tools and methods in their work. Similarly, managers need to understand the principles of design management to effectively incorporate design elements into daily activity. By working together, the two disciplines can create a synergistic relationship that helps organizations achieve better results. Design managers can use the tools and methods of management to ensure that their designs are effective, cost-efficient, and aligned with the organization's goals. Similarly, management can use the principles of design management to make sure that their business, brands, services and products are designed in a way that takes into account user needs and preferences.

2 From Design to Design Management

2.1 A Brief Introduction

The word design has a Latin origin, it comes from the verb "designare" which means to determine. Design uses continual differentiation to make the vague into definite. It has many definitions, as a verb it could mean to work out a structure or form, or sketching, it can also mean to plan or make something using artistic skills, to visualize and invent. It could also mean to have a intend for a specific purpose, to plan, to form or conceive in the mind (in a visual way). As a noun it can assume a plan, a sketch or a preliminary drawing or decorative work [1].

There remains to be a lack of agreement as to the meaning of design that extends further than design research and design education, where the term is used in many ways and tends to relate to different activities and outcomes. Sometimes it is even used as a synonym for innovation, research and development and product development [2]. There is also a lack of understanding found in the world of business of what the real meaning of design is. Bürdek [3] says that businesses across the world recognize the strategic value of design and that in the 80's a group of business economists understood that design had a real economic impact, it was not just concerning design aesthetic purposes anymore. Gorb [4] reflects on if Design Management is to hold its position in the industry it must embrace a wide range of concerns such as marketing and management. He believes that Design Management should concern innovation and the place it holds in the process of creating profit for the business, quality control and maintenance in production and service organizations and the development of effective lines in terms of education, training and development.

Cooper and Junginger [5] says design is criticized for lacking a thorough theoretical base but its practice and theoretical discourse are drawn on a wide and diverse field of knowledge and skills. Walsh mentions the Four C's in design are much like the 4 P's in Marketing (product, price, point of purchase and promotion). With the C's being:

1. Creativity—the creation of something new;
2. Complexity—a decision making based on different opinions and variables;
3. Compromise—balancing multiples and somewhat conflicting requirements;
4. Choice—choosing between different solutions for all levels of the problem [2]

Authors like Kalantzis, Maryand Cope [6] talk about the way design is highly connected with the social sciences, psychology, sociology, management, science, engineering and the humanities and the principles and practices of design concern social change, creative economy, and knowledge society. Design is considered as a process for transformation, it is central in society's agenda.

Research on Design Management (DM) has been broad and still the definition of DM varies according to the perspective of the researcher, whether he or she is a practitioner, design thinker, design manager, design leader etc. The main theories published on Design Management start to appear around the late 70's (1977) according to de Mozota and Wolff [7] The authors refer to Design Management as the space between design science and management science and indicate that it is a forced interdisciplinary field as both designers and managers are not truly interested in it. The reasons they point are threefold:

(1) Academia on both sides have rarely connected;
(2) there is a lack of interest from management for the concrete and the aesthetic perspective and;
(3) the designers lack of interest in management and its measure of value in their activity.

Fortunately, the authors also state that mentalities are changing and that although Design Management research has not yet entered mainstream research in management science there is an emergent role that seems to be gaining importance—the Entrepreneur, which designs and shapes its own company, using design thinking methods and practices and its posture is closer to a designer that of a classic manager. This could indicate that we are leading towards a better understand of Design Management and how it can bring value to businesses. In order to improve design management and management understanding of each other we need to educate managers on design thinking in order to help them make better decisions. We should also foster collaboration and communication between designers and other team members as the design activity is multidisciplinary and transdisciplinary. Designers should be open to understand the business context in which they are working and how their work can impact the business. Designers should be included in strategic planning to ensure that their design decisions are in line with the business goals and lastly design concerns should be heard and considered when making management decisions.

Pribble III [8] believed as Mozota and Wolff [7] that design is a powerful tool and that it should be applied in every area of business to provide a strategic competitive advantage and to achieve its corporate objectives. He recognized the need for more and better design work and refers to it having to begin in a two-way education process—teaching designer students how business works and teaching design to management students. Pribble III suggested that design should be integrated into every area of business, from marketing to operations, to help companies gain a competitive advantage and meet their objectives. Higher education in both design and management could play an important part in creating awareness and understanding of how we could potentially integrate these two disciplines [8].

We can find studies that divide Design Management into three scopes: the strategic, the tactical and the operational, this is done according to the levels at which the design is being managed within the company [9–12].

The main objective of Design Management is to allow the company to nurture an environment where it can achieve its strategic goals in a more efficient and effective way [11, 13]. Design Management benefits design and corporate strategy as it can enhance their creative processes, create an innovative culture and communications for ongoing corporate growth, advancement, and success [12]. If design is managed and used strategically and in a systematic way, the company can secure a competitive advantage by becoming more attractive for the industry. This can be achieved by having designs (products/services or brands) that are highly differentiated, have a user centered approach, circular thinking at its core, better quality, and an appealing aesthetic, that of its competitors. This will increase customer awareness which will potentially increase ROI (return on investment). David Hands [14] and Katherine Best [15] says that implementing Design Management creates added value for clients, business, and all the involved stakeholders, and it can do that by meeting their different interests and needs at the appropriate stage of the design process.

de Mozota and Wolff [7] in their study compared two fundamental works on design management research which are two handbooks: *Handbook,* Oakley et al. [16] and *Handbook*, Cooper et al. [5]. They produced a figure that analysis the words most frequently cited in those handbooks; this provides us with five themes that characterize Design Management (Fig. 1). The words in bold are new ones (as of 2011), in italic they are disappearing.

The authors refer that Design Management is integrating words used in management such as brand, innovation, strategy, and value and that this changes the vision of DM only focusing on managing design projects. Design Management is the strategic, organizational, and operational discipline that focuses on the proactive and integrated management of design activities in organizations. It encompasses the design of a company's processes, products, services, and experiences, and the development

Fig. 1 The words of design management adapted from de Mozota and Wolff [7, p. 4]

of strategies and systems to support them. Design Management is concerned with the design of a company's competitive advantage and its strategic use of design to create value for customers and society. It involves the development of a design-driven culture and the promotion of design thinking within an organization to ensure that design plays a key role in the company's long-term success.

Cooper et al. [5] made a chronological evolution of Design Management and its themes that represent DM (design management) domains and criteria and shows us the evolution of the field in a matrix built around four themes.

Table 1 provides us with the four types of value Design Management can add, the way it can solve problems, how is develops and fuels its design skills and how design leadership can help accomplish the companies' goals. Design Management adds value through aesthetic differentiation, product quality and perception value which increases a company's economic value. It also adds value during the coordination of the process in aiding with problem solving, by using human value as a cultural transformation and by bringing framing skills to strategic value conversations.

Table 1 The chronological evolution of design management and its themes adapted from Cooper et al. [5]

DM adds value through…	Economic value (aesthetics, differentiation) product value (quality) perception value	Process value (coordination, problem- solving)	Human value (human and cultural transformation)	Strategic conversation value (building skills framing problems)
DM solves design problems relating to…	All aspects of company's artifact	Managing innovation	Strategic diagnosis changes in society, in politics	Cultural changes digital transformation design for all
DM develops and fuels design skills in the function of…	Direction Marketing Operations Communications	R&D Interdisciplinary innovation team	Finance Human resources	Every function in the company
Design leadership (design direction, artistic direction) helps the accomplishment of goals such as…	Create a brand and an identity (coherence between design disciplines) Create profit for the company	Create new products and services Improve the innovation process and its efficiency	Make companies aware of design strategy Change for customer oriented and creative culture	Make a company sustainable in a globalized context of societal well-being
Period	**1965–1992**	**1993–2005**	**2005–2014**	**2015–2017**

3 From Design Management to Management

3.1 Design as a Strategic Tool

The role Design Management plays in a company's expertise is firstly based on the design process, the creative capacity designers will visualize solutions and apply them for example in the context of brand creation and customer experience. Design Management is leaning towards prospective methods in a co-design process, it uses usability methods, where skills like: observation, dialogue and empathy during the course of the project help improve both the products and services but also the processes themselves as we could see in Table 1 [7].

Authors de Mozota and Wolff [7], have seen recent trends in management with the emergence of the entrepreneurial spirit, they state that new designers-entrepreneurs (Airbnb), and the issues of work transformation, companies' social responsibility, and the blurry boundaries of industries will change and perhaps bring the gap closer between Design Management research and critical management.

In the following figure the authors represent the two forces of DM which takes into consideration the force of Management toward design (M to d), the force of

Design in management (D to m) and at the center Design Management. They mention Management can reinforce the credibility of design with tools for management the design functions, by implementing performance indicators and by its support and giving space to experiment. Design in management can form a space for innovative systems and help companies see the changes that need to happen. Design is also able to reinforce the conversation between the company and its environment, but can also improve customer orientation, collaboration between participants, develop the creative aspects of corporate culture and give autonomy to the participants [7].

Design has to become part of the company's strategic goal in the initial stages of the strategy development [17]. Design management must affect all levels of company activities. de Mozota [10] sees the implementation of design management as a program of activities inside the company formally set to internally communicate the importance of design for the company's long-term goals. This approach corresponds to the model by Bruce et al. [18], which also describes a sequence of steps that should be taken in design management. Management can use design management effectively by setting clear objectives and expectations, defining the design process and roles, planning resources and scheduling tasks, monitoring the design process, and evaluating designs. Additionally, management should also ensure that all involved are working together and communicating effectively to ensure the successful completion of the design project. The first step is to adopt measures according to which the lead designer creates the initial project concept. The second step is an evaluation of the project concept followed by the development of the solution. The next step is user research, validation of product development, revision, and an assessment of the product design. Other activities are directed at the development of a prototype and its verification, followed by experimental manufacturing, production, promotion, and the product launch on the market.

Figure 2 raises four important issues that are yet to be "solved". How can we measure the value of design beyond the measure of client value and brand perception? How can we think about the products themselves without the company behind them? How can we materialize a company? And finally, how can systems thinking work within the company's structure?

Measuring the value of design beyond client value and brand perception can be done by looking at the customer's experience for example. This can include surveys, interviews, and customer feedback. Additionally, we can look at user behavior data to see how people interact with products, services, and brands. For example, how many clicks or page views a user takes to complete a task. Thinking about the products themselves without the company behind them can be done by focusing on the user needs and the problem-solving capabilities of design. This can include user research, competitive analysis, and usability testing. Additionally, A/B testing can be used to test different versions of the design to find the most effective solution. Materializing a company can be done by creating a visual identity that communicates the company's values and mission. This can include brand design, website design, and print materials. Additionally, we can create a story or narrative to emotionally connect with customers. Systems thinking can be used to evaluate how a company's processes,

	DM	+ DM +	MD
Product and service strategy	Designreinforces user orientation (marketresearch, aestheticvalue, brand)	"Good design" Beauty in utility	Managementreinforces the efficiency of design management in the offer and the brand
Innovation strategy	Designreinforces collaboration between participants (forces systems thinking)	Process Design Co-design Inclusive design	Managementreinforces the credibility of design with the managementtools of the design function
Humanresources strategy	Design changes company culture (more creative) and people's autonomy (creativity)	UX Design DesignThinking	Managementreinforces the pertinence of the design strategy by managing coordination with HR
Company strategy	Design changes the vision between the company and its environment (prospective, research)	Design strategy	Managementreinforces the credibility of the design function by implementing performance indications
Strategic audit	Design opens a prospective conversation between the company and its environment	Critical design Concept Design	Managementreinforces the credibility od design with the support of senior management (research, experimentation)
	• The issue of measuring thevalue of design beyond the measure of clientvalue and brand (perception) • The issue of thinking company and not only "products"	PROBLEMS	• The issue of company's materiality • The issue of systems thinking in the structure

Fig. 2 The two forces of design management adapted from de Mozota and Wolff [7, p. 4]

structure, and culture support its goals. This can include understanding how interdependent parts of the organization interact with each other and how changes in one part of the system can affect the whole. Management should set clear, measurable goals for the design strategy, and use them to evaluate the success of the strategy. When implementing a design strategy, it's important to ensure that the right team is in place. To ensure success, the team should include designers, developers, product managers and marketers. Establishing clear processes and guidelines is essential for any design strategy. This helps ensure that the strategy is implemented in a consistent and efficient manner. Analyzing and measuring the results of the design strategy will help provide insights on what's working and what needs to be improved. Management should also ensure that everyone in the company is aware of the design strategy and the goals associated with it. This will help ensure that everyone is on the same page and working towards the same objectives.

4 Main Conclusions

4.1 Recommendations for Further Work

Today, the concept of 'innovation' is not just limited to technological progress but also includes the design and implementation of new business models. This means that innovation should not just be seen as a one-off event, but as an ongoing process of continuous improvement and exploration. Innovation is therefore often seen as a key factor for economic growth and social wealth. It can be achieved through various means, such as technological advancements, changes in organizational structures and new products and services. By finding new ways to create value, businesses can increase their profits and customers can benefit from improved products and services. Innovation can also be beneficial for society. For instance, it can help reduce poverty by providing new employment opportunities and increasing access to goods and services. It can also help sustainability by helping to reduce waste and pollution. Furthermore, it can help improve public services and infrastructure and create new markets. Finally, innovation can help to make our world a better place. By using new technologies, we can reduce our environmental impact and create a more equitable society. As businesses continue to innovate, we can look forward to even greater benefits in the future.

Design thinking used in a Design Management perspective can help organizations to become more iterative, to anticipate and respond quickly to changing environments and to increase their competitive advantage. It also provides a systematic approach for addressing complex problems and for creating innovative solutions. It is a holistic approach to problem solving that involves understanding the needs of customers, stakeholders, and employees, and using creative and analytical thinking to develop an integrated, comprehensive solution. Design thinking is also an important part of innovation. It can be used to develop new products, services, and business models that are more customer-centric and have greater potential for success. Design thinking encourages companies to look beyond the immediate customer need to identify opportunities for growth, disruption, and increased customer value.

Design and design management have a significant contribution to sustainability issues. By creating products and services that are environmentally friendly and socially responsible, designers can help reduce the environmental impact of consumer goods. They can use sustainable materials, design for durability and reuse, and create products with a low carbon footprint. Design thinking can also be applied to sustainable design, taking into account the entire life cycle of the product or service, from raw materials to disposal. Design management can incorporate sustainability into the design process by establishing metrics to measure the environmental and social impacts of design decisions and integrating sustainability into the design brief. Lastly, design education can play a crucial role in promoting sustainability by teaching students to design products and services that are environmentally and socially responsible. Overall, design and design management can contribute to a more sustainable and equitable future.

Therefore, it is important to develop approaches and tools that are tailored to the specific needs and resources of the entrepreneur. These tools should focus on creating a framework for the entrepreneur to identify opportunities, create new value propositions and develop innovative solutions. Such tools would enable the entrepreneur to quickly and efficiently implement Design Thinking, Open Innovation and Design Management. In order to achieve this, the tools must be based on a comprehensive understanding of the entrepreneurial context and the special requirements of the entrepreneur. The tools must also be easy to use and accessible to entrepreneurs of all backgrounds, including those with limited technical skills.

Author Diwan [19] When it comes to designing solutions for social innovation and social change, a systemic design approach is crucial. This means taking a comprehensive systems approach to understanding and untangling the various factors and components that contribute to complex problems. To achieve this, it is essential to involve the target population that directly faces the problem in the design process, democratizing design and incorporating their suggestions and necessary details into the solution.

The future of design and management is likely to be strongly intertwined. Design management, which focuses on how to effectively use design to create value and achieve organizational goals, has become increasingly important in recent years. Design management also plays a critical role in the development of new products, services, and processes. Additionally, design management is central to successful business model innovation and the evolution of business processes. As technology continues to advance and the global marketplace becomes increasingly interconnected, design management will become even more important. Companies will need to understand how to best leverage design to create value, optimize processes, and create successful products. Design management will be essential to staying competitive and responding quickly to changes in the market.

As we move forward, it is vital to evolve the design education curriculum to prepare the next generation of designers to design robust solutions that meet the needs of the twenty-first century. By adopting a systemic approach, democratizing design, incorporating design research, and evolving design education, we can create innovative solutions that drive social change and address wicked problems in complex systems [19].

References

1. Gancho SPM (2015) The value and importance of design when branding in social media 1–316
2. Walsh V (1996) Design, innovation and the boundaries of the firm. Res Policy 25:509–529
3. Bürdek BE (2005) Design: history, theory and practice of product design, 1st edn. Birkhäuser-Publisher for Architecture: Springer Science + Business Media, Berlin, Germany
4. Gorb P (1990) The future of design and its management. In: Design management—a handbook of issues and methods. Mark Oakley, Ed. Oxford, pp 15–25
5. Cooper T, Junginger R, Lockwood S (2011) The handbook of design management. Oxford

6. Kalantzis B (2011) Mary and cope, "Design in principle and practice: a reconsideration of the terms of design engagement." Des J 14(1):45–63
7. De Mozota BB, Wolff F (2019) Forty years of research in design management: a review of literature and directions for the future. Strateg Des Res J 12(1):4–26
8. Pribble III J (1992) Integration of design and marketing in higher education. University of Colorado at Boulder
9. Cooper R, Press M (1995) The design agenda: a guide to successful design management. New York, NY
10. De Mozota BB (2003) Design management
11. Best K (2006) Design management: managing design strategy, process and Implementation. Ava Publishing SA, Lausanne, Switzerland
12. Ray Holland BL (2014) Managing strategic design
13. De Mozota BB (2003) Design and competitive edge: a model for design management excellence in European SMEs. Des Manage J 2(617)
14. Hands D (2009) Vision and values in design management. Bloomsbury Academic
15. Best K (2009) Gestão de design: gerir a estratégia, os processos e a implementação do design. Diverge Design SA, Portugal
16. Oakley B, Clipson M, Borja De Mozota C (1990) Design management: a handbook of issues and methods. Oxford, Blackwell
17. de Libânio S, Franzato C (2019) Design Baseado em Evidências em organizações da saúde: uma revisão sistemática de literatura evidence-based design in healthcare organizations: a systematic literature review. Hum Factors Des 8(15):114–125
18. Bruce M, Box PO (1999) Effective design management for small businesses. Des Stud 297–315
19. Diwan A (2023) Leading by design in the twenty-first century. Des Manage Rev 34(1):36–40

The Conceptual Design Framework for XR Marketing

Baris Atiker

Abstract The concept of XR (Extended Reality) Marketing is growing rapidly and businesses across many different fields are using virtual and augmented reality more than ever before. Despite the ability of XR technology to create immersive and engaging experiences, there is still a lack of understanding about how marketing experiences should be designed using this technology. The aim of this paper is to explore and analyze the conceptual design framework for creating engaging and immersive marketing experiences in XR. The findings of the study show that storytelling, gamification and User-Centered Design (UCD) are the most effective key elements for designing engaging and immersive XR marketing experiences. Storytelling enables the design of a narrative that captures the consumer's attention. Gamification adds a layer of interactivity and competition to the design, making the experience more fun and memorable. User-Centered Design (UCD) ensures that the experience is designed around the needs and preferences of the consumer, making it more effective and personalized. Ultimately, this research aims to provide a guide on how the design framework can be used to create well-functioning XR marketing experiences.

Keywords Design · Framework · XR · Marketing

1 Introduction

XR is a term for a group of technologies that enable the creation and sharing of immersive experiences. It stands for Extended Reality and includes Virtual Reality (VR), Augmented Reality (AR) and Mixed Reality (MR). XR technology enables people to interact with digital content in a way that seems real, making it difficult to tell where the real world ends and the digital world begins. Kunkel and Soechtig describe this as "virtual and real worlds colliding to create new environments where digital and physical objects and their data can coexist and interact with each other"

B. Atiker (✉)
Aydin Adnan Menderes University, Aydin 09010, Turkey
e-mail: barisatiker@gmail.com

N. Martins and D. Raposo (eds.), *Communication Design and Branding*,
Springer Series in Design and Innovation 32,
https://doi.org/10.1007/978-3-031-35385-7_19

[1]. This can include virtual environments, augmented displays and other forms of computer-generated sensory input.

With the rise of the "metaverse" concept, digital marketing, like all other industries, has found a new playground. Frey et al. define the metaverse as "a system of multiple, interconnected, typically user-created virtual worlds (or meta-worlds) accessible through a single user interface" [2]. The metaverse is often regarded as an embodied Internet that can create an enhanced sense of presence and bring online interaction closer to the real world [3]. Providing a platform and tools to create, access and interact with a virtual world, XR technologies are critical for enhancing realism and immersive consumer experiences along the continuum between AR and VR as defined by Milgram and Kishino [4].

This move toward XR means that marketing needs to be more creative and hands-on, since traditional methods may not work as well. Jessen et al. argue that AR enables a unique form of consumer creativity that differs from previous conceptualizations of creativity through its relationship with consumer engagement [5]. As the metaverse continues to grow and change, XR marketing will be an important part of how advertising and consumer engagement is done in the future.

There is a close and important relationship between design and XR marketing because design is an essential part of creating and shaping the user experience in XR environments and the metaverse. Designers are responsible for creating the look and feel of virtual environments, including the architecture, levels, objects and graphics that make up the immersive experience. They also determine how consumers interact with and navigate the virtual world by designing the user interface and interaction mechanisms. Slater et al. believe that good design is more than just a requirement to immerse consumers in XR environments for effective marketing [6]. Design can enhance immersion in virtual environments by creating a sense of presence. According to the authors, immersion can be enhanced by using high-fidelity visual, audio and tactile cues, as well as storytelling techniques.

Consumer habits are fundamentally changing and are increasingly shifting towards digital consumption [7]. As the 4P theory (product, price, promotion, and place) developed by McCarthy [8] and at the core of traditional marketing is revisited for XR marketing, designers must have a deep understanding of consumer experience and technology to create engaging and immersive virtual environments in the metaverse.

Flavián et al. propose a new taxonomy of technology and experience based on technological (embodiment), psychological (presence), and behavioral (interaction) perspectives to add value to the customer purchase journey and better understand the changing XR customer experience landscape [9]. Similarly, this paper presents a conceptual design framework that addresses interactivity, personal expectations and immersion in a flow according to consumers' behavior.

2 The Conceptual Design Framework

The conceptual design framework (Fig. 1) for XR marketing is based on three key factors: Storytelling, Gamification and User-Centered Design. It also frames attributes called Immersive, Interactive and Personal, which provide a fluid transition between the key elements.

Storytelling and gamification have a core purpose in terms of fostering immersion inside their respective mediums. Immersion, as a notion, relates to the user's interaction with the medium, in which the user feels completely immersed in the experience, resulting in a heightened sensation of presence and engagement. While the shape and structure of these two mediums differ, they share fundamental features in terms of how they elicit and maintain immersion.

The capacity to create and maintain a sense of flow lies at the heart of both storytelling and gamification. Flow is the best sensation of being entirely absorbed in a task or activity, where the person is fully engaged and time seems to fly by. Flow in storytelling is done by using an engaging narrative that captures the user's attention and keeps them engaged with the plot, characters, and setting. Similarly, gamification is based on the usage of game mechanisms that challenge the user while also delivering a sense of progression and achievement, resulting in a sense of flow that motivates users to stay engaged with the game.

Another important parallel between storytelling and gamification is their capacity to instill a sense of agency in the user. The user's perception of control and influence over the experience is referred to as agency, and it is a vital aspect in establishing immersion. Storytelling allows customers to relate with the characters, making them feel invested in the story's outcome. Similarly, gamification allows users to make choices and decisions that influence the game's result, giving them a sense of control over their experience.

Both storytelling and gamification rely on feedback to build immersion. In this context, feedback refers to the user's ability to perceive the outcomes of their activities, whether favorable or negative. Feedback in storytelling is obtained by the user's

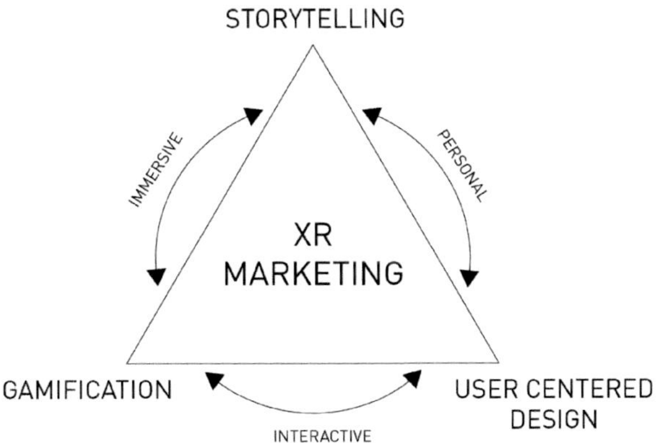

Fig. 1 The conceptual design framework by B. Atiker

emotional reaction to the story's events, where their actions and decisions have a real affect on the characters and the story's outcome. Feedback is achieved in gamification through the use of rewards and punishments, where the user's activities result in good or negative effects.

Gamification and UCD have a focus on interaction design in common. Both approaches prioritize user wants and preferences, rely on feedback to convey information to the user, apply interaction design principles to produce engaging experiences, and are iterative processes involving constant testing and improvement. Knowing these similarities is crucial for designers and developers aiming to create compelling and effective interactive experiences that prioritize the requirements and preferences of the user.

The emphasis on knowing the user's goals and motivations is one of the fundamental similarities between gamification and UCD. Designers in gamification aim to understand the user's motives for engaging with the game and build game mechanics that correspond with those goals. Designers in UCD aim to understand the user's goals and create interfaces that support those goals. These techniques stress user needs and preferences over other factors, ensuring that the experience is relevant and meaningful to the user.

Gamification and UCD share an emphasis on feedback. In gamification, feedback is utilized to provide the user with information on their progress, accomplishments, and failures. Examples of feedback include visual, auditory, and tactile stimuli. UCD uses feedback to aid users in comprehending the outcomes of their activities and the current status of their work. Visual cues, such as progress bars or confirmation messages, as well as audible cues, such as confirmation sounds, can be utilized to convey feedback.

Another thing that gamification and UCD have in common is that they both use interaction design principles to produce engaging experiences. Designers employ game concepts such as points, levels, and badges to create a sense of growth and achievement in gamification. Designers at UCD employ interaction design ideas like as affordances and signifiers to build user-friendly interfaces. Both approaches rely on interaction design concepts to create intuitive and engaging experiences.

User-Centered Design (UCD) and Storytelling are two design methodologies that share a focus on personalization. Both techniques aim to produce experiences that are personalized to the needs and preferences of the user, which can result in increased engagement and pleasure.

Understanding the user's background and perspective is a crucial component of both user-centered design and storytelling. In UCD, designers aim to comprehend the user's objectives, tasks, and preferences in order to create interfaces that meet their requirements. In order to develop stories that resonate with an audience's interests and experiences, storytellers aim to comprehend the audience's preferences and background. Both strategies promote personalization and customisation above one-size-fits-all solutions, thereby ensuring that the user's experience is relevant and meaningful.

Another similarity between user-centered design and storytelling is the usage of personas to portray users. In UCD, designers develop personas to reflect various user types and their demands, ensuring that the interface is suited to the user's requirements. In storytelling, authors develop characters that represent many types of individuals and their experiences, thereby ensuring that the story is interesting and relatable. These approaches leverage personas to generate individualized and tailored user experiences based on their requirements and interests.

The use of user feedback to enhance the experience is a third commonality shared by UCD and storytelling. Both approaches rely on user feedback to identify areas for improvement and adjust the experience repeatedly to better match user requirements.

This framework can be used to gain an understanding of the link that exists between storytelling, gamification, and personalization in XR marketing. The framework focuses on the ways in which these methods collaborate to provide marketing experiences that are both engaging and effective. This framework, at its core, places an emphasis on the significance of comprehending the requirements and preferences of the user and adapting the XR marketing experiences in accordance with those particulars.

2.1 *Immersive Storytelling*

The word "immersive" in XR refers to how involved a user is in a digital experience [10]. An immersive experience aims to make the user feel like they are really there in a virtual or augmented world. This can be done through a combination of visual, auditory and haptic feedback that makes the digital world feel like a real place. The main goal of an immersive experience is to create a sense of realism and allow the consumer to interact with the digital environment in a natural and intuitive way.

Storytelling has long been recognized as a design principle in fields such as user experience design, game design and product design. Using stories can make the user's experience memorable, engaging and meaningful [11, 12]. XR technologies make it possible to create and experience immersive stories that can bring a brand to life. These stories can help convey a brand's values, personality and points of difference to the consumer in a way that traditional media cannot.

Compared to traditional marketing, XR technologies have been shown to make a brand look good while at the same time increasing engagement, recall and desire to buy [13]. Sung states that AR makes it easier for people to share their social experiences, which can lead to user-generated viral marketing and give a business an advantage, especially during seasons when marketing is prominent [14]. Pepsi (Fig. 2) partnered with artist The Weeknd to create an AR portal that allowed consumers to experience the Superbowl Halftime performance in 360-degree video as if they were at the concert, shaping the social sharing experience with a positive brand image.

Contextual relevance is a design factor that focuses on making experiences relevant to the consumer's current situation [15]. This can be done by using information about the consumer's location, time and activities to provide them with information and content for storytelling that is relevant to them in the moment. Designing for contextual relevance is crucial for creating immersive and engaging storytelling

Fig. 2 Pepsi's XR app bridges the gap between product packaging and digital experience

experiences, and this can be achieved with personalization techniques in presence and within the story.

Klein's research on how computer-mediated environments can create successful virtual experiences shows that user control and media richness both help create a sense of telepresence and influence how consumers think [16]. Sylaiou et al. have shown that high levels of "perceived presence" can be linked to feelings of satisfaction and fulfillment that make using simulation systems a pleasant experience [17].

In recent years, numerous social VR platforms such as VRChat, AltspaceVR, Rec Room and Horizon Worlds have emerged, offering users a new format of online social interaction. Barreda-Ángeles et al. emphasize the importance of social connection in XR marketing, stating that consumers are more likely to engage in experiences that allow them to connect with others [18].

Éternelle Notre-Dame (Fig. 3) is a 45-min virtual reality tour inside Notre-Dame, starting from the time it was built to the ongoing restoration after the fire. Accompanied by a builder, people can take an immersive journey together from the Middle Ages to the present day and learn the secrets of the monument as it is painstakingly reconstructed digitally.

In digital marketing, brand authenticity refers to the extent to which a brand's communication and actions and are perceived as reflecting its true character and values by its customers and stakeholders. As a form of immersive media, XR has the potential to create experiences that foster deeper emotional connections between customers and brands. These connections, in turn, can promote authenticity by enabling customers to experience a brand's core values and identity in a visceral way.

Consumers want experiences that are not only interesting and entertaining, but also correspond to their own particular ideals and principles. XR technologies make it

Fig. 3 Sample scene from Éternelle Notre-Dame

possible for brands to develop experiences that fulfill these requirements by supplying immersive and individualized narratives as well as interactions with products and services.

Chen and Lee examine the use of Snapchat for social media marketing, focusing on young consumers [19]. Snapchat attracts young people by offering funny face filters through its AR feature. The results of the study show that Snapchat is a very personal, casual, and fast-paced platform that allows users to experience a brand through information, socialization, and entertainment. As an example, Beats (Fig. 4) launched a sponsored Snapchat Lens over Thanksgiving weekend in 2015.

XR apps can elicit strong emotional responses from consumers [20] as they use visual, auditory, and haptic cues to create unique, engaging and memorable experiences that align with brand identity and connect with consumers on an emotional level. The stories told in XR experiences are directly linked to how people continue to think about and buy from these brands.

The authenticity that brands capture in the stories they create for XR environments also forms the basis of a smooth flow. According to Chen and Li, augmented realism and technological fluidity have a strong impact on consumers' flow experiences and lead to increased cognitive and emotional responses to the brand and/or AR interface environment, as well as purchase intent [21].

Fig. 4 Beats campaign for Snapchat lens application

2.2 *Interactive Gamification*

Interactivity has been defined in the context of technology mediated communication as "the degree to which users can change the form and content of a mediated medium in real time" [15]. XR allows consumers to interact with the virtual environment in a way that is not possible with traditional media. Designers must think about how people will interact with the virtual environment and how this will affect the experience as a whole. This interaction can create brand awareness, increase brand loyalty, and create a deeper emotional connection with the brand. Yim et al. argue that XR marketing will become more interactive and offer new and exciting ways for people to interact with brands and products [22]. This is because XR technologies make it possible to create interactive and unusual experiences that give people a sense of agency and control.

Virtual interfaces are moving away from the traditional 2D plane towards a more immersive 3D space. The 2D window paradigm [23] called WIMP (Windows, Icons, Menus, Pointers), is not easy to fit into a 3D virtual environment because users can now interact with virtual environments in a more immersive way by moving their bodies and making gestures. For example, Ultraleap 3Di (Fig. 5) is a camera that follows the user's hand and lets him or her connect to and control interactive displays without touching them.

A growing number of marketers are using gamification, which refers to the use of game design elements in non-game contexts, such as service experiences, to create value for consumers and improve the buying experience [24, 25]. This can include elements such as points, badges, leaderboards, and rewards in purchase experiences related to products or services. Gamification in XR has received a lot of attention

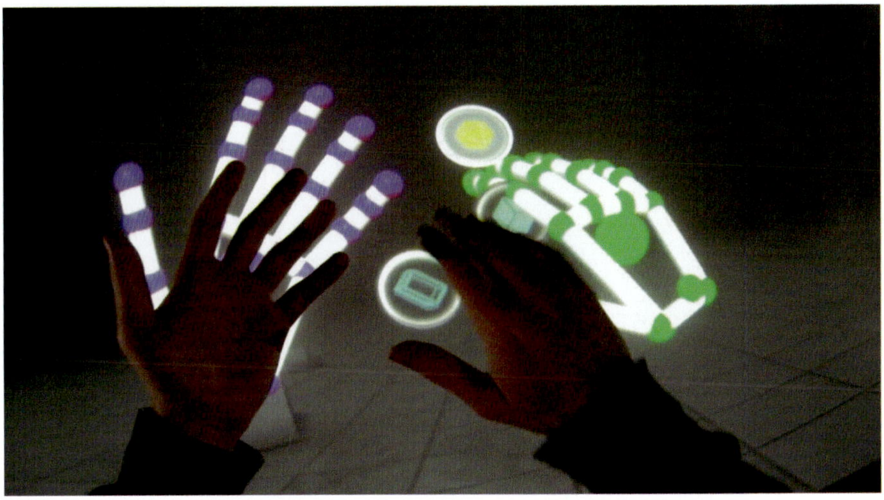

Fig. 5 Ultraleap's no touch interface with advanced hand-tracking

in recent years as a way to get people more engaged and motivated by their digital marketing experience.

One of the first steps of gamification is exploration and discovery. Designers can create interactive experiences by allowing people to explore and learn about XR experiences in their own way. Interfaces that allow people to explore the XR experience and find new content and information make the experience better and more personalized. Gamification is not only about digital technology, as media convergence and ubiquitous computing make it difficult to distinguish between digital and non-digital [26].

"Digital twins" are computer models that simulate, mimic, mirror, or "twin" the life of a physical object, process, or person [27, 28]. Digital twins are therefore one of the best ways to realize the interaction between the physical space and the virtual space [29]. For example, in XR marketing, virtual try-on apps use digital twins to allow people to "try on" products without having to buy them. This can be used for a wide range of products, from clothing and accessories to makeup and furniture. Consumers can look at themselves in a digital mirror using an XR or mobile device, while virtual products are superimposed on their own image. This technology can also be used to customize the product, such as changing its color or size to see how it looks in different variations. Therefore, digital twins are one of the best ways to realize the interaction between physical space and virtual space.

Walmart (Fig. 6) has developed a new strategy called "Be Your Own Model", which allows customers to use their own photos to see how clothes look on them instead of choosing from available models.

In gamification, "social interaction" refers to how people interact with each other through game-like activities and mechanics. This can be done through competition, collaboration, communication, and other types of social exchange in an

Fig. 6 Walmart "be your own model" application

augmented system or game. Deterding et al. state that the relationship between gamification and social interaction is the most important part of creating gamified systems and applications [26]. They point out that social interaction in games can be designed in many ways, including direct player-to-player interactions, information and resource sharing, and the creation of social groups or communities within the game environment.

Fortnite is a next generation platform that uses the sense of presence and digital twins to make digital communication feel more surreal. It is a place where world-renowned music artists appear as digital twins and concert events are organized in the metaverse. At Fortnite's Rift Tour (Fig. 7) event, Ariana Grande took the dream-like stage with her digital twin and was enjoyed by millions.

Research by Potseluyko et al. shows that gamification can be an important part of making XR better in a holistic sense [30]. By adding game-like elements and mechanics to virtual experiences, XR developers can engage people and increase their motivation. By recognizing the unique needs, interests and behaviors of each consumer, companies can design more personalized and positive experiences, which can contribute to consumer brand loyalty and advocacy. However, it is important to keep in mind that gamification needs to be designed carefully and in a balanced way to ensure that it enhances the XR experience rather than detracting from it.

Fig. 7 Ariana Grande's digital twin on rift tour stage by Fortnite

2.3 *Personal and User-Centered Design*

Personalization is important in marketing because it allows businesses to tailor their messages and products to each customer [31]. By making marketing efforts more relevant and engaging, personalization helps customers feel more satisfied and builds stronger relationships with them. Personalization also helps companies understand their consumers on a deeper level and make informed decisions about their products, services and marketing strategies.

User-Centered Design (UCD) is a design method that emphasizes the needs, goals and perspective of the consumer in the design process [32]. This method seeks to understand the consumer's situation, needs and motivations so that solutions can be created to meet their needs and provide them with a good experience.

User-Centered Design is often contrasted with more traditional, technology-centered design approaches that prioritize the design of technology over the needs of the consumer. A user-centered design approach has been shown to make products and services more useful and easier to use, increasing consumer satisfaction and adoption. Therefore, designers and developers who want to create successful and user-friendly XR marketing products and experiences need to incorporate UCD into the design process.

Consumer profiling is the process of collecting and analyzing information about consumers to get a complete and detailed picture of their characteristics, preferences, and behaviors. This process is an important part of modern marketing and customer relationship management because it helps businesses learn more about their customers and provide them with better, more personalized experiences. It can also give companies useful insights into how customers behave and what they like,

Fig. 8 Gucci Town at Roblox

which helps them make smart choices about their products, services, and marketing strategies.

Consumer profiling is becoming a more prominent need, especially for luxury brands. According to Javornik et al., while there are many reasons for luxury brands to use AR, especially those that cater to a more diverse consumer profile, it needs to be used in ways that suit the specific needs of the luxury industry [33]. Otherwise, they risk resembling non-luxury brands and products in XR environments. Luxury brands should pay particular attention to building and protecting product value in XR environments.

Gucci Town (Fig. 8) is marketed on Roblox (an app that allows users to play and make games) as a place where consumers can learn about the luxury brand's history, express themselves and meet like-minded people from around the world.

In the XR world, the actions of the consumer are the main source of personalized data that was previously difficult to access. Data collection has a huge impact on XR marketing because it gives businesses valuable insights into consumer behavior, preferences, and feedback. This information can be used to segment audiences into smaller groups, resonate with them and design experiences that are likely to convert them into customers.

Data can also be used to ensure that marketing messages, experiences and recommendations are relevant and engaging for each individual consumer [34]. Data is a reliable source for monitoring and measuring how well marketing campaigns are working, which helps businesses improve their efforts and return on investment (ROI). User journey mapping, which examines how a customer interacts with a business across different channels, also helps businesses learn more about their customers' journeys and provide them with a better experience.

Mourtzis et al. state that personalization can be used to create unique experiences by allowing the user to adjust and design the products in the XR experience to their liking [35]. This can be achieved using interactive and adaptive methods such as allowing the user to choose their own characters, settings and scenarios.

Avatars are a virtual representation of the physical user in a virtual space. Depending on the type of XR environment, avatars look like anything and are an important part of how social structures are formed in virtual communities [36]. An avatar can be a simple two-dimensional picture of the user or a very detailed three-dimensional model that looks, moves and even shows facial expressions just like the user.

The use of avatars in XR applications is an important part of creating immersive and interactive experiences that allow consumers to connect with each other and interact with digital content in a natural and intuitive way [37]. Often, the user's hand or head movements and inputs are used to control the avatar. This allows users to move, speak and interact with other avatars or digital objects in a virtual environment. Avatars thus enable social experiences such as virtual meetings, events and even games. Avatars also enable anonymity, so people can talk to each other without revealing who they really are.

Ready Player Me (Fig. 9) is a hub that connects users to hundreds of virtual worlds and experiences with a single, fixed digital identity just like a digital twin. It allows users to design their own avatars, enabling creativity and self-expression.

The ability of XR apps to track and monitor what consumers are doing raises privacy concerns [38]. This can make it difficult to enforce accountability and protect against cyberbullying or other harmful behavior. Designers and developers must be careful to protect users' personal information while collecting, storing, and using data responsibly.

Fig. 9 Avatar creation interface from ReadyPlayerMe

XR apps can have a high impact on people's minds, especially when experiences are very immersive and intense. Some people may feel fear, anxiety, or other bad emotions when they are in virtual environments that simulate danger or fear [39]. Moreover, XR applications that rely on social interaction can make people feel isolated and lonely or have other bad feelings if the interactions are not well designed or well managed.

To make sure XR apps are safe, developers and designers should think about the physical and mental impacts of the technology and make sure XR experiences are safe and easy to use for everyone. There should be clear instructions, warnings, and safety information, as well as user testing to find and fix any safety issues. Furthermore, the privacy and security of users should be a top priority and XR applications should be built with the right data protection measures in place.

NXRT's MISHBILD technology is used in the design of the XQ Avatar Porsche (Fig. 10), allowing the user to see their own hands and the interior of the vehicle together while driving in a virtual world. This experience can not only introduce the user to the vehicle, but also provide clear instructions on how to drive safely without harming themselves or others.

Fig. 10 XQ Avatar Porsche experience by NXRT

3 Design Elements for XR Marketing

The most important design component of the XR experience is undoubtedly the interface design. The main goal of a good XR user interface design is to make it easy for people to interact with the virtual world in a joyful way [40]. Design elements like visual, auditory, haptic cues, color, texture, graphics, and movement have a big impact on how people see, interact with, and use these immersive environments.

Keeping a good design flow in the user interface will help the user stay focused on the purpose of the application. The flow and reward should always be guided by level design, and the environment should be limited to a specific space. Clarity and a sense of control are essential interface design elements that can improve the user experience [41].

Clarity is the interface's capacity to effectively communicate its purpose, functionality, and features, whereas control is the user's perception of being in command of the interface. When both clarity and control are present in an interface, the user experience is more likely to be positive, because the user is confident in their ability to use the interface and rapidly comprehends what it offers. This enhances consumer engagement, customer satisfaction, and conversion rates. The interface of Oculus Quest 2 (Fig. 11) for using the platform's applications is tidy yet thorough.

As with traditional marketing, it's important to find out what users want and how they feel about different kinds of messages and communications [42]. Studies have shown that color, lighting, and texture, as well as other visual design elements, have a big effect on how people feel and act in XR environments.

Color can be used to set a mood or atmosphere, draw attention to certain things, and evoke a sense of excitement or calm. It can also give an impression of depth

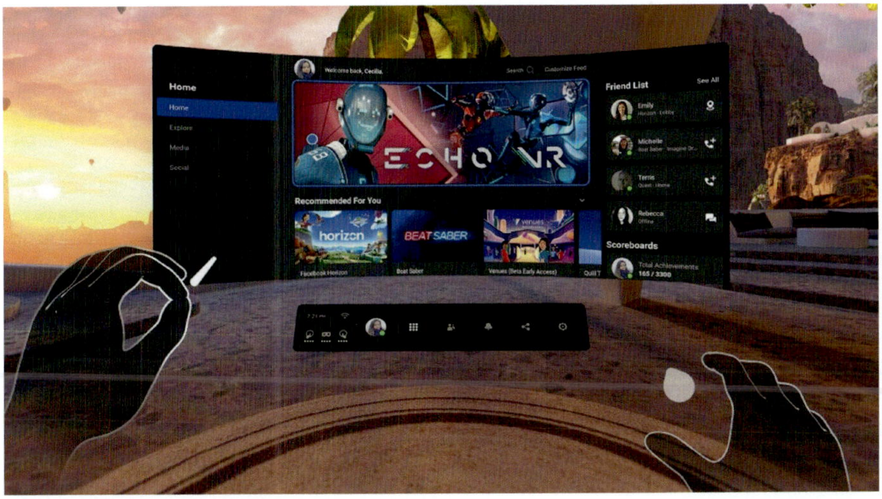

Fig. 11 Oculus Quest 2 interface

and perspective, helping people understand the three-dimensional environment they are in. Additionally, color can be employed in XR marketing to give an impression of depth and perspective, helping people comprehend the three-dimensional environment they are in.

Lighting can also set the atmosphere and mood for XR experiences. For example, darker lighting is often associated with danger or suspense, while brighter lighting makes people feel safe and at ease.

Lupton states that design is an important part of creating a cohesive and recognizable visual identity [43]. This can be done by using consistent design elements and colors that match the visual identity of the brand. Color can also be used to give a brand a consistent look that makes it easy for people to recognize and connect with a certain company or product.

Sound design elements have a big effect on the XR experience as well as visual cues. Gospodarek et al. state that sound can be used to provide important information, set the mood and atmosphere, and make the user feel more immersed in the virtual environment as a whole [44]. Spatial sounds can make virtual environments feel more realistic, while adding background music or sound effects can make the experience more interesting and dynamic. Sound design can also be used to draw attention to specific parts of the XR environment, such as a product being sold, making the experience more memorable and powerful for the consumer.

In order to help Japanese people get back in touch with their local sounds and culture in a new and modern way, Spotify Japan has created the "Sound Tour" (Fig. 12), a series of events that use ambient Spotify codes to trigger special sound effects and music through the XR experience.

It is important to focus on the senses to emphasize and develop the sense of reality and being in XR environments. Design for haptic feedback is becoming an increasingly important part of creating XR experiences, as it makes virtual environments

Fig. 12 Sound tour experience by Spotify Japan

feel more realistic and embedded [45]. Haptic feedback can also be used to simulate vibrations, forces, tissues, and temperatures, among other physical sensations.

Sensory marketing aims to stimulate consumers' senses and influence their perceptions and behavior. Haptic feedback can be used to create subliminal hints that affect how people think about the product in general [46]. Flavian et al. argues that a user's immersion experience is partly based on the interface devices they use. Optical feedback can be used to simulate the user's feeling of walking on clay, sand, or ice, or holding and moving virtual objects. Using such haptic feedback, designers can create a more realistic and immersive experience that allows users to better understand and interact with their virtual environments. Thanks to a patented microfluidic system, HaptX (Fig. 13) gloves use a technology that can provide real contact headsets.

As a fundamental design element, typography can influence how consumers perceive, read and understand text in these complex XR environments. While hardware and software for XR are evolving rapidly, it's a fact that engineers and developers are mostly ignoring typography. The need for more processing power to make the text look correct has long been an excuse. This means that XR designers avoid using text and display it in a way that uses less CPU power, but in XR experiences, as well as visual factors, mood and atmosphere can also be created using typography.

Research has shown that typography in XR environments can affect reading, readability, and overall aesthetic appeal [47]. Clear and legible fonts may make it easier for people to read and understand text in virtual environments, while decorative or fancy fonts can contribute to the visual design and aesthetic appeal of the virtual environment in general.

Fig. 13 Haptx gloves with haptic feedback

As another design element, texture can also influence people's feelings and behavior while influencing the presence and realism. Textures are essential for realistic display of objects and environments, as they often add surface details that are too difficult to directly model [48]. Researchers find that 3D objects and the stylistic textures of the virtual object make people feel safe and comfortable, while sharp- or rough-edged textures can make them feel safe or uncomfortable.

Textures help people understand the physical properties of virtual objects and feel their depth and three dimensions better. Different textures can help direct people to specific objects or places and can create a sense of order and organization by using the same texture repeatedly.

Motion graphics are used to create visual content that changes over time and attracts people's attention. Motion graphics are an important part of the design of XR environments because 3D virtual interactions feel more realistic and make it easier to get lost in. Motion graphics can help users simplify tasks and understand complex information by paying attention to important details or directing them to specific locations [47]. By adding graphics from the real world, users can interact more naturally and get a better feel for the virtual world.

Motion tracking is also an important part of XR applications up to the least moving graphics, as it allows the system to detect and track user movements in real time. Motion tracking is required to place virtual objects above the real world or change their positions and directions. While it is used to combine the real world and virtual objects, this makes it easier for consumers to interact with the virtual objects and environment in a natural and intuitive way. For example, Move.ai (Fig. 14) is an application allowing users to move avatars by extracting 3D motion data from a video.

Fig. 14 Move.ai application is extracting 3D motion data from a video

It is important to remember that design elements in XR environments need to be carefully planned and considered to enhance the user experience. Using too many motion graphics animations that are inaccurate or poorly made for the experience can lead to issues such as anxiety, disorientation, and a feeling that something is not real. Therefore, design elements should be carefully placed in XR environments and should be done to enhance and support the user's experience rather than take away from it.

4 Design Tools for XR

XR applications gain functionality through an effective and efficient combination of hardware, software, and other components. With the right tools, designers and developers can work together to create XR experiences that are engaging, immersive and deliver real value to consumers.

XR applications often require different programs than traditional design tools. "3D modeling" is the process of creating virtual and visually interactive three-dimensional models on a computer [49]. People like 3D applications more than traditional 2D applications because they make the experience more dynamic and interactive. Wu et al. examined how animated and 3D models in virtual reality advertisements influence consumers and found that interacting with 3D models can make viewers more entertained and more likely to have positive attitudes and want to do things like remember products, buy them, and watch more ads [50].

Many file formats such as OBJ, DAE, FBX and GLB have been developed to use and share 3D models in XR applications. In this way, it is possible to use the digital twin of a product across different platforms for marketing purposes. 3D objects and environments can also be animated, creating dynamic and interactive experiences. This is particularly useful in industries such as gaming, education, and training, where consumers can interact with virtual objects and environments to learn new skills or complete tasks.

Another important aspect of XR design and development is prototyping, and design tools play an important role in this process. With these tools, designers can quickly and easily create prototypes of their ideas. This is crucial for testing and refining ideas quickly and making the necessary real-time changes to the design when feedback comes in.

VR prototyping tools such as Vuforia, ARKit and A-Frame have many features and functionalities such as 3D modeling and animation, physics simulation, real-time rendering and user interaction. They enable designers to create interactive and immersive virtual reality experiences that can be used in games, education, training, product design and digital marketing.

Game engines such as Unreal Engine and Unity are used in XR applications because they provide a powerful and flexible platform for creating interactive 3D content. They have advanced tools for creating 3D graphics, animation, physical

Fig. 15 The Matrix Awakens experience by Unreal Engine

simulations and sound effects, making them perfect for XR applications. Furthermore, their game engines are tuned for real-time performance, which is important for XR applications that need smooth, responsive and high-quality graphics. This allows developers to design immersive and interactive XR experiences without compromising performance. For example, The Matrix Awakens (Fig. 15) experience developed by Unreal Engine impressed users with its ultrarealistic imagery.

The use of machine learning and DL in XR is expected to become even more important in the future as these technologies continue to develop and improve. As XR experiences become more complex and interactive, they will require more sophisticated algorithms that can process and understand large amounts of data.

Recently, XR applications have been paired with blockchain infrastructures. A blockchain is a distributed database or ledger shared between the nodes of a computer network. It stores information in a digital format and is best known for its role in systems that use digital currencies such as Bitcoin. It ensures that a data record is accurate and secure and builds trust without the need for a trusted third party.

Blockchain technology offers a number of advantages when used in XR applications. It can make XR experiences more secure, more open, and less centralized. It can also stop counterfeiting and fraud in virtual marketplaces where users can exchange ownership of assets in the virtual world and conduct real business in a virtual environment [35]. Like NFTs, blockchain technology can also be used to verify the authenticity and authenticity of content [42]. This completely changes the way content is created, commoditized, exchanged, and stored for both content creators and consumers [51]. Nike (Fig. 16) collaborated with artists to create a collection of NFT sneakers that didn't really exist, and they fetched hundreds of thousands of dollars.

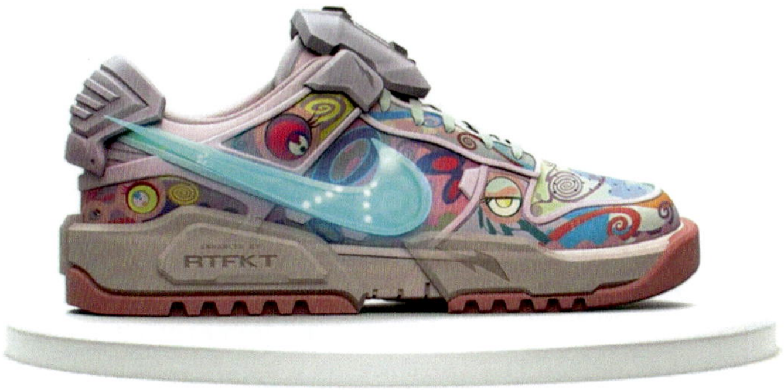

Fig. 16 Nike 'cryptokicks' sneakers NFT sold for $130 K

As with blockchain, the use of Artificial Intelligence as a design tool in XR environments has recently come to the fore [52]. AI is used to create personalized levels and interactions, especially in gamification experiences. This means that XR interactions can be tailored to consumers' needs and preferences. Machine learning (ML) and deep learning (DL) are AI tools used to make XR applications more useful [53]. These algorithms can be used to recognize and track objects, track hands and bodies, recognize and process natural language, understand what is happening in a scene and make predictions. It also offers opportunities to respond to user actions in real time and improve the user experience by understanding what is happening in the scene.

AI tools can collect and analyze data and predict future behavior, allowing marketers to target ads based on what the audience likes and how they are likely to buy. Marketers can use this information to target ads based on what the audience likes and how they are likely to buy [42]. According to Blasco-Arcas et al., consumer data is an important way for companies to learn how to navigate increasingly competitive markets [34].

Finally, collaboration is one of the most important factors in designing and developing XR experiences [28], and design tools play an important role in facilitating this process. Design tools allow designers, developers, and companies to work together on a common goal and make sure that everyone is on the same page about the vision and goals of the project. Collaborative practices ensure that the development process moves smoothly and quickly, and that the final product is of high quality and meets consumer needs. Using design tools that facilitate collaboration, teams can work together to create XR experiences that are new, interesting and deliver real value to consumers.

5 Conclusion

XR technologies are revolutionizing the world of marketing by enabling brands to create realistic, multi-sensory experiences that make people feel more connected to them. It also enables marketers to gather useful insights about how people behave and what they like, enabling them to gain new insights about their target market and tailor their marketing efforts accordingly.

Storytelling is an important part of designing immersive XR experiences. It can transport users into a world that is not their own, grab their attention, make them feel something, and give them an experience they will never forget. In this regard, designers should always work to create a coherent and immersive environment that supports the narrative. This means that everything from visual and audio design to haptics must work together to create a seamless experience. The goal of design is to create an experience that feels natural and intuitive, so the design must be clear so that the consumer can focus on the story, not the technology.

Gamification is widely used in XR experiences to increase user engagement, motivation, and interaction. Designers play a key role in making XR experiences more like games because they must think about consumers, their goals and what makes them tick, as well as the brand story and the XR technology being used. Designers should create environments that encourage interaction and exploration while also guiding the user towards specific goals or learning outcomes. Feedback loops help users maintain interest and motivation by giving them a sense of progress, achievement, and mastery. The relationship between gamification and XR design is complex because designers must find a balance between the interactivity of gamification and the brand value creation goals of the XR experience.

User-centered design is a design approach that places the user at the center of the design process. Through XR marketing, consumers can have immersive, engaging, and interactive experiences. User-centric design is particularly important in marketing, as XR experiences are often complex and require a high level of personalization. The design of XR marketing experiences should be easy to understand and use and aligned with consumers' needs and expectations.

Ultimately, the success of next-generation XR marketing campaigns depends on the effective use of XR technology, immersive storytelling, interactive gamification and user-centered design, which in turn increases brand awareness, consumer engagement and sales.

References

1. Kunkel N, Soechtig S (2017) Mixed reality: experiences get more intuitive, immersive and empowering. Deloitte University Press. https://www2.deloitte.com/content/dam/Deloitte/cn/Documents/technology-media-telecommunications/deloitte-cn-tmt-mixed-reality-2017-en-171109.pdf
2. Frey D, Royan J, Piegay R, Kermarrec A, Anceaume E, Le Fessant F (2008) Solipsis: a decentralized architecture for virtual environments. In: 1st international workshop on massively multiuser virtual environments. Reno, NV, United States
3. Clegg N (2022) Making the metaverse: what it is, how it will be built, and why it matters. https://nickclegg.medium.com/making-the-metaverse-what-it-is-how-it-will-be-built-and-why-it-matters-3710f7570b04
4. Milgram P, Kishino F (1994) A taxonomy of mixed reality visual displays. IEICE Trans Inf Syst 77(12):1321–1329
5. Jessen A, Hilken T, Chylinski M, Mahr D, Heller J, Keeling DI, de Ruyter K (2020) The playground effect: how augmented reality drives creative customer engagement. J Bus Res 116:85–98
6. Slater M, Lotto RB, Arnold MM, Sanchez-Vives MV (2009) How we experience immersive virtual environments: the concept of presence and its measurement. Anuario de Psicologia, 40(2)
7. Shah D, Murthi BPS (2021) Marketing in a data-driven digital world: implications for the role and scope of marketing. J Bus Res 125:772–779
8. McCarthy EJ (1960) Basic marketing: a managerial approach. Irwin
9. Flavián C, Ibáñez-Sánchez S, Orús C (2019) The impact of virtual, augmented and mixed reality technologies on the customer experience. J Bus Res 100:547–560
10. Slater M, Sanchez-Vives MV (2016) Enhancing our lives with immersive virtual reality. Front Robot AI 3:73
11. Norman DA (1998) The design of everyday things. Basic books
12. Robin S (2017) Don't make me think, revisited: a common sense approach to web usability. New Riders
13. Van Berlo ZMC, Van Reijmersdal EA, Smit EG, Van der Laan LN (2021) Brands in virtual reality games: affective processes within computer-mediated consumer experiences. J Bus Res 122:458–465
14. Sung C (2021) The effects of augmented reality mobile app advertising: viral marketing via shared social experience. J Bus Res 122:75–87
15. Steuer J (1992) Defining virtual reality: dimensions determining telepresence. J Commun 42(4):73
16. Klein LR (2003) Creating virtual product experiences: the role of telepresence. J Interact Mark 17(1):41–55
17. Sylaiou S, Mania K, Karoulis A, White M (2010) Exploring the relationship between presence and enjoyment in a virtual museum. Int J Hum Comput Stud 68(5):243–253
18. Barreda-Ángeles M, Hartmann T (2022) Psychological benefits of using social virtual reality platforms during the COVID-19 pandemic: the role of social and spatial presence. Comput Hum Behav 127:107047
19. Chen H, Lee YJ (2018) Is Snapchat a good place to advertise? How media characteristics influence college-aged young consumers' receptivity of Snapchat advertising. Int J Mobile Commun 16(6):697–714
20. Ding N, Zhou W, Fung AYH (2018) Emotional effect of cinematic VR compared with traditional 2D film. Telematics Inform 35(6):1572–1579
21. Chen Y, Li CA (2022) Consumer behavior in an augmented reality environment: exploring the effects of flow via augmented realism and technology fluidity. Telematics Inform 71:101597
22. Yim MY-C, Chu S-C, Sauer PL (2017) Is augmented reality technology an effective tool for e-commerce? An interactivity and vividness perspective. J Interact Mark 39:89–103

23. Smith DC (1975) Pygmalion: a creative programming environment (PhD thesis). Stanford University
24. Huotari K, Hamari J (2017) A definition for gamification: anchoring gamification in the service marketing literature. Electron Mark 27(1):21–31
25. Tanouri A, Mulcahy R, Russell-Bennett R (2019) Transformative gamification services for social behavior brand equity: a hierarchical model. J Serv Theory Pract 29(2):122–141
26. Deterding S, Dixon D, Khaled R, Nacke L (2011) From game design elements to gamefulness: defining "gamification. Paper presented at the proceedings of the 15th international academic MindTrek conference: envisioning future media environments. Tampere, Finland
27. Barricelli BR, Casiraghi E, Fogli D (2019) A survey on digital twin: definitions, characteristics, applications, and design implications. IEEE Access 7:167653–167671
28. Stacchio L, Angeli A, Marfia G (2022) Empowering digital twins with eXtended reality collaborations. Virtual Reality Intell Hardware 4(6):487–505
29. Ke S, Xiang F, Zhang Z, Zuo Y (2019) An enhanced interaction framework based on VR, AR and MR in digital twin. Procedia CIRP 83:753–758
30. Potseluyko L, Pour Rahimian F, Dawood N, Elghaish F, Hajirasouli A (2022) Game-like interactive environment using BIM-based virtual reality for the timber frame self-build housing sector. Autom Construct 142
31. Tang H, Liao SS, Sun SX (2013) A prediction framework based on contextual data to support mobile personalized marketing. Decis Support Syst 56:234–246
32. Chi Y-L (2009) A consumer-centric design approach to develop comprehensive knowledge-based systems for keyword discovery. Expert Syst Appl 36(2):2481–2493
33. Javornik A, Duffy K, Rokka J, Scholz J, Nobbs K, Motala A, Goldenberg A (2021) Strategic approaches to augmented reality deployment by luxury brands. J Bus Res 136:284–292
34. Blasco-Arcas L, Lee H-HM, Kastanakis MN, Alcañiz M, Reyes-Menendez A (2022) The role of consumer data in marketing: a research agenda. J Bus Res 146:436–452
35. Mourtzis D, Angelopoulos J, Panopoulos N (2022) Personalized PSS design optimization based on digital twin and extended reality. Procedia CIRP 109:389–394
36. Book B (2004) These bodies are free, so get one now!: advertising and branding in social virtual worlds
37. Mennecke BE, Peters A (2013) From avatars to mavatars: The role of marketing avatars and embodied representations in consumer profiling. Bus Horiz 56(3):387–397
38. Lammerding L, Hilken T, Mahr D, Heller J (2021) Too real for comfort: measuring consumers' augmented reality information privacy concerns. In: tom Dieck MC, Jung TH, Loureiro SMC (eds) Augmented reality and virtual reality. Progress in IS. Springer, Cham
39. Awada M, Zhu R, Becerik-Gerber B, Lucas G, Southers E (2021) An integrated emotional and physiological assessment for VR-based active shooter incident experiments. Adv Eng Inform 47
40. Sun C, Hu W, Xu D (2019) Navigation modes, operation methods, observation scales and background options in UI design for high learning performance in VR-based architectural applications. J Comput Des Eng 6(2):189–196
41. Low Tze Hui S, See SL(2015) Enhancing user experience through customisation of UI design. In: Ahram T, Karwowski W, Schmorrow D (eds) 6th international conference on applied human factors and ergonomics (AHFE 2015) and the affiliated conferences. AHFE 2015
42. Dwivedi YK, Ismagilova E, Hughes DL, Carlson J, Filieri R, Jacobson J, Jain V, Karjaluoto H, Kefi H, Krishen AS, Kumar V, Rahman MM, Raman R, Rauschnabel PA, Rowley J, Salo J, Tran GA, Wang Y (2021) Setting the future of digital and social media marketing research: perspectives and research propositions. Int J Inf Manage 59
43. Lupton E (2011) Graphic design thinking: beyond brainstorming (Design Briefs). Princeton Architectural Press
44. Gospodarek M, Genovese A, Dembeck D, Brenner C, Roginska A, Perlin K (2019) Sound design and reproduction techniques for co-located narrative VR experiences. In: AES 147th convention. New York, NY, pp 1–7

45. Schölkopf L, Lorenz M, Stamer M, Albrecht L, Klimant P, Hammer N, Tümler J (2021) Haptic feedback is more important than VR experience for the user experience assessment of in-car human machine interfaces. Procedia CIRP 100:601–606
46. Krishna A (2012) An integrative review of sensory marketing: engaging the senses to affect perception, judgment, and behavior. J Consum Psychol 22(3):332–351
47. Atiker B (2021) Exploring the future of spatial typography in immersive design applications. In: Game + design education
48. Dischler JM, Ghazanfarpour D (2001) Survey of 3D texturing. Comput Graph 25(1):135–151
49. Remondino F, Sabry E (2006) Image-based 3D modeling: a review. Photogram Rec 21(115):269–291
50. Wu D-Y, Lin J-HT, Bowman ND (2022) Watching VR advertising together: how 3D animated agents influence audience responses and enjoyment to VR advertising. Comput Hum Behav 133:107255
51. Malhotra A, O'Neill H, Stowell P (2021) Thinking strategically about blockchain adoption risks and risk mitigation. Bus Horiz 65(2):159–171
52. Hackl C, Wolfe SG (2017) Marketing new realities: an introduction to virtual reality and augmented reality marketing, branding, and communications
53. Das A, Day TW, Kulkarni V, Buchanan A, Cottrell K, John NW, Chatterjee K (2022) Towards intelligent extended reality in stroke rehabilitation: application of machine learning and artificial intelligence in rehabilitation. In: Augmenting neurological disorder prediction and rehabilitation using artificial intelligence, pp 309–329

Impact of Social Media on Large Scale Enterprises

Harshit Mittal, Gurpreet Singh, and Pradeepta Kumar Sarangi

Abstract Social media has revolutionised business-customer interactions and brand-building for both traditional large-scale companies and the latest online companies. Established enterprises now have unprecedented opportunities to connect with customers, gather feedback, and cultivate brand loyalty through platforms like Facebook, Twitter, and LinkedIn. At the same time, emerging online companies can leverage social media to establish their brand presence, engage with their target audience, and compete in the digital marketplace. Social media has become an essential tool for businesses of all types and sizes, revolutionising how they interact with customers and build their brands in the modern business landscape. This paper aims to explore the impact of social media on large-scale enterprises, taking into account facts and figures from some of the biggest companies in the world. This research examines how social media affects the operational efficacy of big corporations. Specifically, the study explores how social media use affects various dimensions of business performance, such as revenue growth, customer satisfaction, brand reputation and employee engagement. With the increasing popularity of social media platforms, large-scale enterprises have been leveraging these platforms to enhance their business performance. However, the existing literature on social media's impact on businesses has mostly focused on small and medium-sized enterprises, with little attention given to large-scale enterprises. Exploring New Ways for Large Scale Business Enterprises, including Business Giants and Tech Giants, to Connect with Diverse Customer Pools and what are the benefits and limitations of these new ways of connecting industry with customer?

H. Mittal · G. Singh (✉) · P. K. Sarangi
Chitkara University Institute of Engineering and Technology, Chitkara University, Punjab, India
e-mail: gurpreet.1309@chitkara.edu.in

H. Mittal
e-mail: harshit0841.cse19@chitkara.edu.in

P. K. Sarangi
e-mail: Pradeepta.sarangi@chitkara.edu.in

N. Martins and D. Raposo (eds.), *Communication Design and Branding*,
Springer Series in Design and Innovation 32,
https://doi.org/10.1007/978-3-031-35385-7_20

Keywords Business performance · Large scale enterprises · e-business · Social media · Business marketing · Business innovation · Artificial Intelligence · Economic growth · Productivity · Technological progress · Communication technologies

1 Introduction

The interaction between large-scale enterprises and their customers and brand-building strategies have undergone a significant transformation with the advent of social media. The impact of social media on large-scale enterprises can be seen through the success of companies such as Amazon, Microsoft, and Facebook. In 2020, Amazon reported a 37% increase in revenue, totalling $386 billion, with a significant portion of this revenue attributed to its social media marketing strategy. By leveraging social media platforms like Twitter, Facebook, and Instagram, Amazon has successfully engaged with its customers, marketed its products, and generated sales. Amazon has established brand awareness and fostered customer loyalty through its well-executed social media marketing campaigns, contributing to its sustained success. Microsoft is another example of a large-scale enterprise that has successfully leveraged social media to reach its target audience. In 2020, Microsoft reported a revenue of $110.4 billion, a significant portion of this revenue attributed to its social media marketing strategy. Microsoft employs social media platforms, including LinkedIn, Twitter, and Facebook, to interact with its clientele, promote its products, and drive sales. Microsoft has created brand awareness and has built customer loyalty through its social media marketing campaigns, leading to its continued success. Sehl, k., Social Media for Big Companies [1] Facebook is yet another example of a large-scale enterprise impacted by social media. In 2020, Facebook reported revenue of $85.9 billion, a significant portion of this revenue attributed to its social media marketing strategy. Facebook uses its platform, Instagram and WhatsApp, to engage with its customers, promote its products, and drive sales. Through its social media marketing campaigns, Facebook has created brand awareness and built customer loyalty, leading to its continued success. De Vries, L., Impact of Social Media on Consumers and Firms [2] The capacity of social media to generate brand awareness is among the major effects it has on big corporations. With billions of active social media users worldwide, businesses can promote their products and services across various social media channels, making it easier to target specific demographics. Social media also provides large-scale enterprises with a platform to engage with their customers in real time, addressing their concerns, responding to feedback, and resolving issues quickly. This enhances the overall customer experience, increasing customer loyalty and repeat business.

Moreover, social media provides large-scale enterprises with valuable insights into their customers' behaviour and preferences. Businesses can extract valuable insights into customers' preferences, pain points, and motivations by keeping track of social media conversations and engagement. These insights can be leveraged to inform the development of marketing and product strategies, allowing businesses to create products and services that better meet the needs and wants of their customers. As social media continues to evolve, its impact on large-scale enterprises will continue to grow, leading to increased success and profitability for businesses that embrace it. Edosomwan, The History of Social Media and its Impact on Business [3]. The study by Edosomwan provides insights into the history of social media and its impact on business. It highlights how social media has transformed the way businesses operate, engage with customers, and market their products and services. The study emphasizes the significance of social media for large-scale enterprises and how it has become an integral part of their marketing and advertising strategies. The findings of this study contribute to the understanding of the evolution of social media and its impact on businesses, particularly large-scale enterprises. It emphasizes the need for businesses to recognize the importance of social media in today's digital landscape and adapt their strategies accordingly. The success of companies like Amazon, Microsoft, and Facebook in utilizing social media for their business operations serves as examples of how social media can be leveraged for increased success and profitability.

To sum up, the impact of social media on large-scale enterprises has been significant, resulting in significant changes in how businesses operate and engage with their customers. By leveraging social media, businesses can create brand awareness, engage with their customers in real-time, and gain valuable insights into their behaviour and preferences. Large-scale enterprises such as Amazon, Microsoft, and Facebook have recognised social media's importance and successfully integrated it into their marketing and advertising strategies. As social media continues to evolve, its impact on large-scale enterprises will continue to grow, leading to increased success and profitability for businesses that embrace it (Tables 1, 2 and 3).

2 An Overview of Social Media: A Brief Discussion

Social media is a platform where users create and share content, as defined by Tim Berners-Lee. It is not merely a browsing medium but a collaboration of people sharing ideas and opinions. On social networking platforms like Twitter and Facebook, users can share short messages, images, videos, and other content that their friends and followers can respond to by commenting, sharing, or liking. Social media allows businesses to create a potential market, build credibility, and establish their brand, image, and reputation.

The massive user base of social networking sites makes them attractive to marketers and organisations. Facebook, for instance, has approximately 2.91 billion users worldwide. The broad reach of social media and its relatively low cost offers businesses a distinct chance to connect with a sizable pool of potential customers, making it a crucial element in making business decisions.

Social media has become essential to our daily routines, with multitudes of individuals employing various platforms to interact and establish connections with others. The most widely-used social media networks globally include Facebook,

Table 1 Evolution of digital marketing

Years	Mode of marketing	Impact	Limitation
1990–1993	Prodigy, CompuServe, SMS messaging	Expanded reach, enhanced targeting, increased efficiency	Limited user base, technical limitations, cost considerations
1994–1997	First online display ad, yahoo search engine, email marketing	Enhanced brand visibility, increased website traffic, direct communication channel, cost-effective	Competition, spam concerns, technical limitations, privacy and consent issues
1998–2001	Mobile payments, SEO,SEM and google, google mobile advertising	Mobile convenience, increased website traffic and conversions, measurable results	Changing algorithms, mobile payment security, ad blocking and ad fatigue, dependence on third-party platforms
2002–2005	LinkedIn, WordPress, facebook, google analytics, SEO, YouTube	Professional networking and business connections, content creation and website development, social media marketing and audience engagement, video marketing and visual content promotion	Platform changes and algorithm updates, platform dependence, adherence to platform policies, user behavior and engagement
2006–2009	Twitter, iPhone, Appstore, Tumblr, Facebook Ads	Monetization opportunities, data-driven advertising and targeting, enhanced user experience and convenience, mobile marketing opportunities, real-time communication and customer engagement, increased reach and brand exposure	Platform dependence, privacy and data protection concerns, ad fatigue and ad blocking, platform and algorithm changes
2010–2013	iPad, instagram, internet surpasses newspaper, google +, pinterest, snapchat, visual content, marketing	Enhanced mobile experience, visual storytelling and user engagement, social media marketing and brand promotion, shift in advertising spending, increased user-generated content, visual content marketing opportunities	Platform dependence and algorithm changes, limited demographic reach, shorter content lifespan, content quality and authenticity
2014–2018	Mobile surpasses desktop users, omni channel, wearables	Mobile-first marketing, increased accessibility and connectivity, wearable technology, enhanced targeting and personalization	Device fragmentation, limited screen real estate, user experience challenges

(continued)

Table 1 (continued)

Years	Mode of marketing	Impact	Limitation
2019–2023	Internet of Things, Mobile overtakes online and social interactions, online ad spend equivalent to TV spend	IoT revolution, mobile overtakes online and social interactions, shift in ad spend, enhanced data-driven marketing, new marketing channels and opportunities	Shifting consumer behavior, digital divide, rapid technological advancements

Table 2 Impact of branding/marketing trend on large scale business based organisations

Company name	Category	Previous branding/ marketing trend	Current branding/ marketing trend
Bajaj automobile	Business (company offers products in entry-level, commuter, sports, and super-sports lines)	TV advertising, print advertising, outdoor advertising	Social media (twitter, facebook, YouTube etc.), online advertising, mobile apps
Procter and gamble (P&G)	Business (company manufactures and sells consumer packaged products, with five business segments: fabric care, home care, baby, feminine and family care, beauty grooming, and health care.)	TV advertising, print advertising, radio advertising, trade shows and exhibitions	Content marketing, social media, influencer marketing
IBM	Business (produces and sells computer hardware, software, and offers cloud computing and data analytics services.)	Telemarketing, events and trade shows, print advertising	Social media marketing, email marketing, influencer marketing
American express	Business (prominent issuer of credit cards for personal, small business, and corporate use. They also offer a range of travel-related services, including traveller's checks, credit cards, travel planning, tour packages, and hotel/car rental reservations)	Print Advertisements, Telemarketing, and TV/radio commercials	Digital advertising, social media marketing, email marketing, and content marketing
Ford motor company	Business (the automotive segment includes revenues and costs related to development, manufacture, distribution, service, and electrification vehicle programs.)	TV commercials, print ads, billboards, and dealership promotions	Social media marketing, influencer partnerships

Table 3 Impact of branding/marketing trend on large scale digital based organisations

Company name	Category	Previous branding/ marketing trend	Current branding/marketing trend
Facebook	Social media	Display advertising, self-serve ad platform, page promotion	Mobile advertising, personalized advertising, video advertising, instagram advertising, messenger advertising
Twitter	Social media	Promoted tweets, promoted trends, promoted accounts	Video advertising, sponsored moments, audience targeting, twitter ads manager, brand partnerships and influencer marketing
Amazon	E-commerce	Product ads, display ads, search ads	Influencer marketing, amazon posts, amazon live, sponsored products, sponsored brands
Zomato	Food industry	Search ads, display ads, email marketing	Social media marketing, influencer marketing, content marketing, app notifications, partnerships and tie-ups

YouTube, WhatsApp, Instagram, and Facebook Messenger. Nonetheless, it is crucial to remember that only some social media platforms are created for brand engagement, as certain platforms cater solely to instant messaging, while others have more limited use in specific regions of the world, such as China.

The study by Abuhashesh titled Integration of Social Media in Businesses [4] highlights the widespread use of social media in daily routines and the popularity of various platforms such as Facebook, YouTube, WhatsApp, Instagram, and Facebook Messenger. The study emphasizes that not all social media platforms are designed for brand engagement, as some platforms are primarily used for instant messaging, and others may have limited use in specific regions of the world.

This information is valuable for businesses seeking to integrate social media into their marketing strategies, as it highlights the need to carefully select the appropriate platforms for their target audience and marketing objectives. Understanding the different functionalities and limitations of various social media platforms can help businesses make informed decisions and effectively engage with their audience. It also underscores the dynamic nature of social media, with platforms evolving and changing over time, requiring businesses to stay updated with the latest trends and developments (Figs. 1 and 2).

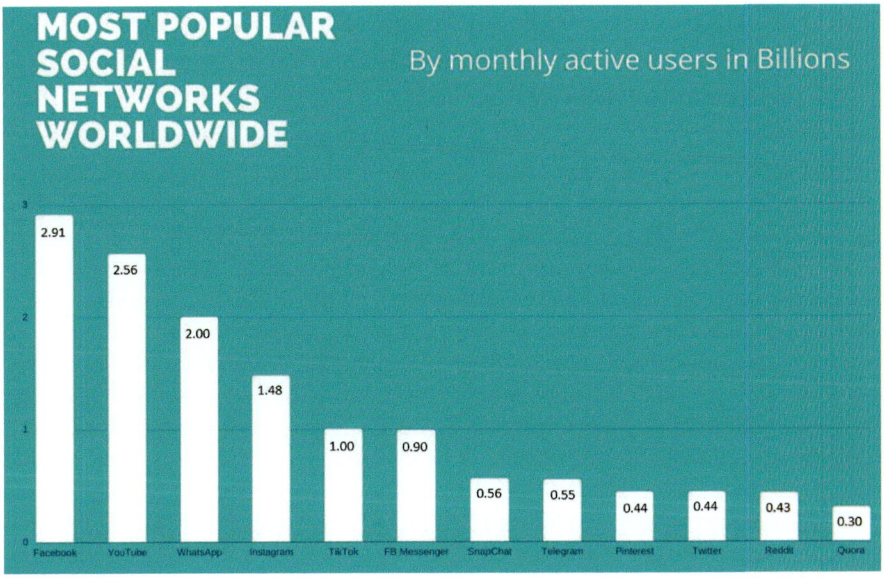

Fig. 1 Most popular social networks worldwide

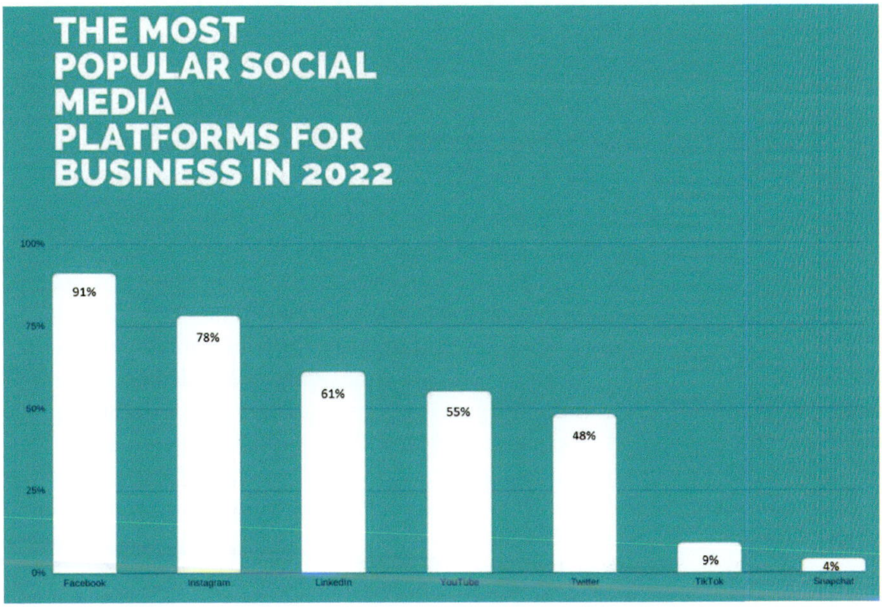

Fig. 2 Most popular social media platforms for business in 2022

3 Exploring the Literature on Social Media Marketing: Categorizing Studies and Investigating the Impact on Large Scale Enterprises

The extensive body of literature on social media marketing (SMM) was synthesized by gaining access to relevant publications through the Scopus search engine. Two keywords, "social media marketing" and "social media advertising," were used to extract publications. The keyword search yielded a total of seventy-one studies, which were categorized into eleven different areas of exploration in SMM. These categories included healthcare and wellbeing, analytics and sentiment analysis, return on investments, advertising, education, small and medium enterprises (SMEs), brand fans and followers, banking, general marketing, music industry, mobile marketing, and RFID. Additionally, the impact of SMM on large scale enterprises will also be discussed individually in the context of these twelve subsections. One notable study in the field of social media marketing is the work by Bajpai, V. titled Social Media Marketing: Strategies and Its Impact [5]. This study provides insights into the strategies and impact of social media marketing. It adds to the existing literature on SMM and offers valuable insights for practitioners and researchers interested in this field. The findings of this study contribute to the understanding of the various strategies used in social media marketing and their impact on different aspects of businesses and organizations.

3.1 The Utilization of Social Media by Large Corporations

Adamopoulos, P. titled The Effectiveness of Promotional Events in Social Media [6] highlights the growing importance of social media usage at the enterprise level. Multinational corporations, such as Disney, operate on a large scale and manage multiple social media channels in different languages and regions. These companies often have separate accounts for different purposes, such as support, marketing, recruitment, and various divisions or verticals. Managing such extensive operations requires a large workforce, multiple agencies, legal oversight, and enterprise-grade management tools, such as Hootsuite Enterprise. Social media policies, guidelines, and style guides are employed to ensure consistent brand messaging and voice across all platforms. Here are some of the primary objectives that large companies aim to achieve through their social media presence:

3.2 Enhance Visibility of the Brand

Social media offers significant benefits for large B2C (business to consumer) companies, as it allows them to amplify their reach and increase awareness for specific

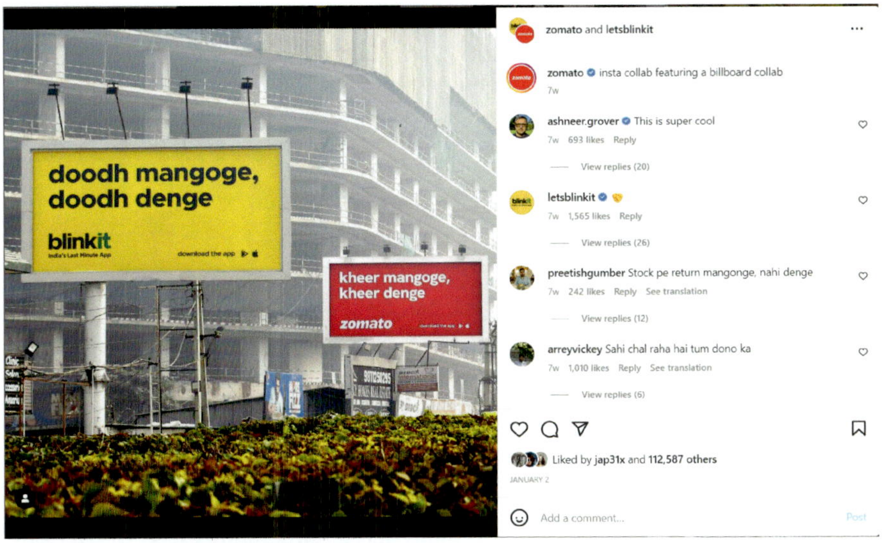

Fig. 3 Ad campaign by Zomato [8]

messages, campaigns, product launches, and other initiatives beyond their existing brand name recognition. Bhanot, S., A Study on Impact of Social Media on Company Performance [7].

Zomato is a food delivery and restaurant discovery platform that utilizes social media to engage with its customers and promote its brand. Here are a few examples of how Zomato uses social media:

1. **Promoting Content**: Zomato uses social media to promote its content, such as restaurant reviews and food-related articles. This helps to keep customers engaged and informed about the latest food trends and new restaurant openings.
2. **User-Generated Content**: Zomato encourages its users to share their food experiences and reviews on social media platforms, which helps to create a sense of community and engagement around the brand.
3. **Influencer Marketing**: Zomato collaborates with food bloggers, social media influencers, and celebrities to promote its brand and generate buzz around new restaurant launches and events. The highly competitive food delivery and restaurant discovery industry Overall, Zomato leverages social media in various ways to connect with its customers and promote its brand (Fig. 3).

3.3 *Establishing a Connection with Targeted Demographics*

Global businesses can target specific market segments on social media by utilizing various platforms and accounts that cater to their intended audiences. Depending on the demographics, different platforms may be more effective. For instance, luxury brands have tapped into WeChat business accounts to attract affluent Chinese consumers, while brands such as Chipotle and Betty Crocker's Fruit Gushers have leveraged TikTok to reach younger demographics.

3.4 What Lessons Can Large Corporations Learn from the Practices of Small Enterprises?

In today's business landscape, "small business" is often synonymous with "good business." This sentiment is evident in the emphasis placed on small enterprises by Facebook executives during a recent earnings call, where they mentioned their work with small businesses at least 23 times. Conversely, large corporations receive a different level of attention.

The ongoing pandemic has also increased people's preference for supporting small businesses. These enterprises typically adhere to customer service principles that have stood the test of time, which many large corporations tend to overlook. As such, megacorps should take note of these best practices and prioritize them accordingly.

3.5 Foster Strong Customer Connections

Customers hold in high esteem the local barista who remembers their coffee order, and this level of personalized service is also achievable for large brands on social media. Reviewing message histories and notes before responding to customer inquiries is important, as this can provide valuable insights into their previous experiences or customer status. For instance, it can be beneficial to know if a customer has faced repeated issues with a particular service or if they are a member of a loyalty program.

3.6 Infuse Personality into Your Brand

In today's business landscape, customers favour personal connections over faceless corporations. Whether in marketing, recruiting, or customer service, individuals want to see the human side of brands. This was affirmed by a Harvard Business Review study, which found that simple actions like signing a message with a customer service agent's initials can significantly improve customer perception. As such, companies must prioritize showcasing the human side of their brand to increase customer engagement.

3.7 *The Importance of Transparency and Ethical Branding for Large Corporations*

Matthews, L. titled "Social Media and the Evolution of Corporate Communications" [9] Large businesses are often lauded for their ethics, which can be easily observed in actions like using donation jars or serving ethically sourced products. However, large corporations may need help communicating their corporate values effectively. Research from the University of Toronto suggests that people tend to judge a business based on its size while also placing increasing importance on purchasing decisions that align with their values. Therefore, large companies must be transparent and genuine in conveying their values to customers. As advised by Pankaj Aggarwal, a marketing professor at the University of Toronto, big businesses need to tell a story that accurately reflects their brand and meets customers' expectations.

3.8 *Corporate Social Responsibility: Supporting the Community*

Consumers favour local businesses to help their community. On the contrary, multinational corporations are often seen as exploiting the communities they operate in. Shockingly, almost 50% of the global companies analyzed in the 2020 Corporate Human Rights Benchmark do not comply with the human rights standards outlined by the United Nations. Big Data: A Road Map for Successful Digital Marketing [10]. To distinguish themselves from these companies, global brands should showcase how they give back to the communities they operate in or benefit from on social media. These companies must highlight their community investments to show their dedication to social responsibility. Illustrations of Effective Social Media Practices by Large Corporations Several well-known brands have consistently received high scores on social media platforms. These include RedBull, Oreo, Nike and KFC. It's recommended that you keep an eye on these prominent brands. Additionally, the following big names should also be on your radar.

4 Illustrations of Effective Social Media Practices by Large Corporations

Several well-known brands have been consistently receiving high scores on social media platforms. These include RedBull, Oreo, Nike and KFC. It's recommended that you keep an eye on these prominent brands. Additionally, the following big names should also be on your radar. Farzana, P., Impact of Social Media Usage on Organizations [11].

4.1 Patagonia

The outdoor apparel brand is privately owned and doesn't manufacture coats solely to sell them. Their marketing strategy isn't focused on promoting their products, which was made clear by their decision to boycott Facebook advertisements last year. According to Alex Weller, the brand's marketing director, their actions form the foundation of their work, including their marketing efforts. Rather than using call-to-actions, Patagonia inspires its audience by highlighting its actions to preserve the planet, using extensive content and panoramic visuals.

Patagonia's approach places a higher value on their vests than just their practical features, such as wind flaps and moisture-wicking fleece. Rather than focusing solely on the quality of its apparel, the company's marketing strategy promotes membership in a community that is dedicated to taking action towards protecting the environment. In this way, Patagonia's marketing doesn't just sell clothing; it promotes a sense of belonging to a community that shares a common goal (Fig. 4).

4.1.1 Main Points to Remember

(1) One important lesson to learn is to avoid marketing just for the sake of it. Having a clear purpose behind your message is essential as not using marketing as a mere promotional tool.

Fig. 4 Social-media campaign by Patagonia [12]

(2) Creating communities based on shared values is a valuable strategy. Connecting with your audience through shared values can foster a sense of belonging and create a loyal following.

4.2 *Sephora*

Sephora has consistently made significant investments in social media. Last year, the beauty company collaborated with Instagram to launch a social storefront that integrates with their loyalty program.

Following allegations of racial bias and criticisms for lack of diversity, Sephora investigated and created an action plan to address the issue. In November, the report was published, specifically acknowledging that a lack of diversity in marketing, merchandise, and retail employees leads to exclusionary treatment.

To address this inequality, Sephora committed to developing marketing guidelines prioritising representation and diversity in marketing and product offerings. Additionally, the company aims to further its 15% Pledge commitment by supporting and promoting Black-owned businesses. This includes their Accelerate Bootcamp program, which is exclusively made up of BIPOC participants this year (Fig. 5).

The promotion of diversity and inclusion will also play a role in this year's instalment of #SephoraSquad, an internal creator program that leverages the influence of social media influencers. Initially introduced in 2019, the program serves as an "influencer incubator" for authentic, unfiltered storytellers who work closely with

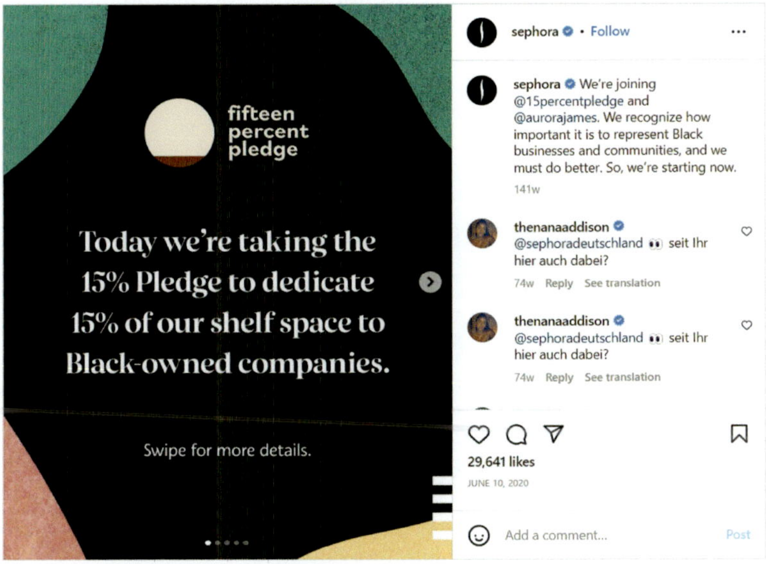

Fig. 5 Social-media campaign by Sephora [13]

the company. Sephora has already seen positive results from its inclusive marketing efforts, with its "Color Under the Lights" campaign leading to an 8% increase in purchase intent and improved brand favorability.

4.2.1 Main Points to Remember

(1) Taking responsibility for errors and directly addressing criticism is important to building a trustworthy and transparent brand.
(2) Incorporating inclusive marketing practices can have a significant and wide-ranging impact on a brand's success.

4.3 Spotify

For some, Spotify is considered more than just a music streaming platform and can be viewed as a social media platform in its own right. This effect is because of Spotify app's introduction of a Stories feature last year and the company's recent acquisition of Locker Room, a move intended to challenge Clubhouse in the live audio realm.

Spotify integrates social media elements directly into its platform rather than just treating social media as a marketing channel. In contrast to Apple Music, Spotify allows for easy connectivity between users, artists, and their friends on the platform. Artist profiles on the app include links to various social media channels, and the platform is seamlessly integrated with Facebook, Instagram, Snapchat, Whatsapp, Twitter, and other similar sites to facilitate effortless sharing and promotion of music (Fig. 6).

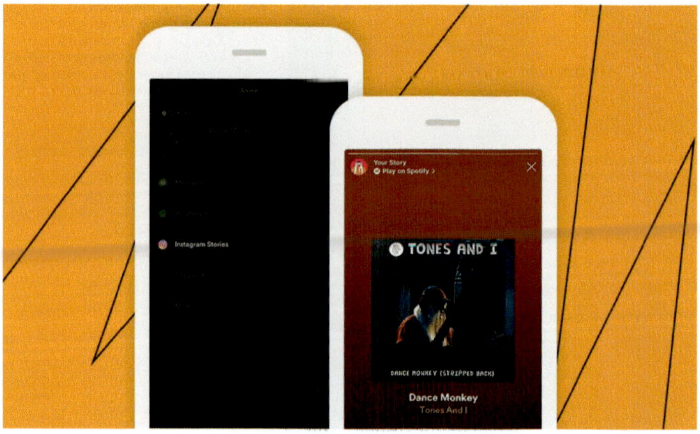

Fig. 6 Social-media strategy of instagram story by spotify[13]

Fig. 7 Post by K-Pop band BTS for spotify[13]

Will Page, former chief economist at Spotify, stated in a recent Facebook study that for younger generations who grew up with social media, their music exploration starts on social platforms, and Spotify aligns itself with this trend by meeting people where they prefer to discover music (Figs. 7 and 8).

Spotify's success in social media is also attributed to its ability to leverage user-generated content and transform artists and listeners into social media marketers. The platform offers promotional tools such as Promo Cards, while its yearly campaign, Spotify Wrapped, encourages listeners to share their personalised music statistics on social media, thereby increasing brand awareness through word-of-mouth marketing.

4.3.1 Main Points to Remember

(1) Engage with your audience on the platforms where they are most receptive.
(2) Empower your audience to become brand advocates by equipping them with the necessary resources and support.

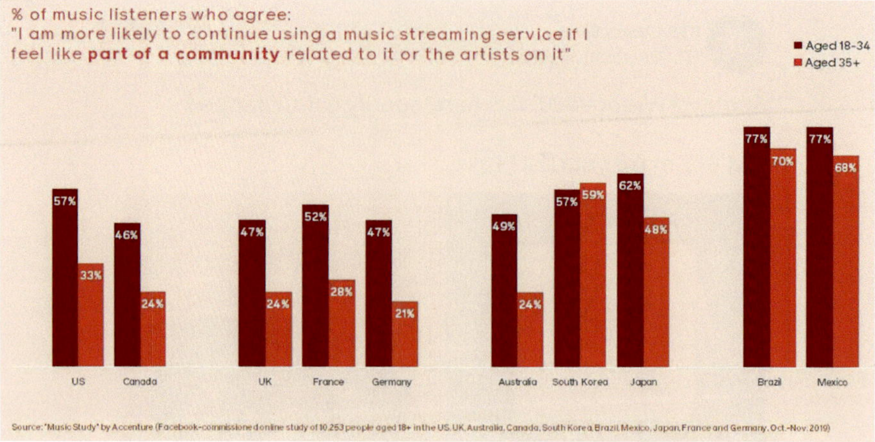

Fig. 8 Percentage of music listeners who agree: "I am more likely to continue using a music streaming service if I feel like part of a community related to it or the artists on it" [13]

5 The Transformative Role of Artificial Intelligence (AI) in Branding, Communication, and Advertising in Digital Marketing

Tan, C., A Study on Effectiveness of Social Media Advertising on Young Adults' Buying Behaviour [14] highlights that Artificial Intelligence (AI) is playing a pivotal role in revolutionizing digital marketing, encompassing various aspects such as branding, communication, and advertising. With advanced machine learning algorithms and data-driven insights, AI is transforming how businesses strategize and execute their digital marketing efforts. AI-powered technologies are enabling businesses to optimize their marketing strategies, personalize brand experiences, enhance communication with customers, and improve ad targeting and optimization. The integration of AI in digital marketing is reshaping the landscape and providing new opportunities for businesses to drive effective marketing campaigns and achieve better results.

In branding, AI enables companies to create personalized and targeted content based on customer preferences, behavior, and demographics. Through AI-powered tools, businesses can analyze vast amounts of data to understand their audience better, allowing them to develop compelling brand messages and experiences that resonate with their customers. AI also enables dynamic branding, where companies can adapt their brand communication in real-time based on changing market trends and consumer preferences, ensuring consistent and relevant brand messaging across different digital channels.

In communication, AI-powered chatbots and virtual assistants are becoming increasingly prevalent, providing automated and personalized interactions with customers. Chatbots can handle customer inquiries, provide product recommendations, and offer personalized offers or promotions, improving customer experience and reducing response times. AI-powered communication tools also allow businesses to analyze social media sentiment and customer feedback, helping them understand customer perceptions, sentiment, and preferences, and adjust their communication strategies accordingly.

In advertising, AI is revolutionizing how companies target and optimize their digital ad campaigns. AI-powered algorithms analyze large datasets to identify patterns and insights, enabling businesses to optimize their ad targeting, placement, and bidding strategies for maximum impact. AI also enables programmatic advertising, where ads are automatically placed and optimized in real-time based on data-driven insights. This allows companies to deliver more relevant and personalized ads to their target audience, resulting in higher engagement, conversions, and ROI.

5.1 The Primary Components of Artificial Intelligence (AI) in the Realm of Digital Marketing

AI comprises several components that underpin other technologies that are used in digital marketing. Machine learning, for instance, is a critical element of AI that facilitates digital marketing on online platforms. Responsive Artificial Intelligence (RAI) [15] It is a computer technology that utilises algorithms to analyse data and improve automated responses. Machine learning contextualises and compares new data with historical data to make decisions based on past actions. In addition, big data and analytics are instrumental in implementing AI in digital marketing because a thorough analysis of extensive user databases is required to improve automated responses and decision-making. By employing big data and analytics, AI can understand consumer data and apply relevant analytics to enhance consumer reach and promote products. These analytics help modify consumer behaviour by catering to particular product and service preferences. Moreover, targeted ads rely on an in-depth analysis of consumer choices and interactions with brands on digital platforms such as social media and websites. AI-powered solutions are employed in digital marketing campaigns to target specific consumer groups and impart marketing intelligence to target audiences. The use of AI, in turn, enables marketers to make more accurate data-driven decisions appropriate for different markets. Bayesian Learning is a technique that marketers use to understand customer response to specific product and service offerings in digital marketing, serving as an example of the strategies employed to leverage AI in digital marketing.

5.2 *Transforming Customer Behaviour Through AI-Enabled Digital Marketing*

AI-enabled digital marketing is reshaping customer behaviour, redefining how businesses approach branding, communication, and advertising strategies. Leveraging the power of artificial intelligence, companies can analyze vast amounts of data to gain deep insights into customer preferences, behaviours, and trends, and tailor their marketing efforts accordingly.

In branding, AI empowers businesses to create personalized and relevant brand experiences by leveraging customer data. With AI-powered tools, companies can analyze customer behaviour, demographics, and preferences to develop customized brand messages, visuals, and experiences that resonate with each individual customer, creating meaningful and memorable interactions that drive brand loyalty.

In communication, AI-driven chatbots and virtual assistants enable instant and personalized interactions with customers. Chatbots can handle customer inquiries, provide recommendations, and offer personalized promotions, enhancing communication channels and creating seamless and convenient experiences that influence customer behavior positively.

In advertising, AI plays a crucial role in optimizing ad targeting, placement, and content strategies. By analyzing customer data, AI algorithms identify patterns and trends, allowing businesses to deliver more relevant and engaging ads that influence customer behaviour and drive conversions. AI-powered programmatic advertising further enhances ad optimization, delivering ads in real-time based on customer behaviour and preferences.

5.3 *Key Concerns and Obstacles in AI and Digital Marketing's Impact on Consumer Behavior*

Dana, L. Social media and consumer buying behavior decision: what entrepreneurs should know? [16] sheds light on the substantial impact of AI and digital marketing on consumer behavior, while also highlighting the key concerns and obstacles that businesses must navigate. Privacy and data security are significant challenges in the realm of branding, as the collection and usage of customer data for personalized branding experiences may raise concerns about privacy and data protection due to the heavy reliance on data analysis in AI.

The impact of AI and digital marketing on consumer behavior has been substantial, but it also presents key concerns and obstacles that businesses must navigate. In the realm of branding, businesses may face challenges related to privacy and data security. As AI relies heavily on data analysis, the collection and usage of customer data for personalized branding experiences can raise concerns about privacy and data protection.

In communication, the use of AI-driven chatbots and virtual assistants may face obstacles in terms of ensuring the accuracy and appropriateness of responses. Businesses need to carefully design and train these AI-powered communication tools to avoid potential misinterpretations, miscommunications, or biases in responses, which could negatively impact the customer experience and brand perception.

In advertising, the increasing reliance on AI for ad targeting and optimization may raise concerns about ethical implications and fairness. There may be challenges related to algorithmic biases, ad fraud, and the transparency of AI-powered ad campaigns, which could result in unintended consequences or damage to brand reputation.

Furthermore, the rapid evolution of AI and digital marketing technologies presents challenges in keeping up with the pace of change, as businesses need to continuously adapt their strategies and capabilities to stay relevant in the dynamic digital landscape. Additionally, there may be concerns around the potential displacement of human jobs in the marketing and advertising industry as AI and automation become more prevalent.

Overall, while AI and digital marketing have transformed consumer behaviour, there are key concerns and obstacles that businesses need to navigate in areas such as privacy, data security, communication accuracy, ethical implications, and workforce displacement. Addressing these concerns and overcoming obstacles is essential for businesses to effectively leverage the power of AI and digital marketing to shape consumer behaviour while upholding ethical standards and maintaining customer trust.

6 Conclusion

Finally we can conclude that the digital era has had a profound impact on large-scale enterprises, revolutionizing how they operate, communicate, and engage with customers..Traditional mediums like television and print media have been the go-to channels for businesses to reach customers, but with the rise of social media and other digital platforms, new opportunities have emerged. One of the benefits of using social media is its cost-effectiveness compared to traditional media. Social media also offers real-time analytics, which enables businesses to track the effectiveness of their campaigns and make data-driven decisions. The new ways of connecting industry with customers, such as social media, television, influencer marketing, and content marketing, offer businesses a range of benefits. These include cost-effectiveness, targeted advertising, real-time analytics, customer engagement, and the ability to connect with diverse customer pools. However, these methods also have limitations, including competition, changing trends, costs, and limited interactivity. Businesses must carefully evaluate their target audience, goals, and resources to determine the most effective approach for connecting with customers and achieving their business objectives. Finding the right balance between utilizing these new ways of connecting with customers while being mindful of their limitations is crucial for successful customer engagement in today's dynamic business landscape. Through a critical analysis of the results against the initial objectives and research question, it is evident that the digital era has brought both limitations and benefits to large-scale enterprises. The limitations include concerns related to privacy, data security, ethical implications, and potential job displacement. However, the benefits are significant, including improved customer engagement, personalized branding experiences, enhanced communication channels, and optimized advertising strategies.

Despite the limitations, the overall impact of the digital era on large-scale enterprises has been transformative, reshaping traditional business practices and opening new opportunities for growth and innovation in the fast-paced digital landscape. It is essential for businesses to carefully navigate the challenges and leverage the benefits of the digital era to stay competitive and thrive in today's business environment.

References

1. Sehl, k. , Social Media for Big Companies: 10+ Inspiring Examples
2. De Vries L (2012) Impact of social media on consumers and firms. University of Groningen, Groningen. Ipskamp Drukkers, Enschede, The Netherlands, Printing
3. Edosomwan S (2011) The history of social media and its impact on business. The J Appl Manage Entrepreneurship 16
4. Abuhashesh M (2014) Integration of social media in businesses. Int J Bus Soc Sci USA 5(8)
5. Bajpai V (2012) Social media marketing: strategies & its impact. Int J Soc Sci Interdisc Res India 1(7)
6. Adamopoulos P (2014) The effectiveness of promotional events in social media, department of information operations and management sciences. In: Workshop on information systems and economics, New York University research paper, USA
7. Bhanot S (2014) A study on impact of social media on company performance, research paper, India
8. https://www.instagram.com/p/Cm6bZ_kpVh4/
9. Matthews L (2010) Social media and the evolution of corporate communications. The Elon J Undergraduate Res Commun USA 1(1 • Winter), 17–23
10. Singh A, Bansal R, Sharma S (2022) (eds) Big data: a road map for successful digital marketing. Walter de Gruyter GmbH & Co KG
11. Farzana P (2012) Impact of social media usage on organizations, pacis 2012 proceedings. Paper 192
12. https://www.instagram.com/p/CktKZC1uaky/
13. https://www.instagram.com/p/CBQyEN5ljJg/?utm_source=ig_embed&utm_campaign=loading
14. Tan C (2021) A study on effectiveness of social media advertising on young adults' buying behaviour (Doctoral dissertation, Tunku Abdul Rahman University College)
15. Khamparia A, Gupta D, Khanna A, Balas VE (2022) (eds) Biomedical data analysis and processing using explainable (XAI) and responsive artificial intelligence (RAI), vol 222. Springer Nature
16. Dana L(2020) Social media and consumer buying behavior decision: what entrepreneurs should know? Management decision
17. Jindal L, Kumar S, Kaushal C, Bhende M, Thakare A, Shabaz M (2022) Aspect-based sentiment analysis employing linguistics content over social media for Web of Things. IET Communications

GPSR Compliance

The European Union's (EU) General Product Safety Regulation (GPSR) is a set of rules that requires consumer products to be safe and our obligations to ensure this.

If you have any concerns about our products, you can contact us on ProductSafety@springernature.com

In case Publisher is established outside the EU, the EU authorized representative is:

Springer Nature Customer Service Center GmbH
Europaplatz 3
69115 Heidelberg, Germany

Batch number: 10756376

Printed by Printforce, the Netherlands